THE PSYCHOPHYSICAL LAB

Yoga Practice and the Mind–Body Problem

by

Ohad Nachtomy & Eyal Shifroni

The authors of this book are not physicians and the instructions, procedures, and suggestion in this book are not intended as a substitute for the medical advice of a trained health professional. All matters regarding your health require medical supervision. Consult your physician before adopting the procedures suggested in this book, as well as about any condition that may require diagnosis or medical attention. The authors and the publisher disclaim any liability arising directly or indirectly from the use of this book.

ISBN: 978-965-92519-6-4

Mudita Books

Text Editing: Barnaby Hutchins and Sivan Goldhirsh
Illustrations: Shira Katz
Cover design: Michal Mer
Graphic Design: Asaf Goral
Photography: Yul Shifroni

The Psychophysical Lab

Table of Contents

Chapter 1

Practical Explorations

Chapter 3 204

A Brief History of Psyche and Soma (Soul and Body):
From Socrates to the Present and Back to Aristotle

Chapter 4

Practice Sequences (with Marked Mental Effects)

Eyal's Preface

Can stretching a limb bring about joy and wellbeing? Can performing headstand improve our thought process and our clarity of mind? Can bending the body forward or backward develop our personality and make us better human beings?

These questions have intrigued me for the last forty years of my yogic journey. On the surface, *asana* (yogic posture) practice looks very much like gymnastics, but clearly there is much more involved and, for my own part, the reply to these questions is definitively positive.

Viparita Karani

When going out in nature, to the sea shore or to the mountains, I like to take in the view upside-down in headstand or just lying on my back on a rock in *Viparita Dandasana* or *Viparita Karani*.

When doing this, I see the view in a completely different way. I tried to capture it with a camera held upside-down but the picture came out just looking normal – it looked like it needed to be rotated, but there was nothing *special* about it... Clearly the experience of seeing is a psychophysical one, and it can't be represented purely visually and can't be captured by an optical device. But what exactly is the reason for that? Is it that we see the view from an unaccustomed angle? Is it the change in circulation in the eyes, and the brain accounting for the difference? Could it be the difference in the weight distribution of the body? Or maybe all of these reasons and more?

It is obvious that the human eye is very different from a camera, since the experience of seeing is embodied – it involves both the body and the mind and cannot be reproduced by an image captured by a camera; it cannot be isolated and observed in other conditions.

Asana practice is an endeavor that involves both body and mind – but where is the boundary between the two? What are the relationships between them, and how do they affect each other? How does a body's posture affect mental state, and how does a mental act (like focusing or concentrating) affect the body?

This book is an attempt to explore these challenging questions, which for me are, and will probably always remain, a mystery. We try to articulate answers that shed light on the intricate relationships between the body and the mind and enrich our *asana* practice. I hope this book will be of interest for anyone who is intrigued by the mystery of human consciousness.

Ohad's Preface

Shirshasana (Headstand)

My first encounter with yoga was as at the age of sixteen or seventeen, as I was growing up in a small kibbutz in Israel. I came across a book entitled *Yoga and Health* by Elisabeth Haich and Selvarajan Yesdudian. I read the book and started practicing. I discovered an experience that was wholly new to me – being with myself and spending time with myself. Yoga did something very positive to me. But I couldn't keep it up.

I rediscovered yoga much later in life. When I was an assistant professor at Tel-Hai College, I met Eyal (who was teaching computer science at the time). I began to attend his yoga classes. What attracted me most to yoga at the time was that it was a *rigorous* practice.

Practicing yoga was mainly a relief from thinking, in general, and from philosophy, in particular. I recall hardly hearing the complicated instructions, not to mention following them in detail. What mattered to me was practicing. I was also rather skeptical about the spiritual aspect of yoga and especially the kind of cheap spiritualism I was worried it attracted.

At the same time, I experienced how my own awareness began to expand and penetrate new vistas through the practice. I slowly rediscovered yoga as a way to be with myself, and began to develop a deeper interest in the practice, slowly improving and observing subtle changes. After a few years, I noticed that yoga practice had become important to me, that it became an important part of my day, and that if I didn't practice, something was missing. It was no longer just a break from work; rather, it had taken on a life of its own.

And then, at some point, Eyal mentioned that we can think of yoga practice as a lab, that we should emphasize observing and attending to the effects of the postures rather than seeking to improve the postures. This suddenly made a lot of sense to me. It connected my growing interest in the practice with my philosophical and reflective interest that had been muted in the background. I thought: A lab, yes. This makes sense. But a lab for what? What is it that we are investigating here? And it struck me that one thing we are investigating in this context is how (in particular cases and exercises) our awareness (or lack thereof) affects the quality of the *asana* – both in the physical sense of quality and in the sensation we have as we are doing it. In this way, we also extend the reach and power of our awareness to affect our practice, so that mute or blind spots in our body become more visible and responsive.

And so it slowly became clear to me that the object of the yoga lab is to investigate the interplay (or mutual connection) between physical and mental aspects of our nature. This, of course, got connected with the formidable mind–body problem, which, as every philosophy student knows, is one of the deepest and most difficult questions that has preoccupied humanity at least since the Greeks and that, to this day, remains unanswered. This is how the idea of writing this book was born.

At this point, Eyal started writing and publishing his books (*A Chair for Yoga* and then *Props for Yoga*). And it seemed to me natural to connect the practical side that Eyal was articulating so well with a theoretical part that I would try to write. Indeed, a synthesis between the practical and the theoretical aspects of this issue seemed like a very promising approach. It took more effort to get Eyal interested in the project, and it was difficult for him to find time to work on it in light of his very tight schedule. But we would meet almost weekly at his classes. And if an idea would occur to me during class, I'd mention it to Eyal at the end. Sometimes, we would discuss it briefly. And so, gradually, we both started taking notes for a future book. I drafted an introduction and we developed a plan: Eyal would write the practical part, and I would write the theoretical part, and the book would come together. But as we started to work in earnest on drafts and share them, an intense exchange ensued. This exchange has resulted, among other things, in the second chapter of this book. For me, this exchange with Eyal was (and still is) a wonderfully enriching and productive process. For as much as Eyal is committed to the path of yoga, and as much as he dedicates all his energy to it, he is also open to criticism and even to skepticism. He never puts off a question. And he is never shy to say that he does not know.

Co-authoring a book can be very difficult and trying. One often debates the formulation of each sentence, and it is not easy to see your sentences get revised in a way that you may not like – not to mention the issues of ego that often come up. But working with Eyal on this book was almost the inverse. Of course, we have many arguments and disputes. But I cannot recall any that was not resolved by a quick discussion. Indeed, Eyal is not only a wonderful yoga teacher and a source of inspiration for me; he is also a friend and a wonderful interlocutor. I hope that the spirit of cooperation and the productive exchange we have had in this process has left its marks in the letters and pages of this book.

Eyal's Acknowledgments

I am indebted to my Guru, the late B.K.S. Iyengar (1918-2014), who created such a deep and insightful method of yoga – a method which became my way of life, and that transformed my life in the most positive way. I wish to thank Mr. Iyengar and his family members, Prashant, Geeta and Abhijata for guiding me in all my visits to RIMYI (Ramamani Iyengar Memorial Yoga Institute) in Pune, India. The word 'Lab' in the title of this book is inspired by Prashant's classes at RIMYI. A main theme in his teachings is that the *asana* practice is about learning and exploring, and that we should carry out experiments and analysis in our practice much as one does in a research lab.

I wish to extend my thanks to the many senior teachers of this method – too many to mention all by name – for giving me further guidance and insights in so many workshops over the last thirty years.

Many people contributed to the composition of this book. First and foremost is my friend, student and co-author, Ohad. Without him, this project would have never been realized. Honestly, when he first mentioned the idea of writing a book about yoga together, I was not inclined, as I was (and still am) absorbed in completing my *Props for Yoga* series, in which two additional volumes are still pending. Ohad patiently and persistently kept pushing the idea forward, until I finally realized the significant and unique contribution this project would make. It has been wonderful to collaborate with Ohad. Our friendship and working relationship have been strengthened through working together on the book!

My dear student, Sivan Goldhirsh, who is a yoga teacher and native English-speaker, did a superb job in reviewing and editing chapters 1, 2 and 4. Sivan has a keen interest and love for yoga and a sensitive ear for language. She read our drafts over and over again, correcting and improving the text as well as contributing many insights. Thank you, Sivan!

Other yoga teachers have read drafts of the book: Michael Sela from Zichron-Ya'akov (Israel), Cecilia Harrison from London, Karin Freschi from Milan and Noga Chepelinski from Buenos-Aires. A nice international cooperation! Thanks to all of you!

Shira Katz, who helps me in managing my yoga center and international workshops, is also a talented graphic designer. Shira did all the illustrated figures of the *asanas* and the props, which contribute wonderfully to the overall look of the book! Thank you, Shira.

My center's teachers: Kym Ben-Yaakov, Liat Bagon, Ravit Moar, Michael Sela, Eleanor Schlesinger and Eleanor Jacobovitz; two other teachers: Atar Rabina and Anat Rachmel, and my daughter, Inbar Shifroni - all modeled for the figures in this book. Thanks to all of you for taking part in this project and for devoting your time in presenting the *asanas* so skillfully!

Atar Rabina, my friend and student, shared her personal story where she describes how yoga helps her to deal with a psychophysical condition she faces – her story appears in Appendix A.

We were fortunate to come across Asaf Goral, a talented graphic designer, who has cared for the appearance of the book as if it were his own! Asaf did an excellent job in designing the graphical layout of this book, while taking care of each small detail. The result is a book that is a pleasure to look at and use!

Yul Shifroni, my daughter, took the photos that were the basis for the illustrations done by Shira – thanks Yul!

I wish to thank all the students in our yoga center—without whom I couldn't have been a teacher! I wish to express my sincere gratitude to all the yogis around the world who read my previous books, gave me warm and constructive feedback and encouraged me to continue to devote time to writing, . It is wonderful to know that my work is of use to people in all corners of the globe!

Last but not least, I wish to thank my wife Hagit for being with me on this journey!

Ohad's Acknowledgments

Much of the inspiration for writing the story of mind–body relations – and the time that enabled me to carry out research for it – is due to a semester at the Institute for Advanced Study (IAS) in Princeton (in the Spring of 2016). Though this was not my official research project there, I received much encouragement from the IAS spirit and its director's encouragement to follow one's curiosity. My discussions with Brooke Holmes, Justin Smith, Heinrich Von Staden, Olaf Witkowsky, Yuko Ishihara, Piet Hut, and Gonardon Ganeri provided further support and encouragement. I am particularly grateful to Giuliano Mori, who read an early draft of this survey and gave me very helpful comments. While serious work on this part of the book was begun at the IAS at Princeton, it was finished it at the IAS in Paris in the fall of 2018. I would like to thank this remarkable institute and its staff, who are extremely welcoming and provide wonderful support.

I presented the main line of argument at talks at the institute for Advanced Study in Princeton, at Bar-Ilan University, at IEA in Paris, and at a conference on The Three Souls in the History of Medicine and Philosophy (in Paris), as well as at Eyal's workshops in Mexico City and Paris. I am grateful to all participants in these events, and especially to Gretty Mirdal, Noga Arikha, Charles Wolfe, Pia Campeggiani, Denis Walsh, Siri Hustvedt, and Justin Smith. My colleagues at Bar-Ilan, Alon Chasid, Alik Pelman, Liat Lavi, and Yuval Dolev offered very useful comments and advice. My student Benny Eisner virtually composed the section on Dennett and Chalmers himself (though I remain responsible for any mistakes). Emmanuel Farjoun read parts of the chapter and gave me extremely critical and helpful comments. As always, my discussions with him are extremely enlightening. Noam Hoffer read through the whole text and provided corrections and comments. Reed Winegar also provided advice on the Kant section. Raphaële Andrault read the second part, and we had very helpful discussions about it. Discussions with Avi Vigderson, Oron Shagrir, and Zohar Yakhini were also useful and important for presenting current approaches in the cognitive sciences and computer science.

Liat Lavi read the whole text, and carefully edited the bibliographical list. Liat also provided extremely helpful comments and references on the second part and saved me from some very awkward points. I also had the pleasure and fortune to discuss this project with Liat from its early stages. I have had the luck and pleasure to work with Liat for many years, and consulting her vast knowledge and curiosity is, as always, extremely rewarding.

I was also lucky to meet Allison Aitken at a visit to Harvard. Allison shares a passion for yoga and philosophy – only she knows so much more about yoga and eastern philosophy than I do. Our meeting and the correspondence that followed encouraged me in thinking that this book might be on the right track – that it would be of interest to those who share these passions. Allison also helped us with correcting the Sanskrit and has drawn our attention to very helpful sources.

Barnaby Hutchins edited the whole text. Barnaby is not only a fantastic editor; he is a reader that any writer can only dream of. He understands what you are trying to say and just puts it in much better words. His intelligence and thoughtful work, as well as his professional engagement with this work, has made it a far better book.

Michal Mer, my dear life partner, advised us on the design of the book, the choice to go with illustrations, the particular character of the illustrations, and the size and shape of the book, as well as the details of the cover design. Michal somehow already had a concept of what this book should look like before it was even written.

INTRODUCTION

In this book, we argue that reflective and mindful yoga practice can go beyond improving and maintaining good health. By engaging both mental and physical capacities it also offers a method, we suggest, of developing and enhancing our whole being. Roughly speaking, according to this view of yoga practice, we use the mind in training the body and the body in training the mind. To put this more precisely, we use our physical capabilities – as well as our limitations – to investigate and develop our mental capacities and potentialities and vice versa. For example, the physical practice of yoga can develop such qualities as endurance, tolerance, balance and equanimity. At the same time, we use our mental capacities of reflection, awareness, memory, and learning to enhance and explore our physical capacities, with the aim of leading to improvements in posture, flexibility, breathing, blood circulation, nervous system functioning, and so on.

We emphasize the point that reflective practice and exploration (on both the physical and mental sides) is an essential part of what we mean by 'development'. For development in yoga need not mean only progress in the sense of measurable achievement, such as maintaining a headstand for a longer duration, or being able to do advanced yoga postures; development also involves realizing our limitations, practicing with less effort and more attention, gaining more confidence and stability – in a sense that goes beyond the time we actually spend on the yoga mat, such that it makes an impact on our overall daily life.

Of course, yoga practice does include difficult physical postures (*asanas*) and intensive breathing exercises (*pranayama*). But we need to ask what these postures and exercises are meant for. What is the point of practicing *asanas* and *pranayama*? While our body is the most immediate medium of the practice, it is not, we suggest in this book, a mere instrument for achieving something else; it is not a means that serves other goals. Rather, we see the body as an essential part of our very identity and nature. Indeed, it is arguable that we cannot make sense of emotional and mental states independently of their bodily expression. For example, if someone says that he or she is in severe pain while his or her physical expression conveys pleasure instead, we would struggle to make sense of what is going on. And so, while we are not practicing for the sake of achieving physical feats of flexibility or certain postures alone, the body should not be seen as a mere instrument for achieving higher ends, so to speak; for, if body and mind are as closely interconnected as we argue in this book, then, in training our body, we also work with our mind. Given this, when we work on, and improve, our physiological capacities, we employ and develop our mental capacities as well. In other words, in training the body through reflective and attentive practice, we can train and develop our whole being.

It would be useful to clarify our approach by distinguishing it from the following two tendencies. One tendency, common in (but not exclusive to) competitive sport, emphasizes the use of the mind in order to improve physical achievement. This attitude is common not only among professional athletes but also among amateur marathon runners, endurance swimmers, weightlifters, and body builders, as well as among some yoga practitioners. In contrast to this, there is a tendency to see the body as merely a means (or an instrument) for housing the mind, and to thereby treat the body, in itself, as having no inherent significance. This attitude is evident in some of the rhetoric about practices of meditation, or in intellectual and scholarly work that tends to neglect the body, seeing it only as something to be maintained, with certain needs (such as nutrition and sleep) that must be fulfilled, but not as an integral part of human development.[1] This approach tends to ignore the fact that even a practice so apparently cerebral as meditation requires sitting still, and that sitting still is not a merely mental affair. Furthermore, an important part of many meditation practices consists of focusing on bodily sensations as well as on our reactions to them. Likewise, in studying and reading, for example, many of our physical (bodily) capacities, such as sight, posture, fatigue, etc., play crucial roles in our very ability to study and comprehend what we read – not to mention our ability to do so effectively. Thus, even our most intellectual capacities require the employment of many physical capacities and are not merely or purely intellectual.

In distinction from both approaches outlined above, our view is that we need not assign priority to the mind over the body, nor to the body over the mind, for the simple reason that human nature consists of both mental and physical capacities that are interconnected and that continuously interact in highly complex ways. We see the practice of yoga as affecting our whole being because we see no separation – and indeed no clear-cut distinction – between mental and physical capacities.

1 This also characterizes certain schools of asceticism in India that interpret *tapas* as self-denial and austerity, seeing the body as something that we need to suppress or even to torture. The Buddha was in such a sect before his awakening (in which he found the 'middle way').

It is, however, very useful to make a distinction between mental and physical capacities. For, as we noted, we employ our mental abilities of reflection, attention, and awareness to improve our practice, and our physical abilities and attributes to acquire mental abilities that allow us to withstand pain, to increase patience, to discern and explore our (physical and mental) limitations, and so on. For this reason, we do not seek to ignore or abolish the distinction between physical and mental capacities – even though the boundaries between them may not be sharp and clear; rather, we see these distinctions as essential to our very nature, and seek to explore the intricate relations between them. The main aim of this book is to offer both the philosophy behind this view and a concrete practical way to explore and experience these intricate relations. We believe that reflective yoga practice should be inquisitive and exploratory – hence, '**the psychophysical lab**'.

The Structure of the Book

The book is divided into four main chapters. The first, practical, chapter presents Explorations: a variety of yoga *asanas* that are meant to explore the relationships between mental and physical capacities. These explorations are of two kinds: in one, we observe the mental effects of physical variations; in the other, we observe the physical effects of mental variations, such as changing the focus of attention and observing its impact on the pose. The Explorations chapter begins with a section for practitioners on all levels followed by a section for more advanced yoga practitioners. The second chapter offers some thoughts on how reflective yoga practice affects and enhances certain important qualities, such as stability, endurance, balance, and equanimity. We also examine the physical and the mental aspects of such qualities and discuss whether and how a physical exercise that enhances, say, physical stability may affect our mental stability. The general question we discuss in this chapter is how yoga practice can be transformative in a way that improves our well-being beyond the yoga mat. The third chapter of the book presents the history of mind–body (or psyche–soma) relations in Western philosophy, in order to better argue for and explain our own approach. It thus provides a historical and philosophical argument for the approach presented above. Finally, the last chapter offers several practice sequences that have marked mental effects.

How to Read this Book

This book need not be read in order. While the four chapters support one another and form a unity, each is also pretty much independent of the others. So, one can, for example, start by trying out some Explorations from chapter 1, then read some of the sections of chapter 2, and then turn to chapter 3. If you are philosophically minded, you can start right away with chapter 3, and then go back to chapter 1 and explore the mind–body relations in a practical manner.Experienced yoga practitioners who have intimate practical sense of the mutual body-mind effects in the *asana*s, can go directly to chapter 2, and examine the discussions given there in light of their own experience, which may ignite an appetite to dive into the philosophical discussion of chapter 3. In short, dear reader, do feel free to select the order of reading according to your own interest, preferences, and inclination.

A Note on the Composition of this Book

This book is a joint endeavor of Ohad, a philosopher and yoga student, and Eyal, a senior yoga teacher and practitioner. While chapters 1, 3 and 4 were written separately – with Eyal composing the Explorations (Ch. 1) and the Practice Sequences (Chapter 4), and Ohad the historical survey of the mind–body problem (Ch. 3) – chapter 2 is a joint effort. The idea for chapter 2 and its composition derives from our ongoing discussions. While Eyal composed the first draft of most sections[2], Ohad made significant contributions in discussing and revising the text. Naturally, due to our differing backgrounds, there are differences in the approach we each take, and in the tone of our writing. Eyal has long devoted most of his time to the practice, study and teaching of yoga, while Ohad – a dedicated yoga student – devotes most of his time to his academic research. Indeed, Eyal usually writes from the point of view of a seasoned teacher, while Ohad writes from that of a student. We hope that these different perspectives enrich the discussion and result in a more interesting exposition.

2 Ohad wrote the following sections: Dealing with Negative Moods, Fatigue, and Feeling Down; Pursuit of Long-Term Goals and Modesty in Realizing Them; and Non-Competitiveness. The rest of the chapter was written by Eyal.

Why Focus on Western (Rather Than Indian) Philosophy?

The reader might wonder why we focus on mind–body relations as they are articulated in the Western tradition rather than in the Eastern tradition in which yoga practice was formed. Indeed, it might be argued that the mind–body problem, as it is understood in Western philosophy, does not even arise in the Eastern tradition. There are several reasons why we think it is very useful (and productive) to discuss yoga practice against the background of Western philosophy in general, and of its entanglement with the mind–body problem in particular.

First, like many (and probably most current) yoga practitioners, we are educated in the Western tradition. It is also worth mentioning that we live, act, think, and practice yoga in the Western world. This means that an essential aspect of the way we think, and indeed an essential part of our very identity, is inevitably shaped by Western thought and culture. Furthermore, dealing with the mind–body problem is not merely a theoretical affair in the Western world; rather, it is also a practical issue that comes up at many junctures, as, for example, when we have to deal with medical institutions that are split along the dividing lines of physical and mental health.

To some extent, one might even argue that yoga practice offers a solution to a Western problem. If so, since we come from the Western side, the motivation for our approach in this book is straightforward. Indeed, we are not alone in this. As things stand, the number of active yoga practitioners in the Western world is surprisingly high, and rapidly rising (one recent study found that around ten percent of the US population actively practices yoga).[3] This suggests that there is a strong need for yoga in Western culture, which in turn suggests that yoga fills a certain lacuna. In this respect too, our approach provides a partial explanation of this curious phenomenon. To put it simply, we, as Westerners are entangled with the question of mind–body relations. Yoga offers a way, a method, a praxis, a lab, which enables us to deal with and study this question in earnest[4].

3 For data on the USA from a 2016 survey, see: forbes.com/sites/alicegwalton/2016/03/15/how-yoga-is-spreading-in-the-u-s

4 Yoga as a psychophysical practice has been conjoined with a great diversity of views throughout its history. This has included (at some point or another) nearly all of the major philosophical systems of India, which are incredibly diverse in their epistemological/metaphysical/theological commitments. So, given its history, conjoining yoga practice with Western philosophy is, we believe, perfectly adequate.

Secondly, without delving too deep into the philosophy of yoga here, let's just note that, although it differs in many respects from Western philosophy, the philosophy of classical yoga[5] (or the *yoga darshana*) is also dualistic. But this dualism is very different from the mind–body dichotomy as it has been understood in Western philosophy since the time of Descartes. Classical yoga (and *Samkhya*) holds that, ontologically, there are two principles: pure consciousness, 'seer', or 'Self' (*purusha*), and unconscious matter or 'seen' (*prakriti*). *Prakriti* encompasses the entire natural world, which is characterized by continuous change, and this includes the human mind, or, more accurately, what Patanjali refers to as *chitta*[6]. *Purusha* on the other hand, is only a 'witness' – it is inactive, unchanged, and unaffected. One must therefore be careful not to conflate the Cartesian dualism of mind and body and the dualism asserted by classical yoga. In yoga, the mind (as long as we understand it as *chitta*) belongs to the ever-changing material world, and as such it is part of *prakriti*. So, for yoga, the body and the mind are just two constituents of the material realm, and there is no sharp distinction between the two[7].

In yogic philosophy, the nature of human beings is described not just in terms of body and mind but also through a model of five *koshas* (layers or sheaths)[8]. What we usually refer to as 'body' is seen as the outermost layer of the human system. It is called the (1) *annamaya kosha* (literally, the 'food sheath'), and consists of the skin, bones and muscles – in short, the anatomical body. This outermost layer encompasses the other four subtler layers or *koshas*: (2) the energetic or organic body (*pranamaya kosha*), (3) the mental body (*manomaya kosha*), (4) the intellectual

5 The *Yoga Sutras* of Patanjali are considered 'classical yoga'. This dualistic view of yoga is shared by the school of *Samkhya* (or *Sankhya*) philosophy.

6 The word *chitta* has no direct equivalent in English. It refers to the active features of the mind which includes the I-maker or ego (*ahamkara*), the intellect (*buddhi*), and the mental faculty (*manas*) that coordinates the sense faculties and faculties of motion and transmits their data to the ego and the intellect. All these components of the *chitta* are part of *prakriti*, which is distinguished from pure consciousness or *purusha*. There's no sentience, or 'lights on' without the consciousness of *purusha*. But pure consciousness is not object-directed, so without the intellect as part of *prakriti*, there would be no intentionality. Also, pure consciousness has no sense of an individuated self, which is afforded by the ego (*ahamkara*). The *chitta* is often likened to the moon, which has no light of its own, but borrows its light from the sun (*purusha*).

7 The mistaken belief that *purusha* (soul or pure consciousness) is *prakriti* causes the painful experience of the mind and body as we know them; realizing the true identity of the soul as separate from *prakriti* brings about liberation.

8 This does not appear in Patanjali's 'classical yoga philosophy', but has gradually become popular in various modern yoga philosophical traditions.

body (*vijnanamaya kosha*), and finally (5) the bliss body (*anandamaya kosha*). Note that in yoga we distinguish between the mental body (*manomaya kosha*), "where the incessant thoughts of human life occur," and the intellectual body (*vijnanamaya kosha*), "where intelligence and discernment can be found."[9]

In his book *Light on Life*[10], B.K.S. Iyengar dedicated a full chapter to discussing each *kosha* separately. In the Introduction to the book, he writes,

> "The physical body . . . is not something separate from our mind and soul. We are not supposed to neglect or deny our body as some ascetics suggest. Nor are we to become fixated on our body – our mortal self – either."

This complex layered *kosha* system is certainly a rich and interesting way to describe our human system. It differs from the common Western model as it places no real boundary between the physical and the mental. Instead, it sees a continuum of layers, advancing from the outermost to the innermost, and from the crude and material to the subtler and more refined. Each layer is in charge of certain functions and exhibits certain capacities: the physical body digests food and carries out the anatomical functions; the energetic or organic body is in charge of respiration and distribution of energy and life force in the body; the mental body has capabilities such as thinking, remembering, assimilating sense input data, calculating, planning; and the intellectual sheath has the functioning of discernment and decision making.

On final analysis, our complex human system can be viewed as a set of capabilities that perform different functions at different levels. But, it seems that this fivefold partitioning is not the only possible way to describe this system. We are dealing with a continuum of capabilities and functions that can be described and dissected in many other ways. As an analogy, think of our color system. How many colors are there? In reality, there is an infinite number of color shades and hues; but our language divides the infinite continuum of light wavelengths into a few defined colors. This is a practical and useful convention, but it doesn't fully express the reality of the color spectrum.

9 B.K.S. Iyengar, *Light on Life*, p. 108
10 B.K.S. Iyengar, *Light on Life*, Ch. 1, p. 5

In any event, this picture seems consistent with the Aristotelian approach we advance here that conceives of human nature – indeed the nature of any living being – as consisting of various capacities that are not clearly distinguished.

* * *

It is also worth noting that the question of mind–body relations played a significant role in both of our personal and intellectual backgrounds. As a philosophy student, Ohad was introduced to this question during his early studies at the Hebrew University in Jerusalem, and has been engaging with it ever since. As a student of computer science, Eyal too was introduced to and engaged with these questions. In fact, Eyal's doctoral dissertation (in Computer Science) focused on artificial intelligence, in general, and the role of language, in particular.[11]

It goes without saying that bringing in Indian and, more widely, Eastern philosophy to address this problem would be highly pertinent and illuminating. But, as this would require space and expertise that we don't presently have, we must refer the reader to other sources.[12]

11 While this may be anecdotal, it might also worth mentioning that, as students at the Hebrew University in Jerusalem we both took (though at different times) a very influential course on the mind–body problem, given by the extremely charismatic, and something mythic, teacher Yeshayahu Leibowitz. Leibowitz was a man of broad knowledge and extreme clarity of expression. He argued with the zeal of a prophet that the psycho-physical problem is simultaneously the most important problem of philosophy and one that cannot be solved. His lectures and character thus instilled a certain sense of mystery and deep engagement with this question. It is perhaps not coincidental that we have decided to deal with this issue only after many years and at a rather mature stage in our careers.

12 See, for example, *Roots of Yoga*, translated and edited by James Mallinson and Mark Singleton, UK: Penguin Random House, 2017, for a broader introduction to Indian philosophy, see Adamson, Peter and Jonardon Ganeri, *History of Philosophy Without Any Gaps, Vol. 4: India*, Oxford University Press (2015), Ganeri, J. (Ed.), *The Oxford Handbook of Indian Philosophy*: Oxford University Press (2017), and *Perrett, Roy, An Introduction to Indian Philosophy, Cambridge University Press (2016)*, which has a number of sections on Samkhya-Yoga philosophy in relation to a number of classic philosophical issues, including the mind–body problem.

Why Yoga?

On top of all this, it is important to recall Pierre Hadot's observation that, "Unlike the Buddhist meditation practices of the Far East, Greco-Roman philosophical meditation is not linked to corporeal attitude" (*Philosophy as a Way of Life*, Blackwell, 1995, p. 59). This remains true throughout the history of Western philosophy, whose methods are generally rather abstract and almost entirely detached from corporeal activity and physical exercise. In this respect, our bringing reflective yoga practice and philosophy together in this book might serve to introduce and provide philosophy with a sort of laboratory context that has the potential to add something new to philosophical reflections on mind–body relations.

Our choice to explore the relationships between mind and body through the prism of yoga is of course affected by our personal engagement with yoga (and more specifically with *Iyengar Yoga*). But, more importantly, we believe that yoga offers an ideal context for studying mind–body relationships. While many kinds of sport and physical activity have positive mental effects, *yogaasanas* are intended to serve as tools for affecting a mental and personal transformation. *Asanas* are not merely body-work; rather, they are designed to explore and affect our state of mind and ultimately our whole personality. *Yogaasanas* encourage intimate knowledge of our body, mind, and breath, and the connections between them. For this reason, they offer a natural, practical laboratory for studying the intimate relationships between physical and mental capacities. At the same time, we believe that much of what we say here, or at least the exploratory attitude we seek to promote in yoga practice, might be relevant and applicable to other physical practices: for example, it seems to us perfectly reasonable that the points we make here should also apply to martial arts as well as, swimming, hiking, or dancing – as long as these activities are done with attention to the qualities and issues we raise.[13]

13 A note by Ohad: I myself swim regularly and also like to run and cycle. I find that extending some of the insights from my yoga practice to these activities is very interesting and useful. For instance, in swimming, I try to focus on the particular bodily sensations and on the overall flow and direction of the body. Elongating and extending one's body seem to work well in reducing resistance and swimming more smoothly. I also try to avoid thinking about how many laps remain and focus on enjoying every moment (as much as possible).

A Note on the Scope of Our Argument

We would like to clarify that we are not claiming that yoga is the only way to employ the body for mental development. Neither do we claim that mental development is not possible without employing the body. It is very possible that certain individuals were born with developed mental skills and it is also possible for people to enhance their mental capabilities without using a structured body practice. Nor do we claim that any type of yoga practice necessarily produces mental enhancement and development. Rather, our purpose is to investigate mind-body relationships through the lens of yoga practice, and to discuss whether and how one can, through reflective and mindful *asana* practice, observe, enhance and develop certain mental and physical capabilities. We provide ample illustration of this in chapter 1, and discuss some pertinent capabilities in chapter 2. The philosophical background and argument is presented in chapter 3.

CHAPTER ONE

Practical Explorations

"Words cannot convey the value of yoga – it has to be experienced".

B.K.S. Iyengar

The purpose of this chapter is to make the investigation of mind and body – mental and physical – more concrete by suggesting a series of Explorations that one can practice on his or her own. These Explorations are rather basic yoga *asanas* (postures), mostly done with props, in which the reader is invited to try out several variations of the same *asana*, but each time with a different emphasis and a different mental focus. The reader/practitioner is then invited to reflect and note the relationships between the change in her or his bodily position and mental state, as well as to observe the feelings she or he has in response to these changes. These reflections and observations serve as firsthand, intimate insight into mind–body relations, not in theory, but through a concrete experience. We think of these Explorations as experiments in one's own **psychophysical lab**.

Introduction[1]

Guidelines for Practice

The Explorations offered here are divided into two groups; the first group (Section 1.1) contains basic *asanas* and is intended for readers who have little or no experience in yoga practice, or for those who have no experience in using the standard yoga props. The second group (Section 1.2) is intended for practitioners who have some experience in yoga and are familiar with basic yoga props. These practitioners can select Explorations from both sections.

The Explorations presented here are samples that are meant to enhance your practice in an inquisitive mode. We haven't tried to be comprehensive, but just to give some clues and ideas for attentive and inquisitive practice. We encourage the reader to use her/his imagination and to make her/his own experiments and explorations. In other words, the idea is to practice as if you are in a lab, and to carry out experiments in order to study yourself – your own body , breath and mind.

The Explorations are quite independent of each other, so that each of them can be tried out separately. Indeed, this part is intended as a practice guide rather than as a textbook; it need not be followed in sequential order. Feel free to pick and choose any Exploration or any small set of Explorations and practice them, according to your time constraints and curiosity.

For those who have no experience in yoga and intend to do several Explorations in one session, we recommend starting with some standing *asanas*, then continue with seated poses, and finally end with supine poses and *Shavasana* (Relaxation Pose). Always spare at least 5 minutes for *Shavasana*, before rushing back to your daily business.

If you are not versed in the jargon of yoga (and especially of *Iyengar Yoga*), then some instructions may seem obscure to you. We have underlined terms that may be unclear, and added explanations for them. In addition, Appendix B contains a glossary of some Sanskrit terms we use (all Sanskrit words are italicized within the book).

In some Explorations you are asked to try out several variations or *asanas* and compare the changes in your body and mind. In such cases, don't stay in each variation for too long, so as not to lose the sharpness of your sensations. In order to keep your memory fresh, move from one variation to the next without delays and without unnecessary movements. This will help you to gain a better comparison.

Chapter 4 contains sequences – you may wish to use them as guides for your practice.

1. Books and texts abbreviations are as follows: BG – *Bhagavad Gita*, LOY – *Light on Yoga*, TOY – *The Tree of Yoga*, YS – *The Yoga Sutras of Patanjali*

A Note About Practicing During Period

During menstruation, women must change their practice. The main guidelines for practice during these days are:

- **Avoid any inversion** (such as Head or Shoulder Stand) – this is because the inversions are a hurdle to menstrual flow.
- Don't practice tiring *asanas* or *asanas* that increase the body's heat (such as strenuous standing *asanas*).
- Don't practice *asanas* that contract the abdominal muscles (such as *Urdhva Prasarita Padasana* – Raised Stretched-Out Foot Pose).
- Don't practice *asanas* that squeeze the abdomen or apply pressure to the abdominal organs (such as *Marichyasana III*).

Instead, practice relaxing poses such as sitting *asanas*, supported forward bends, and supported supine poses.

For more information about practicing during menstruation, refer to books dealing with this subject. Two excellent books that address the subject thoroughly are *The Woman's Yoga Book* by Bobby Clennell and *Geeta S. Iyengar's Guide to a Woman's Yoga Practice* by Lois Steinberg.

Urdhva Prasarita Padasana.
Do not practice during menstruation

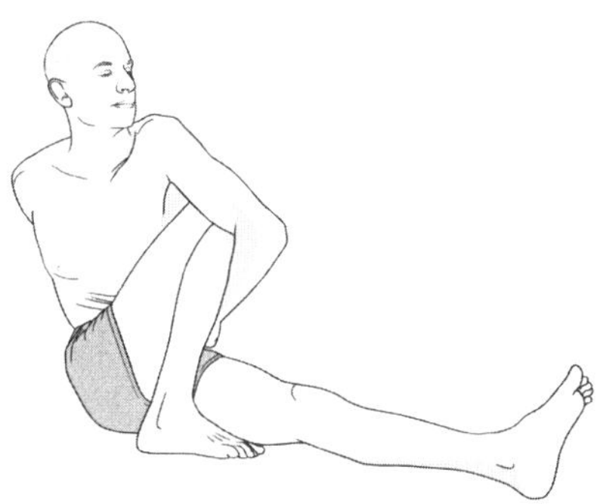

Marichyasana III.
Do not practice during menstruation

A Note on the Use of Props

Yogacharya B.K.S. Iyengar (1918-2014), the founder of the *Iyengar Yoga* method, introduced the use of Yoga Props – various apparatuses, which he invented and adapted over the years, and which were created to enrich practice and to enable every person to benefit from the gift of yoga.

Iyengar defines and explains the usages of props as follows:

"A yoga prop is any object that helps to stretch, strengthen, relax, or improve the ***alignment*** of the body [. . .] I then began experimenting with ordinary, everyday objects such as walls, chairs, stools, blocks, bolsters, blankets and belts [. . .] I discovered that props helped to retain key movements and subtle adjustments of the body by providing more height, weight, or support."[2]

For more information about the use of props, refer to Eyal's books *A Chair for Yoga* and the series *Props for Yoga*.[3]

Alignment is an important principle in yoga practice. To align the body in an *asana* means to position the limbs along lines in a way that minimizes the load on the joints and achieves maximal stability of the skeletal structure. This is important, since it preserves the health of the joints and decreases the muscular effort required to hold the pose.

Alignment refers not only to the physical body, but to our entire psychosomatic system. In his teaching, B.K.S. Iyengar emphasized the importance of alignment and extended it far beyond the physical layer: "When I speak of alignment, it means we have to balance the energy and intelligence evenly throughout the body so that the life force is maintained ever-green and ever-fresh by the practice of *asana*. We have to develop through alignment to enlighten the intelligence in all *asana*, as each *asana* distinctively beams different rays of awareness and attention on intelligence."[4]

2. *Yoga – the Path to Holistic Health*, by B.K.S. Iyengar, pages 182-3
3. These books are available at amazon.com
4. *Astadala Yoga Mala*, Vol. 6 p. 209-210. See also the article *Alignment – a Holistic Principle* in Eyal's blog (eyalshifroni.com/blog)

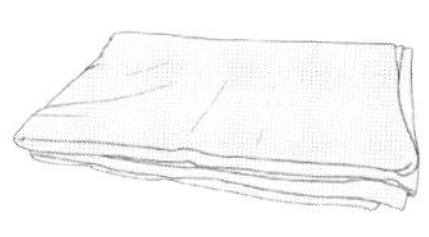

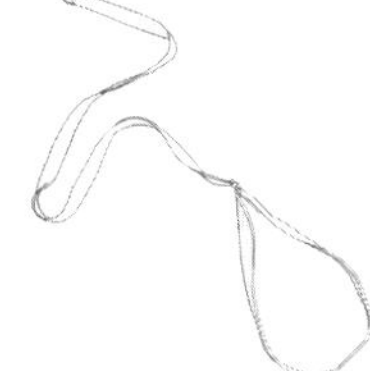

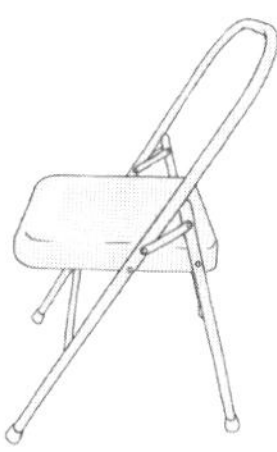

In this book we make use of following standard simple props:

- Yoga sticky mat – a mat is used in all *asanas*, and as such, is not listed for each Exploration
- Yoga belt (or a rope)
- Block (sometimes called 'brick')
- Blanket (preferably made from cotton or wool)
- Bolster (a long, compressed pillow, usually filled with cotton)
- Chair

Props have many applications: they make yoga accessible for the handicapped and the disabled, as well as allowing for restorative practice, which rejuvenates and refreshes our body-mind system.

Additionally, and just as importantly, props are used to explore the *asanas* to a greater depth. In this book, we utilize the props not because one is unable to do the pose without them, but in order to emphasize specific actions and to experience a deeper sensory awareness that may be otherwise obscured. In this type of usage, one typically repeats the pose twice or more, with and without props, and studies one's reactions and responses to successive applications of the same *asana*. The props are used to draw awareness to some bodily region and/or to clarify some action one needs to carry out when maintaining the *asana*. The same *asana* is then repeated without props (or with different usage of props), and the practitioner attempts to recreate the same action or feeling that the props had previously facilitated. By observing these changes and their effects on the body-mind system, one deepens her or his practice.

A Note on Breath

Using the breath is an essential aspect of yoga practice. There are many books dealing with that subject thoroughly: notably, *Light on Pranayama* by B.K.S. Iyengar. Here we only give basic guidelines, and in the Explorations below we will add more guidelines and observations about breathing.

- Breathing (both inhalation and exhalation) should always be done through the nostrils and not through the mouth, unless otherwise impossible due to a temporary cold or anatomical blockage in the nose.
- While staying in an *asana*, never hold the breath; instead, be aware of the breath and maintain its natural, spontaneous flow. The breath should not be automatic or mechanical but should flow softly and smoothly.
- To avoid mechanical breathing, at times, alter the rhythm and the depth of the breath and combine it with your actions. Generally, use exhalation to go further in the *asana*, and inhalation to extend, expand, *open* and *create space* in the body.
- If you feel stressed or breathless, immediately stop controlling your breath and resume natural breathing until the tension is released. If this doesn't help, come out of the *asana*, and relax.

Creating space or *opening* means extending and expanding the anatomical body, in order to increase the dimensions of the joints or the cavities of the body. For example, when extending the spine, we use the back muscles to elongate the spine by lifting the vertebrae and increasing the intervertebral space. This lifts the ribs and increases the volume of the chest cavity and the abdominal cavity. We can also create space in the joints by extending the muscles around the joints or with props (see for example: Exploration A.20: *Vajrasana* – Sitting on the heels). Creating space is an important facet of yoga practice, since it improves breathing and blood circulation, and creates mental relief and exhilaration.

1.2 *Explorations for All Levels*

For the Explorations in this section, there is no need for any prior experience in *asana* practice.

Standing *Asanas*

The standing *asanas* are the best starting point; they provide a stable base from which to explore the other poses safely. They tone, strengthen and flex our organs of action – the arms and the legs. The movements of the arms widen and open the chest, while those of the legs increase the range of movement in the pelvic area. Hence, these poses foster lightness and freedom both physically and mentally.

CAUTIONS

- People with scoliosis should rest the spine against a wall edge to create more awareness of their alignment.
- If you are prone to dizziness, do the pose with your back against a wall.

Exploration A.1

Attending to the Chest and Spine in *Tadasana* (Mountain Pose)

In this Exploration, we compare standing casually, as one may stand in daily life, with standing in *Tadasana* – the mountain pose.

› Stand as you would in a queue during the day, without taking any specific care with your posture.

› Sense the space in your chest as you inhale.

Without changing anything, observe the position of your shoulders, the space in your chest, the flow of your breath, the softness of your eyes, and the state of your brain.

Now do *Tadasana*:

› Widen your toes and feet. Feel the touch of the soles of your feet against the floor and ground your heels, the outer edges of your feet and your toe mounds (see figure).

Imagine each of your feet is like a four-wheeled vehicle. Press down evenly all the eight wheels you are standing on. Now imagine you inject air into these wheels and inflate them.

› Move your tailbone forward into the pelvis and at the same time move the front of your upper thighs back.

› Extend the sides of your trunk upward to your armpits, but release your shoulders downward. Lift your trunk from the lower abdomen and from the base of the spine.

~ *Tadasana* may seem like a simple pose. Indeed, it is not challenging physically; the pose requires no apparent movements of the limbs. However, it requires many actions in order to maintain a stable, open and balanced posture. These actions are not easy to learn precisely because they are subtle.

In his teachings, B.K.S. Iyengar stressed time and again the importance of this apparently simple pose; he taught fine points about this pose even when instructing his most advanced students and teachers. It took me years to learn some of these subtle actions, and I am still exploring this *asana*, and from time to time have new discoveries. ~

› Elongate the spine; roll your shoulders back and down; ***move your shoulder blades in*** and activate your back muscles to widen and ***open your chest***.

Exhale and draw your attention to your spine; then, while inhaling, imagine an external pull, as if a string is connected to the top of your head and gently pulls it up. Feel how this creates space between each adjacent vertebra, as if an air cushion is formed between them. Sense the space in the chest cavity as you inhale.

› Maintain a stable pose but release any tension, especially in the diaphragm, throat, face, eyes and shoulders.

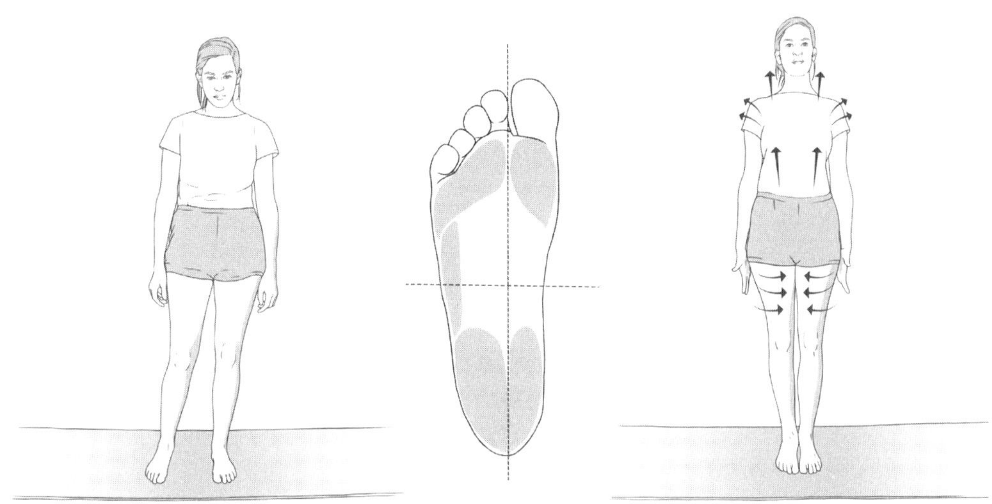

Standing in a slouch posture

Contact of the foot with the floor

Tadasana – the mountain pose

› Mentally connect the front of your brain to the back of your brain, then to your sacrum and all the way down to your heels. At the same time, open and lift your heart center (at the center of your chest). ∫

How was the flow of your breath when doing proper *Tadasana*? How soft were your eyes? What was your mental state? What were the differences between the first, casual, sloppy posture and a proper *Tadasana*?

Opening the chest has enormous effects on our overall disposition. In Chapter 2, we discuss in greater length how opening the chest can rapidly and drastically change our mood. This simple action can take us from gloomy and down to optimistic and cheerful.

When the shoulders are dropped forward, and the chest is sunken, one feels restricted and possibly even depressed to some degree. Indeed, depression is often associated with a rounded upper back and a tendency for a narrow chest. In a depressed mood, we tend to look down, and our breathing is typically shallow.

Sequence 4 (in Chapter 4) illustrates how practicing a sequence of *asanas* can drastically change our mood.

Moving the shoulder blades in means moving them forward toward the front (anterior) part of the body. Imagine someone is looking at your back and you want to hide your shoulder blades from her. Activate your back muscles to move the entire plates of the shoulder blades closer and closer to the ribs at your back. This action opens the chest and improves the breath.

Opening the chest means increasing all three dimensions of the chest cavity, to create more space in the chest.

Exploration A.2

The Foundation of *Tadasana* (Mountain Pose)

In this Exploration we study the effects of an improved *grounding* of the feet on the overall experience of *Tadasana*.

Grounding means improving the contact of the body with the ground (usually the floor, but it can also be a prop situated on the floor). In every *asana*, you should attend to the body parts that touch the ground and make them stable, solid and steady – this is also called 'Earth Element'. Grounding is important, since it allows us to better use the force of gravity to improve our stability and to extend the body upward – just like a tall and stable tree must have firm roots.

› Stand in *Tadasana* and observe your feet and legs.

How did your feet feel (the base of the pose)? How did your legs feel? How much space was there in your chest? How smooth was your breath?

› Now open the sole of the right foot. Bend, and use your fingers to spread and expand the skin of the sole.

› Lift your toes, elongate and spread them and then place them on the floor. Try to spread not only the toes but also the metatarsal bones of the foot

Imagine you spread the skin of the sole of your right foot like spreading a bed-sheet. It should be soft and well spread.

Bending to opening the sole of the foot

› Lift your right heel, extend it back, and ground it. Press equally on the inner and outer sides of your heel.

To press down your heel, imagine you are standing in high-heeled shoes, and then dig this extra height deep into the ground.

› Press the outer edge of your right foot down and lift the inner arch.

› Then stand up, look forward and breathe.

Imagine your right foot is wide and large like a fin. Imagine it has many roots like grass. It is very hard to uproot grass since it has many deep roots. Imagine that each pore of your right sole's skin is like a root grounding you deeply into the earth.

Compare the feeling in the right and left legs; the breath in both your lungs; the sharpness of both eyes.

Did the opening of the skin of your right foot affect your entire right leg? Did it affect your chest as well? Did it affect your eyes?

› After registering your sensations, repeat the same actions on your left foot and stand again in *Tadasana*.

› Observe your breath. ʃ

Did you feel more balance and harmony in the pose once both feet were spread and well-grounded?

~ Grounding the feet in the floor affects my entire pose. After grounding my right foot only, I feel a marked difference between my feet; this difference spreads throughout the right side of my body. I feel that the right side of my chest expands and even the vision of my right eye sharpens. ~

Exploration A.3

Joining vs. Spreading the Legs in *Tadasana* (Mountain Pose)

The 'classic' *Tadasana* (as shown in *Light on Yoga*) is done with the legs joined together. But it is possible to do *Tadasana* with the legs slightly spread apart. In this Exploration, we compare these two variations.

› Join your heels and big toes and stand in *Tadasana* (see Exploration A.1 for basic instructions about *Tadasana*).

› Stay in the pose for a minute or two and take note of your sensations.

› Attempt to center yourself and to keep your body weight distributed evenly between your two feet, avoiding any shifting or oscillations.

Was your body shifting from right to left?

› Close your eyes; keep observing the weight distribution on your feet.

Could you keep yourself centered with closed eyes?

› Now spread your legs to the width of your pelvis and stay in the pose another minute or two.

› Repeat the observations above while your legs are apart. ∫

In which variation did you feel more stable and steady?

In which variation was your concentration better, during the entire time you stayed in the pose?

Observe also how much your body extended and expanded in both variations.

~ In my experience, *Tadasana* with joined legs creates more sharpness and extension, while spreading the legs creates more expansion and relaxation. B.K.S. Iyengar found that vertical extension sharpens our intellect whereas horizontal expansion develops our emotional aspect. In order to develop our personality in a balanced manner, we need to foster both intellectual and emotional capabilities. ~

Exploration A.4

Doing *Tadasana* (Mountain Pose) on Blocks

PROPS
2 blocks

In this Exploration, we compare *Tadasana* on two blocks with ordinary *Tadasana* (with feet on the floor).

› Place two blocks on the floor next to each other and stand in *Tadasana* on the floor, near the blocks.

› Observe the sensation in your legs.

To what extent were your leg muscles active? How sharp was your awareness of the bones in your legs?

› Now stand in *Tadasana* on the blocks. Release your toes over the edges of the blocks.

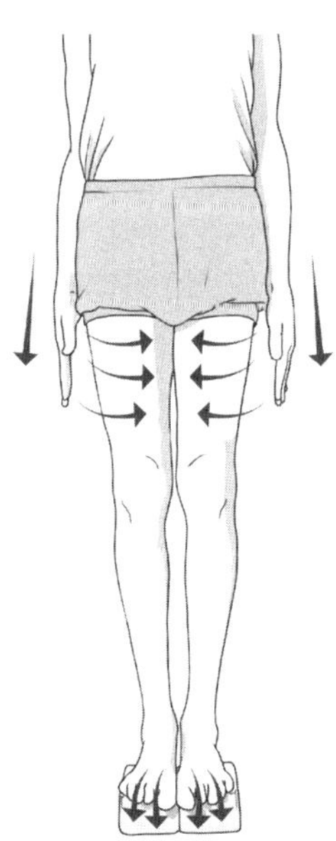

standing on two blocks

What did you notice when you stood on the blocks? Did you have a sharper sensation of the bones in your legs? Did you feel your thigh muscles come closer to your thighbones? Did you notice any change in your field of vision? Was it broader? Sharper? What was your mental state, compared with standing on the floor? Did you feel that you became longer?

It is curious that, for most people, there is a significant, tangible difference between standing on blocks and on the floor. This is a simple case that demonstrates well the integration of the mind and the body in the practice of yoga. While it is hard to say if the effect is of a psychological or physical nature, as most practitioners report, the effect cannot be denied. However, you need not believe us (or other people): try it out and see for yourself.

If you also felt a difference, try to articulate it – everything is the same except that the blocks elevate us a few inches above the floor. What is going on? Clearly some differences in our perception of the pose are likely to account for this difference, for the physiology is almost the same (almost, since the blocks allow us to relax our toes downward).

Exploration A.5

Activating the Arms in *Tadasana* (Mountain Pose)

In this Exploration, we use a belt looped around the arms to activate them; we compare it with *Tadasana* done without a belt.

› Stand in *Tadasana*. Move your tailbone in (forward) and the front of your thighs back. Observe the space in your chest.

How open was your chest? How much did your breath penetrate into your chest and fill it?

› Now take the belt and adjust it to the width of your shoulders. Place the belt around your lower arms, just below your elbows behind the back.

› Stretch your arms (vertically) down and sideways against the belt.

› Use this arm action to open your chest by moving your shoulder blades deep into your chest, but avoid pushing your lumbar spine forward or creating undue tension.

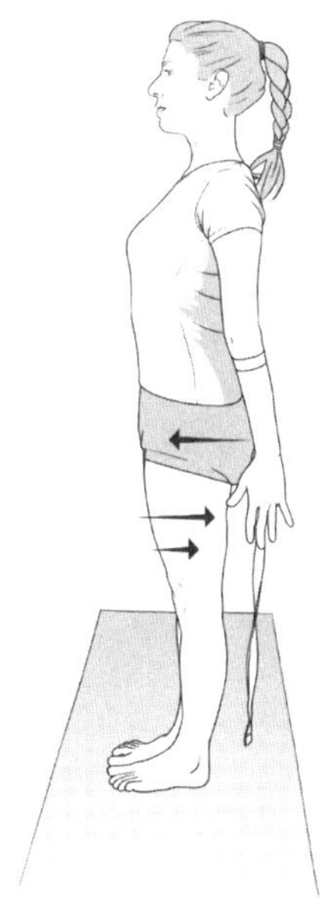

Stretching the arms with a belt

› Observe the effect of stretching your arms against the belt on your experience in the pose.

How did using the belt affect the space in your chest; how deep and smooth was your breath? What happened to your eyes? Were you more composed? More confident? Did you sense greater joy and optimism?

› Do the pose again without the belt, and try to recreate the effects you felt when using the belt. ʃ

~ Generally, we use the legs to work on the pelvic area, and the arms to work on the chest and upper back. In yoga, we use these organs of action (*karmendriyas*) to create space in the trunk. Using the belt helps me to activate my arms and thus creates more opening in my chest. This has a marked effect on the quality and experience of my pose. ~

PROPS
belt

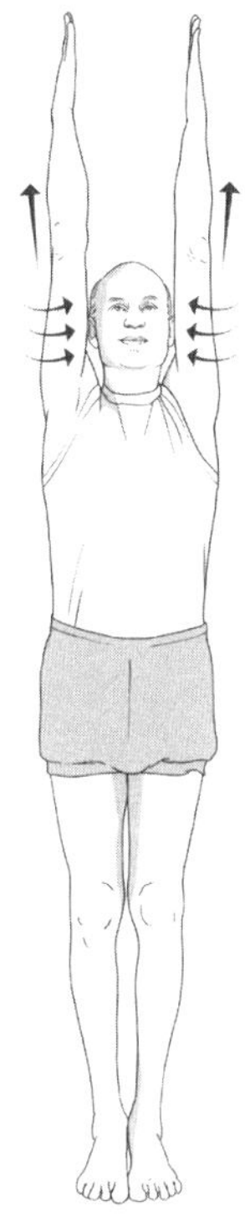

Urdhva Hastasana – Front view

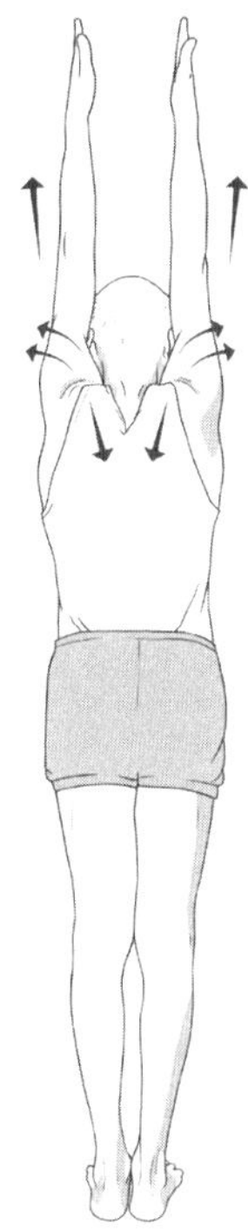

Urdhva Hastasana – back view

Our next pose is *Urdhva Hastasana* – stretching the arms up.

Basic instructions for *Urdhva Hastasana* (Arms Overhead Pose)

CAUTIONS

for *Urdhva Hastasana* and *Vrksasana*:

- If you have high blood pressure or a cardiac condition do not stretch your arms up for more than 30 seconds.
- If you are prone to dizziness, practice with your back against a wall.

› To do *Urdhva Hastasana* (literally, 'arms up pose'): stand in *Tadasana* and stretch your arms up over the head.

› Stretch your arms vertically up, in line with your body and use them to elongate your trunk and to lift and open your chest.

› Connect the action of your arms to your ribs; lift your ribcage but release your trapezius muscle downward. Make sure your neck is not compressed and your throat is soft. ∫

Exploration A.6

Using One Arm to Stretch the Other

We now study the effect of stretching the arms up. We use the arms to lift the entire ribcage and create length in the spine. We compare lifting the arms in the normal way with using one hand to enhance the stretch of the other arm.

› Stand in *Tadasana* and lift your arms up to *Urdhva Hastasana*.

› Use the actions of your arms to elongate the sides of your trunk and to lift your chest.

› Move your shoulder blades, back ribs and thoracic dorsal spine forward into the chest.

› Sensitize the sides of your chest and your outer armpits.

To what extent did the sides of your trunk extend upward? What was the movement of your navel region? Did you experience tension in your throat?

Urdhva Hastasana – Stretching one arm with the other

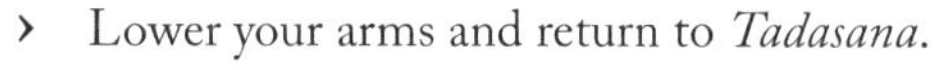

› Lower your arms and return to *Tadasana*.

› Now lift your arms again, and with your left hand hold your right wrist and pull it up; extend up the whole right side of your trunk.

› Then catch your right upper arm and turn it inward (the triceps muscles rolling in).

› Release your left hand and stretch both arms upward at shoulder width.

› Compare the level of extension in the two sides of your trunk.

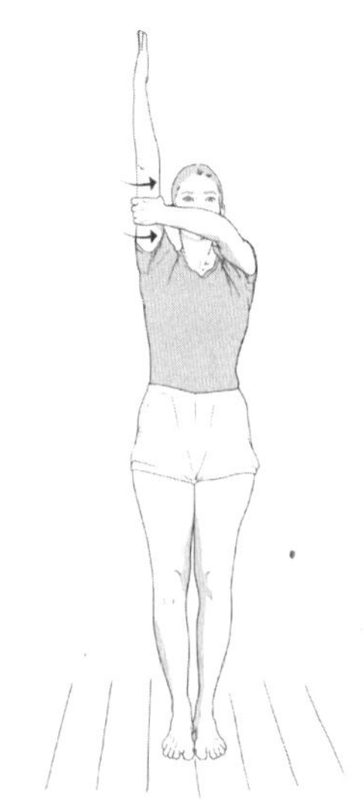

Turning the upper arm inward

Which side felt more extended and enlivened?

Stretching the arms is not done just by lifting the shoulders; if you only lift your shoulders, you are likely to create tension in your throat.

When lifting your arms, connect your upper arms to your shoulders (by moving the deltoid muscles down to the shoulder joints). Imagine that your arms originate from the bottom of your side ribs (rather than from your shoulders). Then while stretching your arms up, lift your entire ribcage. Squeeze your outer elbows in, and extend your inner arms up. Feel the elongation of your spine. Release your jaw and rest your tongue on your lower palate. Keep working with your arms, but release and soften the muscles and skin of your face.

› Now use your right hand to extend and turn your left arm.

› Then stay in *Urdhva Hastasana* and observe the stretch of both sides.

› Exhale, move your arms down and then repeat *Urdhva Hastasana*. Try to achieve an even stretch when lifting both arms at the same time. ∫

Compare the first *Urdhva Hastasana* with the second one. Did you feel better extension and lifting of your chest? What was the movement of your navel region? Did you feel tension in your throat? How deep was your breathing?

I feel that using one hand to lift my other arm helps me to extend the entire side of my body. Doing this first on one side only, creates a clear difference between the two sides of my body. This teaches me how to use the arms in this pose. In addition to the pull applied, touching the muscles of the arm sensitizes them and allows greater activation.

When both arms are used intensively and evenly, there is a uniform stretch of both sides, as if the arms and the trunk are one unit. I feel an upward flow along the sides. The lift of the entire ribcage encourages deeper breath. There is also a lift of my abdominal organs and my navel region naturally moves upward and in (toward my back).

Exploration A.7

Stabilizing *Urdhva Hastasana* (Arms Overhead Pose): Belt Around the Elbows and Block In Between the Palms

In this Exploration we activate and stabilize the arms by looping a belt around the elbows and using a block between the palms. We compare this to doing the pose without props.

We start without using props:

› Stand in *Tadasana* and lift your arms up to *Urdhva Hastasana*.

› Move your outer elbows in (toward each other) and lift your inner arms.

› Maintain the pose for a minute or so and then lower your arms and come back to *Tadasana*.

› Observe the connection between the action of your arms and the extension of your body.

Could you use your arms effectively to create space in your trunk? How much effort did you invest in stretching your arms? How well could you roll your shoulders back and move your arms back to a vertical position (in line with the sides of your trunk)? How was your breathing?

› Now take a belt and adjust its loop to the width of your shoulders.

› Place the belt around your elbows and hold a block between your palms.

› Squeeze the block and stretch your arms up.

› Stay like this for a minute or so; keep your face relaxed and your breathing smooth.

› Compare the first attempt of doing *Urdhva Hastasana* without props to your feelings now.

› You can also try to tighten the belt more and hold the block on its narrow side.

Did the belt and block help you to use your arms more effectively to create space in your trunk? Could you roll your shoulders further back? Did you have better access to your shoulder blades? How much effort did you experience while maintaining the pose? How was your breathing?

~ I feel that the combination of the block and belt helps me to strengthen and stabilize my arms. The belt is especially useful for people who find it hard to straighten their arms. ~

Now, try to do the same without a belt:

› Stand in *Tadasana*. Balance a block on the crown of your head and stretch your hands down.

PROPS
belt
block

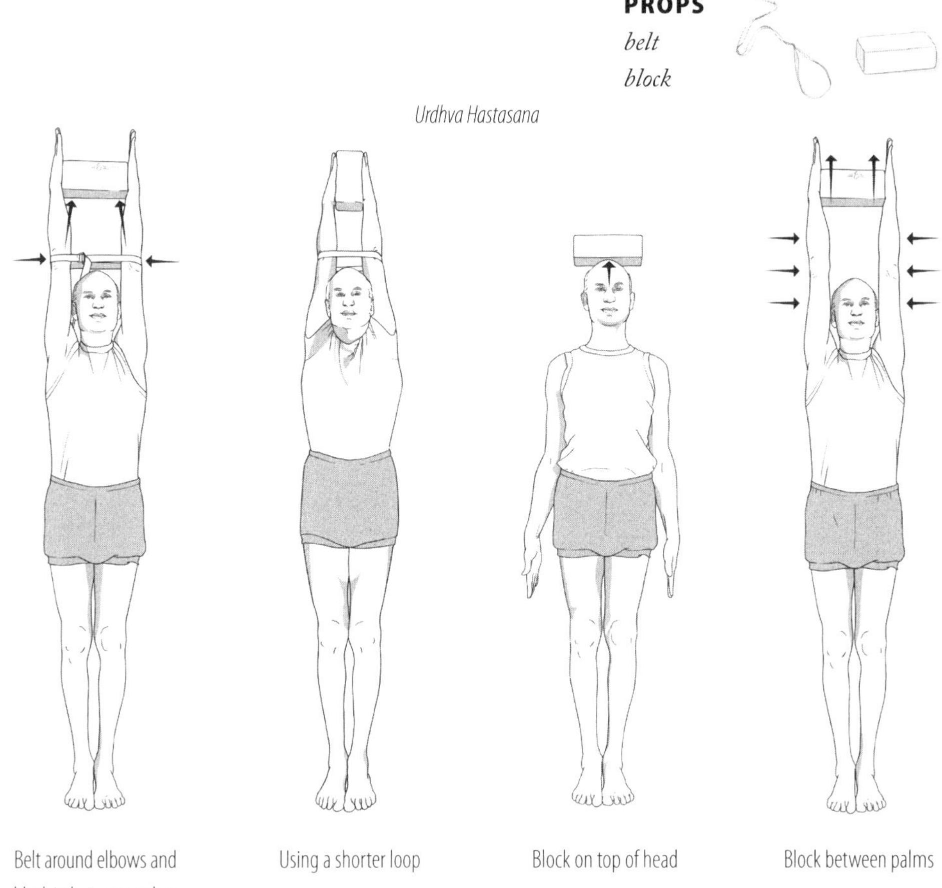

Belt around elbows and block in between palms

Using a shorter loop

Block on top of head

Block between palms

› Carefully extend your spine, to gently push the block up with your head. **Note:** Be aware that you might need to catch the block in case it falls (or use a rubber block).

› Now, hold the block between the bases of your palms, and stretch your arms up. Squeeze your outer elbows in and keep pressing your palms against the block. ∫

~ Pressing the palms against the block (without grasping it) activates and strengthens the arms. Attend to the effect this has on your overall experience of the pose. ~

Notes:

- If pressing the block at the base of your palms is too difficult, bend your fingers and grasp it firmly.
- Move your wrists back and, at the same time, extend your thumbs upward.
- Maintain the verticality of your body. Looking from the side, the joints of the ankles, hips, shoulders, and wrists should all be in one vertical line.

Vrksasana (Tree Pose)

We now turn to a balancing pose called *Vrksasana* – the Tree Pose; this is a slightly more challenging pose since one has to balance the body on one foot.

Vrksasana

"The Ashvattha Tree is a giant banyan tree. Its roots extend deep and wide into the soil. Its trunk ascends, branching again and again carrying its leaves on the outer edge where they face the outer atmosphere, absorbing light, exchanging gases, and receiving the rain, directing its moistening fluid to bathe the entire organism [. . .]. We are the Tree. Our brain is the root, the trunk is our torso, with its spinal cord, and the branches are the limbs – arms and legs."
(*The Bhagavad-Gita*, Ch. XV)

Basic instructions for *Vrksasana*

› Stand in *Tadasana*, lift your right leg and place your heel as high as possible against your left thigh. Place your right foot with the toes facing downward, such that the center of the foot is aligned with the center of your left inner thigh. Press your heel against your left thigh and balance on your left leg.

› Stretch your arms up as in *Urdhva Hastasana.*

› Without turning your pelvis to the right, move your right knee back, attempting to align it (laterally) with your pelvis.

Exploration A.8

Stabilizing *Vrksasana* (Tree Pose – Vision and Balance)

In this Exploration, we study the effect of vision on the ability to balance.

› Do *Vrksasana* four times while trying the following variations:

1. Fix your gaze on a steady point in front of you;
2. Move your eyes from side to side and up and down;
3. Do the pose facing the wall, close to it.
4. Do the pose with your back to the wall, close your eyes, and then move slightly away from the wall, attempting to balance with closed eyes. ʃ

In which variation was your balance better?

~ I find the first variation much more helpful for balancing. Balance is achieved by coordinated activation of many muscles; it is interesting therefore to question why vision is so critical in our ability to balance. Achieving balance requires skillful utilization of the visual system (eyes), proprioceptive system (joint and muscular) and vestibular system (inner ear – equilibrium). ~

Exploration A.9

Stabilizing *Vrksasana* (Tree Pose) Using Focusing

In this Exploration, we focus our attention on two different regions of the body and examine the effects it has on our ability to maintain a well-balanced pose. Note that, here, the difference between the two attempts of the pose is completely internal: we just change the focal region of our attention.

› Do *Vrksasana*, while:

1. Keeping your awareness focused entirely on the foot of your standing leg.
2. Keeping your awareness focused entirely on stretching your fingers vertically upward. ∫

   Note: To aid in keeping your attention focused on the chosen region, you can mentally repeat an instruction for yourself, like repeating a *mantra*. For example, in the second option you can repeat silently: "stretch the fingers, stretch the fingers …", this can help to keep your attention focused.

Just maintaining the pose, without falling, is one thing; good balance is another. We seek to maintain a stable, steady and quiet pose, and to avoid fluctuation.

Were you able to balance without wobbling? In which variation was your balance better?

Exploration A.10

Mountain and Tree

In this Exploration, we repeat *Tadasana* three times: first before doing *Vrksasana*, then after doing *Vrksasana* standing on the left leg, and finally after doing *Vrksasana* standing on the right leg. We study the connection of these two poses and compare the experience of *Tadasana* in these three attempts.

› Stand in *Tadasana* and feel your feet and legs.

› Lift your right leg to *Vrksasana*. Stay in the pose for a minute.

› Lower the leg and stand in *Tadasana*. Observe the sensation in your legs after doing *Vrksasana* on one side.

› Then do *Vrksasana* lifting your left leg. Hold the pose for a minute and then finally come back to *Tadasana*.

What were the differences between the three attempts of *Tadasana*? How did doing *Vrksasana* affect how you felt in *Tadasana* (if at all)?

Sitting *Asanas*

We now explore three basic sitting poses and compare the experience of sitting in a pose for an extended period.

Swastikasana (the auspicious pose) which is sometimes also called *Sukhasana* (the easy or comfortable pose), is a seated pose which is very comfortable and relaxing. It is probably the most common and easiest way to sit on the floor. We first give basic instructions for this pose.

CAUTIONS

For *Swastikasana*:

- If your knees are sensitive, support them with a rolled-up blanket: see *Props for Yoga Vol. II*, p. 32.

Basic instructions for *Swastikasana*

› Use folded blankets or a bolster to have enough support under your buttocks. This allows releasing the knees down, softening the groin, extending the spine upward, and opening the chest. Your knees should be at the same height as (or just slightly higher than) your hip joints – if they do not descend, add under-buttock support.

› Sit such that your sit bones are just on the blanket, but your thighs are not. Spread the skin and flesh of your buttocks sideways, to expose your bones. Align your pelvis such that you sit on the heads of your sit bones.

- Bend your right leg, and then the left and cross them at the middle of your shins. Your legs should form a big triangle. Slide your feet away from you and move your knees closer to each other, such that each knee is resting over the opposite foot.
- To improve the interlock, roll your left calf muscle out, and slide your right shin slightly further away.
- Move your sacral bone into the pelvis and extend your spine up. Lift your lumbar spine, then your thoracic spine and finally your cervical spine up to your head. Maintain your spine, neck and head in one vertical line.
- Release your shoulders, roll them back and down. Release from shoulders to elbows and from elbows to hands. Rest your palms (or the backs of the palms) on your thighs.
- Move your shoulder blades in to open your chest.
- Look forward at eye level. Relax your eyes, inner ears, tongue, lips, jaws and the entire face and head. ∫

Make sure you change the order in which your legs are crossed each time you sit.

Sitting in *Swastikasana*

Exploration A.11

Creating Space in the Chest

In this Exploration, we compare different means of creating space in the chest, with and without using the arms and hands. We observe and compare the mental effects of these different ways of opening the chest.

› Sit crossed legged (*Swastikasana*) with support under your buttocks and place a block on each side of your pelvis.

› Do not activate your para-spinal muscles (the muscles along the spine), but just sit normally.

› Close your eyes and take a few slow, soft, deep breaths.

How much space was there in your thoracic cavity? Did your breath flow smoothly? What was the volume of your natural breathing?

› Now, use your arms and hands to create space in your chest. First insert your thumbs inside your armpits and use your hands to lift the sides of your chest and to move your armpits forward, while rolling your shoulders back and down.

› Then interlock your fingers and stretch your arms above the head.

› Take a few breaths and activate your back muscles to elongate and stabilize your spine.

Using the hands to lift the armpits and move them forward

Stretching the arms up in *Swastikasana*

PROPS

blankets
or bolster
2 blocks

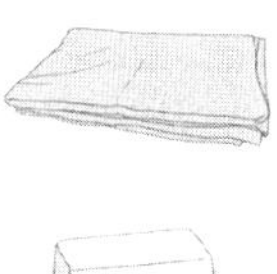

- Then, without dropping the height of your chest, or the length of your spine, lower your arms, and place your palms on the blocks.
- Press your palms down, against the blocks; use this support to lift your chest, but keep your shoulders down. Move your shoulder blades into your chest and widen your ribcage.
- Finally, without collapsing, slowly release the support of your arms and place your hands on your legs, such that your elbows are below your shoulders and the backs of your hands are resting on your thighs.
- Stay in this position for a few minutes without collapsing your chest. You can close your eyes and observe internally. Follow your natural breathing.
- Observe your breathing after placing your hands back on your thighs. ʃ

How did your chest feel when sitting after using your arms to open it? Could you maintain the openness of your chest? Did your breath flow smoothly? Did you note any changes in your emotional state
or in your energy level?

Supporting the palms in *Swastikasana*

Exploration A.12

Using Imagery for Extending the Spine

PROPS
blanket
or bolster

In this Exploration, we use imagery to extend the spine, and we examine the effect of this imagery on the experience of the pose.

› Sit straight in a crossed legged pose (*Swastikasana*) (remember to support your buttocks on a folded blanket or bolster). Place your hands on your thighs.

› Imagine there is a string, connected to the top of your skull, gently pulling you up. Think of your head as an engine pulling the whole train of your spine up. Imagine that this creates a small space, like a small air-cushion, between each two adjacent vertebrae.

› Close your eyes and remain in this position with soft and slow breathing for as long as you feel comfortable.

How did the imagery of the gentle external pull affect your inner state? For how long could you keep this imagery vivid and your spine stable and extended?

I often use imagery in my practice and teaching. I find that it helps to activate the body and to achieve extension with minimal effort. Without thinking directly about the muscles, they become active, thanks to this image of the head being lifted, as if floating above the spine and pulling the vertebrae upward.

Exploration A.13

Focusing Outward and Inward

PROPS
blanket
or bolster

In this Exploration we study the effects of the eyes and vision on our experience in a sitting pose and explore whether and how changing the functioning of the eyes affects the experience of the pose.

› Sit crossed legged on a support. Extend your spine upward and keep your spine, neck and head in one vertical line.

› Look forward at eye level and focus on some external object in front of you. Look very carefully at that object as if you need to draw it. Stay like this for a minute or two.

How sharp was your awareness of your body? Did you sense any tension in your face, eyes, shoulders or other parts of the body?

› Now, with eyes still open, soften the focus of the gaze and start directing your attention inside as if you want to see the space at the back of your skull.

› Then keep mentally observing your back: follow your spine from top to tailbone.

› When you feel that your attention has moved inside your body, allow your upper eyelids to drop. Release them until they gently rest on your lower eyelids, so that your eyes are closed, and your eyelids are softly resting over your eyeballs, which are receding softly inward.

› Observe your bodily areas where you previously felt tension, and consciously relax them.

› Stay quietly in this position while maintaining your inner gaze inside your body, as if your awareness were 'touching' the body from inside.

› Compare these two ways of using your eyes. ∫

When was your breathing smoother? When did you experience more relaxation? What were the differences in your mental state, if any?

When I direct my eyes to the back of my skull, I feel that they naturally become softer and flatter; I feel as if the pupils of my eyes are turned back to observe the inner space of my body. Holding my attention inside my body calms and stabilizes me. In this way, I experience more concentration, poise and tranquility. However (as always), it may be that your experience was different.

Exploration A.14

Using the Breath

In this Exploration, we study the effects of different modes of breathing on our mental state in a sitting pose. We apply *focused, localized breathing*. For example, breathing in the pelvic area, breathing in the chest area, or breathing in the head.

Focused, localized breath means directing your awareness to a certain bodily region, while exhaling or inhaling. An expression like: 'exhale in the pelvis', means: 'direct your attention to the pelvic region while exhaling'.

› Sit crossed-legged on a support. Extend your spine upward and keep your spine, neck, and head in one vertical line. Then close your eyes.

› Breathe in a rather harsh, irregular manner. Every now and then jerk the breath or interrupt it sharply.

What was your mental state when breathing like that?

› Now focus on your exhalation and make it slightly longer. Maintain a steady, smooth flow of exhalation.

Observe the effect of making your breathing smooth on your mental state.

› Now alternate your breathing in the following four manners:

a. Focus on the roots of your thighs and direct your exhalation into your pelvis. Soften the roots of your thighs and make your entire pelvis heavier.
b. Inhale in and through your spine, sharpen it and lift it vertically upward (think of your spine as a pencil that you sharpen by moving the right side of your spine to the left, and the left side to the right).
c. Focus on your chest and inhale into it. Move the skin of your back to touch the flesh, while at the front, move the flesh to touch the skin of your chest. (Note how the skin of the chest fills and touches your shirt, while the skin of your back moves away from the shirt).
d. Focus on your head, skull and brain as you exhale slightly longer. Imagine your breath as water flowing from the top of your head along the roots of your hair, on your forehead and down along the skin of your face – much like the flow of water on your head when taking a shower.

› Observe the effects of using focused, localized breathing on your mental state. Compare the effect of the exhalation with that of the inhalation. ʃ

Can you articulate the differences you sensed? Consider writing down your observations.

PROPS
blanket
or bolster

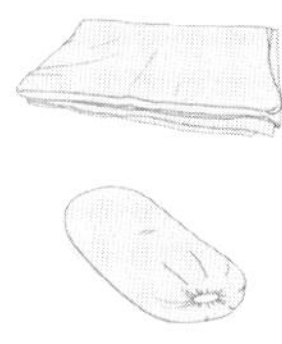

The *Hatha Yoga Pradipika* (a classic ancient text of *Hatha Yoga*) mentions the connection between the breath and the mind as follows:

"When *Prana* moves *chitta* (the mental force) moves. When *Prana* is without movement, *chitta* is without movement. By this (steadiness of *Prana*) the yogi attains steadiness and should thus restrain the *vayu* (air)." (Verse II.2)

In *Light on Pranayama*, B.K.S. Iyengar elucidates the spiritual functions of inhalation and exhalation:

"Inhalation (*Puraka*) is the intake of cosmic energy by the individual for his growth and progress. It is the path of action (*pravritti marga*). It is the Infinite united with the finite. It draws in the breath of life as carefully and as gently as the fragrance of a flower might be indrawn and distributes it evenly throughout the body".

"Exhalation is the outflow of the individual energy (*jivatma*) to unite with the cosmic energy (*Paramatma*). It quietens and silences the brain. It is the surrender of the *sadahka*'s ego to and immersion in the Self". (p. 99-100)

In yoga, the cosmic vital energy known as *Prana* is expressed in the body in five different forms as explained in the following paragraph from *Light on Pranayama*:

"Ancient Indian sages knew that all functions of the body were performed by five types of vital energy (*prana-vayus*). These are known as *prana* (here the generic term is used to designate the particular), *apana*, *samana*, *udana* and *vyana*. They are specific aspects of one vital cosmic force (vital wind), the primeval principle of existence in all beings [. . .]. *Prana* moves in the thoracic region and controls breathing. It absorbs vital atmospheric energy. *Apana* moves in the lower abdomen and controls the elimination of urine, semen and faeces. *Samana* stokes the gastric fire, aiding digestion and maintaining the harmonious functioning of the abdominal organs [. . .]. *Udana*, working through the throat (the pharynx and larynx), controls the vocal cords and the intake of air and food. *Vyana* pervades the entire body, distributing the energy derived from food and breath through the arteries, veins and nerves" (p. 12).

In my experience, focusing the breath in a specific region of my body has deep effects. It brings that region to the foreground of my consciousness and improves its vital functioning.

Exploration A.15

Atma Anjali Mudra – Joining the Palms in Front of the Chest

In this Exploration, we study the mental effect of the simple bodily gesture of joining the palms in front of the chest and lowering the head.

› Sit crossed legged on a support. Round your shoulders and allow your upper back to hunch slightly forward. Lower your head and close your eyes. Take a few cycles of breath.

How deep and smooth was your natural breath in this hunched pose? What was your mental state?

› Now stretch your spine up and open your chest (you can stretch your arms up and/or use blocks for support, like in Exploration A.11).

› With closed eyes and alert attention, move your hands in front of your chest and join your palms.

Did you sense any change in your emotional state as a result of the (action of) joining the palms together?

› Now keep the skin of your palms joined as if merged, and at the same time move the flesh of your palms toward your elbows, as if trying to maintain the least touch possible between your palms.

Did the sensation of your chest change when you did this gentle action? If so, can you describe this change?

› Apply varying amounts of pressure from each hand against the other; try to make them touch with minimal effort and pressure; become more sensitive to these nuances and their effects.

› Keeping your chest wide and well lifted, your shoulders rolled back and down and your shoulder blades tucked in, gently lower your head. Look within (imagine your left eye is drawn into your left lung, your right eye into your right lung and your brain into the space in between your lungs).

› Compare the first time you lowered your head with this second time. ʃ

lowering the head in *Atma Anjali Mudra*

PROPS
blanket
or bolster

In which was there more internalization? More focus and poise?

Joining the palms in front of the chest is called *atma anjali mudra*. *Mudra* means a seal and also a gesture. *Atma anjali mudra* is a *mudra* of gratitude, reverence and respect. Joining the palms symbolizes the unity of the two aspects, the right and the left – which are called in yoga *ida* ('sun quality') and *pingala* ('moon quality'). This *mudra* brings awareness inside, into our emotional center, which is considered to be the seat of our spiritual heart. In India, this gesture is often used to greet other people, instead of shaking hands, and it could mean: "I see the Divine in you."

~ In my experience, the physical action of joining the palms is accompanied by a marked emotional change. Bowing the head enhances further internalization, and expresses respect, surrender, humility and humbleness. By keeping the chest lifted and open, and at the same time surrendering the head down to the chest, we express both vigor and acceptance. ~

Exploration A.16

Embracing the Base in Sitting

In this Exploration we study several ways to use belts for bracing the pelvis and legs in *Swastikasana* (simple crossed legs). We then compare this to sitting without any bracing. We thus examine the effects of the bracing on the stability and the overall feeling in this seated pose.

› Sit crossed legged (*Swastikasana*) on your mat, with no support under your buttocks.

› Observe your sacrum bone and the roots of your thighs

Was your sacrum bone lifted or dropped? Were the roots of your thighs hard or soft? Was your abdomen soft? Was your breathing soft and smooth?

› Now sit on a folded blanket or bolster.

› Take two belts and brace each leg with a belt. Loop each belt from your sacrum to one knee (move the loop over your head down to your sacrum and knee).

Using two belts to embrace the pelvis and knees

› Lift your knees slightly and tighten the belts until you feel ***compactness***, evenness and stability. Then release your knees.

Compacting means making a certain region of the body denser and more condensed. Moving or sucking muscles closer to bones creates compactness. This is healthy for the bones, since it improves their blood supply. It also stabilizes the joints. There are two pairs of ball-and-socket joints in our body – the hip and the shoulder joints – for which compactness is especially important. To prevent dislocation and overstretching of the ligaments that stabilize these joints, it is important to draw the head of the bone (the femur head or humerus head) deep into the socket. This is done by activating the muscles around the joint and also with the use of props (for example, tightening a belt around the pelvis creates compactness in the pelvis). Compacting the pelvis allows the spine to extend better.

› Sit like this for 1-3 minutes and record how you feel; then remove the belts and stay in the pose for a few more minutes. ʃ

What was the sensation in your pelvis after placing the belts? How did this bracing affect the way you

PROPS

2 belts

a folded blanket

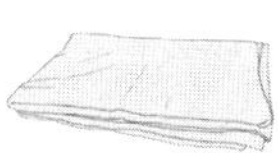

held your spine? Did it affect your ability to extend your spine and keep it stable? How soft were your groin and abdomen? How smooth was your breath? What was the state of your brain and eyes? Were they quieter or less so?

Compacting the base of the pose from outside (bracing) allows me to relax my legs and to expand my pelvis from inside out. When my pelvis and knees are held tight by the belts, there is no need to hold the pose from the groin or abdomen, and as a result these areas remain soft. It also helps me to extend my spine and keep it stable.

Supporting the knees with one belt

We now show two more ways of using belts to brace the legs and pelvis. It is interesting to compare these different options and study their effects.

A. Using one belt to support the knees

- Take one belt and place it around your knees. Adjust its length to firmly support your knees.
- Relax your groin and legs and allow the belt to support them.

B. Using two crossed belts to support the pelvis and knees

- Open one belt and loop it in the second belt.

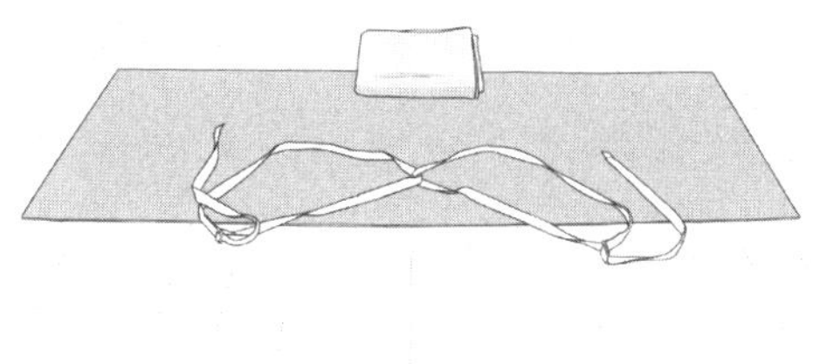

looping two belts

Exploration A.16 cont.

› Place the point at which the belts cross on your sacral band, and brace your knees.

› Place the belts such that buckles are close to your knees.

› Slightly lift your knees and use the two buckles to tighten the belts, then release your knees downward. ∫

Compare sitting without belts with these three methods of bracing the legs with respect to the compactness and stability of the base, the effect on the breath, and the overall experience of the pose.

adjusting the buckles

Using two joined belts

Exploration A.17

Effects of Crossing Alternate Legs

PROPS
blanket or bolster

Sitting cross-legged is asymmetrical. In this Exploration, we alternate the crossing of the legs and observe its effects; specifically, we notice the relation between the crossing of the legs and the sharpness of the vision.

› Sit on a folded blanket or a bolster. Bend your right leg first and then the left, and cross your legs at the middle of your shins.

› Close your eyes and observe the way your buttocks are placed on the support.

› Mentally draw the shape of the contact area of each buttock with the support; also draw the borderlines of these areas.

› Create a mental diagram of the weight distribution over these areas (you may imagine a darker color for heavier regions).

Did you notice differences between your two buttocks? Which one took more weight? Which had a larger contact area?

› Now open your eyes. Keep them relaxed and look forward at eye level, maintaining an unfocused gaze (imagine you are looking from behind your ears rather than from your eyes).

Did you sense any difference in the sharpness of your eyes? If so, which eye had a sharper field of vision?

› Close your eyes again and take a few slow, soft, deep breathes.

Did you sense any difference in the breath to each lung? If so, which lung played a more active role in the breathing?

› Relax for a while, and then change the order of leg-crossing (bend the left first, then the right) and repeat the same exploration. ∫

Which buttock took more of the load or felt more prominent and wider after you changed how your legs were crossed? Which eye was sharper? Which lung became more active?

Observe your mental state at the end of this exploration. Do you feel more balanced?

Exploration A.18

PROPS
belt

Using a Belt to Open the Chest

In this Exploration, we use a belt for rolling the shoulders back and opening the chest, and observe the mood variations while varying the pose.

Crossing a belt behind the back

As mention in Exploration A.1 above (see page 21), opening the chest has enormous effects on our overall disposition. In Chapter 2, we discuss the connection between opening the chest and our mood. We note there that opening the chest can take us quickly from feeling gloomy and down to optimism and cheerfulness.

Opening the chest requires activating the back muscles; we use these muscles to roll the shoulders back, to move the shoulder blades in, to draw the back ribs forward, and to lift the thoracic spine.

› Sit cross-legged on a support, and roll your shoulders forward; let the chest sink, and look down.

› Observe how you feel in this hunched posture.

› Now place an open belt on your shoulder girdle, such that it rests in front of the tops of your shoulders.

› Move the loose ends of the belt under the fronts of your armpits and cross them behind your back.

› Hold the crossed ends with bent arms and pull evenly with both hands.

› Maintain the pull of the belts for a minute or two, and then slowly release the belt. Stay in the pose another minute and check whether you can retain the effect of pulling the belt.

› Observe the space in your chest, the position of your back ribs and shoulder blades and the width of your collarbones.

› Breathe softly, slowly and deeply and observe the smoothness and the depth of your breath. ʃ

Did using the belt to open your chest affect your overall feeling and mood? Did you notice changes in the space of the chest and in your breath while doing the pose with and without the belt?

Exploration A.19

A Block on Top of the Head

In this Exploration, we use a block to turn our attention upward and study the effects this has on the experience of pose.

PROPS

block or any other flat object

› Sit erect on a support. Hold a block and lift it up, as high as you can. Extend your spine upward.

› Carefully place the block on the crown (top) of your head.

Note: You can use any object that has a flat surface and weighs around 500 g (1 lb.); a rubber block is preferable, in case it slips off your head!

› Gently extend your spine upward, as if to push the block higher.

› Stay in this position with the block for a minute or two. Keep corrective movements to a minimum so as not to drop the block!

› Observe the mental effect created by the small weight on top of the head.

What was the sensation of a perfectly erect and balanced torso, with a centered vertical axis, like? How did your eyes react? Did the block give you a sharper sense of centering down?

› Now remove the block and try to maintain its effects as well as observing the differences. ʃ

Sitting with block on top of the head

Exploration A.20

Vajrasana – Sitting on the Heels

Vajrasana is a sitting pose where one sits on one's heels (like the traditional Japanese sitting position). In this Exploration, we compare sitting in *Vajrasana* without any props to using two belts that embrace the legs.

First do *Vajrasana* without props:

› Kneel and join your feet to sit on your heels with your toes pointing back. Keep the knees joined together.

How did your legs feel? Could you keep your heels close to each other? Mentally register your overall feeling in the pose (so as to be able to compare with the next variation).

Now do the pose in a different way, using props:

› Spread a blanket and sit on it in *Dandasana* (sitting on the buttocks with legs extended forward – see figure).

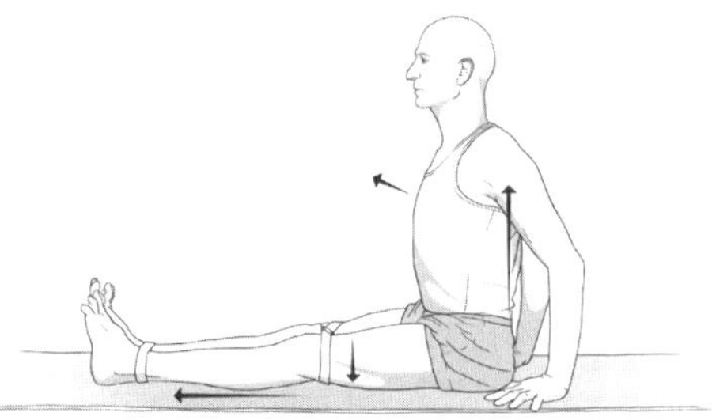

Placing the belts for *Vajrasana*

› Loop a belt around the top of your knees; center the buckle between your knees to make it accessible after entering the pose.

› Loop another belt around your ankles and fasten it to join the ankles loosely; center the buckle behind your ankles, facing the floor, to make it accessible after entering the pose.

Note: Adjust the belts so that your legs are aligned and in contact, but without pressure. The lower belt should keep your inner and outer ankles parallel to each other.

› Kneel and then bend forward to lift your hips and thighs. Slide a folded blanket over your calf muscles until it enters deep into the backs of your knees.

placing the blanket for *Vajrasana*

› Now extend your feet backward and sit on your heels. Spread your metatarsal bones evenly on the floor.

› In each foot, the centerline of the metatarsals (on the top side of the foot) should be pressed to the floor so that the nails of all five toes (including the small toe) touch the floor. Join your big toes and spread your other toes sideways.

PROPS
2 belts
2-4 blankets

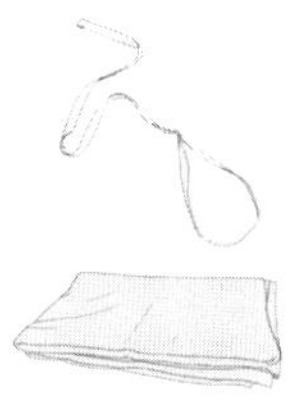

› Rest the back of your palms on your thighs. For longer stays, place a folded blanket on your thighs to raise the palm support.

› Sit straight, roll your shoulders back and open your chest. Relax your face, eyes and jaws and look forward with a soft gaze.

Note: You can add another folded blanket under your buttocks to keep your lower spine erect and make the pose more comfortable.

Vajrasana with belts and blanket behind the knees

› Compare sitting with and without the belts and the blanket behind the knees. ∫

Note: At first, you may experience numbness and some measure of discomfort in the ankles when doing this pose. In this case, use blankets under your shins as shown in the figure on page 61. With practice, you'll be able to sit comfortably for a few minutes.

In which variation did you feel you could have stayed longer? In which did you feel more stable and relaxed?

After coming out of the pose, walk a little and feel your knees. Do you feel more lightness in walking?

The belts keep the knees and ankles joined which, in my experience, allows the legs to relax. In addition, the belts maintain the alignment of these joints, such that the upper legs, lower legs and feet are in one line. This is a healthy movement for the joints – it increases their flexibility without overstretching the ligaments. The blanket behind the knees creates space in the knees and extends their ligaments; this is very soothing. After coming out of the pose, my knees feel 'happier'.

Exploration A.21

Comparing Different Types of Support

In *Virasana*, one sits in between the feet, with knees bent, if possible on the floor (see *LOY* Pl. 89); most children sit in this pose naturally with ease, though, as we get older, we usually need some under-buttock support. In this Exploration, we compare soft (blanket or bolster) support with hard (wood) support, and study the effects of the material used for support on the experience of the pose.

CAUTIONS

- If the ligaments of your knees are injured, use a bolster to support your buttocks, or skip this Exploration.

A. Using soft support

› Kneel with joined knees while keeping your feet spread apart, and place a folded blanket or bolster in between the spread feet.

› As you lower your buttocks, use both hands to separate the calf muscle from the thigh: Starting with the right leg, grip the top of your calf muscle with your right hand, iron it toward your heel and then rotate it outward. At the same time, grip the back of your right thigh with the fingers of your left hand and rotate it inward.

› Arrange your left leg in a similar fashion.

› Sit down gradually; keep your knees joined and lower your thighs symmetrically between the shins.

Note: Be sensitive to your body. If you feel an unhealthy pain in the knees and/or the feet, do not force the pose. Rise on your knees and add another blanket under your buttocks, or use a bolster. Over time, if you practice this pose regularly, you will be able to reduce the height.

› Adjust your ankles and feet such that the inner and outer ankles are equally extended (see that your inner ankles are not shortened) and your feet are extended back, in line with your shins.

› Spread your toes and make sure that your small toes are also touching the floor.

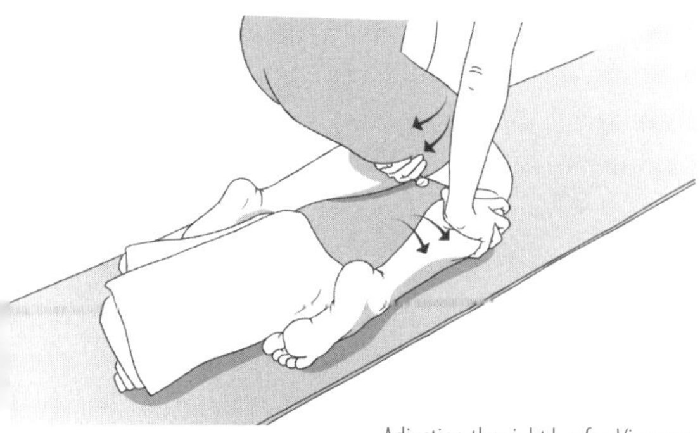

Adjusting the right leg for *Virasana*

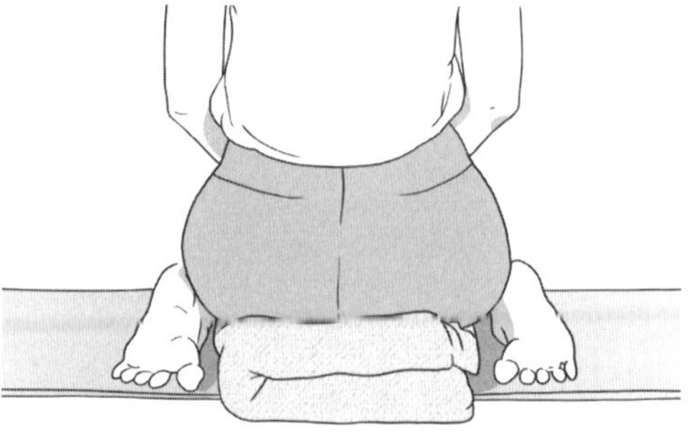

Virasana – Back view

PROPS
folded blanket
or bolster
block

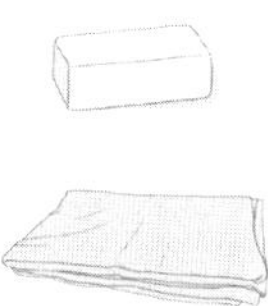

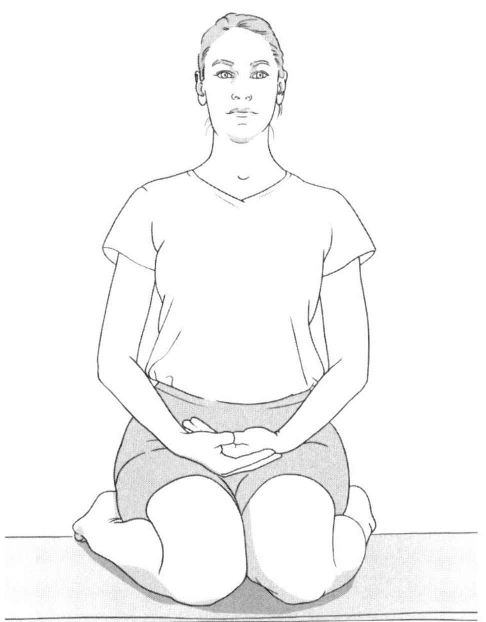

Virasana – Front view

› Release the skin of your knees by gently pulling the skin from under the bottom of your knee to the top of the knee. Turn each knee from inside out. The inner and outer knee should be at the same height.

› Move the flesh of your buttocks sideways, so as to sit on the heads of your sit bones. Lower your outer hips and extend your spine upward; open your chest and look forward. ʃ

Note: You can place a folded blanket or a bolster on your thighs to rest your hands on with more comfort (not shown).

B. Using hard support

› Repeat the instructions above, but instead of blanket or bolster, place a wooden block under the buttocks.

› Compare how you feel when using these different types of support. ʃ

Which support gave more stability and firmness?

I find that a hard support sensitizes the bones, starting from the sit bones up to the spine, while a soft support is 'fleshier'. The bones are the framework of the body, they determine its shape (in yoga, they are considered Earth Element – the solid and steady base of the body), and hence I feel more stability and steadiness with the hard support. The hard support probably stimulates more the sensory nerves and hence creates mental alertness and sharpness.

The soft support is more pleasant and relaxing and is probably more suitable for long sitting, but one tends to sink slightly into it, and hence loses some sharpness. It is important to know these differences in order to select the appropriate support according to the specific need or purpose.

Exploration A.22

Comparing Different Sitting Positions

There are many seated poses, and each one creates a different feeling. In this Exploration, we compare the following three sitting poses: simple crossed legs (*Swastikasana*), sitting on the heels (*Vajrasana*) and sitting between the heels (*Virasana*)[5].

- Sit crossed legged on a bolster (if the bolster is too soft or too thin, place a folded blanket on top).
- Roll a blanket and use it to support your shins as shown.
- Sit on the heads of your sit bones. Lift your sacrum and pubic bone vertically upward from their base.
- Make sure that your knees are both at the same level and well supported.
- Stay in this position for a few minutes, observing your body and breathing.
- Mentally record how you feel and then release the pose.
- Then come out of the pose and sit in *Vajrasana* – you can use two belts and blankets as shown in Exploration A.20 on page 53.
- Stay in this position for the same length of time, observing your body and breathing.
- Mentally record how you feel and then come out of the pose.
- Now sit in *Virasana* on a soft support (see Exploration A.21). ʃ

Sitting cross-legged with support

5. *Vajrasana* and *Virasana* are explained in Explorations A.20 and A.21.

PROPS
folded blankets
bolster
2 belts (optional)

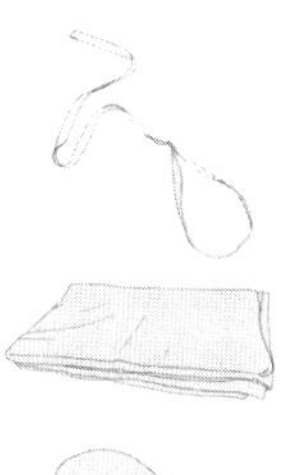

How was your experience in these three sitting poses, with respect to stability, comfort, relaxation, quality of breath, and your overall mental state?

Virasana and *Vajrasana* are symmetrical sitting poses in which the spine can be held upright with ease. There is a large contact area with the floor, which creates stability and feeling of prowess. This is reflected by the name of the poses: *Vajra* means 'diamond' or 'thunderbolt', and *Vira* means 'hero'. The symmetrical nature of these poses creates a sense of centering down. I find that the eyes naturally become quiet and are drawn backward into the skull, and the brain too becomes stiller. However, in both, the base of the pose is narrow, making it prone to sideways tilts, especially in long periods of sitting with closed eyes. Both extend the ankles and improve the flexibility and health of the knees and ankles. *Vajrasana* is easier to perform, and the pelvis is higher, which makes it easier to keep the spine extended. But, after a few minutes, the pressure on the feet may be disturbing. *Virasana* requires more flexibility in the joints of the legs, but, once achieved, it can be maintained for a longer time with comfort.

In *Swastikasana* the base of the pose is wide and stable (*sthira*) – especially if the knees are supported by a blanket and are braced with belts (see Exploration A.16 on page 47).

Comfort and stability in the sitting poses may vary from person to person due to different physical and mental constitutions. Try these variations in order to study how bodily poses affect mental states.

Exploration A.23

Relaxing in *Adho Mukha Virasana* (Child's Pose)

In this Exploration, we start from a sitting position and then stretch the body forward. This is a very basic forward stretch. People with stiff hamstrings find it hard to bend forward with the legs straight, but they can easily bend forward in *Adho Mukha Virasana*.

We study the effect of the head orientation on the experience of the pose. We do the pose twice, first with the top forehead (hairline) resting on the floor, and then with the bottom forehead (eyebrow line) resting on the floor (or on a folded blanket). This might initially seem to be an insignificant difference, which is why it is interesting to explore.

A. Top forehead rested on the floor

› Sit on your heels, spread your knees slightly wider than the width of your waist, lean forward and extend your trunk forward.

› Stretch your arms forward and place the top of your forehead on the floor.

› Mentally record how you feel, the state of your brain and your heart rate, and then come out of the pose.

B. Bottom forehead on the floor

› Now repeat the pose, this time with the bottom portion of your forehead on the floor. If the bottom of your forehead does not descend easily to the floor, support it with a folded blanket.

To get the full relaxation effect, it is essential that your head is horizontal; you can judge this by the orientation of the ears – they should be horizontal (you can touch them to find out, or ask someone to look at your pose and tell you).

You may need to support your forehead on a bolster, inverted chair or the seat of a chair.

› Observe what you feel after staying in each of the above two variations for a few minutes. ∫

Could you feel your brain? In which of the two head positions were you quieter and more passive? Did you also notice any change in your heart rate?

Note: See the following Explorations to learn how to use belts and blocks for this pose.

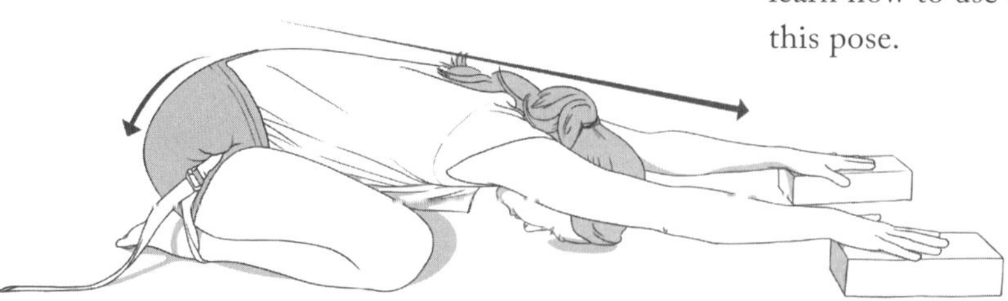

Adho Mukha Virasana with the top of the forehead (hairline) rested on the floor

B.K.S. Iyengar observed that a horizontal head position relaxes the brain and decreases blood pressure. Supported forward bends are used in yoga therapy to treat high blood pressure. This position, where the spine is horizontal and the heart is below it, is typical to four-legged animals. It is probably more relaxing for the heart than our upright posture.

PROPS
blankets
optional:
chair
bolster
2 belts
2 blocks

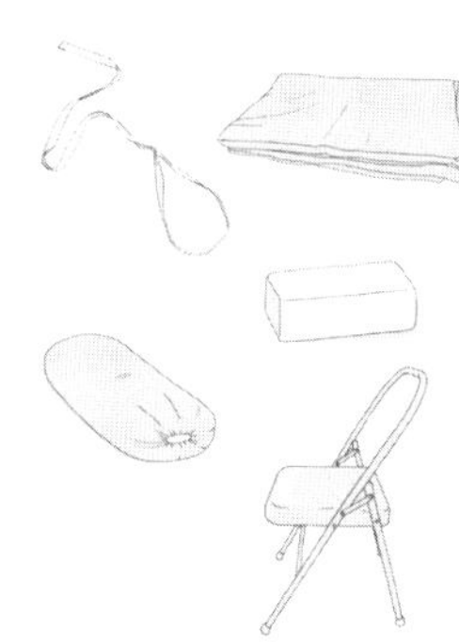

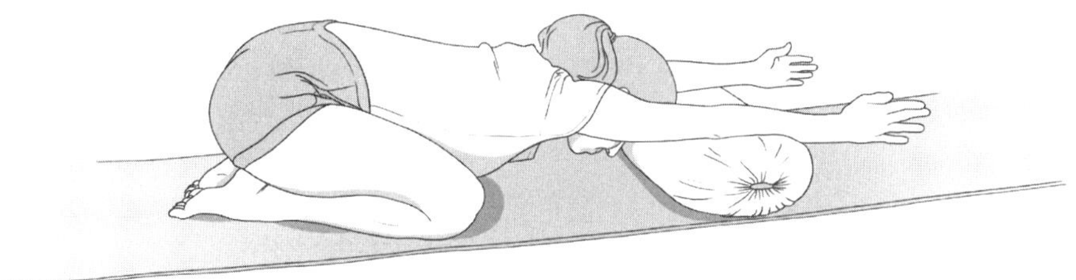

Bolster under forehead and elbows

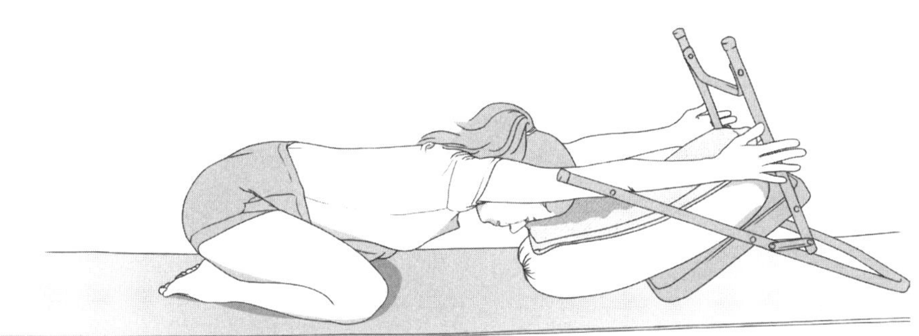

Using inverted chair and a bolster

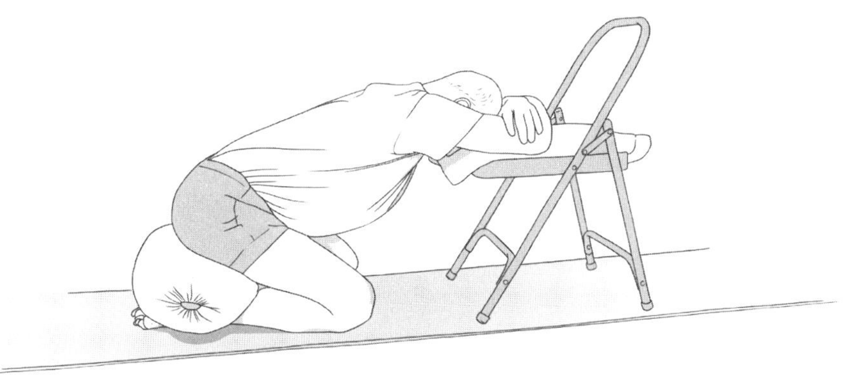

Chair support

Exploration A.24

Stretching in *Adho Mukha Virasana* (Child's Pose)

In this Exploration, we attempt to stretch the trunk forward and have the chest open in *Adho Mukha Virasana*. We start by doing this without support, and then use props support. We then compare the effects of the props on the experience of the pose.

A. *Adho Mukha Virasana* with no props

› Sit on your heels, spread your knees slightly wider than the width of your waist, lean forward and extent your trunk forward.

› Stretch your arms forward and place your forehead on the floor.

Notes:

- Spread your knees just enough to allow your waist to descend between your thighs, but not wider than that. The sides of your trunk should touch your inner thighs.
- If your ankles are stiff, place several stepped blankets under your shins as shown here.

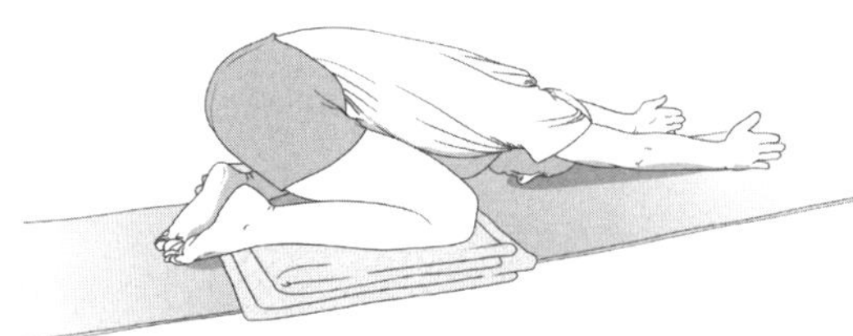

Adho Mukha Virasana - shins on raised surface

› Stay for 2-3 minutes observing your breathing.

› Mentally record how you feel in the pose, and then release and sit.

B. Using belts and blocks

In the second attempt, use two belts and two blocks. The belts are used to anchor the pelvis in place and to keep the buttocks down. The blocks under the palms help to broaden the chest and extend the trunk forward, while lowering the torso to the floor.

› Place two blocks in front of you.

› Sit on your heels and spread your knees. Loop a belt around each top thigh and ankle. Tighten the belts to move the tops of your thighs downward.

Adho Mukha Virasana -
Tying each top thigh to the corresponding ankle

PROPS
2 wooden blocks
2 belts
optional: blankets and bolster

- Bend forward, place your palms on the blocks and stretch forward, sliding the blocks as you go (it is better not to position the blocks on the sticky mat, since its surface has too much friction).

- Raise your head and look forward; extend your arms forward from the armpits and turn your upper arms such that your triceps are rolling in (toward the center of your body) and your biceps are rolling out (away from the center of your body).

- Press against the blocks while broadening your chest and lowering the middle of your back toward the floor.

- Then rest your head down. If it does not comfortably reach the floor, use a folded blanket to support the head, and rest your forehead on it.

- Study the effects of anchoring your pelvis and supporting your hands. ʃ

What was the length of your armpits in each variation (without and with props)? What was the width of your shoulder girdle and collarbones? What was the effect of the stretch on your breathing?

Adho Mukha Virasana with belt for each leg and hands on blocks

Supporting the forehead with a blanket

Supine (reclining) Positions

We now turn to simple supine poses – poses in which we recline on our backs. We explore different variations of supported supine poses as well as *Shavasana* (literally, the Corpse Pose, but usually referred to as the relaxation pose). Supine poses relax the body, calm the nerves and quiet the mind.

Shavasana – the most restorative reclining pose – is where you learn total relaxation. You learn to stay passive but alert, to observe without acting. See the section Relaxation in Chapter 2 for further discussion of this pose,

You may want to read the instructions for entering *Shavasana* in Appendix 1.1.

Exploration A.25

Supporting the Chest on Blocks

PROPS
2 blocks
bolster
blankets

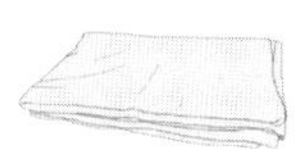

In this Exploration, we use a block or two to support the trunk. We present different variations and compare the effects of different types of support on our breath, on how we feel in the pose, and on our mental state.

A word on blocks

The dimensions of standard yoga blocks are 23 cm × 12 cm × 7 cm (9" × 4.5" × 3"). Wooden blocks are recommended for best support. One can also use blocks made of rubber or foam, but they should be sturdy enough to provide solid and firm support. The effect may vary with the type of material the blocks are made of. For this Exploration, it is best to use wooden blocks.

The block can be placed in three ways:

- Standing (such that the height is 23 cm or 9") – we refer to this as 'Highest-height' block
- Placed on its narrow side (such that the height is 12 cm or 4.5") – we refer to this as 'Middle-height' block
- Flat (such that the height is 7 cm or 3") – we refer to this as 'Lowest-height' block

* * *

We explore placing the blocks to support the back in the following manners:

1. Lowest-height block, widthwise
2. Two Lowest-height blocks, lengthwise (under shoulder blades)
3. Middle-height block, widthwise
4. Two Middle-height blocks, lengthwise
5. Highest-height block under the mid-back with another block to support the head

Take a few minutes to stay in each variation. All of them encourage deeper breathing, so allow your breath to slowly penetrate deeper to the remotest parts of your lungs and diffuse through your body.

There are of course many other possible ways to use blocks for support in *Shavasana*, and we highly recommend you to explore other options. However, we don't recommend exploring more than three or four variations in one session. You need to allow some time for relaxing and absorbing.

1. Lowest-height block, widthwise

› Start by placing a Lowest-height block widthwise under your shoulder blades.

› Support the back of your neck and head with a bolster and/or folded blankets. Your face should be slightly higher than your chest, and the back of the neck should be extended.

› Place your body in *Shavasana* on the blocks (see instructions on 'Placing the body in *Shavasana*' in Appendix 1.1 on page 149).

A widthwise Lowest-height block and a bolster for head support

Exploration A.25 cont.

- Continue lying on the support for 3 to 7 minutes. Observe your breathing and make it soft and smooth.

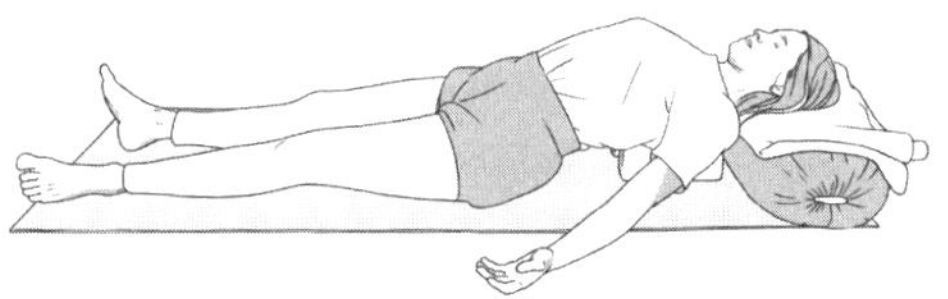

Shavasana with block support

- Record your overall feeling, the degree to which your chest is open, the quality of your breathing, the sensation of your pulse, and so on. Do this for each variation you wish to explore.

Using two Lowest-height blocks lengthwise to support the shoulder blades

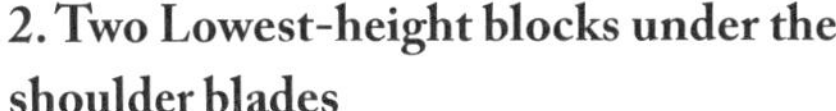

2. Two Lowest-height blocks under the shoulder blades

- Now use two Lowest-height blocks lengthwise; keep a space of 3-5 cm (1-2") between the blocks, such that your spine will be in between the blocks.

Widthwise Middle-height block

3. Middle-height block widthwise

- Continue with a Middle-height block placed widthwise.

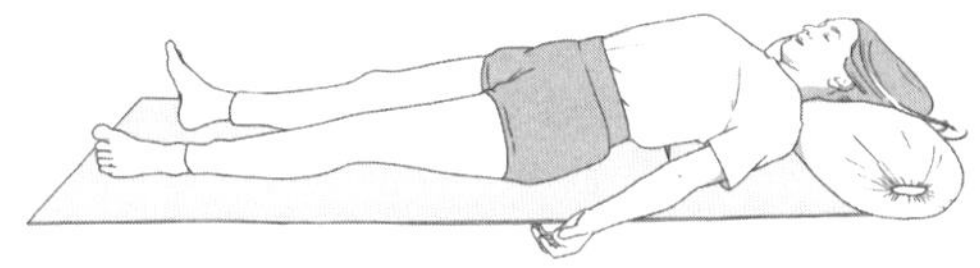

Shavasana on a widthwise Middle-height block

4. Two lengthwise Middle-height blocks

- Continue with two Middle-height blocks lengthwise; here too, keep a space between the blocks. Adjust the blocks such that they support your shoulder blades.

Two lengthwise Middle-height blocks

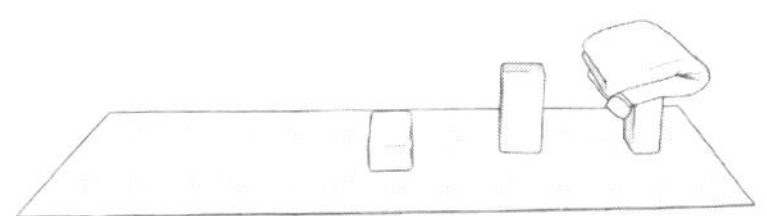

Preparing to use two Highest-height blocks

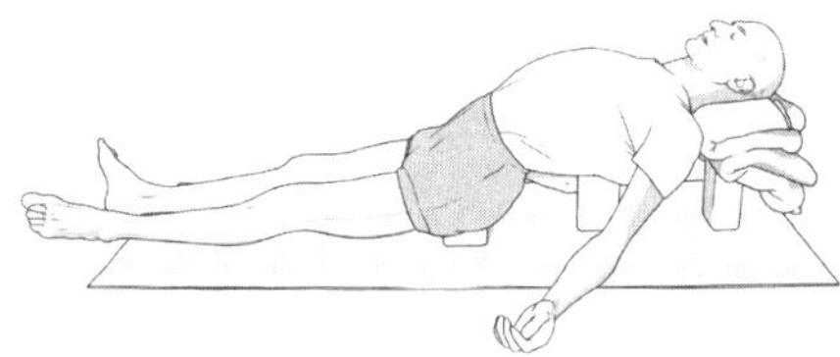

Shavasana on two Highest-height blocks

5. Highest-height block under the mid-back and another block to support the head

This last variation requires more flexibility of the spine. It should open the chest more; try it and see if it works for you. Because the block is placed on its highest side, you may need to support the pelvis; you can do this with another (Lowest-height) block or with a bolster. For head support use 1-2 folded blankets on top of a block.

› Place a bolster or a block widthwise on the mat to support your buttocks, place two Highest-height (standing) blocks to support the mid-back and head. Prepare 1-2 folded blankets next to the mat.

› Sit on the block (or bolster), lift your chest and arch your back until your mid-back is parallel to the block, and then lean your back on the block.

› Adjust the position of the block for head support. Take a folded blanket (or two, if needed) and put them on the block under your head.

› Compare the above five different arrangements of the blocks. ∫

Which of them was most comfortable? Which one created more space in the chest and allowed for smoother breathing? In which did you feel more alert (physically and mentally)? Which was more exhilarating?

The blocks' support maintains the opening of the chest without effort; hence, it encourages natural deepening of the breath. The lungs are opened, and the air penetrates further than it usually reaches. The wood material (hard support) is stimulating. Generally speaking, higher support is more invigorating and exhilarating, while lower support is more relaxing. (See more on this in the following Exploration).

Remember however that people with different (physical and mental) constitutions may respond differently to different supports. It is possible that higher support would not be comfortable for people with stiffness in the upper body, and it may even create tension. You need to know all these options from your own experience and then choose those suited best for your specific purpose and constitution.

Exploration A.26

Supporting the Chest on a Bolster

In this Exploration, we compare lying flat in *Shavasana* to lying on a bolster as a soft support for the back. We can also compare the soft support used here with the wooden blocks support of the previous Exploration.

A. 'Flat' *Shavasana*

› Lie flat on the mat in *Shavasana*. If the back of your neck shortens and your chin lifts, place a folded blanket under the back of your head and neck.

› Stay in the pose for several minutes observing your breathing and your degree of relaxation.

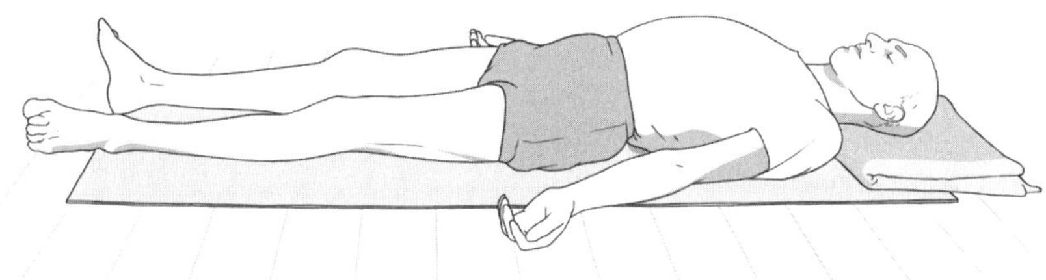

Lying flat in *Shavasana*

B. *Shavasana* on a bolster

› Now place a bolster lengthwise in the center of the mat. Place a folded blanket on the head-side of the bolster.

› Sit on the mat in front of the bolster, then lie on the bolster arranging your body as explained in 'Placing the body in *Shavasana*' in Appendix 1.1 (page 149).

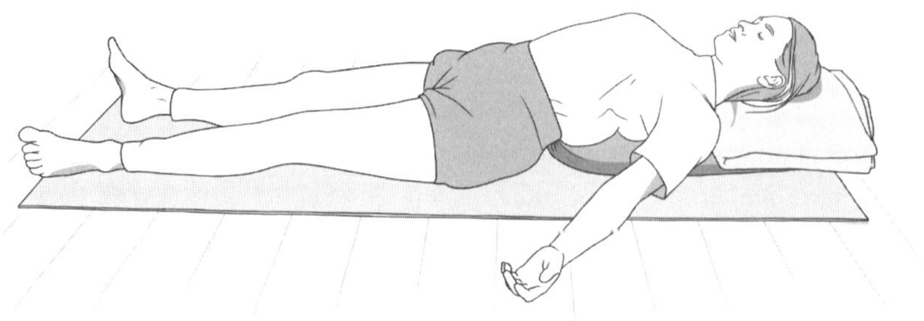

Entering *Shavasana*: spreading the buttocks

PROPS

bolster

blanket

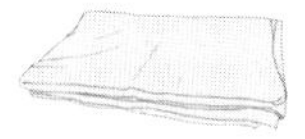

- While lying down, use your elbows to lift and open your chest and to elongate your spine to the head side.

- Verify that your body is placed symmetrically around its mid-longitudinal line: your spine should be in the center of the bolster, your shoulder blades equidistant from the spine, your neck and head in line with your spine, your legs and arms equidistant from the center line, and your feet rolling out evenly.

- Relax your body on the support. Stay in this position for a few minutes, observing your body, breathing and mind. ʃ

What differences did you feel when comparing lying flat on the mat with lying on a bolster, in terms of comfort, width and softness of the muscles of the back, expansion of the chest, quality of breathing and state of mind?

Compare also the feeling of lying on a soft, wide support with lying on a hard, narrow support as in the previous Exploration.

Flat *Shavasana* has an Earth Element quality, the body is close to earth and there is a sense of heaviness. The back muscles soften and spread. However, the chest is not as open as with the bolster-support, and deep breathing may be limited. The support creates space in the chest – hence *Shavasana* on a support is often used for *Pranayama* practice, while flat *Shavasana* is used for complete relaxation.

Comparing hard and soft support, B.K.S. Iyengar found that wide and soft support softens and releases the muscles and tissue of the chest and lungs, while hard and sharp support stimulates the heart. He uses these observations for treating patients with lung and heart problems.

Exploration A.27

Comparing Leg Positions

In this Exploration, we maintain the same position of the upper body, supported by a lengthwise bolster, as in the previous Exploration, but we change the position of the legs and observe whether this affects breathing and the overall feeling in the pose.

We start in *Supta Baddha Konasana* (Reclining Bound Angle Pose – a supine position in which the feet are joined and the knees are spread), using a belt to support the feet and thighs.

› Put a bolster lengthwise in the center of the mat, and then place a folded blanket on the head-side of the bolster. Have a few belts, and, if available, a weight, next to you.

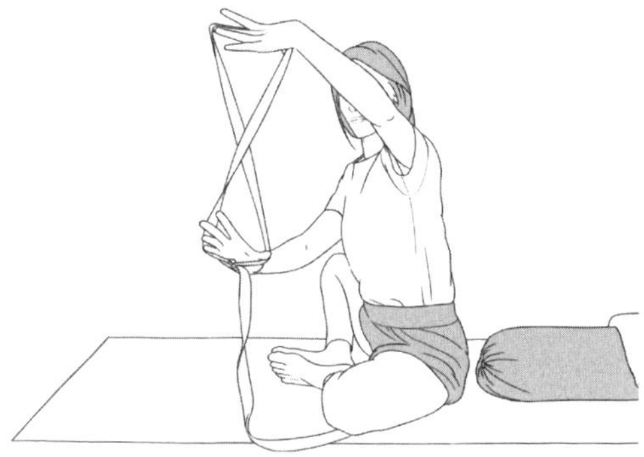

Arranging the props for *Supta Baddha Konasana*

› Sit on the mat in front of the bolster, bend your knees, and join them. Take a looped belt and cross it to form a figure 8. Place the two loops over your knees and move them down until they brace your ankles and the roots of your thighs.

Note: Adjust the belt such that the buckle is easily accessible and allows tightening by pulling toward yourself.

› Spread your knees wide apart and adjust the belt to keep your feet close to the buttocks and to support the outer top thighs.

› Make sure your knees are equidistant from the floor and from the body.

› Now use your elbows to lift and open your chest and, while reclining back onto the bolster, elongate your spine toward your head side.

› Use your hands to lengthen your neck, and place your head on the support. Adjust the folded blanket such that it also supports the back of your neck.

› Stay in *Supta Baddha Konasana* for a few minutes, observing your body, breathing, and mind. Pay special attention to the width of the pelvis and the space in the lower abdomen. Direct your breath to that region.

› Then join your knees, remove the belt and straighten your legs into a supported-*Shavasana*.

What did you feel after straightening your legs? Did it change the way your pelvis and lower abdomen felt? Did it change your breathing?

A supported *Supta Baddha Konasana*

PROPS
belts
bolster
blankets
optional: weight up to 20 kg (40 lbs.)

› After staying in this position for a few minutes with straight legs, cross your legs as in *Swastikasana*. This is *Supta Swastikasana*.

› Stay for a minute or two, observing your comfort, inner space, breathing, and how you feel. Then change the order in which your legs are crossed.

› To come out of the pose, roll off the bolster to your right side, and remain for a minute or two on your right side before coming up.

For the last variation sit, straighten your legs and join them. Tighten your legs together with a belt (you may use more than one belt, for example, two around your thighs and two around your shins).

› Put the weights, or any heavy object, on the top of your thighs. You can easily place 20 kg (40 lbs.) on the thighs.

› Then lie down on the bolster.

› Observe the contrast between flattening and grounding the legs with the lifting and widening of the chest. ∫

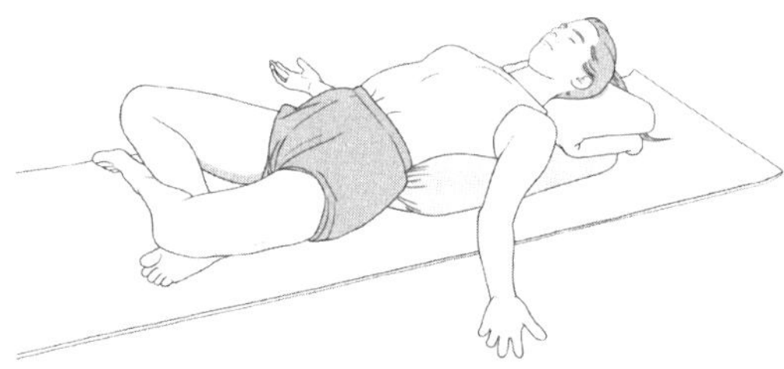

Supta Swastikasana on a lengthwise bolster

Compare the effects of the above three leg positions on how you feel in *Shavasana*. In which one did you experience a deeper relaxation? In which did your breathing flow more smoothly?

The different leg positions work on the *apana vayu*, which is one of the five energy subdivisions of the cosmic energy *Prana*. It is considered one of the most important, since it influences digestion, elimination and reproduction, and it is active in the pelvic and lower abdominal areas.

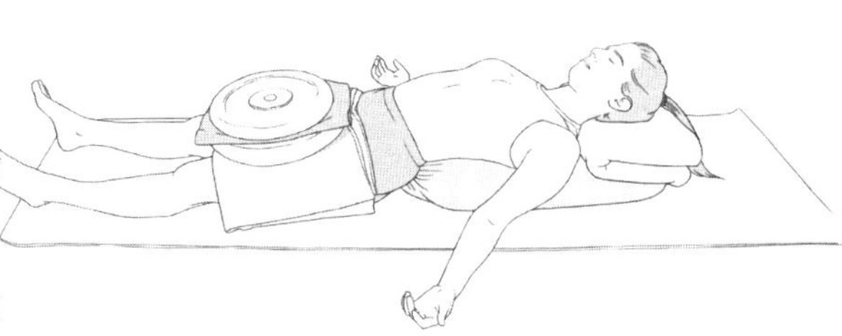

Shavasana on a bolster with braced legs and weightv

Exploration A.28

Comparing Belt Usages in *Supta Baddha Konasana* (Reclining Bound Angle Pose)

In this Exploration, we compare staying in *Supta Baddha Konasana* without using a belt for anchoring the legs. Then we explore three different ways to use belts, and compare the effects of these variations.

A. *Supta Baddha Konasana* without belt

› Put a bolster lengthwise in the center of the mat, then place a folded blanket on the head-side of the bolster.

› Join your feet and spread the knees apart.

› Lean on your elbows and use your hands to extend your buttocks down toward your heels and to spread them. Then lift your chest and extend your spine to your head side, placing it on the center of the bolster.

› Adjust the blanket to support your head and neck.

› Stay in the pose for a few minutes and observe the relaxation of your legs and the space in your pelvic region.

Note: if you feel an unpleasant pull in your groin, place a folded blanket or other support under each outer top thigh.

Now try using belts:

B. Bracing the buttocks and the feet

› Pass a looped belt over your head and lower it to place the belt on your mid-buttocks, over your groin and under your feet.

Placing a belt for *Supta Baddha Konasana*

› Move your heels as close as possible to your buttocks and tighten the belt to stabilize the legs.

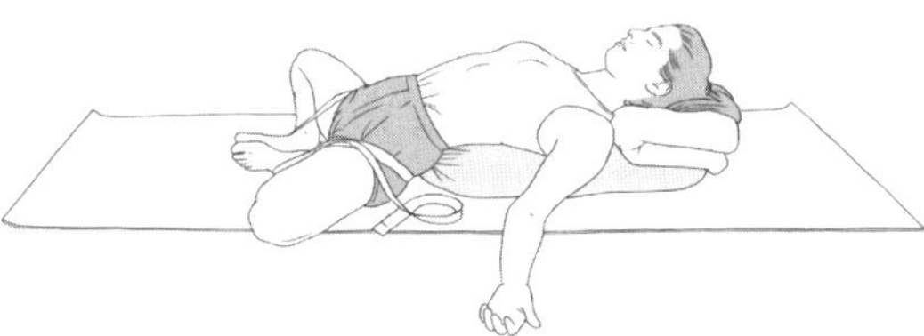

Supta Baddha Konasana - using a belt to brace the buttocks and feet

› Stay in the pose for a few minutes and observe the relaxation of your legs and the space in your pelvis.

C. Using a belt for each leg

› Sit on the mat in *Baddha Konasana* in front of the bolster.

› Use each belt to brace the thigh and shin of one leg.

PROPS
bolster
blanket(s)
2 belts

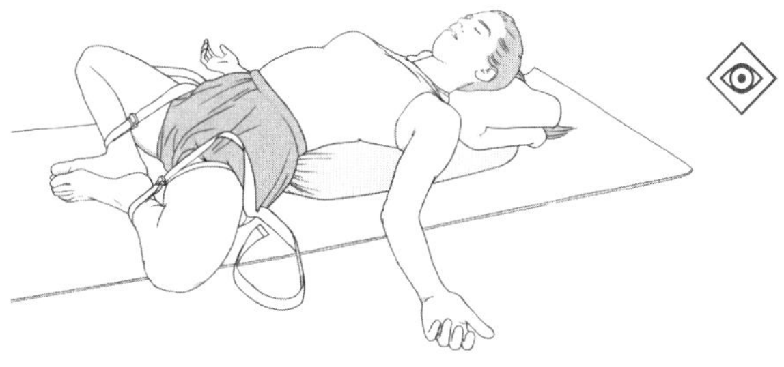

Supta Baddha Konasana - using a belt for each leg

Note: When placing the belts, see that the buckles are adjusted to allow tightening the belts by pulling toward yourself.

› Place the belts on the top of your thighs and ankles and tighten them.

› Stay in the pose for a few minutes and observe the relaxation of the legs and the space in the pelvis.

D. Crossing around the top thighs

Here we use a belt as in the previous Exploration.

› Adjust the belt as in Exploration A.27, and lie on the bolster.

› Stay in the pose for a few minutes and observe the relaxation of your legs and the space in your pelvis. ∫

Compare the variation with no belt with each of the three variations using a belt (or belts). What were the differences in how you felt? In which variation was the lower trunk better extended? In which was the bottom of the pelvis wider?

~ In all three variations in which belts were used, they hold the legs stable and thus enable releasing them. In my experience, using two belts creates space in the bottom region of the pelvis, while using a crossed belt supports the thighs better and creates more compactness. The belt from pelvis to feet helps to extend the buttocks downward and subsequently creates length in the lumbar region. Pregnant and menstruating women should try to use the two-belt option. If needed, one can support the top outer thighs with rolled blankets or blocks. People with tight groins or hip joints may benefit from the crossed-belt option. ~

Exploration A.29

Comparing Arm Positions

In this Exploration, we compare three different arm positions in a supported *Shavasana*. We observe and compare the type of breathing induced by each arm position.

PROPS
bolster
blanket
Optional: weights sticky mat piece for placing the weights.

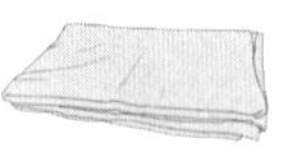

› Lie in *Shavasana* on the bolster.

› Start with your arms extended down in proximity to your body.

› Move your arms and shoulder blades down toward your legs, and roll your outer shoulders down toward the floor.

› Stay in this position for a few minutes while breathing slowly and deeply.

› Then move your arms and stretch them sideways at shoulder level.

› Stay in this position for a few minutes while breathing slowly and deeply.

› Now move your arms upward and extend them over your head; interlock your arms at the elbows and rest them on the bolster.

› Stay in this position for a few minutes while breathing slowly and deeply. ʃ

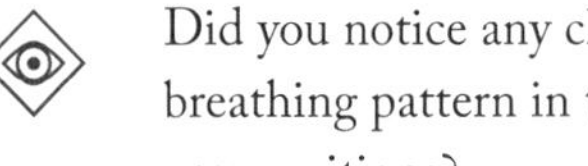

Did you notice any changes in your breathing pattern in the different arm positions?

~ I have noticed a better positioning of the shoulder blades when lying with my arms down, alongside the body. This encourages breath that flows upward, toward the ceiling, from the upper back, to the region of the breastbone.

With arms sideways, the rib cage is widened and expansive widthwise breath is induced, while stretching the arms up and over the head lengthens the chest cavity and narrows it, so that the breath takes a more lengthwise direction. ~

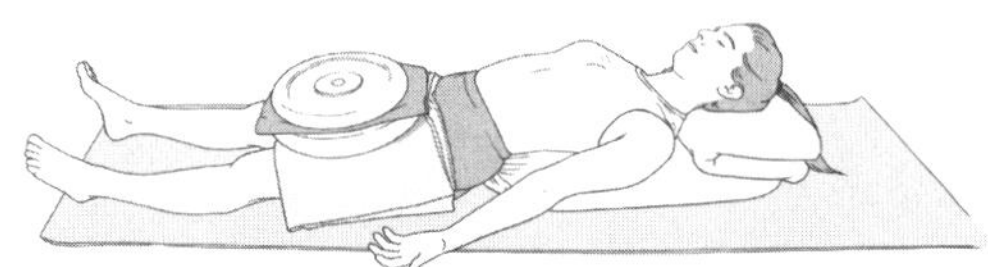

Supported *Shavasana* - arms along the body

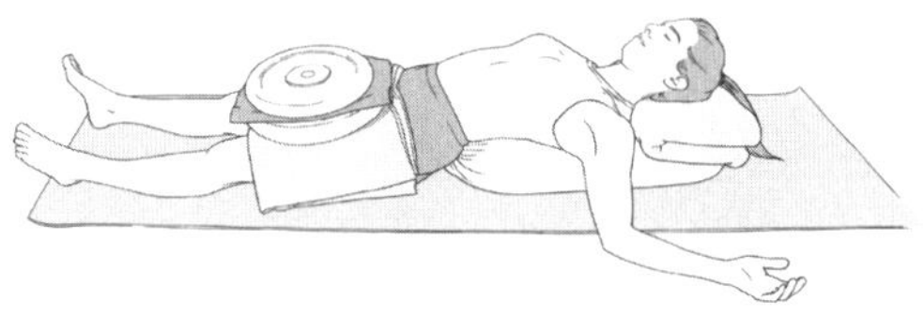

Supported *Shavasana* - arms sideways at shoulder level

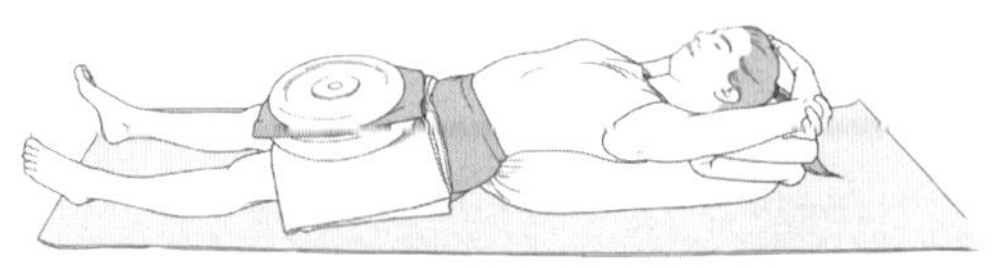

Supported *Shavasana* - arms over the head

Exploration A.30

PROPS
blanket

Changing Focal Regions in *Shavasana* (Relaxation Pose)

In this Exploration, we study how changing the focal point affects the experience of *Shavasana*.

- Lie on your back in *Shavasana*. If needed, use a folded blanket to support the back of your head and neck.

- Focus on your biceps; relax them and allow them to rest on the bones of your upper arms.

- Maintain this focused awareness for a while.

- Then, move your awareness and focus only on relaxing the quadriceps. Allow them to relax on your thigh bones.

- Now try to observe your biceps and your quadriceps simultaneously. Soften these muscles completely.

- Observe whether this changes the experience of *Shavasana*.

- Now add another focal point and also observe the region between your eyebrows (known as the 'third eye'). Relax and soften your eyeballs.

Could you direct your awareness simultaneously to three places, without losing the sharpness of the observation?

What was the effect of this on your *Shavasana*?

Exploration A.31

Experiencing Withdrawal of the Senses (*Pratyahara*) in *Shavasana* (Relaxation Pose)

Pratyahara or the "withdrawal of the senses" is the fifth *anga* (limb) in the Eight Limbs of Patanjali's *Ashtanga Yoga*, as mentioned in his classical work, *The Yoga Sutras of Patanjali*.[6] It is part of the yogi's journey to explore his true inner Self.

In this Exploration, we compare different ways of drawing the senses inward in *Shavasana*.

We explore the following three options:

- Using a head wrap – ideally use an elastic bandage made of cotton (if no bandage is available, use an eye pillow)
- Using a weight – placing a light weight on the forehead
- Blocking the ears – by placing two blocks (or bolsters) on the sides of the head, or by using an inverted bench

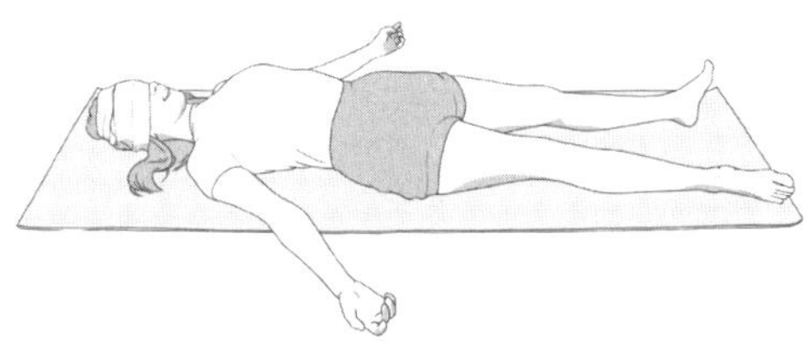

Using head wrap

A. Wrapping elastic bandage

› Sit and hold an elastic bandage in front of your head. Wrap the bandage once or twice around your head at forehead level, then continue to wrap, moving the bandage down until it covers your eyes, ears and bridge of your nose, but not the openings of your nostrils.

› Tuck the edge of the bandage under the wrapped bandage.

› Lie down in *Shavasana*, close your eyes and relax the skin of your face.

Note: When arranging yourself in the pose, you may need to be able to see. In this case, gently insert your thumbs under the bandage by the sides of the nose, and fold it upward. Do not pull the bandage up, as this disturbs the skin of the face.

› Lie down in *Shavasana* (you may want to see the instruction in Appendix 1.1). Allow your eyeballs to soften and recede into their sockets. Relax and widen the space in your inner ears. Look within and listen within.

› Stay in the pose for 5-10 min. ∫

How deep was your relaxation? For how long could you maintain your concentration and the withdrawal of your senses?

6. Patanjali is considered the author of three classic treatises, among them the *Yoga Sutras*, which are the foundations of the classical yoga philosophy.

PROPS
2 blocks
elastic bandage
blanket
Optional: bench and foam blocks

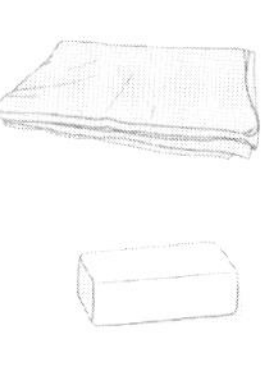

B.K.S. Iyengar introduced the usage of cotton elastic bandages for restorative yoga practice. Wrapping the head with an elastic bandage helps to relax and withdraw the senses, reduces tension headaches, and enhances relaxation.

B. Weight on forehead

- Have two yoga blocks next to you (you can also use a small weight of approx. 1 kg (2 lbs.).
- Lie in *Shavasana* and place one block (or weight) on your lower abdomen and the other on your forehead.

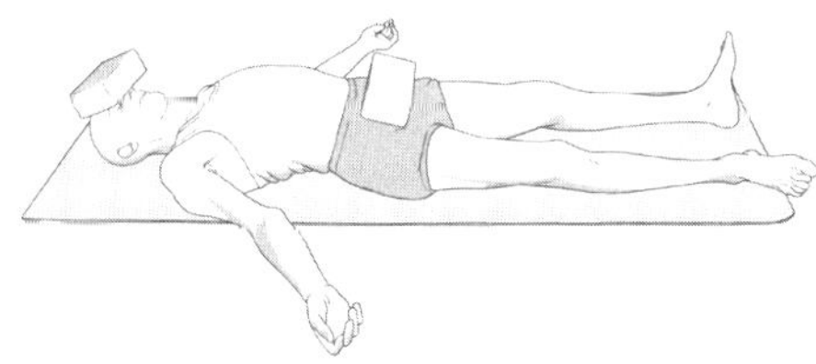

Shavasana with weight on the forehead

Note: Placing a block on the forehead is a little tricky. Move the block until it is balanced and can rest stably on your forehead.

- Stay in the pose for 5–10 minutes.

Observe again: How deep was the relaxation? For how long could you maintain your concentration and the withdrawal of your senses? What kind of feeling did you have in your brain?

Patanjali refers to *vitarka* (self-analysis) and *vichara* (synthesis) as two types of *samprajnata* (thoughtful *samadhi*) (*Yoga Sutra* I.17). In *Astadala Yoga Mala* (Vol. VIII), B.K.S. Iyengar identifies *vitarka* with the frontal brain – the part that plans, analyses, calculates and so on – and *vichara* with the rear parts of the brain, which synthesize and compose:

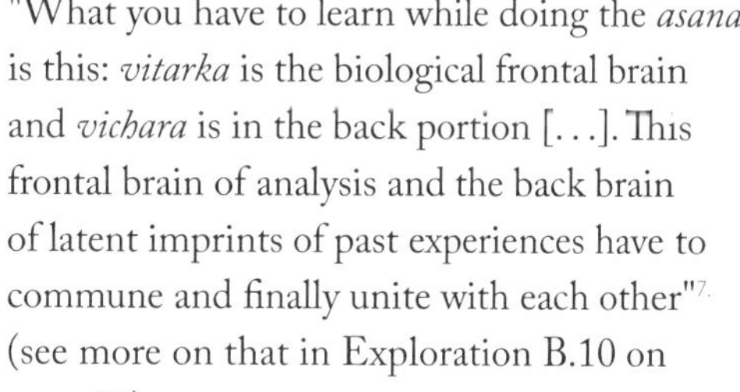

"What you have to learn while doing the *asana* is this: *vitarka* is the biological frontal brain and *vichara* is in the back portion [...]. This frontal brain of analysis and the back brain of latent imprints of past experiences have to commune and finally unite with each other"[7] (see more on that in Exploration B.10 on page 99).

In my experience, the weight relaxes the front brain. I feel that this active part of the brain becomes quiet and recedes to merge with the back of my brain.

7. *Astadala Yoga Mala*, Vol. VIII, p. 22

Exploration A.31 cont.

C. Blocking the ears

We show two ways to block the ears and draw the sense of hearing inward.

› Lie in *Shavasana* and place a block on each side of your head.

› Press on the blocks to apply gentle pressure on your ears and skull.

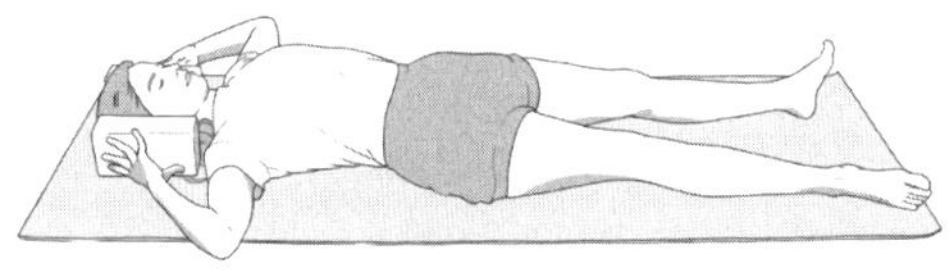

Pressing blocks against the ears

› Then relax your arms and stay in *Shavasana* for a few minutes.

› To maintain the gentle pressure on your ears, use an inverted bench as shown in the figure. Use foam blocks or any other material to fill the gap between the two sides of the bench and your head. ∫

How deep was your relaxation? For how long could you maintain your concentration and the withdrawal of your senses? What kind of feeling did you have in your brain?

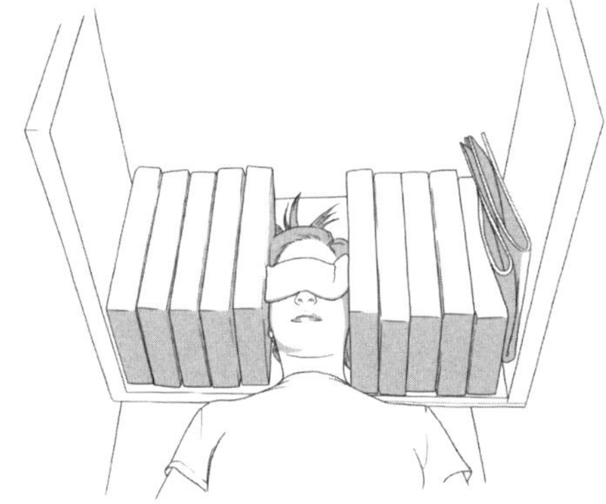

Using an inverted bench to maintain the gentle pressure on the ears

Blocking the ears creates a feeling of inwardness and aloneness, which is an interesting and instructive experience.

1.2 Explorations for Intermediate and Advanced Practitioners

In this part, we present Explorations suited for yoga practitioners already versed in the basic *asanas*. The *asanas* themselves are not very advanced, but some of the observations require sensitivity to subtle nuances that may be difficult for the beginner to observe. We make extensive use of simple yoga props, so you need to be familiar with their usage.

Standing *Asanas*

CAUTIONS

For Standing Poses:

- If you are prone to dizzy spells, vertigo, or high blood pressure, look down at the floor in the final pose. Do not turn your head upward.
- If you have a cardiac condition, practice against a wall. Do not raise your arms, but rest them on your hips.
- During menstruation or pregnancy, you should not jump, should not create pressure on the abdomen, and should not exert and overheat your body. If you are not experienced, avoid standing poses altogether and seek advice of a knowledgeable certified *Iyengar Yoga* teacher.

For *Adho Mukha Shvanasana*:

- If you have high blood pressure or frequent headaches, support your head with a bolster (see *Props for Yoga* Vol. I. p. 52).
- If you are prone to dislocation of the shoulders, ensure that your arms do not rotate outward.
- In advanced stages of pregnancy, practice this *asana* only with a chair or other support for the hands and head.

For *Uttanasana*:

- If you have spinal disc disorder, practice *Uttanasana* only with your back concave.
- In advanced stages of pregnancy, practice only the concave back phase of the pose.

About the Standing *Asanas*

Standing *asanas* are the basis of *Iyengar Yoga* practice. These poses open and strengthen the body, develop flexibility and build the muscle actions required for more advanced *asanas*. By extending the muscles of the legs and groin, one attains free movement at the hips. This allows the spine to extend freely and, in the long run, prevents back pain. The arms become active and one learns to use them to move the shoulders and open the chest. The shoulders are made flexible and the chest broadens. This improves breathing and circulation and keeps the body agile and light, and the mind fresh.

In the following Explorations, we use props to change the geometry of the poses (for example, elevating the feet on blocks in Downward-Facing Dog Pose); this changes the experience of being in the pose, and allows us to examine how changing the body position subtly affects the mental experience. In other Explorations, the same *asana* is repeated twice or more, with different focal points – again, we observe how this may change the experience of being in the pose.

Exploring *Adho Mukha Shvanasana* (Downward-Facing Dog Pose) and *Uttanasana* (Standing Forward Bend)

Adho Mukha Shvanasana, the downward facing dog pose, resembles the spontaneous stretching of dogs; it also resembles a triangle with the buttocks being the apex and the palms and feet the base. Although it's not really a standing *asana* per se, we include it here since it is a fundamental pose which activates all the four principal organs of action (*karmendriyas*) – the arms and the legs – and creates flexibility and strength and encourages deep breathing. It is a very good pose for limbering up; most days, I start my practice with this pose (or as the saying goes: "another day, another dog pose").

We assume you are familiar with the pose; but you may want to refresh your memory and read Appendix 1.2, which explains how to enter into *Adho Mukha Shvanasana*.

Uttanasana is a standing forward bend that activates the legs and releases the trunk and head, hence it can also serve as a very preparation for the other, more strenuous standing poses.

Exploration B.1

Elevating the Feet/Hands in *Adho Mukha Shvanasana* (Downward-Facing Dog)

In this Exploration we try two variations of *Adho Mukha Shvanasana*: elevating the feet and elevating the hands. We compare these two modifications of the pose with doing it in the standard manner, with the feet and hands on the floor.

A. Elevating the feet

› Place two blocks next to the wall. The distance between the blocks should match the width of your pelvis.

› Do *Adho Mukha Shvanasana* with your toe mounds on the blocks and your heels against the wall.

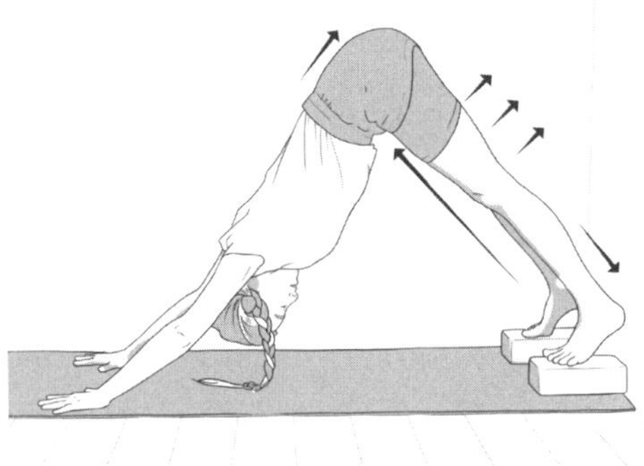

Adho Mukha Shvanasana - feet on blocks

› Lift your buttocks, attempting to sharpen the angle at the sit bones.

Actions:

- Move your legs back to pull your spine back and up.
- Lift your inner thighs and tighten your outer thighs.
- Roll your top thighs from outside in (inner thighs moving back) and separate the sit bones from each other.
- Widen the skin of the back portion of your thighs from inside out.
- Press your heels against the wall.

 Observe the sharpness of the awareness in your sit bones. Could you feel each bone separately?

 Observe the breath in your lower abdomen and pelvic regions. How much did your breath penetrate into and spread through these regions? What was the length and width of the breath in your lower trunk?

› Now step off the blocks and do the pose with your feet on the floor, in the standard way.

 Were you able to maintain the sharpness of the awareness in your buttocks after stepping off the blocks?

 How did you feel while doing the pose with your feet on the floor, compared to when your feet were elevated?

~ B.K.S. Iyengar said that, in *Adho Mukha Shvanasana*, your awareness should encircle the buttocks like snow encircling a Himalayan peak. In my experience, changing

PROPS
2 blocks
wall

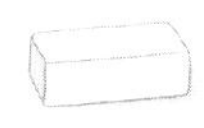

the geometry of the pose by elevating the feet and supporting the heels on the wall enables one to sharpen the angle at the buttocks and to enhance your awareness of the area. The breath can extend in the lower trunk and spread in the pelvic region. This creates mental acuity and increased concentration.

B. Elevating the hands

› Now lean the blocks diagonally against the wall. The distance between the blocks should allow you to spread your hands out appropriately.

› Place your hands against the blocks and enter *Adho Mukha Shvanasana.*

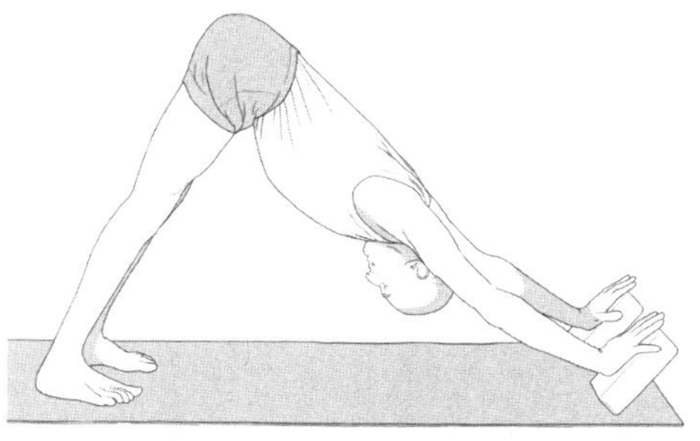

Elevating the hands on diagonal blocks

Actions:

- Roll your upper arms outward (roll your biceps away from the center of your body).
- Move your inner shoulders away from the neck.

How sharp was your awareness in the top of your chest and shoulder girdle?

What was the length of your armpits and shoulders? How much did your breath spread through them?

› Now remove the blocks and do the pose with your hands on the floor, in the standard way.

› Compare your experience in these two modifications of the pose to your experience of doing the pose in your usual manner. ∫

I feel that pushing my hands against blocks helps to shift weight to the legs, to descend my heels and to better activate my arms. This makes the pose lighter: there is more space in the shoulder girdle and the upper chest, and the breath can better penetrate and spread there.

Exploration B.2

PROPS
4 blocks

Elevating *Adho Mukha Shvanasana* (Downward-Facing Dog)

In this Exploration, we do *Adho Mukha Shvanasana* when both the hands and the feet are placed on blocks. We explore whether this kind of support – which, unlike in the previous Exploration, does not change the geometry of the pose – affects the experience of the pose.

› Prepare 4 blocks in a rectangular shape that matches the positions of your hands and feet in *Adho Mukha Shvanasana*.

› Place your hands on the two front blocks and your feet on the two rear blocks.

› Remain in *Adho Mukha Shvanasana* on the blocks for a minute or so and record your experience. Then step off the blocks and do the pose in the usual manner, on the floor. ʃ

Did you experience any difference between the two attempts? If so, try to explain this difference.

~ Although there is no change in the load distribution in the pose (since the hands and feet remain on the same level), I feel a marked change when doing the pose on blocks; most people have the same experience. There are probably a few reasons for that. First, placing the hands and feet on blocks gives a different base for the pose, since the contact with the wooden block is different from that of the mat on the floor. Secondly, there is a proprioceptive effect; the blocks are not a very broad support, and one can sense the recessed space around each limb. The body senses the drop, minimal though it may be, and the experience is thus affected. Thirdly, there is the psychological effect of being elevated from the floor, which probably also affects the feeling. ~

Adho Mukha Shvanasana on 4 blocks

Exploration B.3

Uttanasana (Standing Forward Bend) on Blocks

PROPS

2 wooden blocks

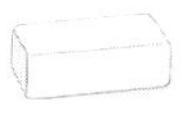

In the two previous Explorations, we studied the effects of grounding the feet or the hands on blocks and experienced the difference between standing on the floor and standing on blocks. Here we observe it in *Uttanasana*.

› Stand on two blocks, inhale, raise your arms and stretch up, and then exhale and bend forward and down into *Uttanasana*.

› Catch your ankles or the blocks with your hands and stay in the pose from 1 to 3 minutes.

What kind of sensation did you have in your legs, especially with respect to the activity in your leg muscles and the sharpness at the bones?

› Stay in this position for a while and then, without lifting your body up, step off the blocks. Then do the pose on the floor, as usual. ∫

Note whether there were any differences in the action and the feeling in the legs. Compare this to doing *Adho Mukha Shvanasana* on four blocks as shown in the previous Exploration.

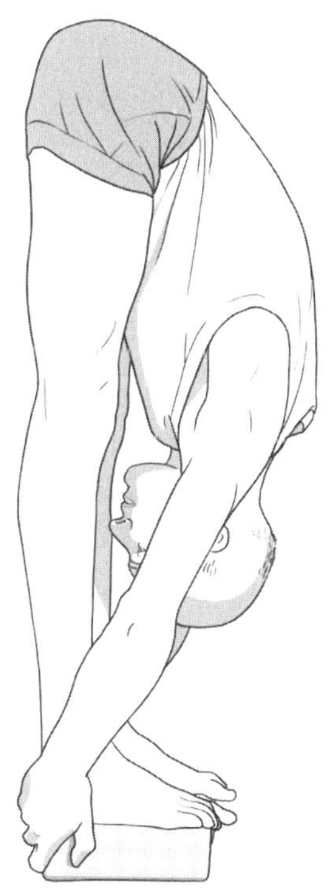

Uttanasana on blocks

Exploration B.4

Arms and Shoulder-Blades in *Adho Mukha Shvanasana* (Downward-Facing Dog)

In this Exploration, we compare doing the pose while anchoring the hands and compacting the shoulder blades with doing the pose without props.

› Place two belts on the floor parallel to one another, as shown in the figure in the next page (you can replace these belts with any two similar objects). The distance between the belts should match the width of your outer shoulders.

› Loop another belt around your chest, across the bottom of your shoulder blades as shown here.

› Do *Adho Mukha Shvanasana* and while in the pose, press the mounds of your index fingers on the belt edges (imagine that someone is trying to pull the belts away).

› Connect the pressure on your inner wrists with your outer shoulders (align them as shown in the figure).

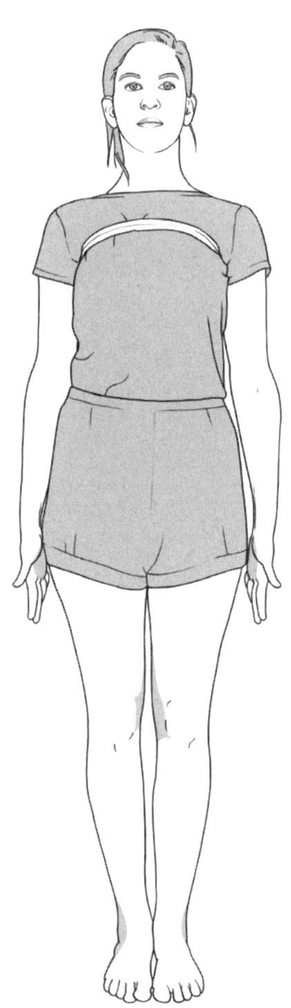

Looping a belt around the chest

Actions:

- Roll each hand from the little finger to the thumb side, such that you press evenly on the roots of all five fingers.
- At the same time, roll your upper arms out (biceps rolling away from the center and triceps toward the center).
- Squeeze your outer elbows in and keep resisting with the elbows (keep them high).
- Move your shoulder blades upward (toward your pelvis) and inward (toward your chest and away from the belt).
- Widen the ribs at your back and, at the same time, draw your lower shoulder blades toward your spine.

PROPS

3 belts (or 1 belt and 2 thin, flat objects)

Feel your arms, especially the compactness of the muscles. Observe the quality of the contact of the muscles with the bones of the arms. What was the degree of extension from your hands to your buttocks? How was your breath? To what degree did you feel stable and relaxed?

› Now do the pose again without using any props (besides a sticky mat). ∫

Did you notice a marked difference between the two attempts?

~ In my experience, the contact of the belt with the shoulder blades sensitizes them and helps to activate and squeeze them in. Pressing on the belts under the hands creates a wringing effect in the arms, which draws the muscles closer to the bones of the arms. ~

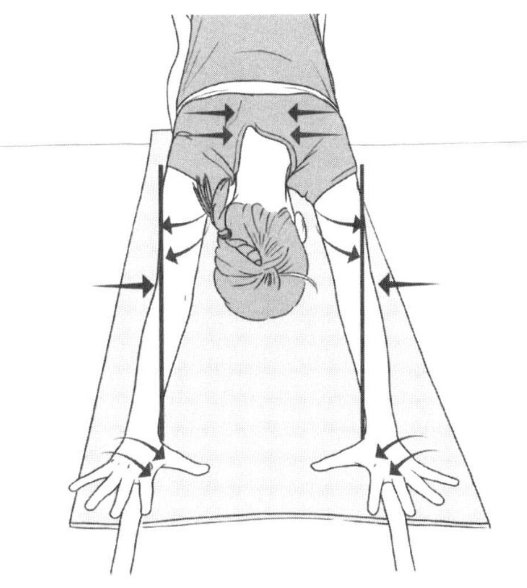

Adho Mukha Shvanasana with belt on chest - pressing the index finger mounds and compacting the shoulder blades

Exploration B.5

From *Uttanasana* (Standing Forward Bend) to *Adho Mukha Shvanasana* (Downward-Facing Dog) with block between the thighs

In this Exploration, we examine the effect of placing a block between the thighs. We compare this with doing the pose normally, without props.

› Stand in *Tadasana* with a block on its lowest-height side in between your upper thighs. Bend to *Uttanasana*; hold the rear side of the block and pull it back.

Uttanasana with block between the thighs

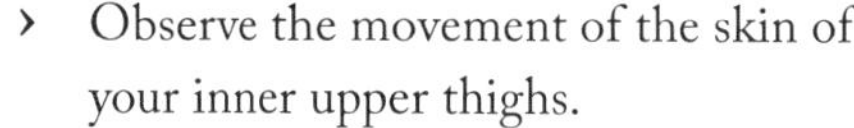

› Observe the movement of the skin of your inner upper thighs.

What kind of feeling did you have in the pelvic region when the upper thighs were rolling this way?

› Now move your hands forward and step forward to *Adho Mukha Shvanasana*. Keep pressing your thighs against the block and attempt to move it back.

› Observe the activation of your thighs, the width of your pelvis and the softness of the abdomen. Observe your breath.

Adho Mukha Shvanasana with block between the thighs (arrows showing actions)

Actions:

- Keep moving the block back and up, and, at the same time, move your outer knees back and descend your outer feet to the floor.
- Verify that your kneecaps are facing forward.
- If a helper is available, she or he can increase the effect by pulling the block gently back and up.

› After 30 to 60 seconds, remove the block and do the pose again without the block. ∫

PROPS

block 

Could you maintain the same action of rolling your thighs in, even without using the block? Could you maintain the sensitivity of the skin of your inner thighs without the block? Did using the block change your experience of the pose?

~ In my experience, pressing against the block teaches one to tighten the outer thighs, while maintaining space between the inner thighs. The increased activation of the thigh muscles makes the pose more stable and creates more space in the lower back and abdomen. This elicits the breath to penetrate this region and to spread there. The reduced pressure on the trunk induces a feeling of relief. ~

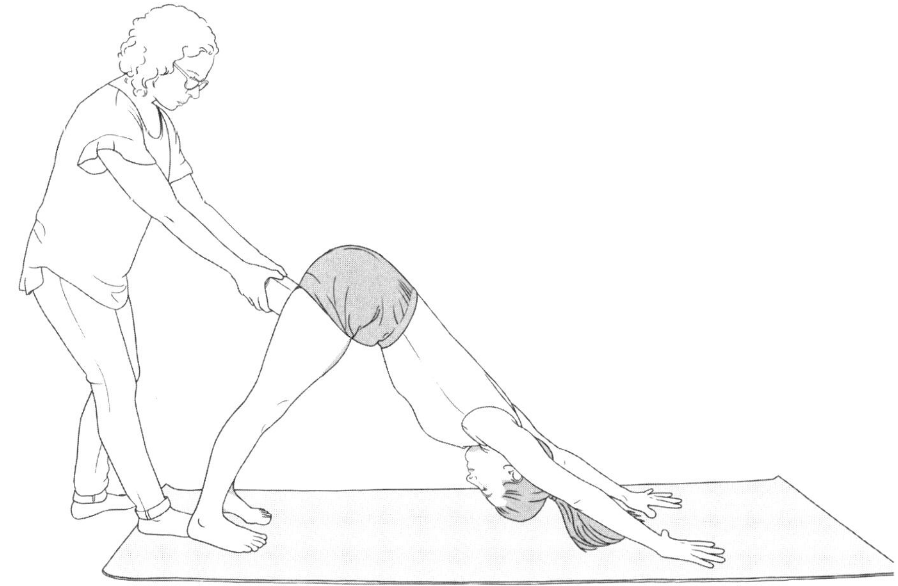

A helper pulls the block

Exploration B.6

Focusing on the Rear Leg in Standing Poses

In this Exploration, we do several standing poses where the legs are spread, such as *Utthita Trikonasana* (Extended Triangle Pose), *Parsvottanasana* (Intense Side Stretch Pose), and *Utthita Parsvakonasana* (Extended Side-Angle Pose), with a belt under the foot of the rear leg. We explore whether pressing the outer foot on the belt changes the experience of the pose.

We give instructions for doing *Utthita Trikonasana* on the right side here, but you can try other standing poses in the same manner. You may even find that, in more challenging poses like *Parsvottanasana* or *Parivritta Trikonasana* (Revolved Triangle Pose), the effect of the belt is even more apparent.

› Place a belt on the floor and step on it with your outer left foot. Move your right leg to the appropriate distance and do *Utthita Trikonasana*, bending to the right side.

› As you bend into the pose keep pressing your outer left foot down on the belt. Observe whether you lose contact with the belt when you bend to the right side.

› Stay in the pose from 45 to 90 seconds, observing the stability of the pose, and then do the other side. ∫

- If a helper is available, ask him or her to gently pull the belt while you enter the pose and while you stay in it. Press down on the belt so as not to allow the helper to slide the belt from under your foot.

Actions in the rear leg:

- Lift the inner leg from your inner ankle to your inner groin, and press your outer leg downward, as if you are attempting to make the leg vertical as in *Tadasana*.
- Move your front thigh backward.
- Imagine that your shin bone can extend through the heel and into the floor.

Were you more attentive to your rear leg when you used the belt (compared to doing the pose as usual, with no props)? How stable was the pose (when using the belt)? What was the state of your eyes while you concentrated on pressing the belt? How was your breathing?

The rear leg provides stability in standing poses. In many standing poses, including *Utthita Trikonasana*, if the rear leg becomes unstable, we drop on the front leg and lose the anchoring of the pose. There is no resistance and hence the stretch is less, and there will be too much load on the right leg. B.K.S. Iyengar said that in standing *asanas* the rear leg is "the brain of the pose." The touch of the belt helps me to keep my awareness focused continuously on the rear leg and maintain its stability. This changes my experience of the pose since there is more stability and balance. Focusing on the sensation at the outer rear foot also helps me to concentrate better. Keeping a strong focus on this rear foot, I try to shift my awareness to other regions of the body, without losing that focal point.

PROPS

belt or any other thin, flat object

Utthita Trikonasana with a belt under the outer foot of the back leg

Exploration B.7

Awakening the Shoulder Blades in Standing *Asanas*

In this Exploration, we try out some standing poses with a belt wrapped around the top chest. The belt is used to sharpen the awareness around the chest and to activate the shoulder blades. We then attempt this action without the belt and study the mental effects of directing awareness to the chest area.

We recommend that you try other *asanas* with the belt around the chest and observe the effect. You'll probably find that the belt is helpful for many other *asanas* (Headstand being a good example).

CAUTIONS

- Do not practice the *Virabhadrasana* (hero) poses if you have a cardiac condition, palpitations, heartburn, diarrhea, or dysentery.
- Anyone with menorrhagia or metrorrhagia should avoid these *asanas*.

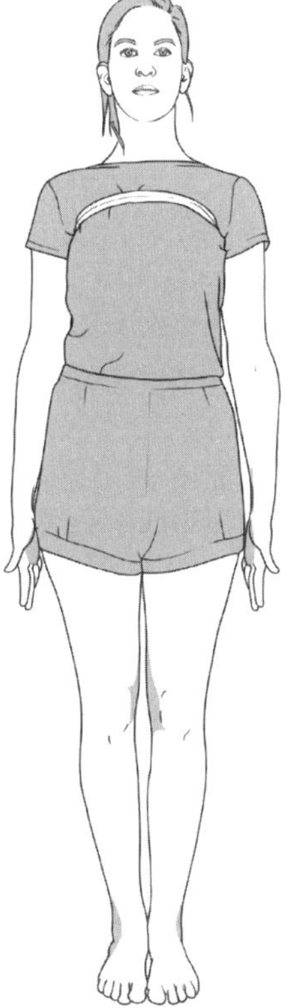

Tadasana with belt on top chest

› Wrap a belt around your chest such that it is above the nipples and over the center of the shoulder blades. Tighten the belt so that it will stay on the chest, but not too much (i.e., not so much as to restrict your breathing).

› Stand in *Tadasana* and observe the contact of the belt with your chest.

Note: If a partner is available, he or she can help you by tucking your shoulder blades under the belt and tightening it from the back. This way, the belt can be adjusted more precisely.

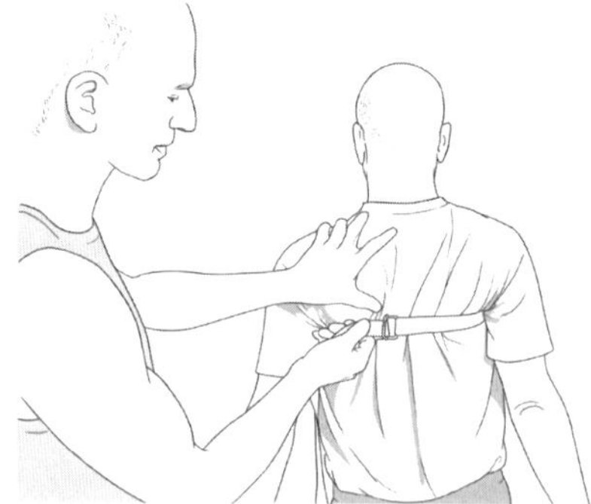

Partner adjusts a belt around top chest

Where on the circumference of the thorax was the contact firmer? Did you feel the same contact on the right and left sides?

PROPS
belt
optional: block

Utthita Trikonasana with belt around the chest

~ When I use the belt and open my chest, the skin at the front comes in contact with the belt, while the skin of my upper back moves away from the belt. ~

› Stand in *Tadasana*, inhale, and jump and spread your legs into *Utthita Hasta Padasana.*

› Turn your right leg 90° outward, to *Parsva Hasta Padasana.*

Compare the contact of the belt with your right and left shoulder blades. Which was in better contact?

Could you maintain the same contact of your chest with the belt after jumping to *Utthita Hasta Padasana*?

› Now bend into *Utthita Trikonasana* on the right side. Keep moving your shoulder blades in and maintain the contact between your chest and the belt.

› Keep observing the contact of the belt with your right and left shoulder blades.

Actions for the shoulder blades:

- Move your shoulder blades down along your back and in toward your back ribs.
- Attempt to move your shoulder blades away from the belt.
- Draw the bottom portion of your shoulder blades in toward your spine.

› Do the pose on the left side, then come back to *Tadasana.* Take a few cycles of breath and observe the space in in your chest.

Could you move both shoulder blades away from the belt evenly? How did the belt touch the skin of your chest? How was your breathing? How did you feel when doing the pose and focusing on your chest?

› Now remove the belt and repeat *Utthita Trikonasana.* ∫

Could you maintain the same sharp awareness in the chest and action of the shoulder blades without the belt?

Exploration B.7 cont.

~ Often when doing *Utthita Trikonasana* on the right side, the right shoulder blade tends to move backward, and the right side of the chest shrinks and recedes back. The belt sensitizes this region and helps me to correct this tendency. It helps me to activate the right shoulder blade and to move it in; then the left side of the chest remains just above the right side, and not forward. When this is achieved, I can turn my head and look up, without tensing my neck. ~

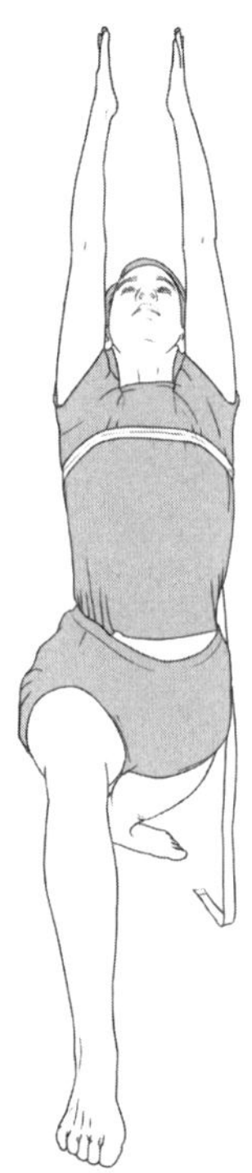

Virabhadrasana I with belt around the chest

We continue to explore *Virabhadrasana* (Hero Poses) *I* and *III*

› Jump and spread your legs wide apart. To proceed to *Virabhadrasana I*, turn to your right: turn your left leg in, and your right leg out. Turn your pelvis until both sides are aligned.

› Your left foot should turn about 30° inward and your pelvis should turn 90°, so that it's facing to the side.

› Move your buttocks down, widen your left buttock to the left and tighten the mid-buttocks inward.

› Bend your right leg to square your right knee. While bending the right leg, make sure to move forward from your tailbone, and not from your lumbar.

› Keep extending your spine upward, move your shoulder blades in, and inhale to expand your chest.

› Observe again how your chest touches the belt.

Which parts of the circumference of your thorax were in contact with the belt?

› Now continue to *Virabhadrasana III*. Keep moving your buttocks away from your back and widening your left buttock.

› Observe again the contact between your chest and the belt.

Could you keep the expansion of your chest?

› Now repeat *Virabhadrasana I* and *Virabhadrasana III* on your left side.

› Then remove the belt and do these poses again, and compare doing it without belt to what you felt with the belt.

~ The *Virabhadrasana* poses (*I, II* & *III*) are asymmetrical poses, and it is challenging to move both shoulder blades evenly into the chest. I feel that the belt helps me to correct this unevenness and to perform a more balanced pose. ~

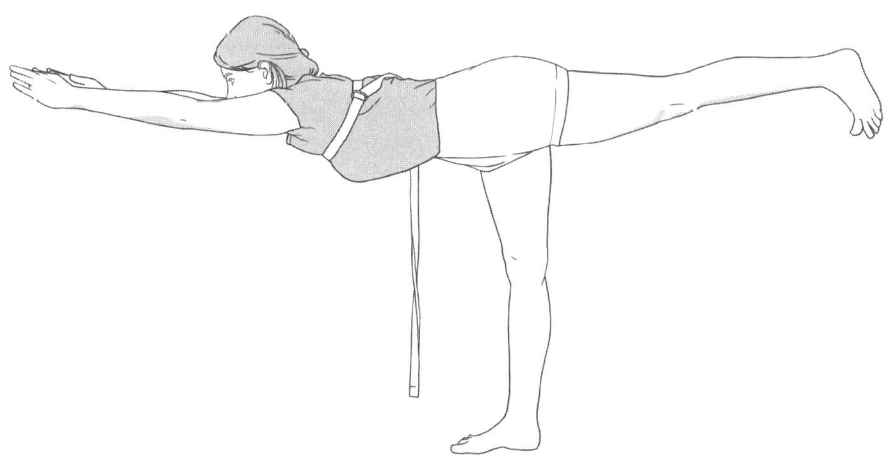

Virabhadrasana III with belt around the chest

Exploration B.8

From *Dharana* to *Dhyana* in *Utthita Trikonasana*

In this Exploration, we repeat *Utthita Trikonasana* three times and in each attempt direct the awareness to a larger area of the body. We observe the effect of expanding the awareness from a focused narrow location (the middle finger) to a long line.

- Do *Parsva Hasta Padasana* on your right side and focus your awareness exclusively on the middle finger of your left hand. Now bend into *Utthita Trikonasana* on the right side. When bending to the right, don't allow your awareness to shrink in that finger.

Parsva Hasta Padasana. Extending to the middle finger

Utthita Trikonasana - focusing on the middle finger

- Repeat on your left side, this time focusing on the middle finger of your right hand.
- Come up and rest in *Tadasana* for a few moments.
- Again, do *Parsva Hasta Padasana*, this time expand your awareness along your entire left arm, from your armpit to the middle finger.
- Bend laterally into *Utthita Trikonasana* to the right side, keeping your awareness moving along that same line.
- Repeat on your left side; this time, expand your awareness along your right arm, to the middle of your right hand and through the middle finger.
- Come up and rest in *Tadasana* for a few moments.
- On the third time, before you commence, open your chest wide. Imagine that the center of your chest is a source of light, which radiates from its center simultaneously out to both arms. Imagine that this radiation is projecting beyond both middle fingers outward to space.

The triangles in *Utthita Trikonasana*

PROPS

2 blocks

wall

The center of the chest is considered in yoga the center of the spiritual heart and the seat of the *buddhi* (intelligence). This is the location of the *anahata chakra* – or the Heart *chakra*. Imagine this *chakra* is a source of light, which radiates throughout your entire body.

› Do the pose again to your right side. As you bend laterally to your right, keep this radiation expanding from the center of your chest and throughout both middle fingers.

› Maintain both arms inline – this line, which is horizontal in *Parsva Hasta Padasana* should be vertical in *Utthita Trikonasana.*

› Come back to *Tadasana*, rest for a while and then repeat on your left side. ∫

Could you keep your attention solely on the designated body region without allowing it to shift to other body parts or to wander?

Compare the first attempt in which you concentrated on a small area with the third attempt where you expanded your awareness, allowing it to widen sideways. What was the state of your eyes? Were they stable? Did you gaze outward at some external place or did you feel your gaze was drawn inward? How was your breathing?

Focusing on one point is *dharana* (concentration); spreading the awareness along the body may lead to *dhyana* (meditation). Iyengar explains the difference between concentration and meditation in the practice of *asana* as follows:

"Focusing on one point is concentration. Focusing on all points at the same time is meditation. Meditation is centrifugal as well as centripetal [. . .] if you spread the concentration from the extended part to all the other parts of the body, without losing the concentration on the extended part, then you will not lose the inner action or the outer expression of the pose, and that teaches you what meditation is. Concentration has a point of focus; meditation has no points. That is the secret".[8]

Did you feel you were absorbed in the *asana* when widening your awareness, allowing it to spread into space? Did you experience a meditative state?

8. *The Tree of Yoga*, p. 39-40

Exploration B.9

Grounding the Standing *Asanas*

In this Exploration, we take a close look at the weight distribution on the feet and the effects it has on the feeling of the standing poses. We divide each foot into four quarters, as shown in the following figure.

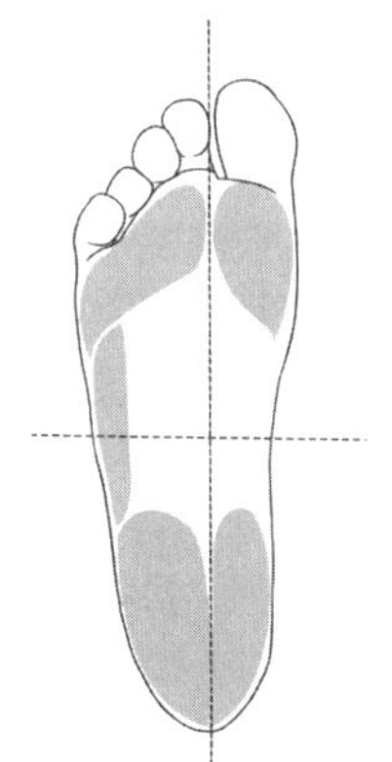
The four quarters of the foot

› Stand in *Tadasana* and rock slowly back and forth to shift your weight from the back portion to the front portion of your feet. Then, alternately, press more strongly on the outer edges of each foot and then on the inner edges.

› Learn to isolate these four quarters of each foot and to control the pressure you apply to each of them. Observe the effects it has on the experience of *Tadasana*.

What were the reactions you observed when pressing the various parts of your feet?

What happened when you pressed the front edge of your heel and the rear portion of your toe mounds simultaneously? Did you feel the arches of your feet lift?

› Now do *Utthita Trikonasana* focusing on the foot of your rear leg (left leg when doing the *asana* on the right). Press only one of the quarters of that foot at a time and study the effects it has on the pose.

How did the stability and alignment change when you shifted weight from quarter to quarter? What was the effect of pressing your heel heavily down? What was the effect of pressing the outer part of your foot? And so on.

I feel that (when doing the *asana* on the right) pressing my left heel down moves my leg backward (toward the wall behind me) and hence increases my stability and balance in the pose. Pressing the outer edge of my left foot lifts the inner portions of my left leg, and hence creates more space in my pelvis and abdomen. Pressing the inner edge of my left foot lengthens the inner leg, which tends to shorten when the foot isn't on the floor (as in *Ardha Chandrasana* – Half Moon Pose).

Pressing both the front edge of the heel and the back portion of the toe mounds lifts the arch of the foot and distributes the weight more evenly along the feet.

› Do *Utthita Trikonasana* again, but this time focus on the foot of your front leg.

What was the difference between the two feet? Can you focus simultaneously on both feet?

Note: In the front leg of *Utthita Trikonasana*, the back of the heel tends to be heavy and the front of the heel becomes light. This may cause extra pressure on the Achilles tendon (at the back of the ankle). To counter this, bend your leg slightly, shift weight to the front part of your heel and then straighten your leg by pressing on your toe mounds and the front of your heel. You can also try lifting your toes; this helps to press the toe mounds more strongly.

Vrksasana

Vrksasana: right knee aligns with the left leg

Try also *Vrksasana*:

› Lift your right leg into *Vrksasana* and observe carefully the weight distribution in your feet. ∫

What did you sense in your left foot (standing foot)? What did you sense in your right foot?

~ Standing in *Vrksasana*, I feel that my weight tends to shift to the outer foot of the standing leg. I counter this by pressing my inner heel in order to move my leg to a more vertical alignment (so as not to lean too much sideways). The balance becomes more delicate and harder to maintain; however, the more I succeed in balancing my weight along the four quarters of that foot, the taller and lighter my pose becomes, and the better the energy flows upward.

Observing the lifted foot, I feel that my inner foot presses harder on the inner thigh of my standing leg. When I press the outer foot (of the lifted leg), my lifted knee moves sideway and there is a better opening of the pelvis. ~

You can now explore the weight distribution on the feet in other standing poses. It is especially interesting to observe this in balancing poses like *Ardha Chandrasana* and *Virabhadrasana III*.

Exploration B.10

Shifting Awareness in *Virabhadrasana II*

We already studied (in Exploration A.31, see page 76) front brain awareness (*vitarka*) and rear brain awareness (*vichara*). Actually, Patanjali mentions four types of awareness, namely: *vitarka*, *vichara*, *ananda* and *asmita* (*sutra* I.17[9]). B.K.S. Iyengar identifies these types of awareness with the different parts of the brain:

> "We know the brain has four chambers. As I read and re-read the *Yoga Sutra*, I thought that Patanjali divides these four lobes of the brain as four parts of intellectual development. These are analytical part (*vitarka*), the part that reasons and synthesizes (*vichara*), the part of bliss (*ananda*), and the fourth part as the seat of the individual self (*asmita*)".[10]

> "It is said that the front brain is the analytical part (*savitarka*), while the back of the brain is the old, reasoning area (*savichara*). The base of the brain is the seat of *ananda*, and the crown of the head of the individual self, *asmita*".[11]

He then connects this with the practice:

> "When we direct our eyes looking forward from the corner of the temple in its normal field of vision, the frontal brain is working with analysis (*vitarka*). But when we spread our ocular awareness from the back corner of the temple, near the ear, the back brain is brought into play and works with synthesis (*vichara*). The front brain can dismantle because of its powerful penetration. The back brain is holistic and reassembles [. . .]. While working in *asana*, if the action is 'done' solely from the front brain, it blocks the reflective action of the back brain [. . .]. Whenever *asana* is done mechanically from the front brain, the action is felt on the peripheral body, and there is no inner sensation, there is no luminous inner light. If the *asana* is done with continual reference to the back of the brain, there is reaction to each action, and there is sensitivity. Then life is not only dynamic, but it is also electrified with life force".[12]

9. *vitarka vichara ananda asmita rupa anugamat samprajnatah* - Practice and detachment develop four types of *samadhi*: self-analysis, synthesis, bliss, and the experience of pure being.
10. *Astadala Yoga Mala*, Vol. VIII, p. 81
11. *Light on the Yoga Sutras of Patanjali*, p. 65. (*sa* means with)
12. *Light on Life*, p. 39

In this Exploration, we perform *Virabhadrasana II* four times, each time emphasizing another type of awareness by activating the corresponding part of the brain.

- Do *Virabhadrasana II* bending your right leg. Sharpen your gaze as if to take in as much visual information as possible. Aim to look from the front corner of your temple, as if you could extend your eyes forward (*vitarka* awareness).

- Then repeat the pose. This time allow your gaze to soften and become a little fuzzy in the front. Keep your eyes open, but instead of focusing forward, withdraw your gaze inward. When doing the pose on your right side, direct your inner gaze to your left arm. Physically, you are still looking to the right, but as if looking from the back corner of your temples, near your ears.

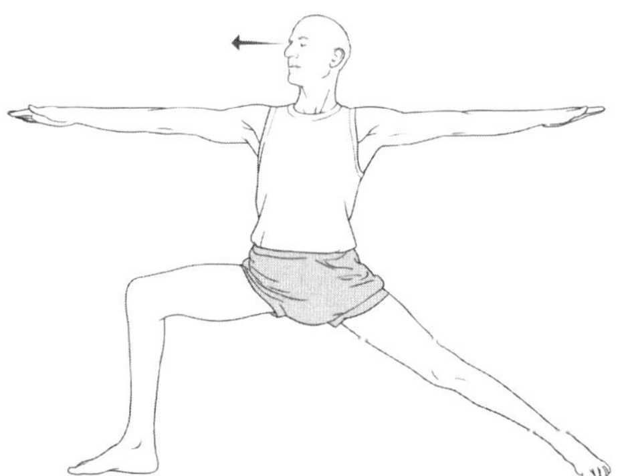

Virabhadrasana II with *vitarka* (front brain) awareness

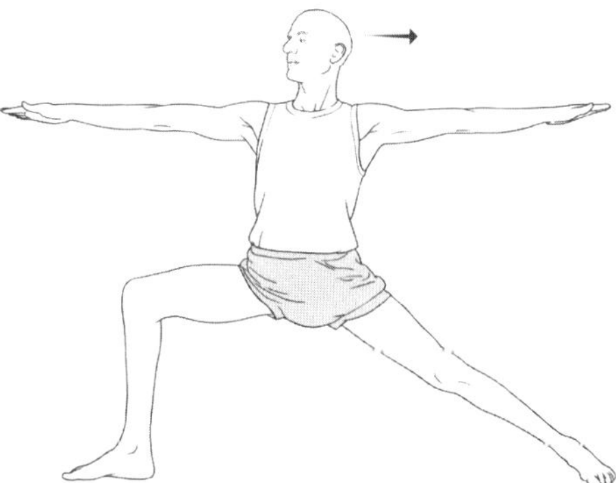

Virabhadrasana II with *vichara* (back brain) awareness

- Stay in the pose for 40-60 seconds while reflecting on the experience of doing the pose with this type of awareness. Then come up and do the pose on the left side.

- Come back to *Tadasana*, and rest for a while. Observe how you feel.

- Stay in the pose for 40-60 seconds while reflecting on the experience of doing the pose with this type of awareness (back brain awareness – *vichara*). Then come up and do the pose on the other side.

- Come back to *Tadasana*, and rest for a while. Observe how you feel.

Exploration B.10 cont.

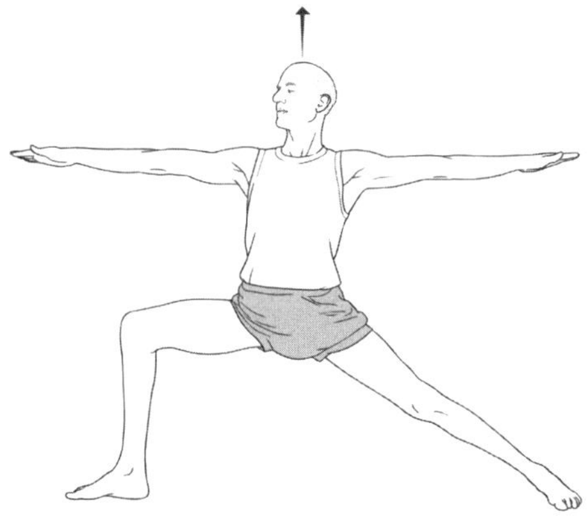

Virabhadrasana II with *asmita* (top brain) awareness

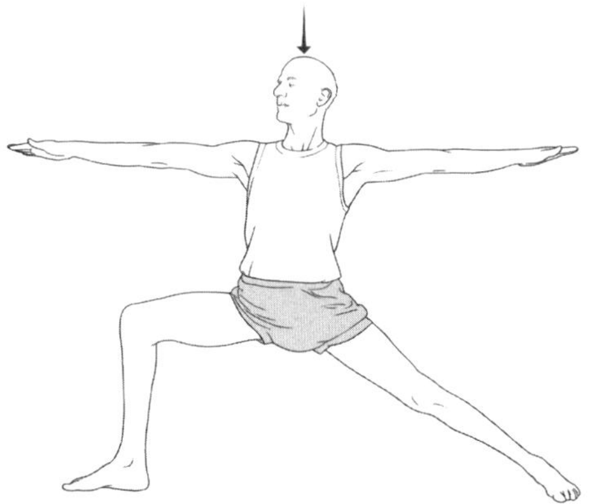

Virabhadrasana II with *ananda* (base of the brain) awareness

› Repeat the pose again, this time concentrating on the top of your head, as if your eyes are drawn upward to observe the crown of your head.

› Stay in the pose for 40-60 seconds while reflecting on the experience of doing the pose with this type of awareness (upper brain awareness – *asmita*). Then come up and do the pose on the other side.

› Come back to *Tadasana*, and rest for a while. Observe how you feel.

› Now do the pose again (this is the fourth time). Relax your eyes and allow them to descend as if looking toward the center of your heart. Let your awareness rest in the base of the brain.

› Stay in the pose for 40-60 seconds while reflecting on the experience of doing the pose with this type of awareness (base of the brain awareness – *ananda*). Then come up and do the pose on the other side.

› Come back to *Tadasana*. ʃ

Compare your mental state in all of these four attempts of *Virabhadrasana II*. Try to articulate what you felt, and what the differences were.

~ Widening the vision without focusing on any external object, as if attempting to look inside, makes my eyes soft and flat. This changes my mental state and allows for more reflection. Moving my eyes up creates a strong feeling of 'I-ness', maybe even an egoistic pride. Relaxing my eyes to the base of the brain creates a feeling of bliss. ~

Exploring Sitting *Asanas*

Sitting is fundamental for yoga practice; we sit for meditation, we sit for practicing *Pranayama*, and we sit for chanting OM at the beginning of every yoga class to prepare mentally for practice and study. Sitting *asanas* allow for long stays with stability, balance and evenness. They help develop correct alignment, extension and openness as well as concentration and mindfulness.

The root of the word *asana* in Sanskrit, *as*, means 'sitting'. So, in a sense, we should do all the other *asanas* – standing poses, forward bends, backward bends, twists and so on to prepare ourselves to sit with stability, comfort and balance, or, in another sense, to do all *asanas* with the mental quality of stability and serenity we experience while sitting.

Sitting is like coming home, returning to ourselves. When we sit properly, it is not only the body that sits – the mind joins in and sits with the body. With our center of gravity closer to Mother Earth, we become stable and quiet. In this relaxed, neutral state we can observe our tendencies: we can face our impatience, boredom, restlessness, agitation, etc. We can also follow our breathing and just enjoy being in the 'here and now', savoring the state of being present at the present moment.

In *The Hero's Contemplation*, Pisano writes:

"The organs of action (arms and legs) are conditioned to ensure survival. In sitting *asana*, the legs are reposed in different ways and learn to become quiet and free from the desire for movement linked to defense, aggression or escape".[13]

This quote is equally true for the other organs of action (speech, and the organs of elimination and reproduction), which also become quiet in sitting.

13. The Hero's Contemplation, p. 258

Exploration B.11

Compacting the Legs in *Dandasana* (Staff Pose): Belt from Sacrum to Heels

In this Exploration, we use a belt to brace the legs. We compare doing *Dandasana* using the belt to compact the legs, with *Dandasana* done without a belt.

CAUTIONS

For *Dandasana*:

- If your spine has a tendency to sag or if you suffer from asthma, support your spine against a wall.

Dandasana rolling the thighs in

› Sit in *Dandasana* and spread your buttocks by rolling each thigh from outside in.

› Loop a belt from your sacrum to your heels.

› Bend your legs slightly and tighten the belt such that when you straighten your legs the belt will be well stretched.

› Extend the backs of your legs and push your heels against the belt.

› Stay in the pose for 2-3 minutes observing your breathing.

Actions:

- Extend the backs of your legs and press them down to the floor. Draw your knee caps up toward your pelvis and flatten your front thighs.
- Observe your legs: the fronts of the legs should face up, and the centers of the back of the legs, from buttock to heels, should press into the floor.
- Press your inner knees down; then, without lifting them, press your outer knees down as well. Your kneecaps should look identical and should face directly upward.
- Press your palms or finger tips down to the floor, extend your spine upward, make your back concave, and widen your chest.

Observe the connection between the compactness of your legs and the sensations in your trunk. How much could you extend your spine? How much space did you have in your chest? How was your breathing?

› Now do the pose without using the belt, attempting to activate your legs as if still pushing against the belt.

› Compare the experience of the pose with and without the belt. ∫

PROPS
long belt

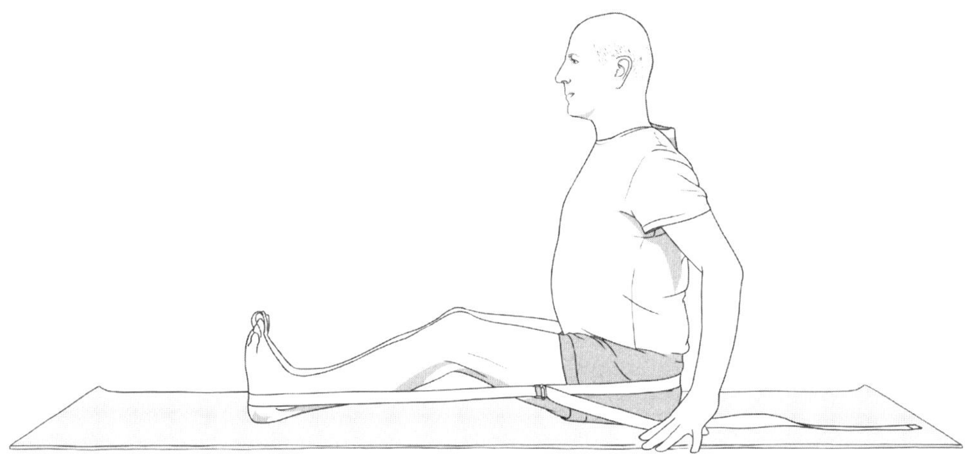

Adjusting the belt

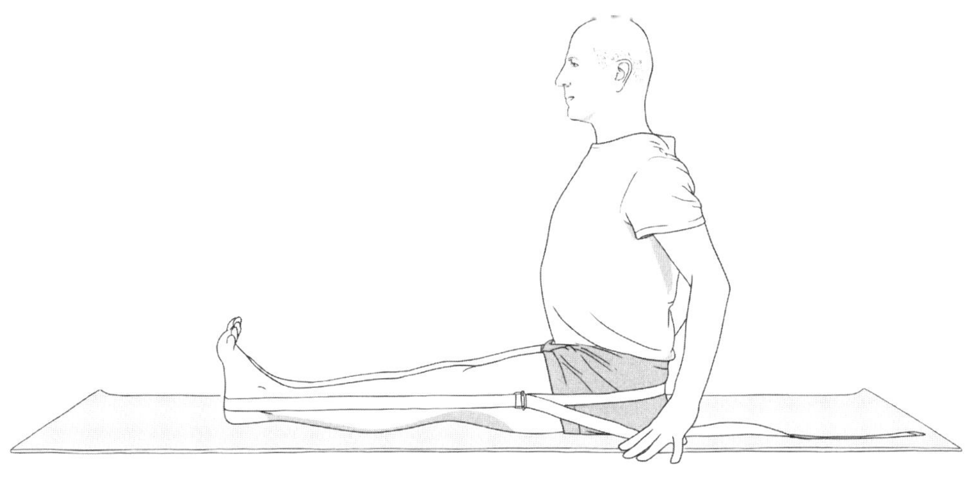

Dandasana with belt from sacrum to heels

Exploration B.12

Compacting the Pelvis in *Dandasana* (Staff Pose): Belt Embracing the Pelvis

In this Exploration, we study the effect of using a belt to make the pelvis more compact; we explore this in *Tadasana* and in *Dandasana*. Afterwards, you can keep the belt on, and explore its effects in all standing *asanas*, as well as other *asanas*.

We have two pairs of 'ball and socket' joints: the shoulders and the hips joints. These joints allow a great deal of movement. The shoulders allow the arms to move freely, but they are prone to dislocation. The hip joints are stronger, but they carry a much greater load, so even a slight dislocation there weakens the ligaments and make the thighbone (femur), and especially the neck of the femur, vulnerable. Therefore, an important action in all *asanas* is to draw these bones (humerus and femur) into their sockets. We need to activate the muscles around these joints and use them to stabilize these joints. Compacting the hip joints keeps the thighbones in place and helps to extend the spine and open the chest. Here we use a belt to create such compactness and study its effects.

› Stand in *Tadasana*.

› Loop a belt around the middle of your pelvis. Bend your knees slightly and tighten the belt so that it presses against the greater trochanters (the two boney bulges on the sides of the pelvis) and touches the middle of your pubic bone.

› Use both hands so that the belt is tightened evenly on both sides of your pelvis.

Note: If one hip joint feels weaker than the other, tighten the belt from that weaker side toward the 'good' side.

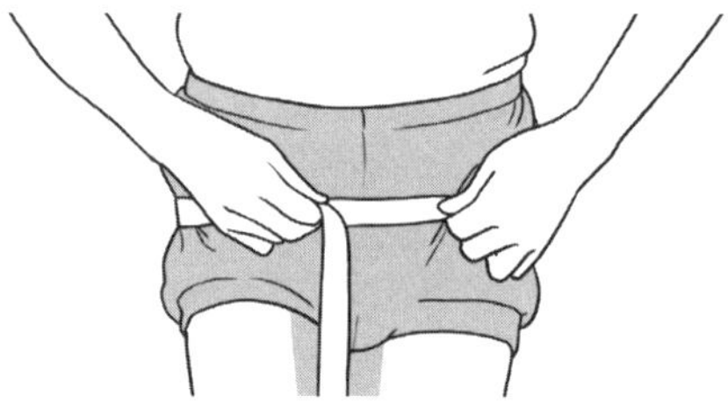

Tightening a belt around pelvis

› Wrap the remaining end of the belt around your pelvis and tuck the edge in the wrapped belt, so it will not hang on the floor. ∫

Did you notice a connection between making the pelvis compact and your stability and ability to extend your spine and open your chest?

Next, we sit with the belt in *Dandasana*. After sitting for a while with the belt wrapped around the pelvis, we will release it and stay in the pose without the belt. To ease the releasing of the belt, before sitting, unwrap the extra loops you made (leave the first loop tight) and verify that the buckle is placed forward, so that it is easily accessible.

PROPS

belt

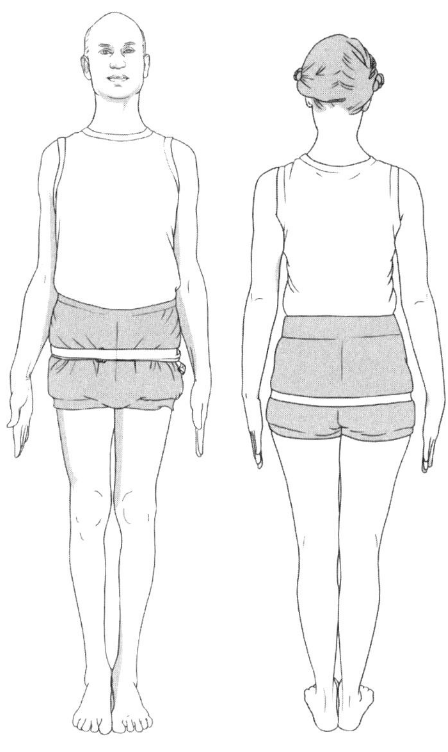

Belt around pelvis - front view Belt around pelvis - back view

› Use the edge of the belt as a measuring tape and mark the length of your lower abdomen, from your pubic bone to your navel, while standing in *Tadasana*.

› Sit in *Dandasana* with the belt tight around your pelvis. Measure again the length of your lower abdomen.

› After a while, release the belt and stay in the pose for a few more moments. ʃ

Were you able to maintain the length of the lower abdomen when you sat down in *Dandasana*?

Observe the effect of releasing the belt. Could you keep the same compactness around your hips? When you unfastened the belt, did your spine drop? Did your chest shrink?

~ It's quite amazing how the abdomen shortens when we sit down. I use my arms and legs to extend my spine upward; still, I can't quite keep my lower abdomen the same length it is in *Tadasana*.

Whenever I ask my students to sit with the belt and then to release it, they feel a very marked difference. The belt helps them to keep their hips tight and to lift their trunk upward; often, they express their wish to keep the belt in place (which surely can be done). The belt teaches us the importance of this compactness. It takes some practice to learn to use the muscles in order to achieve a similar effect (although, admittedly, not as sharp) without the belt. ~

Dandasana with belt around the pelvis

Exploration B.13

Sensitizing the Base of the Pose: *Dandasana* (Staff Pose) With Buttocks and Heels on Blocks

In this Exploration, we do *Dandasana* with the buttocks on one block and the heels on another block. We compare this with *Dandasana* done normally, sitting on the floor.

› Sit in *Dandasana* on the floor and place one block next to your buttocks and another block next to your heels.

› Now sit on the blocks, with your buttocks on one block and your heels on the other block.

› Observe the sensation of your two sit bones and two heel bones when pressing them against the blocks.

Actions:

- Roll the fronts of your thighs from outside in, as shown in the Exploration B.11. Move the flesh of your buttocks sideways to expose your sit bones.
- Extend the backs of your legs up to your heels; extend your Achilles tendon. Press the backs of your heel bones down against the block and open the backs of your thighs and knees.

Note: In order to better use your arms, you may want to add two blocks for the hands.

What was the extension of the back of your legs and the activation of your legs? Also note the experience of the pose when sitting higher and pressing against the blocks.

› Now get off the blocks and do the pose again on the floor.

› Compare how you feel while doing these two variations of the pose (with and without the blocks). ʃ

CAUTION

Hyper-extended knees:

- If your calf muscles drop too much down to the floor, then the knees are hyper-extended. This is unhealthy for the knees.
- If you cannot prevent your calf muscles from moving down, support them with a rolled-up blanket to prevent unhealthy locking of your knees. Once your calves are supported, contract your quadriceps and move your front thighs down toward the floor.

PROPS

2 blocks

Dandasana on two blocks

Heels on block with shin support (for hyper-extended knees)

Inversions

CAUTIONS

Do not practice inversions during menstruation.

In addition, avoid practicing inversions if you suffer from:

- High blood pressure
- Eye or ear problems
- Heart disease
- Dizziness or nausea
- If you have a neck injury, or neck pain, you can still practice inversions with props, but do so only under the guidance of an experienced *Iyengar Yog*a teacher.
- Some of the Explorations of *Shirsasana* (Headstand) that are given below are advanced; practice them only if you can stay in *Shirsasana* at least 5 minutes, without using a wall.

> "Whatever nectar flows from the moon which is divine form, it is all swallowed up by the sun. Hence the body decays."
>
> "There exists a divine process by which the sun is duped…"
>
> "If one's navel is high and palate is low, then the sun is above and the moon below. This position, the inverted pose (*Viparita Karani*), is to be learned through the instructions of a Guru."
>
> *Hatha Yoga Pradipika III*, 77-79

The above quote from the classical book of the *Hatha Yoga*, describes symbolically the extraordinary benefits of the inverted poses. The downward flow of the nectar is “swallowed up by the sun,” which causes the body to decay. Inverted poses reverse, or at least slow down, this process. Indeed, the inverted poses - the unique gift of yoga - are a great boon. These poses take us on an inner journey to the core of our being. They penetrate deep within and touch and heal us at a deep level, where our fears are hidden, yet also where our powers and joys can be found.

Inverted poses stimulate and balance the two control systems of the body: the nervous system and the hormonal (endocrine) system, and thus affect our entire psychophysical system. In addition, they benefit other functions of the body, most notably, blood and lymph circulation, but also breath, digestion, excretion and more. They charge us with energy while engendering focus, poise and equanimity.

Exploration B.14

Checking the Stability of *Shirsasana* (Headstand): Hanging a Belt From the Toes

In this Exploration, we use a belt looped around the big toes and hung down, much like a pendulum, in order to assess the stability of the pose.

PROPS

belt

(the length of the belt should be at least equal to your height).

› Take a belt, make a small loop and insert your big toes into the loop.

› Tighten the loop around your big toes and adjust the buckle to be in between the tops of the toes.

› Come up into *Shirsasana*. When coming up, try to keep the belt aligned with the center of your body and hanging just in front of your nose.

Notes:

- You have to come up with both legs joined, but you can bend your legs to come up.
- If you can't manage to arrange the belt directly in front of you, ask someone to help you align the belt.

› Stay in *Shirsasana* a few minutes, while watching the belt and trying to keep it still. Initially the belt may swing, but the more you stabilize your legs and keep them still, the more the belt will also become still. ∫

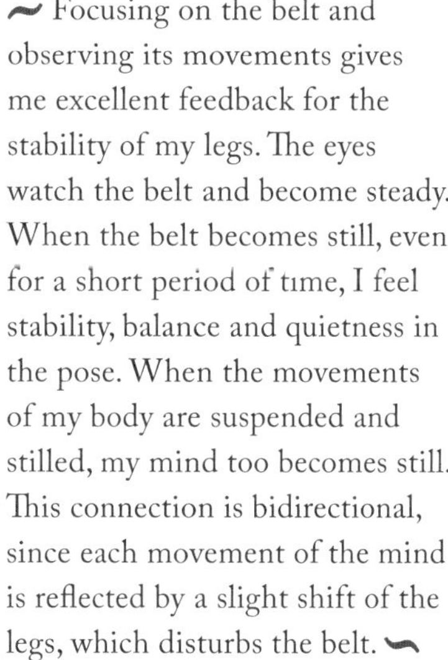

Shirsasana with belt hanging from the toes

While you focused on the belt: How stable were your eyes? What was the quality of your breathing? What was the state of your mind?

Challenge

Tie a small weight (about 2 kg. or 4 lbs.) to the end of the belt, such that the weight is hung just a few centimeters above the floor. This makes it much more difficult to keep the belt still, since every movement is amplified by the weight.

~ Focusing on the belt and observing its movements gives me excellent feedback for the stability of my legs. The eyes watch the belt and become steady. When the belt becomes still, even for a short period of time, I feel stability, balance and quietness in the pose. When the movements of my body are suspended and stilled, my mind too becomes still. This connection is bidirectional, since each movement of the mind is reflected by a slight shift of the legs, which disturbs the belt. ~

Exploration B.15

Using Imagery in *Shirsasana* (Headstand)

In this Exploration, we use imagery and study its effects on the experience of *Shirsasana*.

› Do *Shirsasana* and imagine a string is connected to your ankle bones and gently keeps pulling them vertically upward. ʃ

What was the effect of this image on the action of your legs? How did this affect your experience of the entire pose?

~ I feel that this image helps me to stretch my legs up, with minimal effort. It also gives me a sense of direction, since my legs follow the vertical direction of the pull. As long as I can keep this imagery alive in my mind, the action of my legs is less muscular; instead, there is a surrendering to the imagined external pull. This keeps my legs stretched and stable without hardening them, and without exerting too much effort. When my legs are stretched upward, my abdomen lengthens and softens, and I feel a gentle massaging of my abdominal organs. ~

Shirsasana

Exploration B.16

Shirsasana (Headstand) Facing the wall

This Exploration may be challenging psychologically – since we usually come out of *Shirsasana* by lowering the legs forward. When doing *Shirsasana* facing the wall, close to it, it seems like the way to come down is blocked. This makes one face the unseen, unknown territory that is behind oneself, and which may create an instinctive fear. Staying in the pose in this way gives us an opportunity to explore this instinct and our reaction to this potentially stressful situation. Intellectually, we know that we can come out of the pose, just as we entered it, so we can learn to overcome the fear, to relax and to remain calm.

› Start by kneeling with your side to the wall. Place your head down inside your cupped hands.

› Twist your lower body as you climb up the wall. Stretch your legs up and support the tips of your toes against the wall.

› Move your legs one by one away from the wall, and balance. ∫

How did you feel when you were in the pose? Did you feel fear? Insecurity? How was your breathing? How were your eyes?

Entering *Shirsasana* facing the wall

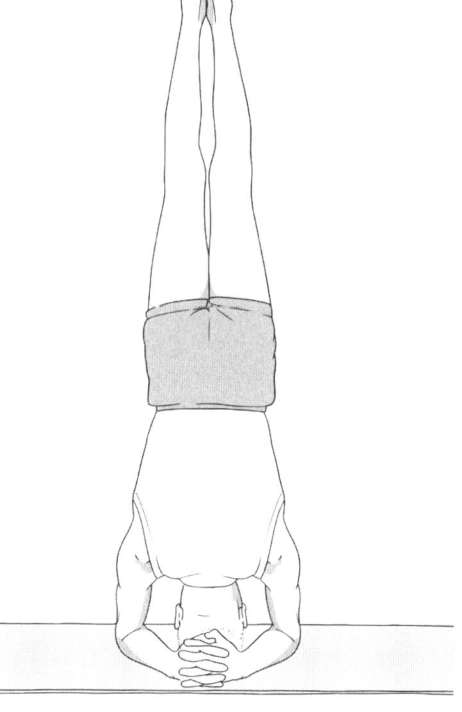

Shirsasana facing the wall

Exploration B.17

Opening the Chest in *Shirsasana* (Headstand)

One of the challenges of *Shirsasana* is to move the thoracic dorsal spine and the shoulder blades into the body. Failing to do so may create pressure on the vertebrae of the neck, which, over time, may lead to injury. It also causes stress and discomfort. If the arms are weak or injured, or if the upper back is curved (excessive kyphosis) or the trapezius muscle is stiff, this action becomes difficult, and in some cases a support is needed. In this Exploration, we use blocks to support the thoracic spine and the shoulder blades, and we experience *Shirsasana* with this support. Then we compare it to doing the pose as usual, without support. Even if you can do the pose without support, using the blocks can help you achieve a better pose, and it teaches you the actions of the arms and upper back in *Shirsasana*.

The blocks can be arranged in several ways. Each person may need a slightly different arrangement, depending on his/her size and structure, on the degree of movement in the shoulder girdle, and on the type of blocks used.

› Place a Highest-height block[14] next to the wall and place one or two blocks on top of it.

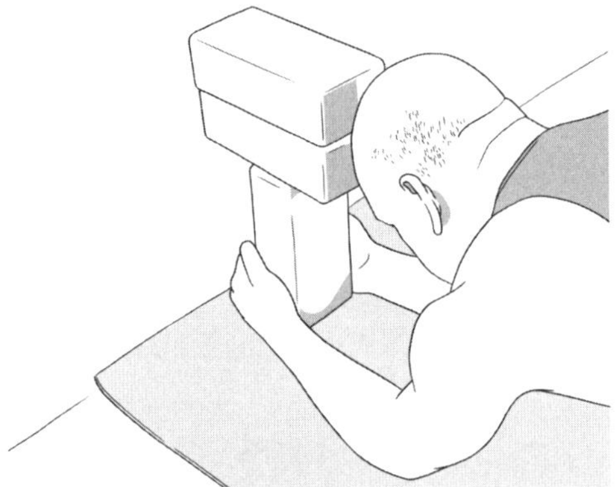

Supporting the thoracic dorsal spine with two Lowest-height blocks on top of a Highest-height block

Notes:

- People with short upper arms can do this variation with one block on top. Try it with one block and with two and find out what works better for you.
- Experiment to find the correct position of your head in relation to the vertical block. You should feel the blocks supporting the vertebrae in between your shoulder blades while the crown of your head rests on the floor. Excessive projection of the horizontal blocks makes it difficult to lift your legs into the pose.
- You can study more ways of arranging the blocks in *Props for Yoga Vol. III, Inverted Asanas.*

› Instead of interlocking your fingers, hold the bottom block firmly.

› Place your head about 5 cm (2 inches) away from the vertical block and go up into the pose. ʃ

Observe the stability and opening of your chest when standing on your head with this support. How was your breathing? Were your eyes soft?

Compare this to doing *Shirsasana* without blocks.

14. See explanation about block-positioning in p. 64.

~ The blocks improve my *Shirsasana* significantly. With this support, I find it much easier to keep my shoulder girdle stable, and I feel that my head is almost floating. My neck can be released down from the shoulders toward the floor. There is a feeling of relief combined with stability. The cellular memory of this experience helps me to improve my pose when I practice without the blocks. ~

PROPS

2-3 blocks

wall

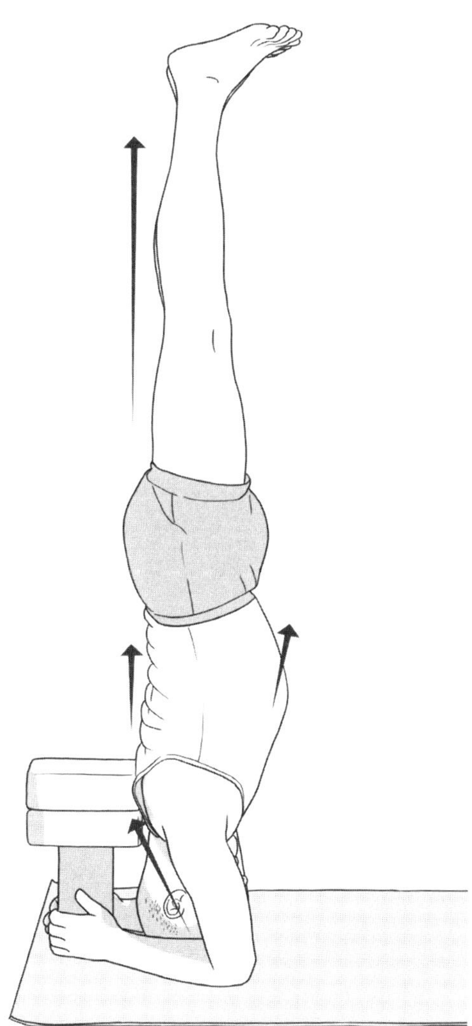

Shirsasana with block support - two Lowest-height blocks on top

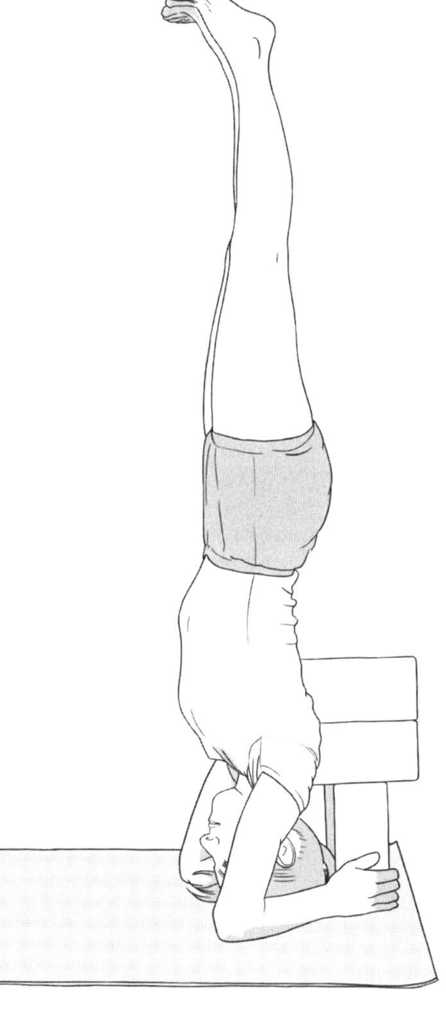

Shirsasana with block support - two Middle-height blocks on top

Exploration B.18

PROPS
belt

Focusing on a Line Stretching Forward: A Belt Under The Top of the Head

In this Exploration, we place a belt along the center of the mat and do *Shirsasana* with the edge of the belt under the top of the head. While in the pose, we gaze along the belt and observe the effects this has on the pose.

› Stretch a belt along the center of the mat.

› Place the top of your head on the edge of the belt and go up into the pose.

› Look forward and make sure your eyes are following the line of the belt.

› Close one eye at a time and check whether the images you get from your left and right eye are symmetrical.

› Then open your eyes and keep observing forward along the belt. Keep your eyes soft and steady.

› Feel the belt under your head and check whether it is exactly under the center of the top of your head. ∫

How did you feel when following the straight line extending forward?

My experience is that observing the belt and following its line indefinitely, mentally widens the horizons of the pose. My eyes become quiet and stable, and I feel evenness and balance in the pose.

Shirsasana with a belt under the top of the head

Exploration B.19

Doing a Pose Before and After *Shirsasana* (Headstand)

In this Exploration, we do *Utthita Trikonasana* (Extended Triangle Pose), then practice *Shirsasana*, and then repeat *Utthita Trikonasana* again. We compare the experience of being in *Utthita Trikonasana* before and after *Shirsasana*, and check whether and how the performance of *Shirsasana* changes the experience of the pose that follows it.

In this exploration, we briefly touch upon the important subject of **sequencing**, which is very fundamental in *asana* practice. We'll revisit this subject when introducing some practice sequences in Chapter 4.

› Do *Utthita Trikonasana* (on both sides) and note how you feel. Pay particular attention to the level of relaxation in your eyes and the state of your mind.

› Then do *Shirsasana*. If possible, stay in the pose for at least 5 minutes.

› Come down, wait a while with your head down, and then stand up and repeat *Utthita Trikonasana*. ∫

Did you notice any differences in the experience of the two attempts of *Utthita Trikonasana*? If so:

- Were these differences of a physical or mental nature?
- Can you describe these differences and explain why they happened?

Exploration B.20

Exploring the Effect of Timing in *Shirsasana* (Headstand)

In this Exploration, we do *Shirsasana* several times, with different timings, and study the effects of timing on the experience of the pose. Unlike most of the other Explorations, don't attempt to do this Exploration in one session; do it instead over a period of several days, otherwise the previous attempts may affect the experience of those that follow.

CAUTION

- Do this Exploration only if you can stand for 8 minutes or more on your head.

› During 4 consecutive days, do *Shirsasana* for 1, 3, 5 and then 8 minutes (and if possible, more). Upon coming out of the pose, write down your feelings, describing both physiological and psychological effects. ʃ

Compare the notes of these 4 days. In what ways does timing affect the experience of the pose? Can you explain why the duration makes a difference?

~ Both physiological and psychological processes take time. I feel that the effects of being inverted increase dramatically with time. I would even say that they increase at a greater than linear rate. For example, staying for 5 minutes vs. 1 minute seems to increase the effects more than five times. It would be interesting to verify this subjective feeling empirically for some affected parameters, but I think that the observation itself is evident to anyone who practices *Shirsasana* regularly. At times, I stay in the pose for 30 minutes; this has a very deep effect indeed! (But caution – don't attempt this if you are not ready). When coming down, my legs are numb, and it takes a minute or two until I can stand on them again… ~

Exploration B.21

Exploring Different Dupports in *Sarvangasana* (Shoulder Stand)

PROPS

2 bolsters
5-6 blankets
belt
2 blocks

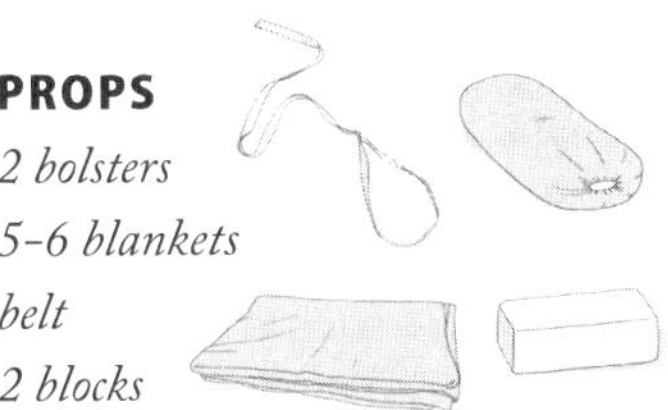

To practice *Sarvangasana*, one should use a platform to raise the shoulders and upper arms, above the level of the head, which rests on the floor. This prevents pressure on the vulnerable neck vertebrae and allows one to lift the upper back and open the chest. If you are not familiar with this way of doing the pose, carefully read Appendix 1.3 on page 153.

In this Exploration, we examine the effects of three different types of support:

- 5-6 blankets;
- 2 bolsters;
- 1 bolster, 2 blocks and 2 blankets.

Don't do this Exploration in one practice session, but in three consecutive sessions. After each session, write down what you felt when doing the pose on the type of platform used. At the end of the three sessions, compare your notes.

CAUTION

- Doing *Sarvangasana* when there is a cervical spine disc protrusion is risky. If you suspect you have this condition, consult a knowledgeable certified *Iyengar Yoga* teacher.

A. A platform of blankets

We start with a platform made of 4-5 blankets. We also use a block and a bolster on either side of the platform, to verify the alignment of the body, before going up into the pose.

This arrangement is depicted in the following figure. We assume you know how to do *Sarvangasana* on a platform (detailed instructions for making this arrangement are given in Appendix 1.3).

Setting a platform of blankets with a block and a bolster

Exploration B.21 cont.

› Start from *Halasana* and adjust such that you are supported on the tops of your shoulders.

› Lift your legs (one by one or both together) and stretch up into *Salamba Sarvangasana*.

<u>Actions</u>:

- Stretch your legs up and lift your back from your upper back to your buttocks.
- To keep the body straight and vertical tighten, your mid-buttocks inward and move your front thighs up and back.

› Stay in *Sarvangasana* for a few minutes.

How did you feel in the pose done on the blankets? Was it comfortable for the neck? Could you raise your upper back and open your chest? How was your breathing? What was the general experience of the pose? Write down these observations.

› Lower your legs into *Halasana*. Your toes should land on the centerline of the block. Stretch your arms back on the bolster and hold it.

› Stay in *Halasana* for 1-2 minutes.

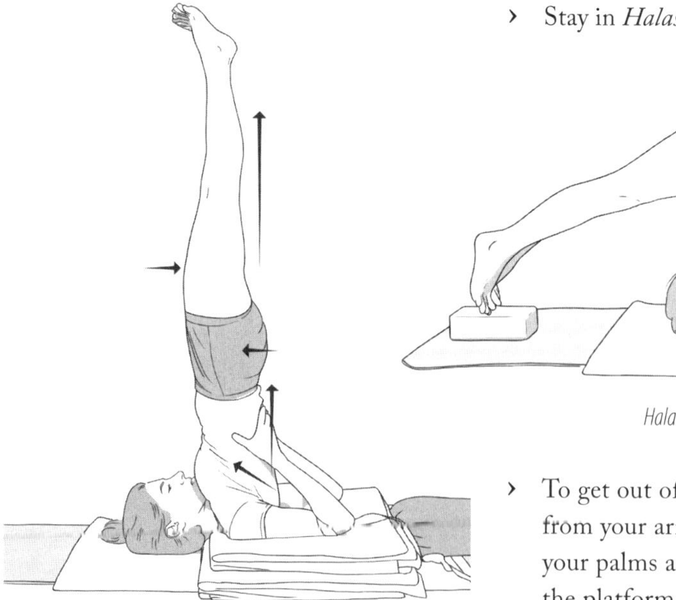

Salamba Sarvangasana I

Halasana with toes on block

› To get out of the pose, remove the belt from your arms, support your back with your palms and slowly roll your back to the platform, until your pelvis rests on the bolster.

› Slide from the platform to the head side until your shoulders rest on the floor, but your chest is still on the platform. You can bend your legs and rest for a minute or so, before rolling to the right and coming out of the pose. ʃ

Coming out of *Sarvangasana*

B. Platform of 2 bolsters

› Spread a blanket and place on it two (even sized) bolsters next to each other. One bolster serves as shoulder support and the other as elbow support. The blanket should extend beyond the head-side bolster so as to soften the contact between the head and the floor.

› Lie on the bolsters such that your shoulders rest on the centerline of the front bolster and your neck is fully supported by the rounded edge of that bolster.

› Go to *Halasana*. Place the belt on your elbows and go up to the *Sarvangasana*.

Note: When using bolsters, support the entire back of your neck on the platform (rather than just the lower third as in a platform made of blankets). ʃ

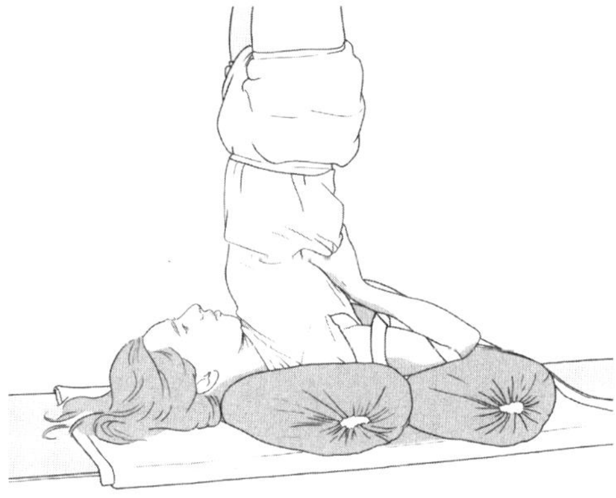

Using two bolsters as a platform

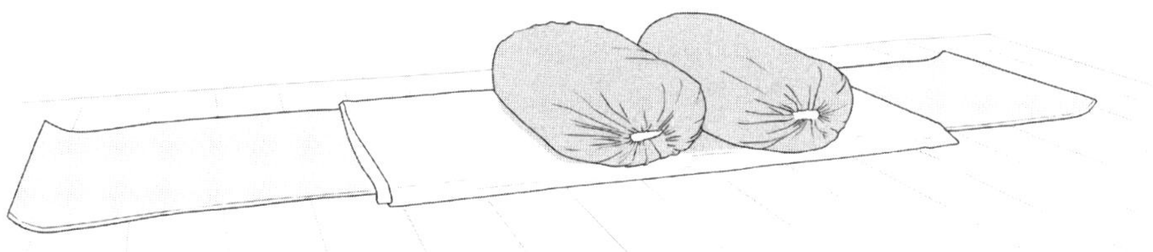

Using two bolsters as a platform

Exploration B.21 cont.

How did you feel in the pose done on the bolsters? Was it comfortable for your neck? Could you raise your upper back and open your chest? How was your breathing? What was the general experience of the pose? Write down these observations.

C. Platform of 2 blocks and a bolster

For the third option, replace the bolster that supports the shoulders with two blocks.

- Spread a blanket on your mat and place on it two blocks. Space the blocks slightly, such that each one will support a shoulder.
- Place a bolster next to the blocks for elbow support.
- Spread a folded blanket on the blocks, for cushioning.
- Do *Sarvangasana* as before. ∫

How did you feel in the pose done with your shoulders on blocks? Did you feel the shoulders better than in the previous attempts? Was it comfortable for your neck? Could you raise your upper back and open your chest? How was your breathing? What was the general experience of the pose? Write down these observations.

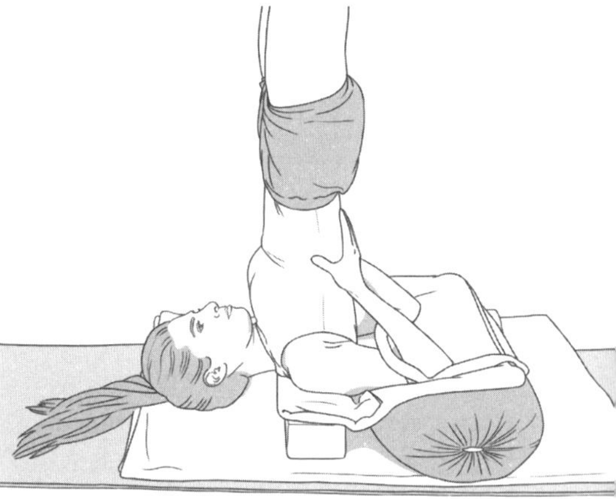

Sarvangasana on two blocks and a bolster as a platform

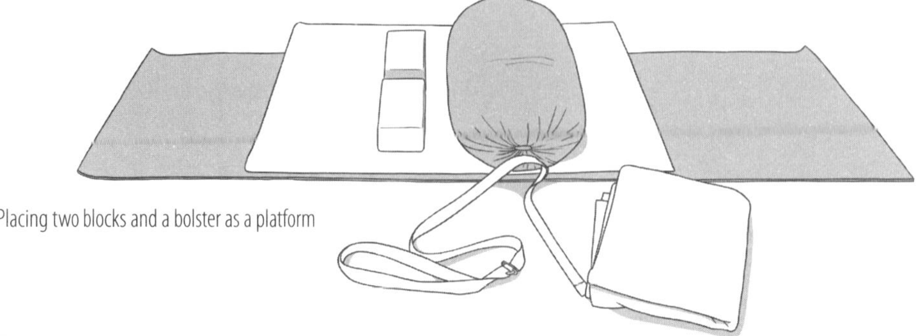

Placing two blocks and a bolster as a platform

~ Bolsters are thicker and softer than a blanket-platform; hence they are more comfortable. This comfort is soothing and makes it very 'friendly'; one can stay longer in the pose. This enables doing the pose even when the neck is sore or the shoulders are very stiff. However, I feel that the bolsters lack the stability and resistance that the blankets provide; the shoulders and upper arms slightly sink into the bolsters and hence the lift of the trunk is compromised. The higher support also reduces the *jalandhara bandha* (chin lock) effect of the pose (which is created when the upper chest is in contact with the chin).

Blocks are the opposite of bolsters in this respect: they are hard and provide resistance for the downward push of the shoulders. This type of hard support helps to adjust the shoulders at their very tops and, consequently, allows for a better lift to the upper back and for the chest to open further. I feel that it brings alertness and mental sharpness.

I usually use blankets, since they are neither too soft nor too hard and provide an appropriate base for the pose. But, from time to time, according to the specific needs of the day, I use bolsters or blocks to achieve the effects mentioned above. ~

Exploration B.22

Overcoming Fear in *Adho Mukha Vrkshasana* (Full Arm Balance): Bolster Against the Wall

Inversions tend to arouse insecurity and fear. This is especially the case for *Adho Mukha Vrkshasana*. Some students, although able to hold themselves on their arms, are reluctant to jump up with the back to the wall. They are afraid of losing control and banging their head into the wall. Magically, a bolster placed against the wall helps to overcome this fear. Obviously, there is some psychological barrier that needs to be crossed here. In this Exploration, we use a bolster against the wall and observe its effects. In Chapter 4 we offer a sequence (4.1) for building confidence.

› Place a bolster vertically against the wall.

› Place your hands on either side of the bolster, equidistant from both the wall and the bolster. Spread your fingers wide to broaden your palms.

› Bend one leg and use it to jump up. Keep your other leg straight and use it to swing your body up into the pose.

› Once you are up, join your legs, push your palms down against the floor, stretch your entire body up, and slide your heels up the wall.

› Lift your sit bones toward your heels and move your tailbone inward.

› Move your head forward to lengthen the back of your neck and look up as if you want to see your toes. Move your shoulder blades in and tighten them toward your back ribs. At the same time, do not project your lower ribs forward, but lift them and keep them close to the wall.

Preparing for *Adho Mukha Vrkshasana* with bolster leaning on the wall

Actions:

- When looking up, move your shoulder blades in and extend your armpits.
- Lift your deltoid muscles to your shoulders and open your armpits. Suck these muscles toward your armpits, and at the same time resist with the elbows (as if moving them toward the wall).

› Then, without dropping your chest, release your head and let it hang. Look forward; relax your face and breathe smoothly

› Stay in this position for 30-45 sec. and then come down one leg at a time and recover in *Uttanasana* with spread legs. ∫

PROPS
wall, bolster

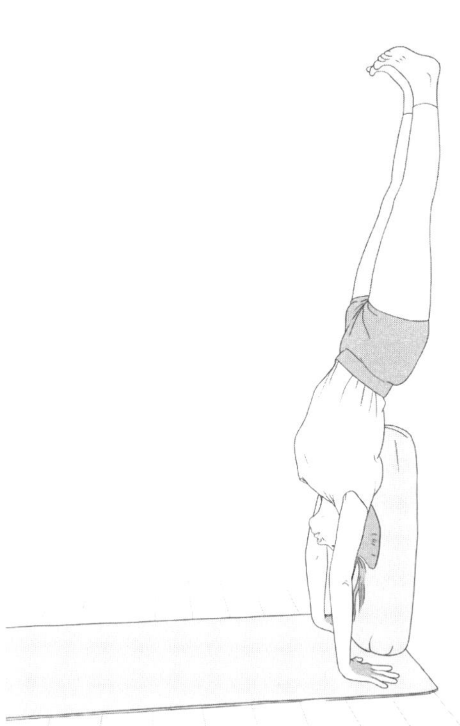

Coming up with bolster support

Adho Mukha Vrkshasana -
looking up to move the shoulder blades in

Notes:

- Notice which leg you use for jumping up into the pose. Then try to jump with your other leg. Practice the pose an even number of times and change the leg each time.
- Once you master jumping into the pose with one leg, try to jump with both legs concurrently. When doing so, concentrate on lifting the entire pelvic girdle rather than bringing your feet to the wall.

~ The soft bolster, being more 'friendly' than the hard wall, helps to overcome the fear of hitting the wall when jumping up into the pose. Some of my students who could never jump into this pose, learned to do so with the help of the bolster (even if they didn't actually touch the bolster at all). The very presence of the bolster helps to overcome the psychological barrier of jumping into an unfamiliar, topsy-turvy pose. After a few times using the bolster, most students gain enough confidence to jump into the pose without it.

So, using this simple support helps to overcome a deep-rooted fear. ~

Forward Extensions

Forward extensions are calming and cooling and have pacifying and relaxing effects. They lower blood pressure, bring relief from anxiety, and quiet and focus the mind. In bending forward, we intimately fold into ourselves and find in ourselves the sustenance we tend to seek outside. Our vision is neutralized, and the auditory sense drawn inward: "In forward extensions, abandoning the head towards the knee and beyond symbolizes surrender and capitulation of all strategies. Frontal brain perception dies away and makes way for the humility of the earth. One is crowned by one's own vacuity."[15]

We start here with some leg stretches that prepare for forward bends.

Supta Padangushthasana is a good starting point to work on the extension of the legs, and to prepare them for the seated forward extensions. This pose has many other benefits. It creates space in the sacral band and hence relieving lower back pain. It also strengthens the bones of the legs and opens the backs of the knees; hence, it is also healthy for the knees.

Supta Padangushthasana I

15. Cristian Pisano, *The Hero's contemplation*, p. 292

Exploration B.23

PROPS
belt

Stabilizing *Supta Padangushthasana I*

In *Supta Padangushthasana I*, we stretch one leg up while keeping the other leg stable on the floor. The lifted leg is the one that moves, that is seen, and that is felt more prominently. However, the other leg is just as important as it provides stability and stillness. In this Exploration, we turn our attention not to the lifted leg, but rather to the unseen leg that remains on the floor. We observe the mental effects of directing our attention there.

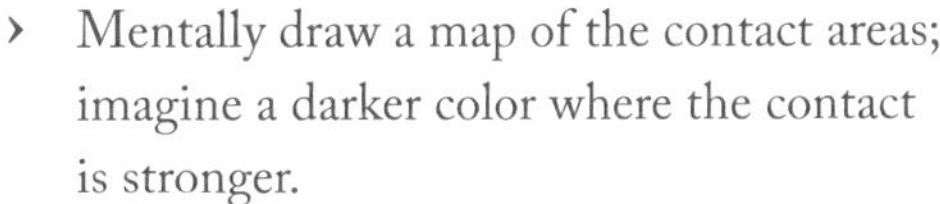

Eka Pada Supta Pavana Muktasana

› Start in *Supta Tadasana* (a reclining *Tadasana*). Broaden the contact of the backs of your legs with the floor. Press the legs down to increase this contact area.

› Mentally draw a map of the contact areas; imagine a darker color where the contact is stronger.

› Keeping the contact between your left leg and the floor unchanged, bend your right leg into *Eka Pada Supta Pavana Muktasana*.

› Now place the belt on the heel of your right leg, pull the belt, and straighten your leg by pushing your heel against the belt

› Again, don't allow the left leg to move.

When moving your right leg up, were you able to maintain the same level of contact between your left leg and the floor as you had experienced in *Supta Tadasana*? Lift your head and look at your left leg: Did it roll outward? Did the thigh lift? Did the leg shorten?

What was your mental state when you were concentrating on the contact between your left leg and the floor? What was the state of your eyes? How was your breathing?

Yoga is an inward journey; it teaches us not to be overly impressed by outward appearances and images or overly distracted (or influenced) by movements happening outside in the world. We learn to observe inside and to study our own mentality (*svadhyaya* – self-study). *The Bhagavad Gita* says that "When the mind runs after the roving senses, it carries away understanding, even as a wind carries away a ship on the waters [. . .]. What is night for all beings is the time of waking for the disciplined soul; and what is the time of waking for all beings is night for the sage who sees" (II.67, II.69).

The lifted leg is visible and moving, so it draws our attention. It tends to pull the other leg and cause it to lift slightly and lose its contact with the floor. The challenge is to keep attending to the bottom, unseen leg, and to keep it stable. This is primarily a mental action, since only by directing continued awareness to that leg can one keep it stable.

Exploration B.24

A Soft and Supported *Paschimottanasana*

In this Exploration we stay passively in *Paschimottanasana*, allowing gravity to pull the trunk closer to the legs. We note the experience of surrendering to gravity.

This way of performing the pose is combined in Sequence 4.5 – Restoration (see p.346).

› Spread a blanket and sit on it in *Dandasana*. If needed, sit on a folded blanket.

› Place a blanket folded two or three times under your knees (this support for the knees helps to soften the back ribs and allows for more freedom in moving the trunk forward).

› Place a bolster on the top of your shins (this is used for head support). If you are stiff, place a chair over your legs for head support.

› Optionally, you can place another thin blanket on your upper thighs (this is used to support the abdomen).

› Place a block or two in front of your feet.

› Bend forward into *Paschimottanasana* and catch hold of the block(s). If you can't reach that far, use a belt wrapped around your feet to catch hold of instead.

› Rest your forehead on the bolster and remain quietly in the pose.

› If you want to use weight, ask somebody to place the heavier weight on your mid-back, and the other weight on the back of your head (not shown).

› Stay in the pose for 3-7 minutes with closed eyes and smooth breath. ∫

Actions:

- Keep your legs extended but don't stretch them with force; think of your thighs as being very heavy, but keep them soft.
- Widen your front ribs and slide them forward. Soften your abdomen and diaphragm and breathe smoothly.
- Soften your back ribs and allow the weight to gradually flatten them.

While staying in the pose, reflect on the process of quieting and surrendering to gravity. What was your state of mind when you came out of the pose?

PROPS

3 blankets
bolster (or chair)
block or two
optional: Two sand bags, one of 10–15 kg (20–30 lb.), and the other of 2–4 kg (4–8 lb.)

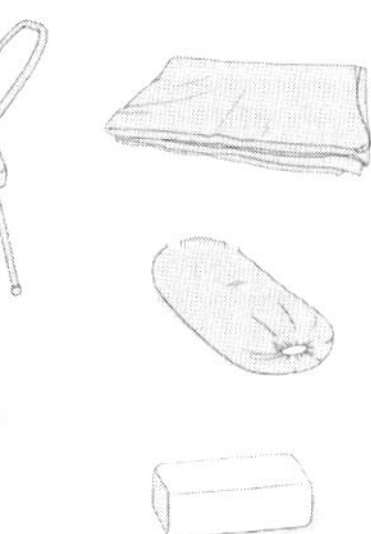

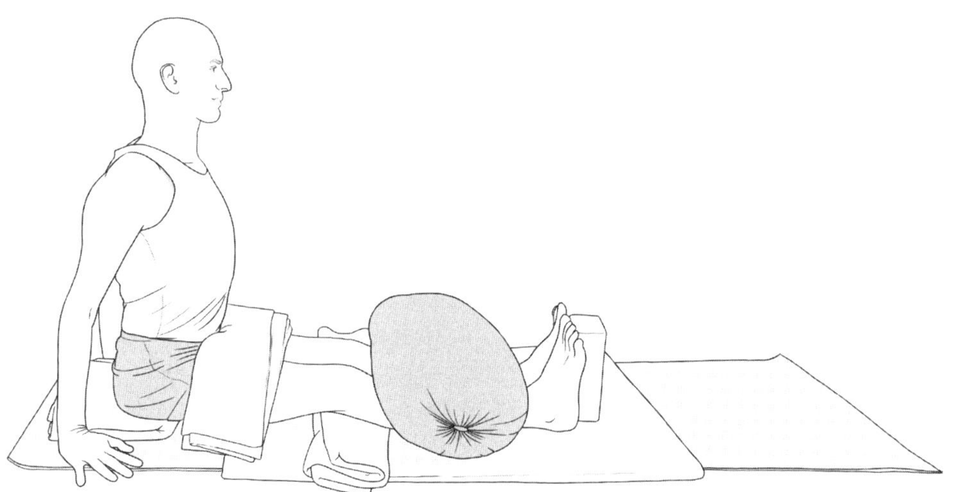

Preparing for a restful *Paschimottanasana*

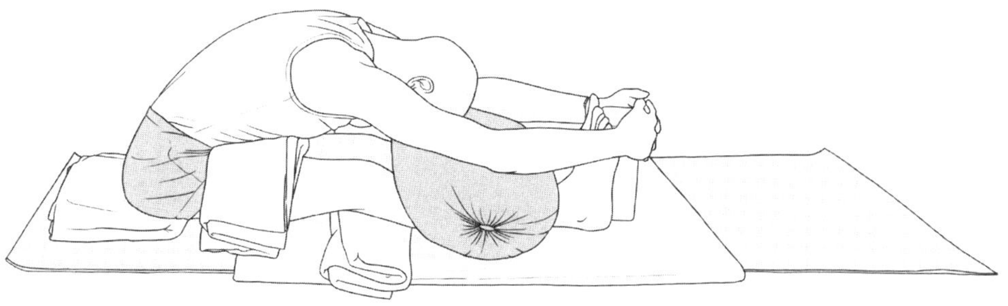

A restful *Paschimottanasana*

Back Bends

Back bends are thrilling and fascinating. The back can never be seen and hence it always remains somewhat mysterious – an unknown territory which can be exciting but also frightening. By practicing back bends, we delve into this territory and thus overcome this natural fear and build our confidence. Developing our awareness and sensitivity to the back of the body helps to go deeper into meditation.

B.K.S. Iyengar said that the breath and the circulation are the two gates for sound health. Back bends expand the chest, thus improving the breath and circulation (of blood and lymph). Christian Pisano writes, "Backward extensions put us in contact with this region (the back). According to Sri B.K.S. Iyengar, backward extensions are a means of introversion for the yogi."[16]

Opening the chest, where the *anahata* (heart) *chakra* resides (considered in yoga to be the seat of the soul), has far-reaching effects on our mood. It counters depression and anxiety. Bobby Clennell writes, "Anxiety and depression can weaken immunity, so it's important not to allow depression to take hold. Back bends elevate mood. They direct the mind outward, lift the chest, and lift the spirit."[17]

16. In: *The Hero's Contemplation*, p. 324
17. In: *Yoga for Breast Care*, p. 19

Exploration B.25

Supporting the Chest on a Block

PROPS
block
Optional: blanket

In this Exploration, we use a block to lift and open the chest, much like Exploration A.25 (see page 64), but there we did it in *Shavasana*, and hence we used a support for the head. Here we do it as a supported backbend, so we arch the back over the block. We compare the effects of using the block to open the chest in 3 ways, and then compare it with *Supta Tadasana* (Reclining Mountain Pose). You can also compare this Exploration with A.25.

Variation 1: *Supta Tadasana* (not shown)

› Lie on the mat, extend your buttocks and your legs toward your heels and extend your spine to the head-side.

› Keep your legs stretched and joined, but don't harden them.

› Stay in the pose for 2-3 minutes.

› Then sit down and observe your chest region. ʃ

How much space there was in your chest? Did you feel your chest as light or heavy, narrow or wide? How did this affect your breath and your overall feeling?

Variation 2: A Middle-height widthwise block[18]

› Place a Middle-height block widthwise on the mat.

› Lie down, extend your legs, and place your shoulder blades on the block.

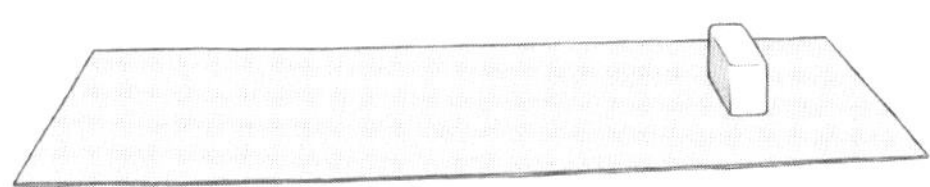

Middle-height block widthwise on the mat

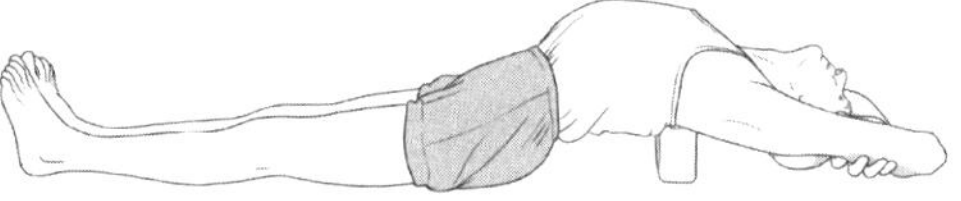

Using a widthwise block under the shoulder blades

› Elongate the spine and neck and arch your back over the block.

› Interlock your arms at the elbows and extend them over your head.

› If possible, support the back of your head and your elbows on the floor; otherwise, use a folded blanket to support them.

› Stay in the pose for 3-5 minutes. ʃ

18. see explanation about block-positioning in p. 64.

Exploration B.25 cont.

Actions:

- Before arching your neck back, be sure to lengthen it; move the back of your head away from your trunk.
- When lying on the support, suck your shoulder blades into your chest, as if you want to avoid being heavy on the block.

Placing a lengthwise block

Variation 3: *Supta Baddha Konasana* with a Middle-height lengthwise block

› Now place the block lengthwise to support the thoracic spine.

› Lie down while extending your spine and placing your thoracic vertebrae on the block.

› Bend your legs and join your feet to *Baddha Konasana*.

› Interlock your arms at the elbows and extend them over your head.

› If possible, support the back of your head and your elbows on the floor; otherwise, use a folded blanket to support them.

› Stay in the pose for 3-5 minutes. ∫

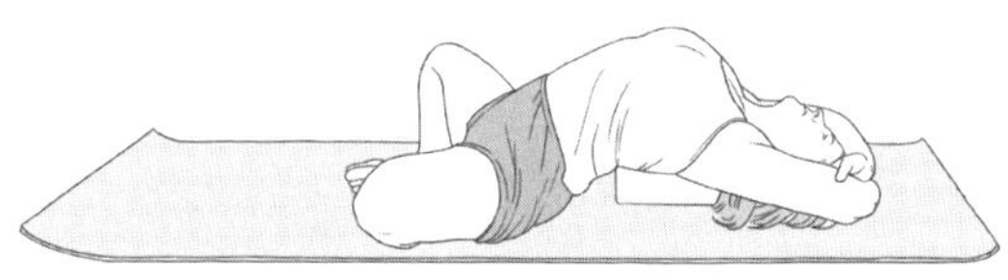

Using a lengthwise block under the thoracic spine

Actions:

- When lying down, extend and expand your back; move your back ribs away from the spine and toward your head.
- Suck your thoracic spine into your chest, as if you want to avoid the block.
- Extend your cervical spine before arching the neck.

Variation 4: *Setu Bandhasana* (Bridge Pose) on a Highest-height block

> **Note:** *Setu Bandhasana* (LOY Pl. 296) is a very advanced *asana*; even with prop support, it is still quite challenging. If you find it too challenging, skip it.

› Place a Highest-height block on the mat. Sit in front of the block and arch your back.

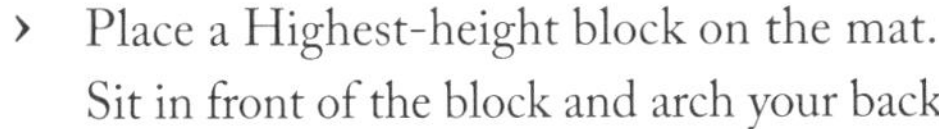

› Recline to place your mid-back – just under the region of the heart – on the block.

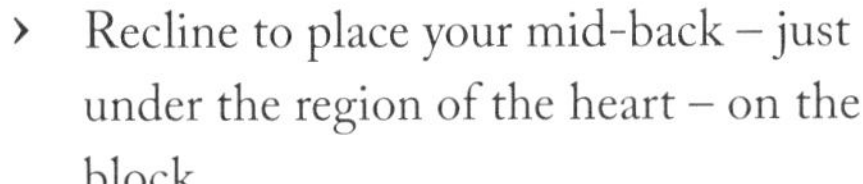

› Lift your pelvis as high as possible, extend the spine, and arch backward.

› As you do so, you may tilt slightly the block. Support the back of your head on the floor (or on a folded blanket).

› Extend your arms over the head or interlock them at the elbows.

› Stay in the pose for 2-4 minutes.

Actions:

- Breathe deeply and slowly to expand your chest.
- Tighten your legs at the knees and keep lifting your pelvis.

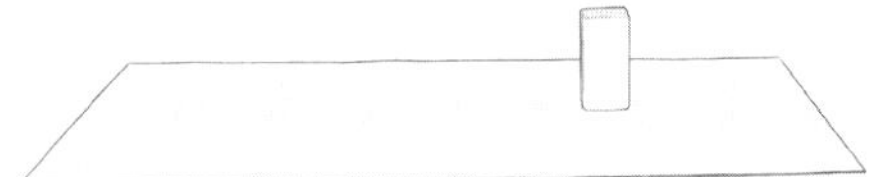

Placing a Highest-height block for *Setu Bandhasana*

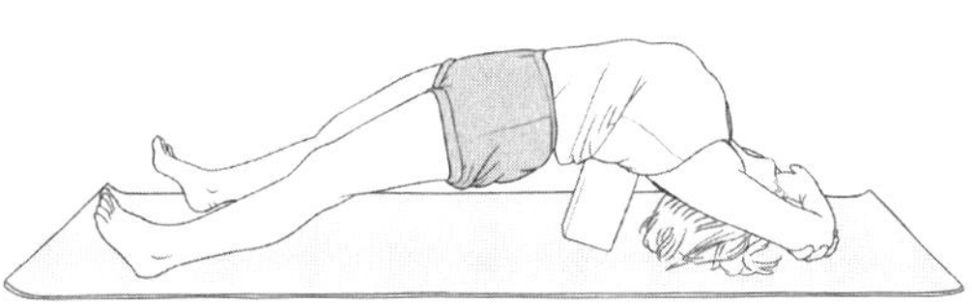

Supported *Setu Bandhasana*

Now repeat *Supta Tadasana*:

› Lie in *Supta Tadasana* as in variation 1 above. ∫

What were the differences between the four variations? Could you maintain the opening of the chest in the final *Supta Tadasana*? What were the differences, if any, between the first and the final *Supta Tadasana*?

Exploration B.26

Chest and Pelvis Awareness in *Ushtrasana* (Camel Pose)

In this Exploration, we repeat *Ushtrasana* twice, each time directing the awareness to a different region of the body. We use the sensation of touch and the breath to focus the awareness in the specific bodily region and observe the mental effect it has.

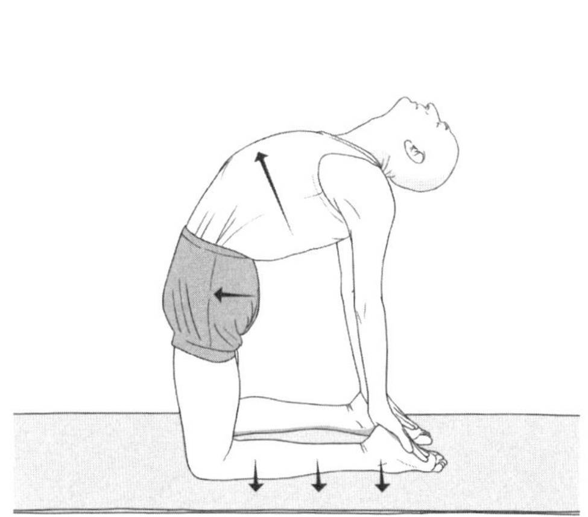

Ushtrasana

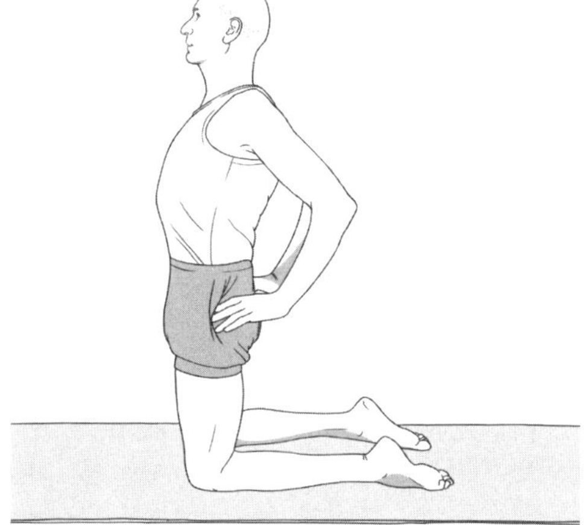

Kneeling with hands on pelvis

The same type of exploration can be done in other back bends, for example, in *Bhujangasana* (Cobra Pose) or *Urdhva Dhanurasana* (Upward Bow Pose), but since we use touch to sensitize other body parts, we want to have the hands free, and *Ushtrasana* is ideal for this.

› Kneel and place your hands on the pelvic girdle, such that your thumbs are on the region of your sacrum. Use your thumbs and fingers to push your sacral bone into your pelvis and to widen the skin of your sacral band.

› Direct your breath to the pelvic region. Imagine that the pores of the skin of your pelvis are like nostrils and you inhale into your pelvis and exhale from there.

› Extend your gluteal muscles down and move your tailbone in.

› Wait there until the awareness in your pelvis is sharp and stable.

› Then start to arch back into *Ushtrasana*. As you arch, keep moving your tailbone into your pelvis and extend the spine up from the front of your tailbone.

› After arching back, move your hands to place them on your feet and stay in the pose for about one minute, all the while breathing into your pelvis and keeping your awareness in that region.

Note: If your hands don't reach your feet, place two blocks next to your feet, and use them to support your hands.

› Then come out of the pose, sit on your heels, and stretch forward to relax. ∫

Actions:

- Press your shin bones and the top parts of your feet down.
- Press down your outer knees and outer feet, and lift your inner thighs. Roll the tops of your thighs inward.
- Tighten your mid-buttocks; suck your anal mouth in and up – these actions move the tailbone in.
- Press your hands down against your feet and lift the chest.
- Move your trapezius muscle and shoulder blades down (toward the mid-back).

› When you are ready for the next attempt, kneel again, this time placing your hands on the sternal region. Imagine the breath of your inhalation touches your palms. Use your inhalations to lift and widen your sternum (breastbone). Imagine that your heart center spreads to occupy the entire chest and touches your sternum from inside.

› Wait in this position until the awareness in your chest is sharp and stable.

› Then start to arch back into *Ushtrasana*. As you arch, keep lifting your sternum. Don't allow the sternum to disconnect from your hands.

Placing the hands on the breastbone to focus the awareness in the chest region

› Use your inhalations to intensify the lifting and the spreading of the chest. Use your exhalations to draw the skin of your back toward your spine and to suck the vertebrae into your body.

› Keep this feeling of lifting your heart center such that it doesn't lose contact with your sternum.

› After arching back, move your hands and place them on your feet. Stay in the pose for about 1 minute, while breathing into your chest and keeping your awareness in that region. ∫

Exploration B.26 cont.

Actions:

- Lift your back ribs and widen them away from the spine (but move the skin of the back toward the spine).
- Elongate your neck before arching it. Move your trapezius muscle down, toward your lower back, and the back of your skull up.
- When moving your hands to your feet, don't drop your sternum; keep it lifted to maintain its contact with the skin of your chest.
- When moving back to reach your feet, resist with the back of your thighs. Attempt to keep an angle of 90° at the back of your knees.

Compare the two attempts of *Ushtrasana*. In which one did you feel more freedom in your back and could arch better? How was your breathing in these two attempts? How was your concentration?

~ Moving the tailbone in and lifting the chest are two important actions that must be done in backbends to prevent pressure on the lower back. Working on these two regions simultaneously helps to extend the spine evenly and harmoniously and to form even arching along the spine. I feel that using the touch of my hands helps me to sensitize and activate these areas. Thinking about lifting and widening my heart center prevents any pressure on my lumbar spine. It also brings lightness to my pose and uplifts my spirit! ~

Exploration B.27

PROPS
2 blocks

Comparing Different Hand Orientations in *Urdhva Mukha Shvanasana* (Upward-Facing Dog Pose)

In this Exploration, we do *Urdhva Mukha Shvanasana* three times, each time alternating the orientation of the hands. We compare the effects of turning the hands in these three directions on the experience of the pose.

We start by studying the following hand and arm actions in *Tadasana*:

› Stand in *Tadasana* and flex your hands at the wrist, such that your palms are facing down and your fingers are pointing forward.

› Extend your arms downward and allow your shoulders to move down with them. At the same time, lift your armpits and chest.

› Observe the movement of your shoulder blades and the sensations in your abdominal region, around your navel.

› Then turn your hands 90° out, such that your fingers are pointing sideways (nor shown). Again, observe your shoulder blades and abdomen.

› Finally, turn your hands out more until your fingers are pointing backward. While doing so, keep observing your shoulder blades and your abdomen. ∫

~ In my experience, lifting my armpits and chest draws my navel in and up. This is a nice feeling, since it relieves the load from the abdomen. This should always be felt in backbends. We shouldn't allow the abdominal organs to press into the abdominal wall. Turning the hands 90° out lowers the shoulder blades and moves them closer to the spine. Finally, turning the hands backward moves the shoulder blades in. But there is a certain price to pay for the increased movement of the shoulder blades. Could you feel that? ~

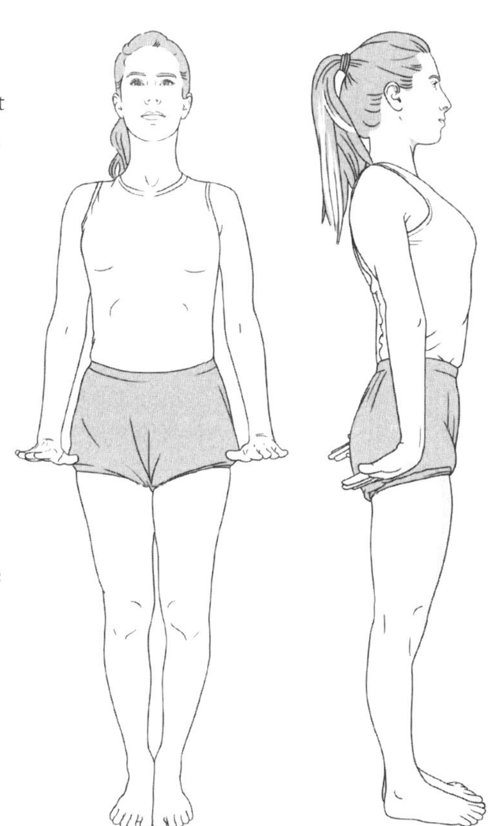

Tadasana with palms facing to the floor and fingers pointing forward

Turning the hands to point the fingers back

Exploration B.27 cont.

Now try the same three directions of the hands in *Urdhva Mukha Shvanasana*:

› Place your hands on blocks with your fingers pointing forward. Adjust the distance between the blocks such that your upper arms are slightly wider than your chest (so your chest can move forward in-between your upper arms).

› Push into the blocks and lift up into *Urdhva Mukha Shvanasana*.

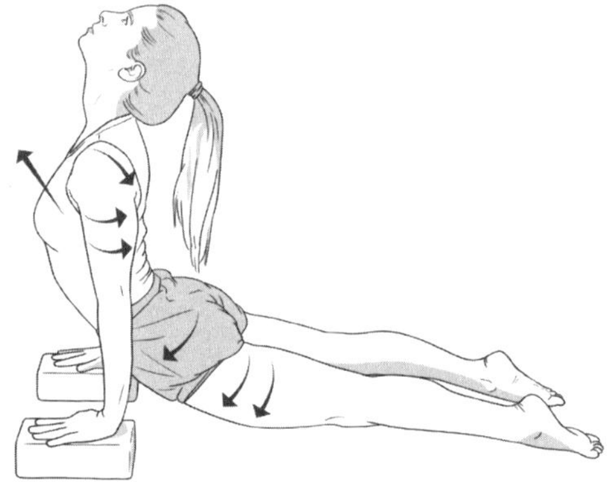

Urdhva Mukha Shvanasana on blocks, hands forward

Actions:

- Move your front thighs up and open the backs of your knees. At the same time, roll your upper thighs in, such that your outer thighs are cutting down toward the floor.
- Keep your buttocks wide and tighten the mid-buttocks inward. Move your tailbone in and extend the front part of your tailbone upward along the spine.
- Push your hands down to lift the chest.
- Turn the skin at the tops of your hands from the little finger side inward, toward the thumb side. At the same time, roll your bicep muscles from inside to out.
- Roll your shoulders back and keep your arms vertical. Without lifting your shoulders, lift and open your chest.

Note: We assume you are familiar with this pose and hence give here only a few basic instructions.

How much could you move your shoulder blades in (forward toward your chest), and how open was your chest? In which direction did your navel move?

› Now turn the blocks and your hands 90° out and do *Urdhva Mukha Shvanasana* again.

› Finally, do the pose once more with your hands turned backward.

› Compare the feeling in the shoulder blades/chest and the navel in all three versions of *Urdhva Mukha Shvanasana*. ∫

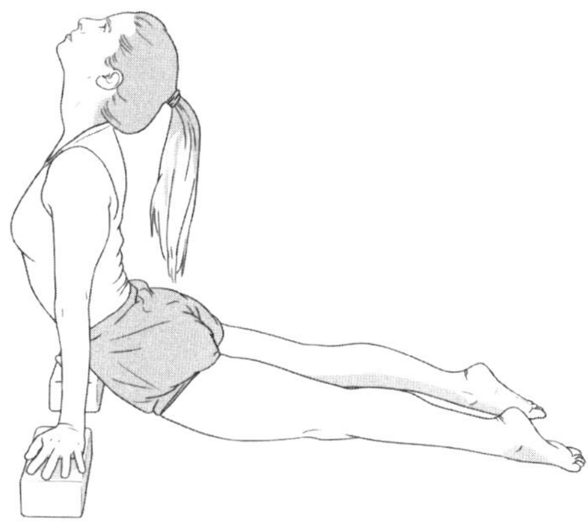

Urdhva Mukha Shvanasana on blocks, hands turning outward

In which of the hands variations did you feel more movement in your shoulder blades and more opening in your chest? In which did you feel more softness in your abdomen?

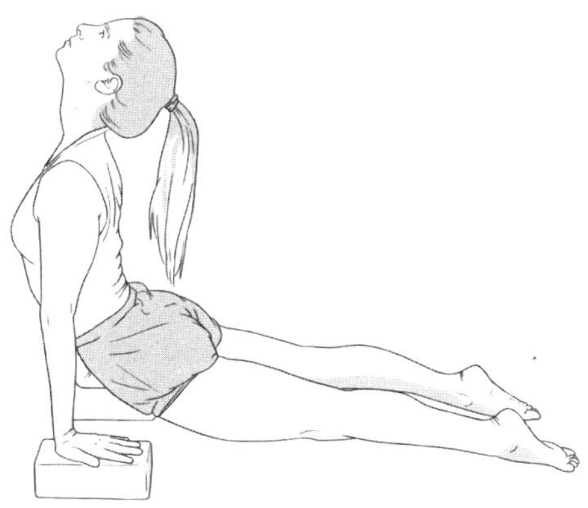

Urdhva Mukha Shvanasana on blocks, hands turned backward

Turning my hands out helps me to move my shoulder blades down and in and to squeeze the latissimus dorsi muscle from the sides toward my spine and forward. These are important actions one needs to perform in backbends; however, there is a price to pay for this variation. As you turn your hands increasingly outward, the abdomen tends to bulge slightly, as if the organs are being pushed toward the abdominal wall. This creates some tension and hardness in the abdomen. As mentioned, in a well-done pose, the navel region should move in (toward the back) and up, and the abdomen should not be tight or hard.

In order to get a balanced pose, you should learn, in the standard pose (with the fingers pointing forward), to roll your biceps out (without losing the pressure of your inner hands down to the blocks or the floor). This will open your chest without creating tension in your abdomen and will allow you to stay longer in the pose, with deep breathing and exhilaration. Of course, in the learning stages, trying out different orientations helps to understand and develop these actions. Turning the hands out or backward, makes it easier to rotate the biceps out and hence to move the shoulder blades in, especially if one's shoulders are stiff, so all three variations are very useful and worth doing.

Exploration B.28

Comparing *Viparita Dandasana* (Upward Facing Staff Pose) With *Setu Bandha Sarvangasana* (Bridge Pose)

In this Exploration, we compare two back bends which, from outside, may look quite similar, but when done, feel very different.

Start with *Viparita Dandasana* on a chair (or a bench):

› Place the chair at an appropriate distance from the wall.

› Place a block next to the wall (to support your feet); place a bolster on the other side of the chair and prepare another bolster or a few folded blankets within reach (these will be used for *Setu Bandha Sarvangasana*).

  Note: To prevent slippage, it is recommended to place a sticky mat (or a mat piece) on the chair.

› Sit on the chair facing the wall and slide your pelvis under the backrest. Catch the backrest, lean on your elbows, arch your back and lift your chest.

lying on the chair before sliding to *Viparita Dandasana*

› Slide toward your head side until the bottom of your shoulder blades are supported by the edge of the seat.

› Remain with knees bent and feet on the floor for a while, then straighten your legs, rest your heels on the block, and press your feet against the wall (adjust the distance if needed).

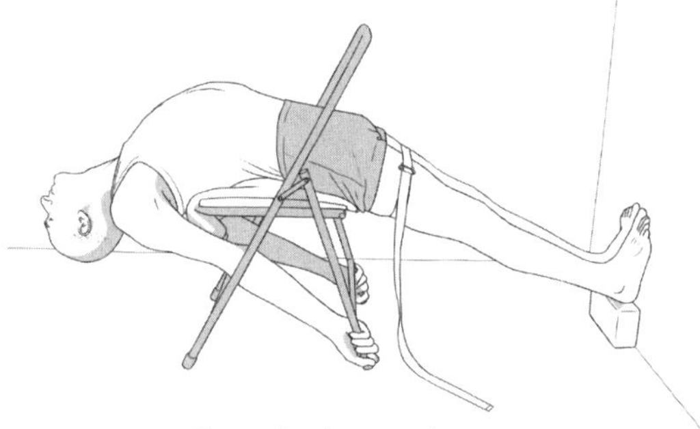

Viparita Dandasana on chair

› Insert your arms in between the front legs of the chair and catch the back legs or the back rung of the chair. Pull to roll your shoulders back and to increase the arching of your back.

Notes:

- When sliding into the pose, use the sticky mat you placed on the chair to catch the skin of your upper back and move it down toward the mid back. This helps to release the neck.

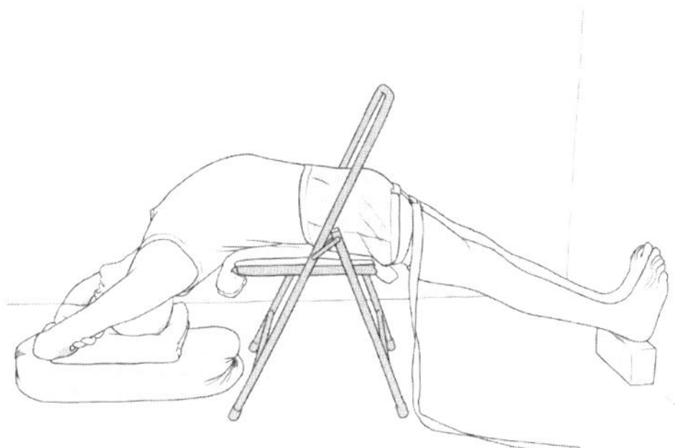

Viparita Dandasana on a chair, arms over the head and head support

PROPS

chair, bench or any similar object (even a bed can work)
a bolster or two
blankets
block
belt
wall

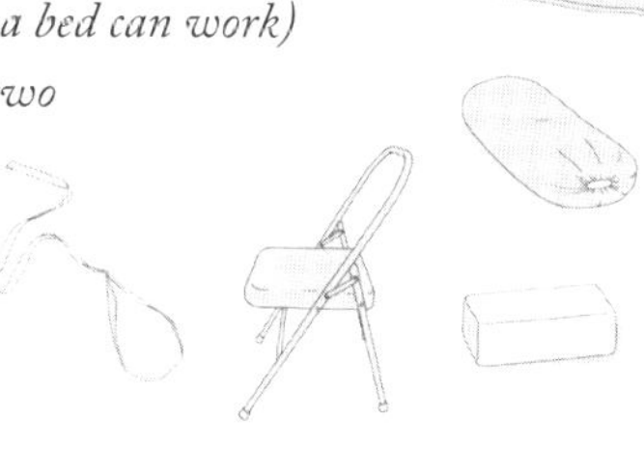

- Allow the body of your shoulder blades to slide off of the chair, but keep their bottom edges on the seat. This allows the upper back to arch and the neck to release.

› After 2-3 minutes, stretch your arms over your head, release your head down, and adjust the bolster to support the top of your head (use an additional blanket if necessary). Stay in this position for another 2-3 minutes.

› To come out of the pose, bend your legs and place your feet on the floor. Catch the backrest. Inhale, and while exhaling lift yourself.

If you experience pressure on youı lower back, try to place a block under your sacrum, as it often helps to move the tailbone in:

› Sit on the chair with the block nearby.

› Place the block under your pelvis.

› Arch back to *Viparita Dandasana*. Lift your tailbone as if to avoid the block.

› Another option is to elevate the feet to the level of the seat.

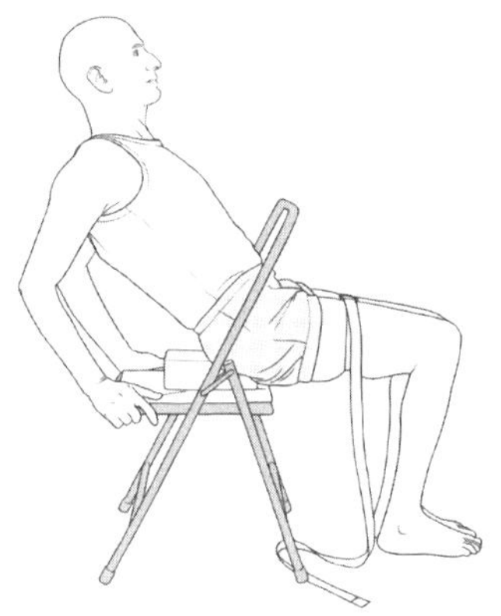

Placing the block under the sacrum

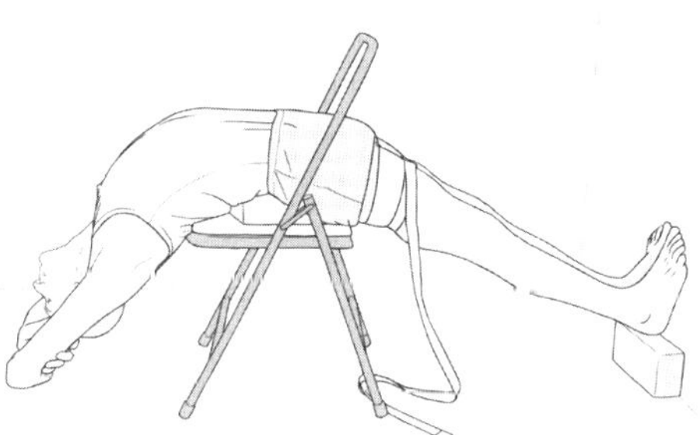

Viparita Dandasana with block under the sacrum

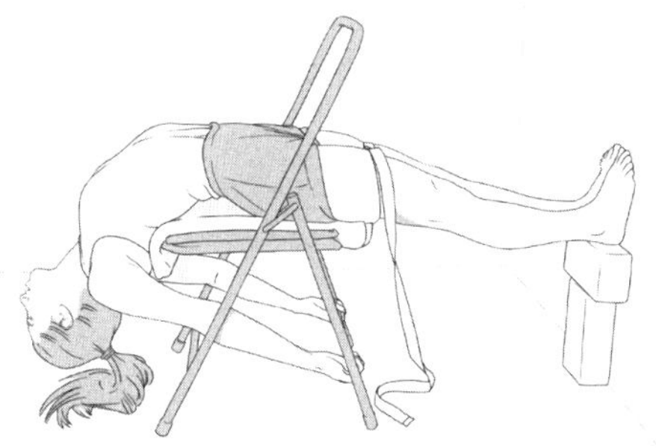

Elevating the feet to the level of the seat

Exploration B.28 cont.

Actions:

- Extend the back of your legs to the wall and move your front thighs down (toward the floor).
- Activate your arms and pull the chair to roll your shoulders back and further arch your upper back.

After staying in the pose for 4-7 minutes, continue to *Setu Bandha Sarvangasana*:

› Lift your head, take the extra bolster you prepared next to you, and place it on top of the first bolster.

› Slide more to your head side and rest the tops of your shoulders and the back of your head on the bolsters.

Note: If the support is not high enough for your shoulders to rest on it, add a blanket or two.

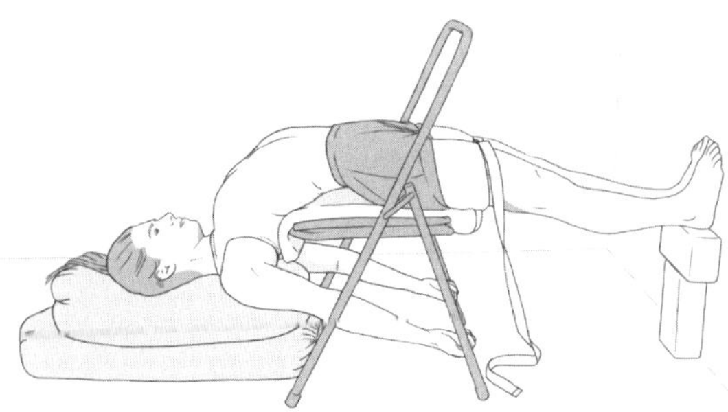

Elevating the feet to the level of the seat

› Stay in the pose for 4-7 minutes breathing slowly and smoothly, and observe how you feel. Compare what you had felt when staying in the above two poses. ∫

Which pose was more invigorating? Which more relaxing? How did your breathing react?

~ *Viparita Dandasana* resembles *Shirsasana*, since in both of them the head is vertical, and the top of the head is on the floor. *Setu Bandha Sarvangasana* resembles *Sarvangasana*, since in the two poses the head is horizontal and the top of the shoulders and the back of the neck and head are on the floor.

Shirsasana is a 'sun' posture; it warms the body and stimulates the organic body and the mind. *Sarvangasana* on the other hand is a 'moon' posture; it pacifies and cools the body and the mind. These differences can also be experienced in comparing *Viparita Dandasana* with *Setu Bandha Sarvangasana*. I feel that *Setu Bandha Sarvangasana* induces quietness and introversion, and prepares me well for *Shavasana*, while *Viparita Dandasana* stimulates the nervous system and prepares me for action. In *Setu Bandha Sarvangasana*, my gaze is directed inside, toward my chest, and my eyes tend to close, while in *Viparita Dandasana* the eyes are stimulated, and the vision becomes sharp. ~

Twisting *Asanas*

Prashant Iyengar said that the twisting *asanas* "twist the body and untwist the mind." This is a very vivid experience for anyone who practices twisting. Physically, the challenge is not big; twists don't require the same level of strength and flexibility as required, for example, by backbends, or arm balancing. But twists create a balanced ambience of quietude and serenity. They require more releasing and letting go than direct muscle activation.

Twists stimulate the digestive fire and cleanse the digestive tract, thus ensuring the proper working of the essential functions of digestion and assimilation. They aid detoxification by squeezing and twisting the abdominal area, much like wringing out a wet towel. Twisting the spine also twists the spinal cord (the tube of nervous tissue running inside the spine), thus vitalizing and energizing the entire nervous system.

In the Explorations below, we experience the special characters of the twisting *asanas*.

Exploration B.29

Bhardvajasana I (Simple Seated Twist Pose) on Chair With and Without Anchoring the Pelvis

When twisting the trunk, the pelvis should remain fixed and stable (otherwise, we just turn the whole body, rather than twisting the spine). In this Exploration, we perform two variations of a supported form of *Bhardvajasana*, done sitting on a chair. In the first variation, we use belts to anchor the pelvis to the chair to prevent its movement. Then we do the pose again without this anchoring.

› If necessary, adjust the height of the seat of the chair to match the height of your knees, such that when sitting, your thighs are parallel to the floor, and your shins vertical. Then sit on the chair facing the backrest with your legs under it.

› Place a block between your thighs and press on it (this helps to stabilize the pelvis region).

Note: If the seat is higher than your knees, put some support under your feet. If your knees are higher than the seat, then place one or two folded blankets on the seat.

› Tighten a belt around the seat of the chair and the tops of your thighs.

› Twist to your right. Stay for a minute or so, attempting to increase the twisting action with each inhalation.

› Then come back and twist to your left.

Actions (twisting to the right side):

- Roll your right shoulder back. Hold the seat behind you with your right hand and pull it as if you want to lift the seat. Use this to move your right shoulder blade in and to widen your right collar bone.
- Hold the backrest of the chair with your left hand, bend your left elbow, and roll your biceps out, to move your left shoulder blade in. Widen your left collar bone as well.
- Mentally observe your ribcage: the ribs tend to move laterally to the right – move the mid-ribs from right to left, and lift the left side of your trunk (up to the armpit, but without lifting your left shoulder).
- When inhaling, lift both sides of the chest evenly and extend your spine upward; when exhaling, twist further.

› After twisting twice to each side, release the belts and repeat the twist, this time without the belts. Compare the two. ʃ

In which attempt was the twist deeper? In which did you have more inner penetration? In which did you experience more stability and concentration?

PROPS

chair
belts
block

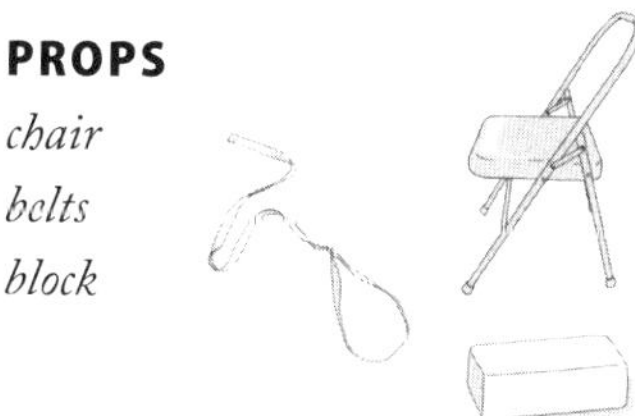

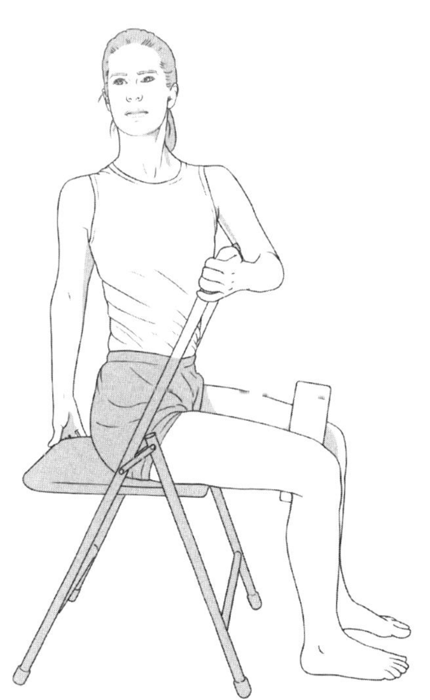

Sitting for *Bhardvajasana* on a chair

Tightening the belts to fix the pelvis in place

Exploration B.30

Fixing the Gaze in *Bhardvajasana* (Simple Seated Twist Pose)

PROPS *chair or blanket*

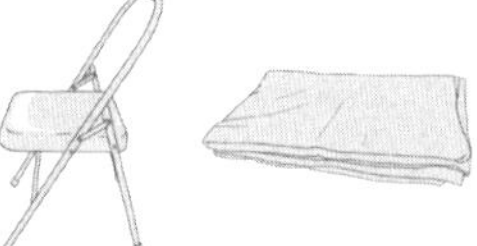

In this Exploration, we keep the direction of the head and eyes fixed, while twisting the trunk sideways. We observe the mental effects of separating the movement of the trunk from that of the head.

› Sit for *Bhardvajasana* on a chair, or on the floor. If you sit on the floor, start by folding your legs to the left side; support your right buttock with a folded blanket, to prevent your body from tilting to the right.

› Before you start twisting, look forward and observe a fixed point on the wall in front of you.

› Start turning your trunk to the right side, but keep your gaze fixed on the same point in front of you.

› To deepen the twist, inhale, lift the trunk and then exhale and use your arms to turn further. However, don't turn your head, but keep looking forward.

› Stay in this position for a minute or so, and then return to the center and repeat on the left side.

› Observe your mental state when deepening the twist. ʃ

Actions:

- When turning to the right, the left knee tends to move forward. If you sit on the chair, avoid this by resisting with the head of your left shin bone; when sitting on the floor, press down your left knee. Stabilize your pelvis, so it won't slide forward.

Can you describe the experience of twisting when gazing at the same fixed point? How smooth was your breathing?

~ I feel that keeping the gaze and the head fixed while twisting creates a very special effect. When twisting to the right, for example, the right side of the trunk is moving away from the right eye and from the right hemisphere of the brain. This is a very unusual experience, since we are accustomed to turn the body and the head together. Effectively, the neck is turned to the opposite side than the trunk. The head remains steady, which creates quietness and tranquility. ~

Sitting for *Bhardvajasana* on a floor

Pranayama

In *Yoga in Action – Intermediate Course I*, Geeta Iyengar writes,

"The respiratory system is the gateway in purifying the body, mind and intellect. It is the main tool in the practice of *Pranayama*. Through the practice of *Pranayama*, we learn to commune with our own breath, *prana* (vital energy), mind and self" (p. 100).

CAUTIONS

- *Pranayama* should be practiced only after getting a certain degree of control over the body by practicing *asanas*. Before attempting the Exploration in this section, read carefully *Light on Pranayama*; especially chapters 19, 22 and 26.
- *Pranayama* is very subtle but very effective. It affects deeply our respiratory and nervous systems as well as our mind. Be careful and patient in this practice. If you practice *pranayama* hastily or forcibly, you may harm yourself.

Exploration B.31

Comparing *Ujjai* Inhalation with *Pratiloma*

Note: For this Exploration, you should be well versed in *Pranayama* practice. If you don't know how to use the fingers for digital *Pranayama*, then skip this Exploration.

› Sit in any comfortable position with your back erect and your chest well lifted and open.

› Lower your head down to form *jalandhara bandha*.

› Exhale fully and then take a slow, soft and deep *Ujjai* inhalation.

› Now take a few normal breaths and observe your sensations.

› Exhale fully and then take a slow, soft, deep inhalation with your left nostril blocked. Block your right nostril partially and inhale through it.

› Again take a few normal breaths and observe your sensations.

› Exhale fully and then take a slow, soft, deep inhalation with your right nostril blocked. Block your left nostril partially and inhale through it.

› Take a few normal breaths and observe your sensations.

› Repeat the above cycle (*Ujjai* and *Pratiloma* inhalations through the right and left nostrils) 2-3 more times, and then raise your head.

What was your experience after inhaling through two open nostrils? How was it different from breathing through one partially block nostril?

Did you notice any changes between *Pratiloma* through your right nostril and *Pratiloma* through your left nostril?

Appendix 1: Further instructions for some poses

1.1 Placing the Body in *Shavasana* (Relaxation Pose)

› Place a folded blanket on one end of your mat to support your head.

Note: The height of the head support depends on the flexibility and shape of your shoulder region and upper back. The support should enable the back of your neck to extend and your head to be horizontal. If the back of your neck shortens and your head is tilted back (so that the chin is lifted), there will be tension in your throat and you'll find it difficult to direct your senses and your brain inward (into the body) and to relax.

› Sit in the center of the mat, lean back and support yourself on your elbows.

› Use your hands to extend your buttocks toward the legs, and to widen them away from the center.

› Then, while extending your spine to your head side, place it on the center of the mat.

› Widen and spread your back on the floor. Move your shoulders down, away from your neck.

› Roll your arms from inside out and your outer shoulders toward the floor.

Note: Correct placing of your shoulders is crucial since it keeps the chest open and allows for smooth breathing.

› Now catch the back of your head and move it away to extend your neck. Then arrange the head support such that it supports the back of your neck and head. The edge of the folded blanket should touch the top of your shoulders, but not be under them. This support allows the throat to relax, and it quiets the nervous system.

› Rest your arms symmetrically sideways at an angle of about 45° from your body.

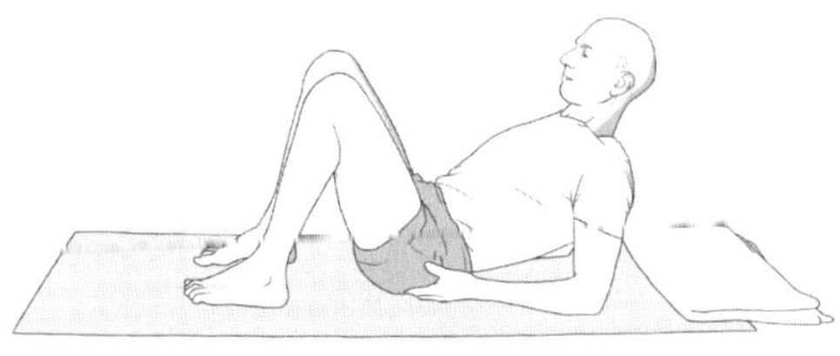

Entering *Shavasana* - spreading the buttocks

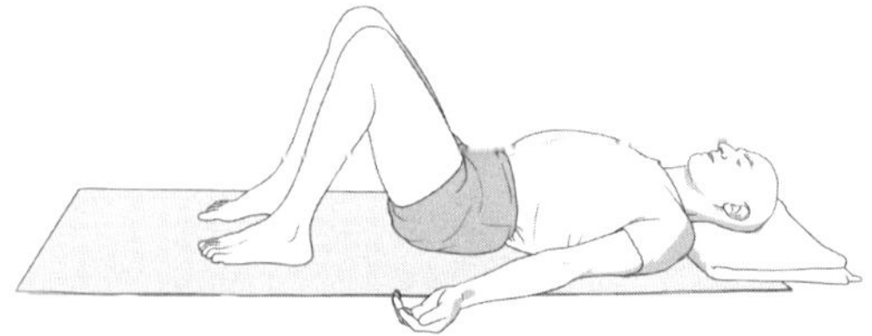

Entering *Shavasana* - placing the upper body

Note: If you have adjusted your shoulders properly, your palms should face upward, and your thumbs and little fingers should be at the same height.

› Now slide your heels away, extend the backs of your legs fully, and then release your legs, allowing them to roll freely sideways. Don't spread your legs too much; your feet should be about pelvis-width apart.

› Lift your head, observe your body and verify that your shoulders are at the same level, that your legs and arms are equidistant from the center line, and that your feet are rolling out evenly. Adjust your pose if necessary.

› Now rest your head by placing the center of the back of your head on the blanket. Close and relax your eyes and look inside.

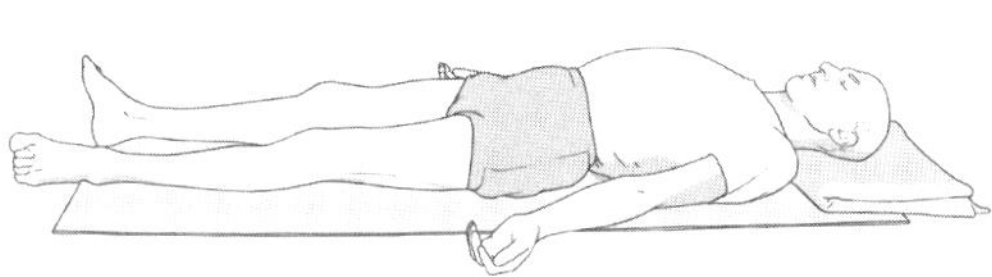

Entering *Shavasana* - placing the upper body

› Scan your body from feet to head, observing and relaxing each part. Use soft, smooth exhalations to aid in the relaxation process. ʃ

Note: For a complete description of *Shavasana*, please refer to B.K.S. Iyengar's book, *Light on Pranayama* Ch. 30.

1.2 Entering *Adho Mukha Shvanasana* (Downward-Facing Dog Pose)

› Stand on the front portion of your mat. Bend your knees and bend forward to place your hands on the mat.

› Place your hands such that your finger tips are aligned with the edge of the mat and the distance between the inner parts of your wrists matches the width of your outer upper arms (see figure on p. 86). To center yourself on the mat, observe that the distance between your hands and the edges of the mat is equal on both sides.

› Spread out your fingers and widen your palms. Place your hands such that your middle fingers are pointing forward.

› Step your feet back and spread them to the width of your pelvis. Observe that the distance of your feet from the edges of the mat are even on both sides.

› Bend your knees, lift your heels and look forward. (1)

› Move forward until your arms are vertical. Turn your biceps outward (away from the midline of the body), and your triceps inward (toward the midline of the body).

› Keep looking forward, lift your deltoids to your shoulders, elongate your armpits, and move your shoulder blades in to curve in your thoracic spine as much as you can.

› Press your palms against the mat and stretch back. Without dropping your elbows, move your front thighs back to pull your trunk back and up.

› Straighten your legs and lift your buttocks as high as possible.

› Keep your shoulder blades in (toward the back ribs) as you extend your spine back and up (away from your hands).

› Open the backs of your knees and descend your calf muscles and heels down to the floor. (2)

› Release your head and let it hang freely. Relax your neck and face. Maintain the pose with smooth breathing. (3) ʃ

Note: These are just very basic instructions; there are many more actions one needs to do in entering and staying in the pose; these should be learned from a competent teacher.

(1) Extending back to *Adho Mukha Shvanasana*

(2) Making the back concave

(3) *Adho Mukha Shvanasana*

1.3 Using a Platform for *Sarvangasana*

We explain here how to make a *Sarvangasana* platform from blankets and how to align the body before going up to *Sarvangasana*.

Use a platform long and wide enough to support your shoulders and elbows: a platform of 50 × 50 cm (20 × 20 inches) is sufficient. The height should be about 5 cm (2 inches). In addition, we use a block and a bolster for checking alignment here. A belt is used for keeping the elbows at shoulder-width. Here is how to set a platform from 5-6 blankets:

- Spread a blanket on the mat. This blanket allows your head to slide so that your neck will not contract, as well as providing some padding for the back of your head.
- Create a platform by stacking 4-5 blankets on top of the spread blanket.
- Align the rounded edges of the blankets to form a unified, smooth edge, on which the base of the neck will be supported. This is the 'head-side' of the platform.
- Place a block in the center of your mat on the head-side of the platform, and a bolster lengthwise on the other side of the platform. Measure the distance of the block from the platform by sitting on the platform as shown in the figure.

measuring the distance between the block and the platform

- Adjust a belt to the width of your outer shoulders and place it near the platform.
- Lie with your upper back on the platform and pelvis on the bolster, spine in the center of the platform, such that the lower third of the neck is supported on the platform, and the back of the head is on the cushioned mat. Leave a gap about three fingers wide between the tops of your shoulders and the edge of the platform.
- Make sure that both shoulders are equidistant from the edge of the platform and that the center of your body is aligned with the center of the mat (hold the edges of the mat to verify this).
- Lift your legs and roll over your head to *Halasana*. Your toes should land on the block. If this is not the case, correct by moving your legs until you feel the toes resting on the center of the block.

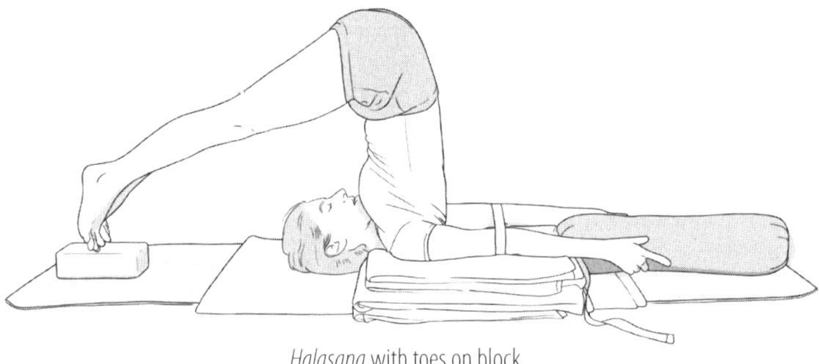

Halasana with toes on block

› Place the belt on your elbows.

› Interlock your fingers, move your shoulders back, one at a time, and roll the outer part of each shoulder down, until you rest on the tops of your shoulders. Make sure your neck is relaxed and can stretch freely away from the platform. If needed, adjust the distance of your shoulders from the platform edge.

Note: This step is critical – do not go up to *Sarvangasana* until you have adjusted yourself on the top of your shoulders.

› Stretch your arms back along the sides of the bolster. Check that both arms are positioned evenly in relation to the bolster.

Now your arms and legs should be aligned symmetrically, in line with the centerline of the platform and the mat.

Actions:

- Look up to verify that your two legs meet above the centerline of your face.
- Move your shoulders inward, i.e. toward each other, to support yourself on your outer shoulders.
- Move your upper back forward until the top of your chest touches your chin.

› Now fold your forearms to support your back with your palms. Turn your hands such that the fingers face your spine and your thumbs support the sides. Press your upper arms down and use your hands to lift your back ribs and open your chest.

Palms position for *Sarvangasana*

› Lift your legs up, tighten your mid buttocks and move your thighs back until your body is straight. ʃ

Note: See further instructions in *Props for Yoga, Inverted Asanas*, Vol. III.

Actions:

- Join the tips of your middle or little fingers to verify that both hands are placed symmetrically around your spine and that they support your back at the same height.

CHAPTER TWO

Developing Mental and Physical Capacities Through Yoga Practice

"Where does the body end and the mind begin? ...
They cannot be divided as they are inter-related ..."

B.K.S. Iyengar (in *Light on Yoga*)

Introduction

It is often said that *asana* practice is transformative. While this sounds good, it is rarely specified what this transformation consists in. And it is even rarer to find an account of how such a transformation can come about as a result of *asana* practice. In this chapter, we address this important issue. In sections 2.1- 2.15, we focus on several ways in which yoga practice can contribute to the cultivation and enhancement of positive qualities such as stability, endurance, pain tolerance, confidence, and equanimity, and can help us to deal with issues such as mild depression, fear, and anxiety. In sections 2.16-2.19, we expose tendencies such as competitiveness and laziness that often come up in the context of yoga practice, and discuss whether the practice can help us transform such tendencies.

In line with the main theme of this book, we pay particular attention to the relation between the physical (bodily) aspect of capacities such as stability and flexibility, and their mental corollaries, exploring the mutual relations of physical and mental advancements. For example, we seek to address questions such as how the physical stability that we gain on our yoga mat might affect our mental stability and how it might further affect our conduct in daily life. More generally, we try to explore how the practice and advancement of certain qualities on the mat can be extended and carried over into daily life. These observations and reflections draw on our own personal experiences, as well as on those of other practitioners and students. If successful, they might go some way toward substantiating the idea of yoga practice as transformative (an idea that otherwise risks seeming empty).

We should clarify from the outset that the capacities and features we focus on here are examples and case studies. We are certainly not trying to be comprehensive.

There is also some overlap between the features that we are discussing. Indeed, sorting and classifying them is not easy. We have tried to order the discussion in the way that makes the most sense, but we still feel that the order, as well as our choice of features, remains somewhat arbitrary. Of course, readers might well have more interest in some features rather than others, and so one should feel free to read according to one's own interests.

* * *

In his Foreword to B.K. S. Iyengar's fundamental book, *Light on Yoga*, Yehudi Menuhin, the renowned violinist and one of Iyengar's first western students, writes,

> "The practice of Yoga over the past fifteen years has convinced me that most of our fundamental attitudes to life have their physical counterparts in the body. Thus comparison and criticism must begin with the alignment of our own left and right sides to a degree at which even finer adjustments are feasible: or strength of will will cause us to start by stretching the body from the toes to the top of the head in defiance of gravity. Impetus and ambition might begin with the sense of weight and speed that comes with free-swinging limbs, instead of the control of prolonged balance on foot or hands, which give poise. Tenacity is gained by stretching in various Yoga postures for minutes at a time, while calmness comes with quiet, consistent breathing and the expansion of the lungs. Continuity and a sense of the universal come with the knowledge of the inevitable alternation of tension and relaxation in eternal rhythms of which each inhalation and exhalation constitutes one cycle, wave or vibration among the countless myriads which are the universe...
>
> [Yoga] is a technique ideally suited to prevent physical and mental illness and to protect the body generally, developing an inevitable sense of self-reliance and assurance. By its very nature it is inextricably associated with the universal laws: for respect for life, truth, and patience are all indispensable factors in the drawing of a quiet breath, in calmness of mind and firmness of will."

Indeed, every seasoned yoga practitioner knows the exhilarating experience that comes with widening and opening the chest in backward bends; the quiet contentment that flourishes from prolonged and gentle stretch of the muscles in forward bends; the mental balance and concentration that accompanies the attempt to balance the body on one foot or on two hands; the sense of stability and confidence that results from standing on strong and well-toned legs; the freshness and lightness that settles from free moving joints; the poise that grows from listening to the internal sound of the breath; the tranquility and stillness that spreads from staying quietly in an inverted pose like *Shirsasana* (headstand); the willpower and mental discipline that builds up from adhering to a daily practice in spite of all the surrounding 'noise' that distracts us.

In what follows, we discuss some examples that, in our view, demonstrate how the practice of yoga fosters both mental and physical capabilities. If, as we believe[1], mental and physical capabilities are intertwined, and are developed and enhanced simultaneously, there is no wonder that *asana* practice can affect our entire personality.

2.1 Dealing with Negative Moods, Fatigue, and Feeling Down

(Written by Ohad)

A central theme of this book is that our feelings and emotional states are strongly related to our bodily states and behavior. If this is indeed so, then working with our body will affect our mental and emotional state. This connection is very evident when we feel down or even slightly depressed. Usually, such a state has clear physical (bodily) and behavioral manifestations: the shoulders drop and tend forwards, the chest closes and constrains the breath, the back curves, and the gaze tends downwards. The tendency to curve our spine and drop our shoulders is most evident in the long hours we spend sitting (for many of us, working in front of our computers).

In practicing yoga, one constantly works against such tendencies. We seek to straighten and elongate the spine; and to create space in the chest by rolling the shoulders back and down, and moving the shoulder blades forward (toward

1 Our argument for this is given in chapter 3.

the back ribs). As anyone who practiced yoga knows, this can have a sharp and immediate effect on mood (see in particular Explorations A.1, A.5 and A.11 and also Practice Sequence 3). The immediate effect is clearly felt.

But there are also more subtle long-term effects that are perhaps less noticeable. Given this immediate connection between our posture and emotional state, it is probably no exaggeration to say that one can help to combat a tendency for slight depression by seeking to open the chest and roll the shoulders back. But, is it really this simple? To a degree, yes. And this can come as a revelation, since many of us suffer such moods. Of course, this applies mainly to lighter forms of down feeling, and we certainly do not want to suggest that this method should be taken as an easy remedy for depression in general. At the very least, if one suffers from more severe depression, one is unlikely to have the energy and desire to work consistently on posture. Indeed, we are not thinking of severe or clinical depression here, but of the more transient negative moods that affect most of us from time to time.

Accordingly, what we want to suggest is that persistent yoga practice can be very effective in dealing with non-clinical mood issues of this kind, such as feeling down or loss of energy. For example, I often get up in the morning with a sense of disorientation, feeling down, and a lack of purpose. But when I manage to sit down, straighten my back, and open my chest, an immediate change begins to take place. The rest almost happens by itself. A sense of orientation and optimism slowly reigns over fatigue and disorientation. At this point, a desire to practice usually kicks in, and this fills me with energy that helps me start the day in a much better mood.

Viparita Karani

Over the years, I've learned that starting each morning by practicing yoga not only has a positive effect on that particular day, but also has a long-term effect. It has also taught me a skill that allows me to deal better with episodes of something like slight depression or negative mood that come up from time to time. Thus, when I'm feeling tired and crushed, I do a few poses (I usually do a headstand followed by *Viparita Karani*) and, most of the time, this suffices to recover my energy and regain a positive attitude.

Since the psychophysical connection in this case seems fairly clear, explaining the long-term effects is also straightforward. If we can improve our regular posture, so that the spine is kept straight, the shoulders rolled back, and the chest open, we breathe with more ease and tend to feel better. Inducing such a change in our habits of posture, however, is far from being easy and far from quick to happen; rather, it is more likely to take years of practice to change deeply ingrained habits. But one can certainly experience gradual change. A practice along the lines described above gives us a skill to help deal with such recurrent moods of fatigue and feeling down.[2]

2.2 Flexibility and Agility

The practice of yoga definitely improves the body's flexibility and elasticity, but does it improve mental flexibility? This is an interesting question, which is difficult to answer objectively. It is quite clear that not everyone with a flexible body has a flexible mind. There is surely no simple correlation here. Some are naturally flexible and some are not. Some are flexible in their shoulders and some in their pelvis. And then there is the difference between natural flexibility and working to improve flexibility. It may be that working on the flexibility of our body enhances our mental flexibility, such that we are more willing to accept change, quicker to accommodate to changing circumstances, more open to new ideas, and more able to see things from different perspectives.

My subjective answer to this question is yes. I feel that the practice of yoga definitely contributes to my mental flexibility, agility, and lightheartedness. How can this feeling be explained?

2 There is some scientific evidence that yoga practice helps dealing with depression of this kind. See for examples the References we listed at the end of the book.

Well, there are a few factors in the practice of yoga that can improve the mind's flexibility. First, yoga leads to more freedom of movement, and when your body moves more easily and with greater comfort and lightness, it might be that your approach becomes lighter and your interactions become less rigid. Second, yoga offers a wide variety of movements, far beyond our habitual 'normal' movements of walking, standing, sitting and lying (and, for some, running). We find ourselves in unfamiliar positions, and we see ourselves and the environment from different angles and points of view, while our body assumes many forms - forms that human bodies don't usually take, forms that resemble a variety of creatures. We see the world for a little while like a frog, and then like a snake, and then like a dog, and so on. We habituate ourselves to changing views and perspective. This may contribute to opening our minds and being able to see other people's points of view and perspectives.

Inversions, like headstand and shoulder-stand, stand out in this respect, since they give us the possibility of seeing the world from a totally different - literally inverted - angle and height. Being upside-down, we see things differently. Often, when I practice on the beach, I see the waves and people passing by, from zero height and upside-down; this is a unique experience.

But inversions are not the only example. Most adults never bend backwards, so this body position is totally unfamiliar to them. Backbends change the way we perceive our environment. For example, in *Ushtrasana* (Camel Pose), our gaze is opposite to the direction of the front of our body, and again we see the world upside-down.

Ushtrasana

In forward bends, we see our own body from a different proximity and angle. When bending forward, we come close to our legs and can see them very intimately. Advanced forward bends like the Turtle Pose (*Kurmasana*) or placing one leg behind the head (*Eka Pada Shirsasana*), put us in a position in which our limbs are situated in a highly unusual way. This again changes our perception.

Supta Kurmasana *Chakorasana*

Lateral twists (like *Marichyasana III*) also place us in an unfamiliar position, especially if we twist the trunk and the head in opposite directions.

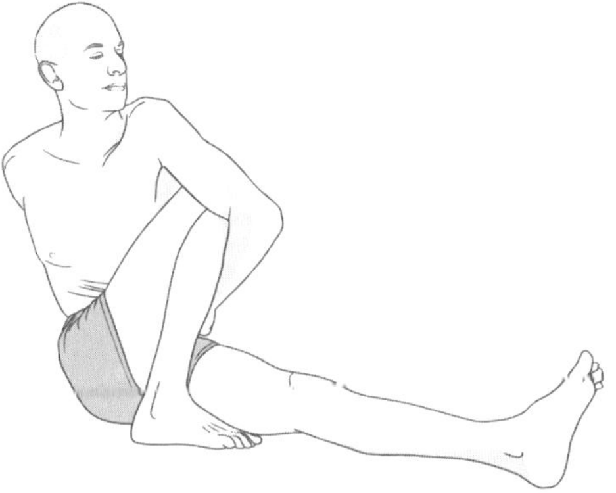

Marichyasana III twisting the head opposite from trunk

When we position our body in all these unusual forms, we are also likely to flex our mind, since our body position generates a particular state of mind. When we have a wider variety of bodily postures, we become accustomed to experiencing a wider variety of mental states, and to shift more easily from one state to another.

A mindful practice also allows us to expose some unconscious behavioral patterns and habits. These habits make our behavior an automatic response. But such behavior is often not the most efficient or healthy, and hence may cause a lot of suffering. Once these constricting and unhealthy patterns and habits are seen, one can learn to let go of them. Seeing where we are attached to constricting and limiting habits, views, and ideas, and unsound beliefs and interpretations, enables us to become freer. We thus learn to 'let go', both physically and mentally, and to develop a greater ability to choose our responses and to act in a more skillful manner.[3] Given all this, I am indeed convinced that the practice of yoga contributes to mental flexibility: working on the suppleness of the body contributes to making the mind less rigid. But, of course, this, like many other skills, requires a conscious choice by the practitioner to relate what is learned in practice to life beyond the practice.

2.3 Confidence and Courage

A practice of standing poses improves the sense of grounding. I can recall the feeling of standing and walking on strong legs which had struck me when (in 1982) I shifted from *Shivananda* style yoga to *Iyengar Yoga*, and started to work a lot on standing *asanas*. This practice with emphasis on strength and posture helped me to improve my confidence in interacting with other people and with the world in general. This improved grounding affected me physically as well as mentally. That a change in style of yoga practice should have such effects might sound surprising, but think of the way in which someone with strong, stable legs walks in contrast to someone whose legs are (for whatever reason) shaky. The confidence that comes from being able to rely on your legs to hold you, and on your agility in reacting to various things that come in your way is familiar to all of us.

3 Recent research shows that concentration and meditation improve the plasticity of the brain. So, even this aspect of the practice can potentially make our mind more flexible and adaptable.

Balancing poses make up another family of *asanas* that enhance courage and confidence. When we learn to balance on one leg in poses such as *Vrksasana* (Tree Pose), *Ardha Chandrasana* (Half Moon Pose), and *Utthita Hasta Padangushthasana* (Extended Hand-To-Big-Toe Pose), our stability and confidence increases. The Hero Poses (*Virabhadrasana I, II* & *III*) in particular strengthen the body, open the chest, and induce feelings of power and courage. It is said that *Shiva* - the Lord of yoga - gave us these poses in order to help us face fear.

It is normal to struggle with balancing at first, but as one gains more control, one experiences how what at first had seemed so difficult, even impossible, becomes possible. And then it starts to become natural, something that comes with very little effort. This lesson may well extend to other tasks we face in our daily lives.

Inverted poses and backbends are often more challenging psychologically than physically. Some students who can easily support themselves on their arms are still afraid to jump up to *Adho Mukha Vrksasana* (Full Arm Balance) by a wall. *Shirsasana* (Headstand) also causes concern and anxiety - some students feel very uneasy about going upside-down. It seems that the unfamiliar orientation of the body creates a mental obstacle. Some students have been practicing *Shirsasana* for years, but only with their back against a wall. What is behind us seems unknown; we do not see what is there, and the fear of falling backward might arise (this becomes evident when standing facing a wall - see Exploration B.16).

This is also the case for some backbends that we never ordinarily perform in daily life. We often bend forward, and we sometimes twist, but we are not accustomed to bending backward. This might be one reason why backbends tend to raise anxiety and fear. Often students are reluctant to attempt even simple backbends because they are afraid of hurting their backs.[4] Dropping from *Shirsasana* to *Viparita Dandasana* (Upward Facing Staff Pose), or arching back from *Tadasana* (Mountain Pose) to *Urdhva Dhanurasana* (Upward Bow Pose) is also mentally challenging. Even advanced students who practice these poses regularly (from the floor), are afraid to drop back, into the unknown territory behind them.

4 While in fact, a forward bend may be more problematic for the lower back.

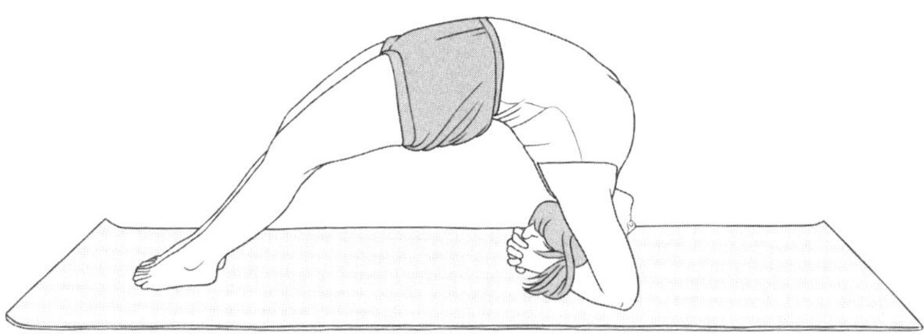

Viparita Dandasana (Upward Facing Staff Pose)

Urdhva Dhanurasana (Upward Bow Pose)

By working on these poses steadily one can slowly overcome the mental barrier and learn to extend one's limits; practice turns these frightening movements into a territory of well controlled actions. It seems reasonable to assume that this increased confidence propagates into our life beyond our yoga practice in various ways. The lesson of making what seems impossible possible, strengthens personality and builds confidence: we develop the ability to accomplish tasks that previously seemed impossible. It also teaches us that such achievements do not come straight away; rather, they require patience and persistent practice, in which progress comes incrementally, in very small steps, sometimes too small to even notice. But then all of a sudden one can balance in *Shirsasana* away from the wall, or perform backbends without fear. As we know from other fields of learning, sometimes slow and patient study pays off at once when various things connect together and click. This brings joy and satisfaction that derives from an inquisitive and patient attitude to life.

2.4 Joy

Asana practice can show us that there is joy to be found in attending to simple activities, without needing to rely on extravagance or expense, and without depending on extreme stimuli or adventure. Releasing tension from the body and quieting the mind gives rise to spontaneous joy. We can draw much joy simply from a feeling of sound health and calmness. Our worries and problems seem less salient, and we can appreciate the health and happiness that we do have.

We learn to appreciate the subtle and refined joy of staying calmly and passively in a pose while observing the gentle touch of the breath in the membranes of our nostrils. We don't need to jump from cliffs or to dive deep into the ocean in order to be happy. While the latter are by no means bad in their own right, being dependent on such things would disturb our happiness. When we are quieter and more focused, we can also enjoy the wonders of nature and the beauty of art. These are simple joys that do not require expensive and sophisticated means and do not, on the whole, generate more cravings.

This is the practice of *santosha* (contentment), the second *niyama* in *Patanjali*'s *yoga sutras*[5]. Craving for indulgence and depending upon external, elaborate enjoyments create uneasiness in the mind. When we achieve the object of our desire, or the experience we crave, there is a temporary relief and we experience joy. But this joy is short-lived, since our mind will soon start to crave something else. The relaxation we experience by attaining the object we desire is only temporary. Patanjali includes in the *yamas* the practice of *aparigraha* or non-craving, non-possessiveness, and non-hoarding. *Aparigraha* means living a simple life without unnecessary possessions and consumption. This is opposed to being consumed by the pursuit of success, fame, fortune, etc. *Aparigraha* and *santosha* are two sides of the same coin; *aparigraha* is a restraint; and *santosha* is the positive practice of fostering contentment. It is a practice of gratitude for what we have, which helps us not to be over agitated by inevitable losses, pain, failures, etc.

5 Patanjali is a legendary figure, considered as the author of three classic treatises, among them the *Yoga Sutras*, which are the foundations of the classical yoga philosophy.
We use the abbreviation YS for the *Yoga Sutras*.

Both *santosha* and *aparigraha* are important components of *asana* practice. A mindful practice teaches us not to crave 'success' or be devastated by 'failure' in a given pose. Cultivating contentment with where we are in a given pose also involves not being rocked by the fact that we are in a different place every day with our practice (some days we can nail the arm balance, some days not; some days our balance feels perfectly poised, other days we're just off). When we relinquish (or lessen the strength of) the attitudes of attachment and aversion, a sense of equanimity naturally arises.

Yoga can connect us to ourselves and quiet the endless scampering of our mind. From this quietness, we can derive great joy. Not the pleasure of obtaining something or achieving some goal, but the simple joy of being alive, the basic appreciation of each new breath. A feeling of health, energy, delight and tranquility is all that is needed to transform a moody mind into a joyful one.

2.5 Effort Management

Our next example of a quality that can be developed by attentive and mindful yoga practice is the ability to manage the effort we invest in attempting to accomplish a task, first in the context of yoga practice and then in life beyond the practice. When Patanjali talks about *asana*, he says that,

> Perfection in *asana* is achieved **when the effort to perform it becomes effortless** (YS, II.47).

The notion of effortless effort is central in *asana* practice, but it may sound like a contradiction. Let us then try to explain it. There is certainly an effort in the performance of *asanas*, but as one becomes more mature in one's practice, one finds (as expressed in the above *sutra*) that one can perform the same *asanas* with less and less effort. As much as it is important to invest effort, it is also important to learn how to release effort, without compromising the quality of the *asana*. Making an effort in performing a task is very intuitive for us; making less effort is less so. Too much effort, however, may undermine progress, since it hinders the ability to stay quietly in the *asana* in an absorbed and reflective mood.

In *The Tree of Yoga*, B.K.S. Iyengar asks, "When you are practicing a pose in yoga, can you find the delicate balance between taking the pose to its maximum extent, and taking it beyond that point, so that there is too much effort creating wrong tension in the body?" (p. 39).

It is quite surprising that, often, one can make more progress in an *asana* not by working harder but by releasing unnecessary tension, softening and letting go of unneeded actions, and decreasing the level of effort. This also enables one to stay in the *asana* for a longer time and with less fatigue. When we maintain an *asana* for an extended period of time, say doing *Shirsasana* (Headstand) for more than five minutes, we need to balance our efforts, so that we won't get too tired too soon. In any task, we need to balance between using too much force (over-doing), and using too little force (under-doing). We should try to pace ourselves and to invest the minimal amount of energy required to perform the pose well.[6]

When attempting new or challenging *asana*, undue tension and effort are produced. In order to stay calmly in the *asana*, one must create space for breath and relaxation. Only then does the attitude of penetration and observation desired in yoga become possible. One should observe and identify rigidity, contractions, hardness and resistances. Once these are identified, we should seek to release them without compromising the quality of the *asana*.

The breath is an important tool for achieving this. When one is able to turn rough breath into smooth and soft breath, then one can decrease muscular effort and can stay in the *asana* with more ease and become more absorbed in it. This absorption brings about a state of joy and sometimes even bliss, so that instead of thinking when to come out, one just wants to stay in the *asana*. When this happens, there is no need to exercise willpower and no psychological effort is required. As B.K.S. Iyengar puts it, "When a wise action comes, you no longer feel the effort as effort - you feel the effort as joy."[7]

6 Observe here how different this attitude is from the common attitude in working out and seeking to burn as many calories as possible. Here, the whole objective of the practice is very different.

7 In the chapter "Effort, awareness and joy", *The Tree of Yoga*.

But in fact, this is not unique to yoga. We all know that studying new skills requires a huge investment of time and energy. But once we are more skilled, things flow with much less effort. Managing effort is a highly desirable quality in life. We are accustomed to achieving goals through action and effort. However, tensions, undue stress, and extra effort do not contribute to achieving our goals; on the contrary, they waste our energy and diminish our health. Think, for example, of facial tension that often comes up. Yoga practice teaches us how to let go of extra effort, strain, or unnecessary actions. When we learn to invest the minimal amount of effort in our practice, we may also be able to manage our efforts in other tasks better. This will make our actions more effective and our work more productive.

Yoga practice also teaches the importance of rest and how to pace ourselves in accordance with the external environment, and also with respect to the different periods of our life. We seek to gauge our energy level and to use it in a skillful way.

2.6 Handling Stress, Pain, and Similar Issues

The ability to release physical tensions is intimately connected with our ability to face various kinds of difficulties, even situations of crisis, with a more balanced and calm attitude. In the practice of *asanas*, one is confronted with many limitations, difficulties, frustrations, fears, and challenges, which can produce rather stressful situations. Such situations affect us both physically and mentally: we tend to hold our breath, stiffen certain muscles, or distort our face with grimaces of pain or unease. We often experience excessive muscular stretch, and various aches and discomforts. Undue effort or tension may also over-load and irritate our heart. Learning to deal with these in our practice can help us to handle stress and difficulties in life. But how, in the practice, should we deal with pain and stress?

B.K.S. Iyengar has two sayings that summarize very concisely the attitude of yoga to pain.[8] The first is: "The philosophy of pain is to conquer it". This suggests that we shouldn't be afraid of pain. Pain is an unavoidable part of life, and we better learn to be with pain without being overwhelmed by it. This is the *tapas* part.

8 Quoted in the booklet *Guruji Uwach* by Nivedita Joshi.

The second is *svadhyaya* (self-study): "Pain comes to guide you; pain is your Guru". This means that we have to listen to pain and learn from it - to let the pain guide us as a Guru. Indeed, pain may tell us that something went wrong; it forces us to examine and analyze the reasons for it, and to learn how to avoid it. In some cases, pain should cause us to come out of the *asana*, since, if we don't, we might injure ourselves. But we need to be observant here, since, often, we don't come out of an *asana* because of harmful pain, but because of some disturbance or restlessness the pain causes. For example, a mild stretch in the hamstrings is a common experience in *Supta Padangushthasana* (Reclining Hand-to-Big-Toe Pose). If we don't overstretch, there will be no injury. Naturally, our attention is drawn fully to the stretched muscle. However, we can learn to distribute our attention to the entire body and become absorbed in the *asana*. This will allow us to stay and bear the pain. The pain may still be there, but it will not be at the forefront of our attention, and it will not disturb us as much. In fact, after a while, we may not even notice it.

Consider another example. We may decide to stay five minutes in *Adho Mukha Shvanasana* (Downward Facing Dog); this is challenging, and muscular force alone is not enough to sustain the *asana* for the full time. But, we can learn to use our breath to help us overcome discomforts and tensions that may build up during this time. We attend to the fatigued regions of our body and use inhalations to overcome the fatigue. Or we use exhalations to release tension. We can learn to stretch our limbs with less muscular force by allowing our awareness to extend and spread into the entire body.

Gradually we also learn to recognize and mitigate our automatic response to pain and stress, and, with time, are able to keep our face and throat relaxed, our flow of breath smooth and our heart rate normal. We learn to be with unpleasantness without resistance and aversion. It's ok to feel unpleasantness: it comes and goes, and we can be with it without immediately reacting. This takes patience and attention - but it is an essential part of our practice.

This attitude and awareness may gradually become available to us in our daily life as well. We identify such tensions more quickly, even in the midst of our daily interactions, and learn to use our breath and connect with our body in order to release these tensions and reduce their impact. We learn to accept life's inevitable sorrows and difficulties, which may at times overwhelm us, or even break our spirit if we encounter them unprepared. This training can change our attitude, and allow us to respond in a more skillful manner, to remain calmer, and to handle life's contingencies more effectively and with less stress.

2.7 Stability and Balance

Patanjali defines *asana* with the terms *sthira* - which means stability, steadiness, firmness, and *sukha* - which means happiness, pleasure, ease, or bliss (YS II.46). These terms have both physical and mental senses. Are these senses related? Often, in the practice of *asanas*, one loses one's stability when one's mind starts to wander (think, for example, of a standing pose like *Parsvottanasana* - Intense Side Stretch Pose). Achieving a stable pose certainly requires concentration and attention. But does achieving stable balance in a pose help to develop **mental** stability and balance?

Balance and stability are intimately connected. If someone somehow manages to stay in *Vrksasana* (Tree Pose) while constantly shifting and wobbling, we wouldn't say that he or she is well balanced. Balance in a pose implies staying in a pose quietly and stably.

In Exploration A.3 we compared standing in *Tadasana* with joined vs. spread legs. You probably have found that spreading the legs increases your stability, but this kind of stability can be heavy and dull, and doesn't require concentration and alertness. Joining the legs in *Tadasana* makes the pose less stable, but brings more sharpness and lightness; keeping the body still is much more challenging, but this is precisely what helps us to develop our attention and concentration. Many *asanas* create such challenges and invite us to achieve stability in it.

Balance in an *asana* is often achieved by constantly adjusting the body to the underlying shifts that are taking place. This is a very organic, adaptive process. Even in a seemingly stable and anchored sitting pose, the spine needs to be held stable, without collapsing, on the one hand, and without rigidity and tension, on the other. This requires one to continuously adjust and balance, since the organic nature of the body is subject to constant changes, and if we lose attention, we tend either to drop or to hold the spine with too much force and tension.

Yoga offers a variety of balancing poses: on one foot (e.g., *Vrksasana* - Tree Pose); on one foot and one hand (e.g., *Ardha Chandrasana* - Half-Moon Pose); on two hands (e.g., *Adho Mukha Vrksasana* - Full Arm Balance); on the head and forearms (e.g., *Shirsasana* - Headstand); on two forearms (e.g. *Pincha Mayurasana* - Feathered Peacock Pose), and so on. All these *asanas* teach us to balance in positions we do not normally encounter in daily life.

Balancing on narrow base is a bit like walking on a tightrope. For example, in *Adho Mukha Vrksasana*, (Full Arm Balance; literally means downward-facing tree) - especially when done without leaning on a wall - there are always some minor shifts and movements. These occur because of the organic nature of our muscles, the ongoing movement of the breath, and the constant fluctuations (*vrittis*) of our mind. To maintain balance, one must therefore constantly adjust by manipulating many large and small muscles, starting from the hands and up to the feet, and one must also still the mind.

If, in a balancing pose, you think 'I will never be able to make it', or even 'oh, I balance so well!', then your balance will tend to weaken. Focusing only on the balancing task, without such self-conscious thoughts, opens the door to achieving better balance.

The more advanced *asanas* present a greater challenge, and require a more refined attention. For example, in *Parsva Hasta Padangushthasana* (Side Hand-To-Big-Toe Pose), the lifted leg is stretched away from our center of gravity, and hence balancing is more challenging than in *Vrksasana* (Tree Pose).

The advanced *asanas* are mentally challenging because they require more effort and put us in more stressful positions. Keeping our mental composure and focus in these *asanas* therefore requires more maturity and practice. The maturity required here is a maturity of both mental and physical capacities.

Other Types of Balance

Parsva Hasta Padangushthasana

There are many more types of balance that one learns while practicing *asanas*; there is a necessary balance between movement and stability, compactness and expansion, hardness and softness, and flexibility and strength. We need to stretch our muscles, but at the same time to strengthen them. We need to maintain a delicate balance between over-doing and under-doing, between over-exertion and laxity.

Another type of balance is counterbalance, a balance that is achieved by pulls in opposite directions, by simultaneously performing an action and a counter-action. For example, in *Tadasana*, the action of moving the front thighs back and that of moving the tailbone forward, form such a pair of actions. The front to back alignment and balance in the pose is maintained by balancing these two actions.

Alignment and Balance

Another important facet of balance in *asana* is aligning the left and right sides of the body. Our body is anatomically symmetrical around its median line.[9] In Exploration A.3, we explored finding balance in *Tadasana* by balancing the body's weight evenly on two feet. In symmetrical poses like *Tadasana* or *Paschimottanasana* (Seated Forward Bend), we learn to extend both sides of the body evenly. Other poses take us out of symmetry, and present a challenge in

9 B.K.S. Iyengar called this median plane 'the divine plane', since by extending evenly both sides of the trunk, we sharpen the central line, which is the spine, and find harmony and poise in the *asana*. He further emphasized correct alignment, by saying that 'alignment leads to enlightenment'. Indeed, with proper alignment, the mind becomes balanced and neutral - it doesn't take sides; it isn't biased and it displays no favoritism, but accepts and allows for everything with evenness.

maintaining the left-to-right symmetry. For example, in *Utthita Trikonasana*, when bending to the right side, one often tends to shorten the right side of the trunk. The challenge is to bend from the pelvis (rolling the pelvis over the femur heads), and to extend both sides of the trunk evenly. This enables us to better stretch the spine and to create more space in the trunk. The same challenge is posed by many asymmetrical poses. In *Janu Shirsasana* (Head-to-Knee Forward Bend), the bent leg pulls one side of the trunk away from the symmetrical shape of *Paschimottanasana*. Still, we need to strive to adjust the body in order to move both sides of the trunk evenly forward.

It often happens in daily life that we find ourselves off balance. Such situations challenge us in ways that are similar to these asymmetrical *asanas*. When one succeeds in balancing the left and right, some new quality emerges. This quality can be likened to the quality that emerges from balancing the field of vision of the two eyes when looking at a 'Magic Eye' picture. Initially one sees only two-dimensional figureless shapes. But, when finding the correct balance, the figures magically 'pop up' out of the flat surface and appear to be three-dimensional.

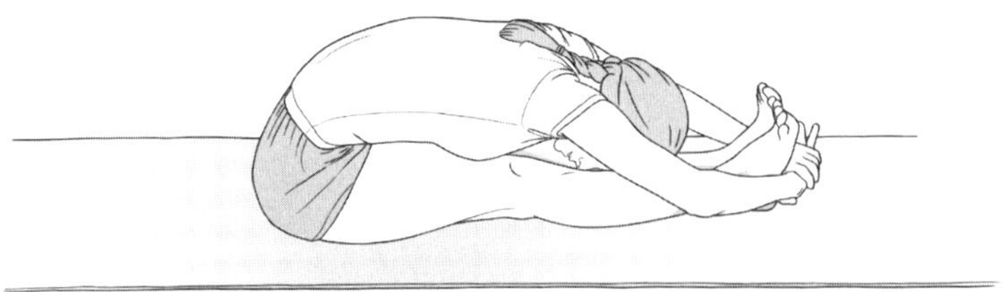

Paschimottanasana

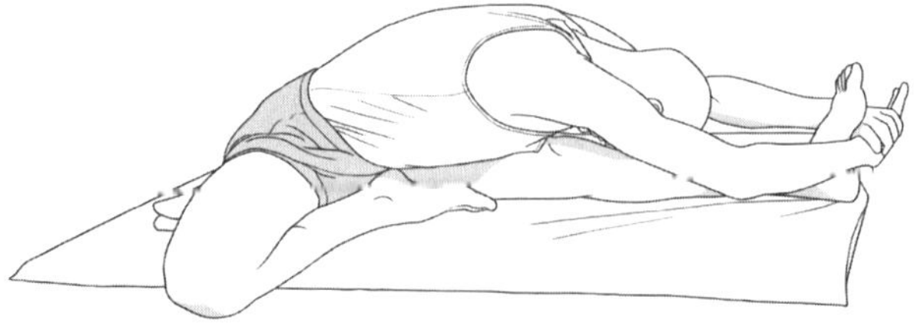

Janu Shirsasana

Balance Between Over- and Under-Doing

As discussed above, *asana* is a balance between stability (*sthira*) and comfort or ease (*sukha*). Similarly, we need to balance effort (*prayatna*) and letting go of effort (*shaithilya*) (YS II.47). We seek a 'middle-way' (via media) between these seemingly opposite attitudes. This requires tremendous attention and concentration, since our bodily reactions change as we stay in the pose. We have to learn to constantly monitor the level of effort and the amount of stretch in our body, and to fine-tune them, so that the *asana* will be effective without being harmful. We need to avoid overstretch on the one hand, and laxity on the other, to hold the *asana* without rigidity, but without collapsing.

The result of learning to balance effort and non-effort, says Patanjali, is acquiring immunity to dualities (YS II.48). It seems as though Patanjali is telling us here that when one learns to stay on the middle-way (which changes constantly) between these opposites, then one is less affected by dualities, such as success and failure, and is able to keep a balanced mind amidst difficult circumstances and eventualities. Or as Yehudi Menuhin says[10], "The practice of Yoga induces a primary sense of measure and proportion." This sense of measure and proportion helps us to develop intellectual and emotional balance as well. This is equanimity - a quality we discuss later in this chapter.

Long-Term Balance

Still another kind of balance is a long-term one. It is the skill of maintaining a balanced state of mind over time. In the practice, this may turn into finding a sequence of *asanas* that leaves us in a *sattvic* state of tranquility and quietness. We learn this as we mature in our practice and learn how our body and mind react to different sequences of *asanas*, and as we find sequences that are balanced in this way - neither too heating nor too cooling; not exhausting, but deep enough to create a mental and emotional transformation.

10 in the Foreword of *Light on Yoga*.

Learning to achieve balance in our practice may also help us to maintain a balanced state in other activities during our working day, a long hike that we take on our day off, or other events that occur throughout our lives. As B.K.S Iyengar writes in *Light on Life*: "Balance does not mean merely balancing the body. Balance in the body is the foundation for balance in life. In whatever position one is, or whatever condition in life one is placed, one must find balance."[11]

As we have seen, yoga practice offers ample opportunities to practice different types of balance. While it is not easy to explain how the extension beyond the mat works, in our experience, developing these sorts of balance in the practice can help us to achieve a more balanced mind in our daily life. But this is something each practitioner should explore and find out for him/herself. Achieving mental and emotional balance in all circumstances, is equanimity, a topic we discuss in the following section.

2.8 Tolerance and Equanimity

When Krishna teaches yoga to his disciple, the warrior and yogi, Arjuna, he tells him that "yoga is equanimity" ("*samatvam yoga ucyate*", BG, II.48).[12]

Equanimity, or evenness of mind, is the capacity to remain composed, even when facing difficulties, disappointments, sorrows, insults and failures. It is the ability to keep a stable and undisturbed mind when facing dualities (*dvandva*) such as success and failure, pleasure and pain, gain and loss, and fame and condemnation. We are all subject to experiencing such polarities in our daily life. We are strongly affected by our natural (e.g. weather changes[13]) and social environments, over which we have only limited control.

All these vicissitudes tend to shake our mental and emotional stability. Often emotions like anger, sadness, worry, and insult distract and upset us. Our natural

11 B.K.S. Iyengar in *Light on Life*, p. 43.

12 "Fixed in yoga, do thy work, O Winner of wealth (Arjuna), abandoning attachment, with an even mind in success and failure, for evenness of mind is called yoga" (From *The Bhagavad-Gita* by S. Radhakrishnan).

13 This is demonstrated, for example, by the issue of temperature control in yoga studios - often a controversial issue which raises a lot of frustration and dissatisfaction.

reaction to pain and discomfort is aversion and rejection (*dvesha*), and our natural reaction to pleasure and satisfaction is clinging and attachment (*raga*). But, since we sometimes have to face pains and failures, we better learn to face these vicissitudes more calmly.

It is obvious that no one can succeed in everything one does, avoid pain and loss, and always be praised. Most current theories, however, tell us that we ought to maximize success over failure - to be a 'winner' rather than a 'loser'; some utilitarian theories of morality tell us that the whole point in life is to seek pleasure and avoid pain; and a cardinal assumption in economics is that human beings lead their whole lives in order to maximize gain and minimize loss. While these theories tend to mix descriptive claims with normative ones, the yogi's attitude is rather different. Our wellbeing should not depend on the contingencies of the stock market or whether our article is accepted for publication, whether our book sells well, or whether our favorite soccer team wins or loses. We seek to ground our wellbeing in our own ability to withstand and accept contingencies and inevitable changes and events that come our way. It is not that we don't care about such things. Of course we do. Equanimity is not apathy, dullness, or indifference. We do want to feel the joys and sorrows of life; we care, but we try not to let successes or failures undermine our stability and confidence. In this sense, keeping the mind stable through the changing circumstances and vicissitudes of life is a key feature for maintaining wellbeing.

But how can the practice of *asanas* support achieving equanimity?

In the previous section, we discussed some of the capabilities that are relevant here: Handling Stress Pain and Other Difficulties and Stability and Balance. Here, we discuss another quality that is relevant to fostering equanimity, and that can be developed through the practice of *asana*, which is being able to forbear discomfort through **non-reactivity**.

Non-reactivity is the ability to respond to stimuli in a non-automatic way, so that one can apply judgment and discernment. As already mentioned, in the practice of *asana* we often face situations of stress and discomfort. Our habituated, automatic reaction (our automatic pilot, so to speak) tells us to avoid this inconvenience and to immediately come out of the pose. But the ability to forbear states of discomfort and unpleasantness is something we can develop through *asana* and meditation practices. We learn not to fear pain and discomfort and to deal with them without reacting in an automatic manner and without immediately moving. We observe and study them, as well as our reaction to them, with interest and curiosity. In observing pain, we should first try to determine whether it is harmful; if it is, we should change something in the pose or come out of it.[14] But often a pain is caused by a healthy, mild muscle stretch. In such cases, we can stay in the pose and observe the nature of the pain: What is the source of the pain? Can I stay in the *asana* and relax into it? Can I maintain my breath flowing smoothly? This kind of reflective practice can enhance our pain tolerance and help us to contain pain and, more generally, to learn to deal with pain in daily life.

In daily life, we often encounter inconvenient or even painful situations - sometimes such situations cannot be avoided. We tend to react by distracting our attention from the experience, by moving away, or by seeking some pleasure or satisfaction (grab something from the fridge, turn on the TV or attend to our smartphone). Can our practice teach us to handle such challenging situations better? Not to shut-off, and not to lose our peace of mind?

Modern communication technology increases our reactivity, since we are constantly available and since we tend to feel that an immediate response is expected. But the immediate response is not necessarily the best one. Mindful *asana* practice can help us to be less reactive, to remain more connected to whatever situation we encounter, and to delay our automatic reaction. By this, we acquire a larger degree of tolerance and are able to **respond** more skillfully, rather than to **react** automatically.

Equanimity is achieved when one is able, on the one hand, to accept inevitable pain and discomfort more calmly and, on the other, to be grateful and content with the simple joys that life offers us, as discussed in the section on Joy.

14 Deciding whether certain pain is harmful or not is a very delicate issue. We discuss it in the *Ahimsa* section.

2.9 Persistence and Ardency

tatra sthitau yatnah abhyasah	Practice is the steadfast effort to still these [the mind's] fluctuations
sa tu dirgha kala nairantairya satkara asevitah dridha bhumih	Long, uninterrupted, alert practice is the firm foundation for restraining the fluctuations[15]

As Patanjali points out in the above two *sutras* (YS I.13-14), being able to maintain a regular, uninterrupted routine of practice (*abhyasa*) is the key to success in a *sadhana* (spiritual quest). This has two aspects: **persistence** - bringing ourselves back to the practice day after day; and **ardency** - practice with zeal and enthusiasm.

Many students, even while enjoying yoga, find it hard to include regular practice in their daily routine. They stop practicing, or they practice on and off without being persistent. There are many obstacles we face that can make it hard to persist in the *sadhana*. Patanjali mentions nine such obstacles (YS I.30).[16]

Persistence

It is sometimes said that the hardest *asana* of all is unfolding our yoga mat. This simple action requires strong determination and willpower.

This is a choice that we make, and like any other choice, it necessarily means that we have to give up many other things. If we choose to invest our resources (time, energy, money) in a certain activity, we give up many other options in which we could have invested these resources. So the question is not **whether** to give up, but rather, **what** to give up.

15 All the English translations of the *Yoga Sutras* are taken from *Light on the Yoga Sutras* of *Patanjali* by B.K.S. Iyengar.
16 "These obstacles are disease, inertia, doubt, heedlessness, laziness, indiscipline of the senses, erroneous views, lack of perseverance, and backsliding".

Often we are too busy to find time for practice, or too tired, or too lazy, or it's too cold, or ... (you probably can add to this list...). So many things can distract our attention and take us away from the practice. To bring ourselves to unfold the mat and start practicing may not be easy. This is why one needs to develop self-discipline.

Even now, after almost 40 years of practice, many mornings I still hear these voices that tell me: "oh, today I have so many things to do, maybe I should give up the practice just one day," or: "today I lack energy, shall I rest one day?" I have learned to hear these voices, but not to listen to them. Once I decided to commit myself to the path of yoga, I know I must persist in my daily practice - otherwise it wouldn't be possible to pursue the subject deeply. So, whether I feel like it or not, I bring myself to the practice. Usually, after the first *Adho Mukha Shvanasana* (Downward Facing Dog Pose), the practice flows and I don't need to exercise too much willpower to keep it going.[17]

Ardency

The second aspect involves bringing energy and enthusiasm to the practice. Some students are persistent in attending their weekly class for many years, but if they lack ardency and enthusiasm, they will not make significant progress. Progress doesn't necessarily means being able to do more advanced *asanas*, but rather to develop the psychophysical capabilities discussed here such as balance, confidence and sensitivity. Patanjali points out that such progress can be achieved with "long, uninterrupted, practice."

17 In my article *Establishing and Structuring Self-Practice* published in *Iyengar Yoga News*, No. 26, Spring 2015 & No. 27, Autumn 2015, I included practical advice that may help to establish sound self-practice, including fixing a place in your home for yoga practice, hanging a recommended practice sequence on the wall, prioritizing yoga according to its true value for your life, making yoga a habit and practicing it with religious zeal, making the practice interesting and enjoyable, using a timer to develop endurance, adapting the practice to current conditions and circumstances, using recorded guidance, and, last but not least, taking support from family and friends when needed. Maintaining a routine is important, and since traveling can be a big obstacle for people who frequently travel away from home for their work, I also included tips on how to keep the practice going when one is not at home.

Patanjali also uses the terms *tapas* (YS II.1), a strong determination and burning zeal to practice and transform, and *samvega*, which refers to those who are supremely vigorous and intense in practice. He says that for these *sadhakas* (spiritual aspirants) the goal is near (YS I.21). These qualities can be developed in the practice of *asanas*.

Every practitioner knows that staying in an *asana* often requires overcoming an urge to come out, because of discomfort or stress. Staying in the *asana* in such cases requires strong determination and willpower. How can our practice foster determination and willpower? Well, one can say that there is circularity here, since in order to start practicing, one already needs to exercise willpower.

However, as in any process of fostering and education, progress is achieved in small steps that gradually create a snowball effect. Thus, we can approach this issue by supposing a gradual and slow process of increasing the time we stay in the *asana* and the quality of practicing it. Remember that many small steps in the right direction gradually make a big difference. An action in the right direction (even when using an external support of some kind, such as a timer) has a certain momentum that makes the next subsequent action or decision in the right direction just a bit easier and more natural.

This is true for any process of habituation: by persistent and ardent practice, one develops willpower; with sufficient willpower, one can persist with one's long-term goals. Once one develops self-discipline, willpower is no longer needed. Once a habit of practicing is formed, the fruits of the practice are enough to sustain and intensify it. Instead of using an external chronological timer, one then uses an internal psychophysical timer that determines when it is the right time to come out of the *asana* in a more natural manner.

This is true for any serious path a person is committed to, whether in the realm of art, science, sport, or business. You choose to do what you know will be beneficial for you in the long run, and not to follow your transient whims, and, subsequently, you develop the ability to resist many temptations that deter you from your track.

If one persists with this day after day, and month after month, with zeal and trust, the self-discipline developed for yoga practice will effect a broader character change: what started as a particular discipline for a particular practice will become a more general discipline, applicable not just to yoga but to a much wider variety of practices and tasks.

2.10 Awareness and Sensitivity

Awareness may be directed both internally and externally. Internally, we need to be aware anatomically (e.g., the position of our limbs in space), physiologically (e.g., our breath and heartbeat), and mentally (the feelings, emotions and thoughts that occupy our mind). Externally, we need to be aware of our environment, of other people around us, and so on.

Awareness and sensitivity are closely related to concentration and mindfulness. If your mind is scattered, jumping all over, then your awareness is weak, and your sensitivity may be compromised. If you are constantly busy with your own worries and plans, you won't notice other people and won't appreciate their feelings and concerns.

In self-practice, we can become more attuned, and develop our internal awareness. In class, our awareness also needs to be external: we need to listen to the instructions of the teacher, to relate to the other students, and to be considerate with the space we are in and the yoga props we are using.

Sensitivity is connected to awareness. When we enhance our internal awareness, we become more sensitive to messages received from our senses, our breath, and our proprioceptive system. The skin is the largest sense organ and, in *asana* practice, it is very important to pay close attention to sensations of the skin. In most *asanas*, the use of the eyes is limited, since we can see only a small portion of our body (in headstand, for example, we can see only our elbows). Hence, we have to become sensitive to the messages received from our skin and from our proprioceptors.

The actions we perform in yoga are meant to increase our sensitivity. We act in order to feel more. We learn to observe the effects and the reactions to the subtle actions we make. It wouldn't be an exaggeration to say that what one feels in *asana* practice is as important as what one does.

Since the world we live in is constantly changing, an important facet of sensitivity and awareness is to be aware of the changes that occur both inside us and in our environment. Often, we don't notice changes as they occur, or we miss minute changes and notice only after a long series of minor changes has eventually made a greater difference. For example, when living with people we know, we usually don't notice how their appearance changes. But, if we see an acquaintance after not having seen them for a year or so, we can see that they have changed. How is that we don't notice the changes as they occur? This is due to lack of sensitivity to minute, subtle changes.

Patanjali writes (YS III.15) that a yogi can notice successive sequential changes as they take place. This is definitely an amazing *siddhi* (extraordinary, paranormal attainment) which requires a highly developed sensitivity and tremendously sharp memory.

We can develop this capability through *asana* practice, at least to some extent. In headstand, for example, one needs to constantly lift the shoulder girdle; this is a deliberate muscular action, which needs to be refreshed every now and then. Often, our shoulders slowly lose their grip and drop, but we only notice it after they are already collapsed. With continuous practice, we learn to monitor the state of our shoulders more closely, and to notice any slight change, in order to correct it immediately. We learn to be more attentive to the process and to identify changes much more rapidly. This increased sensitivity is a boon in our life, since if we don't notice changes as they occur, it may be too late to respond.

The sensitivity we acquire in our practice makes us more sensitive to other people and to the circumstances we face. Sensitivity is an important ingredient of intelligence. It is the basis for empathy for other people and for the natural world around us. And this empathy is the basis for compassion (*karuna*).

2.11 Motivation and Surrender or Acceptance Without Stagnation

When practicing an *asana* we strive to achieve a correct, perfect posture. This requires many actions and adjustments, so that we align our body properly, according to the requirements of the *asana*. But while staying in the *asana*, a dilemma often arises: will we continue to keep adjusting and correcting forever? Or, is there a stage where we can remain in the *asana* peacefully, without having to constantly fine-tune, adjust and correct?

There is a tension between doing the *asana* 'good enough' and wanting to be 'perfect'. Of course, when the body position is wrong, we need to correct it, but if we constantly strive for perfection, we may find ourselves caught in a cycle of persistent action and dissatisfaction, and we'll never be able to stay peacefully in the *asana*.

Probably, most of us will never be able to do many of the *asana*s shown in books like *Light on Yoga*; and even the *asanas* that we can do, we'll never be able to execute them with such perfection and elegance as presented in these books. But does this mean that we cannot enjoy the positive effects of the *asanas*? Shouldn't there be a state, where we are content with our performance of the *asana*, where we feel we are doing well enough and can resist the urge to keep changing?

In daily life, one often faces similar situations: can I be content with who I am and what I have, or do I always have to struggle to improve? Can I accept myself as I am right now, without needing to correct anything? Perfectionism can be very tiring indeed, and at some point we need to learn to stop; to let go of the endless struggle to transform and improve. But this makes me recall B.K.S. Iyengar saying: 'Do not stop trying just because perfection eludes you. Nothing is perfect, you can always improve; that is creation of life, creation of interest". (*Guruji Uwach*)

This tension also exists in any spiritual quest, since in order to reach mental peace one needs to accept oneself. It is said that each one of us is already the Buddha; we are perfect just as we are, and this acknowledgment must be there, or else we will ever remain unsatisfied and harsh with ourselves.

In the *Yoga Sutras*, Patanjali says that the two means to reach a peaceful mind (*vritti nirodha*) are *abhyasa* and *vairagya* (YS I.12-16). *Abhyasa* is a continuous effort (*yatnah*); *vairagya* is desirelessness (or freedom from desires) and renunciation. While these seem to call for action in opposite directions, they are two sides of the same coin. We need *abhyasa* since we have many problems, and usually we don't perceive ourselves as the Buddha; we are often confused and deluded and need to practice in order to transform ourselves, so that we attain better clarity and discernment. However, if we are too ambitious and eager to improve, there will be a desire and restlessness; we will always struggle and never be peaceful. Thus, both *abhyasa* and *vairagya* are necessary, and one will not get far with only one of them.

Our practice can educate us to achieve the correct balance between these seemingly opposite attitudes. We can learn to balance our natural, positive tendency to improve and progress with the need to be content with who we are and where we are right now. When we are absorbed in an *asana*, there is no duality - there is neither *abhyasa* nor *vairagya*. Language is dualistic, but perhaps our experience can be more unified and holistic. We can learn to be content with where we are, but still have a healthy motivation to make progress. We need not expect any immediate results. Somewhere in the back of our minds, we know that right actions and right attitudes will lead to good outcomes; but we are not hankering after any specific reward or result.

When we orient our practice in this way, we may learn acceptance that is absent of stagnation. We will be able to accept our shortcomings and limitations, without regressing to frustration and desperation. This will also help us to accept the limitations of others with more tolerance and compassion.

2.12 Concentration and Meditation

Concentration (*dharana*) is the ability to keep the mind focused on a single object or action (See YS III.1). In the case of *asana* practice, we focus on the body and the breath. We are called to observe and monitor carefully the position of the limbs and joints, the level of stretch, the flow of our breath, and so on. We have

..y and make sure that we maintain correct alignment. Doing a ...ne limbs are not aligned correctly may cause wear and tear of joints, ...is, and ligaments, which, in the long run, may injure them. But more ..nportant in this context is that maintaining a precise alignment requires constant attention and observation. When we are uncompromising about precision, we can't ponder the past or worry about the future. We need to attend continuously to the actions and adjustments needed to maintain the correct alignment. This keeps us focused in the present moment.

Asana practice develops concentration if it is done mindfully and attentively, and if one stays in the *asana* for an extended length of time.[18] While staying in an *asana*, sometimes concentration is lost and one notices that distracting thoughts come up and he or she is no longer attending to the actions that should be performed. The challenge is to come back, time and again, to the present moment - to feel the body and the breath, and shift the attention back to the actions of the *asana*. One should ask oneself: Can I maintain my concentration and alertness? Can I maintain an uninterrupted flow of breath? Can I find stillness in the action? Can I release unnecessary tensions? Can I stretch to my limit, without overstretching?

Often when losing concentration, we come out of the *asana* casually without a deliberate decision to do so. This is another aspect where we can work on improving our concentration. Can we be attentive and come out of the *asana* mindfully and deliberately, at the right time, and not because some thoughts have just crossed our mind?

This requires practice. Concentration can be seen as a 'mental muscle' that needs to be exercised and strengthened. We know that activating a muscle strengthens it - this is the idea behind physical practices. In the same way, returning again and again to the object of concentration is a mental practice, a mental effort, which strengthens our capacity to concentrate.

18 Generally speaking, *asanas* are postures which are held for an extended length of time. But, there are forms of yoga that emphasize the *vinyasa* type of practice, in which a sequence of *asanas* is done dynamically, in succession, with a relatively short stay in each *asana*. But this doesn't characterize yoga practice in general.
The exact timing of staying in an *asana* varies according to the *asana* being performed, and to one's capability, experience, and purpose.

Concentration brings about tranquility and clarity. When our attention jumps from place to place and from one idea to another, we cannot delve deeply into exploring and developing an idea or an insight. Concentration creates mental quietness. Concentration is required in order to be productive in any task one performs. In the context of yoga practice, concentration makes it possible to meditate and to deepen our self-study (*svadhyaya*).

Asana practice can teach us not only *dharana*, but also *dhyana*, or meditation. Meditation refers to a wide spectrum of practices, and, unlike concentration, it doesn't necessarily have a specific goal (such as keeping the attention focused on a single object). Generally speaking, meditation requires presence in the moment and awareness of whatever happens, moment after moment. In some of the practical Explorations (for example Exploration B.8 on page 95), you could sense the difference between focusing on one action or location, and allowing the awareness to spread and cover a wide area of the body, or the entire body. This last type is a meditative *asana* practice.

2.13 Relaxation

Yoga practice can teach us to relax physically - i.e. to relax our muscles and organs. It can also teach us to relax mentally - to be calm and tranquil. This capability is connected with abilities we have already discussed, such as concentration and releasing effort and tension. As noted in the section on Managing Effort, relaxation is an important aspect of practicing any *asana*. But the main *asana* in which we practice complete relaxation is *Shavasana* (literally, the Corpse Pose, but usually referred to as the Relaxation Pose). At the end of each practice session, *Shavasana* is practiced and it is here that one learns the art of relaxation. It might seem that lying down without doing anything is a waste of time, but, actually, *Shavasana* is one of the most important and difficult poses. Its difficulty is not of course physical, but mental; and it is difficult precisely because there isn't any physical action involved. When the body is passive, the mind tends to be active. So we need to practice and learn how to relax our busy (and sometimes hectic) mind.

It might seem easier to relax the body than to relax the mind. On a deeper level, however, we become aware of the connection between relaxing the two. In the practice of *Shavasana*, we begin to identify more and more tensions in the body - tensions that were previously imperceptible. By deep concentration and observation, we release these bodily tensions. This requires focused involvement of the mind, and in this process the mind also relaxes, such that body and mind are relaxed together; it is a mutual process. As the mind becomes stiller and steadier, our observation penetrates deeper, and this enables us to release the body further. Nowhere is this mutual influence of relaxing the body and mind more obvious than in the musculature of the face. A thought that passes through the mind creates some reaction in the face, a minor contraction or tightening, which can be observed in *Shavasana*. On the other hand, relaxing the facial muscles enhances mental passivity and relaxation.

In *Light on Pranayama*, B.K.S. Iyengar writes, "*Sava* in Sanskrit means a corpse and *asana* a posture. Thus *Shavasana* is a posture that simulates a dead body, and evokes the experience of remaining in a state as in death and of ending the heart-aches and the shocks that the flesh is heir to. It means relaxation, and therefore recuperation. It is not simply lying on one's back with a vacant mind and gazing, nor does it end in snoring. It is the most difficult of yogic asanas to perfect, but it is also the most refreshing and rewarding."[19]

Shavasana requires the art of not-doing, not-acting - just being in the present moment, without drifting to the past (through memory), or to the future (through plans). In our busy life, it is important to learn to pause and relax. Deep relaxation is probably among the healthiest things we can do. The body is a wondrous machine - the internal organs that are responsible for our health do their job orderly without our conscious intervention, but stress is harmful to their proper functioning. The ability to relax deeply during activity is beneficial to the healthy functioning of our mental and physical capacities. We practice relaxation in all *asanas* while our body is active, but chronic especially in *Shavasana*, when our body is passive.

In *Yoga - the Path to Holistic Health*, B.K.S. Iyengar writes: "If you suffer from stress, you may experience indigestion, irritable bowel syndrome, headaches,

19 *Light on Pranayama*, p. 232 (Chapter 30).

migraine, a feeling of constriction in the diaphragm, breathlessness, or insomnia... **Yogic methods of deep relaxation have a profound effect on all the body systems.** When a part of the body is tense, blood flow to that area decreases, reducing immunity. Yoga works on that area to relieve tension and improve blood flow to the entire body, stabilizing the heart rate and blood pressure. Rapid, shallow breathing becomes deep and slow, allowing a higher intake of oxygen, and removing stress from the body and the mind."[20]

2.14 *Ahimsa* and Other *Yamas*

Ahimsa (or non-*himsa*), the practice of non-violence or non-injury, is the first and foremost precept in Patanjali's *Astanga Yoga*. It is the first precept of the first limb (*yama*) of the eight limbs of yoga (or *ashtanga*).

It is easy to talk about *ahimsa* theoretically; however, even if you respect the rights of other people and do not mean to do any harm intentionally, what happens when somebody, even unintentionally, steps on your toe? Surely that hurts - but what is your reaction? Do you become angry with that person? Do you react with (deliberate or non-deliberate) animosity? Or maybe you don't act outwardly, but internally develop anger, which is also a kind of injury (first toward yourself).

We need to ask ourselves: can we observe *ahimsa* even when other people threatening to violate our rights by being aggressive or violent toward us or toward people who are dear to us?

Absolute *ahimsa* is not at all easy; developing an attitude of non-injury conflicts with many of our survival instincts developed by evolution over millions of years. At least on some levels, the survival principle and the mechanisms of natural selection seem to reward the strong and the aggressive, and therefore encourages *himsa*. With our current technology, violence can bring about the destruction of all human life on this planet. As Mahatma Gandhi supposedly put it, an eye for an eye will make the whole world blind.

20 *Yoga - the Path to Holistic Health*, p. 179. Emphasized by authors.

It is true that in the practice of yoga we can also injure ourselves. Injuries in yoga practice usually result from practicing with the wrong attitude and with wrong expectations for the practice. Injuries usually occur if we are overly ambitious, or when we are not sufficiently attentive. In distinction from inner motivation, ambition is a problematic drive, since it is achievement-oriented, and thereby lends itself to an attitude where 'the ends justify the means.' Motivation, on the other hand, is a positive attitude in which we make an effort in order to improve and transform ourselves. So, although we have an intention and orientation, we are focused on the path without worrying so much about what we achieve. Overly ambitious impulses may drive us to sacrifice our wellbeing and health in the pursuit of achieving some external goal (such as showing off an advanced *asana* in order to impress, or just staying too long in an *asana* to prove to ourselves that we can).

Even with the right motivation, we are still susceptible to injury in the first stages, because we are not familiar with the limitations of our body and haven't yet developed the required sensitivity. "Insensitivity means that part of the body is dull - that it has no awareness - and this is the part where pain will develop."[21] Initially, our awareness may be limited, and we may cause ourselves light injuries. These can usually be recovered from quickly if one practices in a non-*himsa* manner.

For instance, one of the things we learn from pain is to respect our limitations. By learning to listen to our body and respect its limitations and shortcomings, we practice *ahimsa* toward ourselves. In yoga, we turn inside and study our motivations, and this is a good laboratory for observing our tendency for ambition or greed (*parigrah*). The *asanas* tend to punish us very quickly if we practice carelessly, and if we try to achieve or impress without respecting our true capacity. The *asanas* are a very powerful tool, and if we don't use this tool with judiciousness and prudence, we are likely to get injured quickly.

For example, in trying to achieve a backbend, we might overuse our lower back, instead of working from the tailbone and the thoracic spine. In this case, we 'steal (*steya*) from the lower back' and overuse its movement, which can result in injury.

21 From *The Tree of Yoga* (p. 40) by B.K.S. Iyengar.

So, in the practice of *asanas*, we can actually practice all the *yamas*: be truthful with ourselves (see next section on *satya*); not stealing (*asteya*); be disciplined and restrained with ourselves (*brahmacharya*); and not be greedy or possessive (*aparigraha*). A mindful *asana* practice offers an opportunity to test our motivations. We can acquire intimate knowledge of ourselves. We can learn to accept and respect our limitations and to be considerate and true to ourselves. From this, we can develop consideration towards others. Just talking or hearing about the *yama* isn't enough; change comes with repeated practice, done with awareness and reflection.

In *The Tree of Yoga*[22], B.K.S. Iyengar discusses two sources of possible violence in an *asana*: deliberate and non-deliberate (or negligence): "In your practice you will find within your own body that one part is violent and another part non-violent. On one side is deliberate violence because the cells are overworking. And on the so-called non-violent side there is a non-deliberate violence, because there the cells are dying, like still-born children."

The cells of the body need attention; to keep them healthy, we must bring a fresh supply of blood to each and every cell - neglecting to do so will harm us in the long term. The interesting point here is that negligence, being heedless, or being non-attentive are also forms of *himsa*, and can create injury. To practice *ahimsa*, we need to develop attention and sensitivity - otherwise, we may injure ourselves or others, without intending to, and without even being aware that an injury has occurred.

The practice of *ahimsa* is not only of restraint. *Ahimsa* "is more than a negative command not to kill, for it has a wider positive meaning, love. This love embraces all creations for we are all children of the same Father - the Lord." [23] Ultimately, developing *ahimsa* requires spiritual awareness, acknowledging the similarity between all human being, and even our similarity with all sentient beings. Only when we see this commonality - when we see ourselves in others and others in ourselves - can true *ahimsa* blossom. The practice of yoga should ultimately foster in us this awareness of brotherhood and sisterhood and open our hearts to universal, unconditional love. So, the first step in the path of *ashtanga yoga* (i.e. *ahimsa*) is also the last: achieving this first precept requires that we walk the yogic path to its very end.

22 In the Ch. Effort, awareness and joy.
23 From the Introduction to *Light on Yoga*, B.K.S. Iyengar.

2.15 Truthfulness and Sincerity (*Satya*)

Satya - the second of the *yamas* - means truth, truthfulness, honesty, sincerity, and authenticity. It means living honestly, being sincere to yourself, not deceiving others, being truthful in thought, speech, and deed. It is the virtuous restraint from falsehood and from distortion of reality in one's expressions and actions. It lies in not holding nor expressing falsehoods, exaggeration, distortion, fabrication, or deception. How can one develop such a quality through the practice of yoga?

Being true to yourself in the practice means respecting your limits, accepting the inevitable changes that occur from day to day and especially with aging. It means not pretending that you can do what you can't; it means not showing off in order to fool others. In teaching, it means not pretending that you have invented something that you did not - you should acknowledge honestly the teaching you've received, express gratitude to your teachers, and avoid producing an impression that you know everything.

Being sincere in practice means also embracing the entire subject of yoga, and not choosing to practice only what you like - not 'cutting corners' whenever there is a difficulty. It means practicing all aspects of yoga with the same open-minded approach and equal seriousness.

If you practice with that honesty and genuineness, then you are practicing *satya*. By being true to yourself you will become true to others. This attitude will propagate to your daily life and make you a more honest and trustworthy person.

2.16 Observing and Transforming Tendencies

Yoga practice offers a wide space for self-study (*svadhayaya*): we can observe our mental and emotional tendencies - the distractions, pettiness, self-centeredness, as well as our strength, kindness, and open, heartedness. By observing these, we recognize what there is, what the reality of our nature is. This requires great sincerity and acceptance; but only by knowing what there is can the process of transformation take place.

The tendencies exposed while practicing may differ considerably if we practice in a group setting or if we are practicing individually at home. Although both offer ample space for reflection, there are important differences between the two.

Tendencies in a Class Setting

Whether we like it or not, group practice brings about our tendency to compare ourselves with the other students. This may involve (or give rise to) tendencies such as competitiveness, desire to impress and excel, envy, pride, and feelings of superiority or inferiority. We all need some acknowledgment and attention; we want to be seen, and we want to be recognized. Our desire to impress, to receive affirmation, and to be loved is a very basic and fundamental one. You can observe it clearly in children who have not yet learned to suppress this tendency. However natural, this is a wrong motivation for yoga practice, as it takes us away from ourselves and from the inner work required by yoga. It can also lead to injury.

In the final analysis, any comparison is alien to yoga - since in yoga each person progresses on one's own path and at one's own pace; progress in yoga is subjective. It may well be that your neighboring student in the class, who can hardly bend forward in *Paschimottanasana* (Seated Forward Bend Pose), is progressing more than you are, even if you can fold down over your legs. Maybe he is absorbed and is able to release his stiffness and to advance slightly, and for him this is a big step forward. Yoga is not a performing art and is not about showing off. For this reason, the external appearance is not the main thing.

In yoga class, we can recognize these tendencies and look at them more closely. This is possible, of course, to do so in any type of a group setting. However, *asanas* by nature encourage self-observation and study. Such observation may be difficult to do when the practice is dynamic or in a competitive environment. Many types of sport strengthen the competitive drive and are therefore not appropriate for the study of this competitive tendency of ours.

Tendencies in Home Practice

A group setting, while potentially raising the above-mentioned tendencies, is still preferable for most students. Why? Because when practicing alone, we are more exposed to character dispositions. There is no teacher to give us instructions, and there are no others around to motivate and energize us. We are on our own, with our own tendencies and wandering minds. These tendencies are categorized in yoga into three qualities (*gunas*), namely, *tamas* (laziness, dullness, heaviness, resistance to change), *rajas* (activeness, dynamism, restlessness, agitation) and *sattva* (purity, serenity, clarity). Personal practice is important precisely because when we are alone these traits and tendencies tend to manifest, and the practice allows us to observe them and deal with them.

On some days, the *rajas guna* is dominant; we feel restless, impatient or agitated. On these days, we may leave our phone next to us while practicing, and allow it to interrupt our practice flow; we are susceptible to endless distractions and find it difficult to concentrate on practice.

Another tendency connected to *rajas* is ambition. We may find ourselves struggling hard to achieve some difficult pose, fighting with the *asana* and with our body without consideration. We are focused on the external goal and not enjoying the path. We want some immediate achievement, so we disrespect the natural pace in which the progress should occur.

On other days, the *tamas guna* may be dominant: we feel heavy, dull or lazy. It will be hard to bring ourselves to even begin practicing, and even if we do begin, our practice lacks energy and enthusiasm. We may also find ourselves holding a negative attitude towards our body, such as dissatisfaction with the length of our legs or our weight. We may also feel pessimistic, which will make it difficult for us to endure and accept challenges in the practice.

Finally, there are days when the *sattva guna* is dominant - and we feel bright and focused; practice flows without difficulties, allowing us to dive deep within ourselves and to experience the joy of it.

In our practice, we should seek to strengthen the *sattva* on account of the *rajas* and *tamas*. If, at the end of the practice, we are left feeling as *rajasic* or *tamasic* as we were when we started, then the goal of practice was not achieved in that session.

Even in a class setting we may encounter these tendencies, to a certain extent. Although the teacher provides the overall framework, each student has a great deal of freedom and choice over how to perform the poses, and needs to make many choices on how to implement the instructions given. For example, the teacher may instruct the class to do *Trikonasana* (Triangle Pose), while adding several technical points, but the teacher can't specify the exact actions to be taken, and can't define exactly how far to bend, at what pace, or how to combine the breath with the movement, etc. All of these nuances are under the student's responsibility and control. The student can decide to go slowly and carefully or try to stretch to the limits of their capacity. So, the qualities of *rajas* or *tamas* may manifest even when practicing in a group, and a mindful practitioner should observe them.

2.17 Extending the Practice Beyond the Mat

Often, at the end of a yoga class, we feel calm and serene, but when the class is over, we quickly return to our habituated pattern of behavior. When encountering some difficulty or unexpected event, we instantly lose all our serenity. When driving back home after class, if another car accidently cuts into our lane, our stable and quiet mindset may rapidly turn into impatient aggression or frustration.[24]

How then can one better integrate the practice into one's life? How can we keep our balance and tranquility even when we are out of the yoga studio? How can we not only practice more mindfully, but also live more mindfully? These questions are of utmost importance as many practitioners find it difficult to relate their yoga experience with the way they conduct their daily lives.

24 In large workshops, where each participant brings one's own yoga props, the peace of mind can evaporate rapidly upon searching for the props; if you are missing a belt or a blanket, the relaxation may turn quickly to worry and resentment.

The word for mindfulness in Sanskrit is *smriti*, which literally means 'that which is remembered.' It also means 'memory' - in order to be mindful, you need to overcome your forgetfulness. You need to remember to come back to the present moment, to remember to stop in the midst of an activity or interaction, take a slow breath, center down and reconnect with yourself. This can change the quality of your life drastically, since you will no longer lose yourself in undesired chains of events, and be able to respond much more skillfully to the challenges and unexpected events of life.

A good way to extend the practice to daily life is to set up small reminders throughout the day - small daily activities that can serve as prompts to pause, breathe and reconnect with ourselves.

This should start immediately in the actions we do once your yoga class is over. How do you roll your mat? How do you fold your blankets and arrange the props you have been using? Are you as attentive while doing this as when you did the yoga poses? In *pranayama* classes, we often use elastic (cotton) bandages for wrapping around the head; when the class is finished, I tell my students to do a 'bandage rolling meditation'; to take time and concentrate on the action of rolling the bandage before starting to chat and move around.

When walking out after class, try to stay a little longer under the effect of the yoga - take time to savor the fresh air, or to appreciate the view, before rushing on to your business.

To be more mindful in your daily life, designate a few actions that you do regularly during the day, as reminders to pause and come back to yourself. For example, each time you enter your car, you can take five mindful breaths - it takes only a few seconds, but can help you to start your drive more calmly. Or, when you stop at a red light, instead of waiting impatiently, you can again attend to your breath - no need to close your eyes, but simply sense the breath moving in the nostrils. All you need is a tiny reminder. With persistence, this will turn into a habit which has the potential to change your life.

Personally, I adopted the habit of pausing and watching my posture and my breath before every meal - this is a good opportunity to practice gratitude, to contemplate how lucky we are to have this food, and to quietly thank all the people (and other creatures) that took part in its production and preparation.

We can also be helped by technology, for example, by using a mindfulness app, which allows setting an alert to come up at certain intervals. While sitting at your desk in the office, every time you hear the bell, pause, maybe stand up, stretch, or breathe more slowly with awareness. This can change the experience of your work day.

I am convinced that, if one practices yoga persistently, a significant transformation will occur. If you find yourself in a stressful or frustrating situation, you might remember to reconnect with your bodily sensations, to center yourself at the spine, and to restore your balance and calmness. Yoga often seems like isolated, individual (and some would even say egoistic) practice, but, in my experience, when you change positively and become calmer, more balanced, and more considerate, it will radiate outside and affect your relationships with other people. The people with whom you are interacting will feel this change in you, and will respond better to you. The inner calmness and harmony will affect them and the good you achieve will spread around you.

2.18 Pursuit of Long-Term Goals and Modesty in Realizing Them

(Written by Ohad)

One of the things that I like and appreciate about practicing yoga is that it sets long-term challenges and a systematic method for working towards achieving them. This is essential for developing a realistic sense of slow but persistent progress. At the same time, one cannot help feeling that some of the poses are so difficult and challenging that, at some juncture, they are bound to feel impossible to achieve. And to some extent, this is true. Yet, if one persists in practicing, one will experience improvement and progress (depending, of course, on the intensity and quality of the practice). At the same time, being able to perform some of the poses will continue to seem very far away and likely to remain impossible, at least for the time being, and perhaps entirely. This might certainly cause frustration.

I have experienced improvement in some poses and almost none in some others. After years of practice, I can now do Full Arm Balance away from the wall, which I find almost miraculous, but can hardly do other simple and basic *asanas* such as *Paschima Namaskarasana* (joining the palms behind the back).

Even if progress may be very slow - or non-existent in some cases - I feel that the long-term course set by yoga practice has a significant and healthy impact on one's wellbeing. On the one hand, one feels that a serious and dedicated practice pays off and yields results; on the other, one realizes that, even if you dedicate the rest of your life to practice, there will be a lot to improve, learn, and achieve, not to mention poses that will remain ever elusive. Indeed, there is no point in the future where I'll say: Now I've reached the goal. Now I can stop and rest. This would be very foreign to the spirit of yoga. For the point of the practice lies in the practice itself and not in anything external to it; it is an activity that allows one to observe and attend to one's attitudes and development on both physical and mental levels. Since we always change, mature, and age, our mental and physical capacities change as well. Thus, there are always new things to learn and observe.

For me, this complex trajectory of slow progress through attentive practice helps to instill a sense of modesty and a realistic attitude towards other challenges in life. It encourages one to pursue very difficult and long-term challenges while maintaining a sense that the pursuit itself (with a reflective and investigative attitude) might be more important than the external goals one sets. I believe that this applies both in professional and personal life. For instance, if one is a writer, one develops the sense that writing takes an immense investment of time and effort. And while this investment would pay off, there will always be books that I would like to write but never have the time or capability to write. If one is an architect, the same applies to projects. Even if one is an avid traveler and hiker, a similar attitude might be useful. Any hike is important and valuable, but one must realize that there will be many places one will never be able to reach in one's lifetime. If one likes to read, reading itself is precious and pleasurable - even if there are many books one will never be able to read. The curiosity and the motivation to do and achieve ever more is healthy and positive; but it needs to be mitigated by a sense of modesty and a realistic perception of one's limitations. The practice of yoga helps to instill such an attitude.

The magnitude of the challenges that lie ahead of us should not deter us from pursuing them. But we should not delude ourselves either. It takes work and persistence. It does not come by itself. Nor does progress come in quantum leaps. With time, one develops a sense that the practice itself is the true benefit rather than achieving this or that goal. The engagement in a lifelong process of taking care of oneself, observing and learning oneself - in both physical and mental dimensions - is the real fruit of the practice.

2.19 Non-Competitiveness

(Written by Ohad)

This leads to another feature of yoga practice: it is not a competition. Unlike many kinds of sport or other physical exercise, and against a very natural tendency we all have to compare our achievements and performance, advancing in yoga cannot (and need not) be measured against those of other practitioners. While there are clear standards by which we can assess how well we perform an *asana*, there is no sense in ranking one's performance against that of other practitioners. This is not only because people greatly differ in their physical conditions and abilities, such as strength and flexibility, but also because one does not gain anything in being better than someone else, nor lose anything in performing 'worse' than someone else, say, in performing Full Arm Balance. Progress can be measured only against one's previous practice. Since performing an *asana* correctly and elegantly requires a lot of mindful practice and the exercise of many abilities, it can certainly be regarded as an important achievement on both physical and mental levels. But since the aim of yoga is self-development, there isn't any point in comparing yourself to others. In short, there isn't any sense in running yoga competitions.

Of course, nothing is more natural in a yoga class than looking around the room observing other practitioners. It goes without saying that there is much to learn from the way others perform, both for negative and positive lessons - this is often a part of class demonstration. But evaluative comparison with the way that others perform - better or worse than me - is pointless. For some, *Urdhva Dhanurasana* (Upward Bow Pose) comes easy, and for some it is impossible;

for some *Shirsasana* (Headstand) is rather natural, while for others it seems extremely frightening. We need to learn our capabilities and limitations in order to improve and undo hang-ups and obstructions. The deep insight to draw from this is that, since the ultimate goal of the practice is self-development, competition doesn't make any sense in this context.

2.20 Some Additional Words About the Practice of Yoga

As we see it, yoga practice can go beyond improving the psychophysical capabilities discussed above; it can also make us better human beings, in a sense of being more humble, considerate, and compassionate. Discussing how this can come about would require another book project. But we do not want to close this chapter without mentioning this important moral aspect.

An important facet of the practice was termed by Patanjali, *ishavara pranidhana*, which is the fifth (and last) *niyama* he mentioned. *ishavara pranidhanais* usually translated as 'surrender to God', but yoga doesn't require a belief in God. In the yoga *sutras*, *ishvara* is described as a being totally free from conflict, unaffected by actions and untouched by cause and effect, and as the unexcelled seed of all knowledge (YS, I.24-25). In an article on *Kriya Yoga*, Gary Kraftsow write 25:

> "the word *pranidhana* is a technical term usually translated as 'surrender' ... The implication of this word is the profound recognition of that which sustains us and gives meaning to every dimension of our lives. It is a kind of faith – in the sense of the 'place' where we put or give our hearts. It implies an element of self-sacrifice – the sacrifice of our own self-importance."

Ishavara pranidhana can therefore be seen as a practice of fostering humility and reducing our tendency for self-centeredness and self-importance; it also suggests opening our heart to other human beings and to the wondrous nature around us.

25 In: *Iyengar the Yoga Master*, p. 240.

We believe that practice along the lines suggested here – and especially the daily confrontation with, and recognition of, our limitations – can develop these attitudes, so that our practice will make us more capable as human beings, that is, it will also contribute and enhance the moral aspect of our nature.

We now turn to a historical survey of the mind-body problem since its inception in ancient Greece and to a philosophical discussion of how it can be resolved.

CHAPTER THREE

A Brief History of Psyche and Soma (Soul and Body): From Socrates to the Present and back to Aristotle

Introduction

It would have been nice if the pre-history of the relations between the psyche and soma (the soul and body) were simple and easy to state. It is tempting to think that things were clear and simple in the beginning and then became messy and complicated over the course of history. But the history of psyche and soma relations, as well as the precise meaning of these terms, seems to be messy and complicated from the very beginning, that is, from the early texts in which these terms appear. Thus, in early Greek literature and mythology, the terms are already used in a variety of ways, which resist simple description in a single and clear statement. Yet the very nature of our enterprise here – to abbreviate the story of the relations between mind and body – demands some simplicity and clarity. And so, if we want to be clear, we must simplify. Clarity requires simplification. And simplification, in turn, requires ignoring some of the historical complexity. In practice, this means that we must focus on some texts and ignore others.

While I would very much like to begin our historical survey with a clear and simple statement about the way psyche and soma were used in early Greek texts, I also want the reader to realize that here, as well as in the rest of this historical section, clarity comes at a cost, namely that we focus on what we can state clearly and ignore many other complexities. Indeed, what we seek to achieve in this short historical survey is far from a comprehensive presentation of all positions and subtle changes that took place from ancient Greece until the present day. This would be far too presumptuous. Rather, we only seek to present and highlight the most influential ways in which human beings in the western tradition have conceptualized the relations between soul and body, psyche and soma, with an eye to showing the tangled route by which we have come to understand these relations today. As we already noted in the preface, this really amounts to a presentation of how we understand an important aspect of our human nature. Obviously, even this is a daunting task that requires much more space and time than we have here. As such, one might wonder why we go to the trouble of writing such a complicated and challenging story in the first place.

We go into this because we believe that the history of the problem is essential for its resolution. In other words, the history of the problem is essential for understanding how it was formed and how it might be resolved, and the extent to which such a resolution is possible. To paraphrase Herbert Spencer, we believe that in order to understand the mind we need to examine how our conceptions of mind and body have evolved.[1]

To put our approach rather crudely, we think that the most promising model for conceptualizing psyche-soma relations has been lost on us because of the way these relations were conceptualized through the rise of modern science and philosophy, and especially by Descartes' influential work. Thus we seek to recover a version of Aristotle's approach that has become almost inaccessible to us. We do not, however, suggest simply going back to Aristotle. Rather, our approach is strongly influenced by Wittgenstein's work in focusing on language-use and by stressing a non-reductive approach and distinguishing it from the reductive approach that seeks to explain the mental in terms of the physical. This reductive approach is certainly the most prevalent today in philosophy and the cognitive sciences, and it is simply taken for granted in most brain studies. To a large extent, the Cartesian mind–body dualism has been transformed into a brain-body dualism, so that scientists seek to understand the mind in terms of the brain. We discuss these issues in the second part

Let us then begin with a rather neutral statement of how the terms 'psyche' and 'soma' are used in the Homeric literature. It is strangely appropriate to begin our survey with the context of death or, more precisely, with how a person's death is depicted by Homer: upon death, the psyche, which is similar to breath or air, leaves the body (soma) and passes to the house of Hades, where it leads a shadowy existence. In Hades, the psyche is without a body, but still retains some of its previous identity. Thus, for Homer, psyche is depicted as the life-principle that departs the body upon death and persists as an image or a shadow in Hades (the house of the dead) (see *Psyche* and *Soma*, p. 13).

This picture of the soul, as departing the body upon death, remains powerful and influential even now. It also highlights one of the most important functions attributed to the soul, namely, a life-giving-principle – that which animates a body, without which it is instead a mere corpse. At the same time, this portrayal also highlights the difference between two central contexts in which the relations

1 Spencer, H. (1890). *Principles of Psychology*, 3rd Edition. London: William and Norgate, p. 291.

between psyche and soma are considered: in the context of living beings (or life), psyche and soma may seem intrinsically connected (or at least conjoined), whereas in the context of death the psyche may appear separable from the body and might have (so to speak) a life of its own.

This may also serve to point out that psyche-soma relations may be understood rather differently in the context of life, where health and medical concerns are prominent, and in the context of death, where religious, moral, and metaphysical concerns may become more prominent. Indeed, even radical dualists such as Plato and Descartes adopt a different tone when they discuss the context of medicine and well-being; and radical monists, such as Aristotle and Spinoza, may hesitate and make some ambiguous statements when they consider the context of death.[2]

Thus, in discussing the mind–body problem, it is important to be sensitive to the context – medical, metaphysical, moral, or scientific – in which the question is discussed. In the other parts of this book, where we discuss yoga practice and its impact, we mainly focus on the context of well-being. In the current part, however, we situate the question in a much broader context. We seek to enrich the practical side of exploring mind–body relations with the fascinating history of these concepts. But this part serves not only to enrich and give deeper meaning to the practice; it also serves to provide the rationale for the approach we take in this book, namely that exploring our human nature – and ultimately seeking to improve our well-being – requires an intelligent exercise of both mental and physical capacities.

2 "While the distinctness of the soul and the body as separate substances is stressed in works such as the *Phaedo* and the *Meditations* in which the central issue is the survival of the soul after the death of the body, a very different conception of the relationship appears when the issues of health and disease come to the fore." (cited from *Psyche and Soma*, eds. Wright and Potter, OUP, 2000, p. 2).

Early Origins – Which Was Discovered First, the Body or the Mind?

In a debate among scholars of ancient philosophy, an interesting question came up: was the mind discovered before the body or the body before the mind?[3] It might seem odd to think that the mind or the body were discovered at some point in history, as if humans could live either without a body or without a mind – but the point concerns the discovery of the concepts of mind and body. And, however strange, it does seem possible to ignore these concepts. In other words, the question concerns the awareness and recognition of our body and/or a mind as essential features of our nature – of how we understand ourselves as human beings.

It may seem obvious that we have a body, for we normally sense our body. We certainly seem aware of it when something goes wrong, as when we are ill or in pain. But even when all goes well, we are constantly preoccupied with sensations of pleasure, or discomfort, fatigue, and hunger that we tend to associate with our body. It may be less obvious that the very recognition that we have a body, and that we have such sensations, presupposes something like a mind – a sensitive ability and some reflexive awareness of ourselves as having a body as an essential part of ourselves. While having a body may seem more intuitive and obvious to us than having a mind, the very observation that we sense ourselves as having bodies reveals that we also use our sensitive and reflexive capacities for this very recognition.

This short discussion brings out an interesting point. Can we have a concept of a body without that of a mind? Perhaps the very articulation of the concept of a body requires that of a mind, and perhaps the very articulation of the notion of mind presupposes the notion of a body. If this is the case, we might say that body and mind serve to define one another, such that one cannot say what a body is without reference to a mind, or what a mind is without reference to a body. We want to put this proposal on the table and note that it may serve to resolve the historical question of primacy as well as the question of conceptual priority briefly discussed above. To put this crudely, if each concept – of the mind and body – requires the other for its very definition, there is no sense to the question of primacy for they come together.

3 See Bruno Snell, *The Discovery of the Mind*, trans. T. G. Rosenmeyer (Cambridge, MA: Harvard University Press, 1953); Bernard Williams, *Shame and Necessity*, Sather Classical Lectures, Volume 57 (Berkeley: University of California Press, 1993).

We shall return to this idea. But at present, we turn to explore some of the early and most influential conceptualizations of the relations between the soul (or mind) and the body as constitutive aspects of our human nature. Indeed, a close attention to historical texts reveals that conceptualizations of the self and of mind–body relations have not always been seen in the same way. In fact, in our cursory exploration of the history of these relations, we will attempt to show not only different conceptions of mind–body relations but also how we have come to be entangled in this as a problem. As noted, this survey is also intended to highlight an attractive approach to a question that is usually left out of sight from our current perspective.

Whether it ultimately makes sense or not, the debate concerning the discovery of the mind raises interesting questions: which, body or mind, is more fundamental for understanding the self, of who we are, and how we understand our peculiar nature as human beings? As we shall see, the early founders of western philosophy, Socrates and Plato, identify the true self with the soul, or, more precisely, with the rational aspect of the soul. This is also the case for many thinkers who follow, including Descartes and, to a large extent, Kant. According to these views, being a moral agent requires the use of reason in deliberating between alternative courses of action. This is particularly clear in Leibniz, for instance, according to whom a non-reasoned choice cannot be regarded as a choice at all.

Outline

Identifying the true self with the soul or the rational aspect of the soul is an extremely important feature of the Western tradition and culture. Going back to Socrates and Plato (section 1) will provide us with some of the sources for the moral precedence given to the soul over the body. More generally, Plato's work will serve here to present the dualistic model of the relation between psyche and soma, emphasizing the rational aspect of the soul as the defining feature of human beings. As we shall see in section 2, in Aristotle, as well, the rational aspect of the soul serves as the defining feature of human beings. But, in Aristotle, the psyche is conceived in a radically different way. For Aristotle, the psyche is not a thing or an entity. Rather, 'psyche' serves as a name for a large array of capacities (and powers) that characterize living beings. Since living beings have different capacities, their psyches differ accordingly. Thus, all living beings have a capacity for self-nutrition, but only animals have senses (and sensitive capacities) and only rational animals (or human beings) have the capacity for speech and reasoning. The most important feature of Aristotle's view is that any of these psychic capacities is inseparable from the organs that serve their execution. Thus, the capacity of seeing is intrinsically related to that of the eye; and the capacity of hearing to that of the ear. This implies a model in which psyche and soma concern particular capacities that are functionally related, as sight is related to the eye, such that they are inseparable from one another.

In Plotinus (section 3), we shall find an influential version of Platonism that emphasizes the connection between the soul as the source of goodness and matter as a source of evil. Augustine (section 4) picks up this Neoplatonic thread and reconciles it with the ascendant Christian framework in the fourth century. And what Augustine does for Plato's views of the soul in the fourth century, Thomas Aquinas (section 5) will do for Aristotle in the twelfth century, that is, he reconciles the Aristotelian conception of the soul with the Christian framework. While this Christian version of Aristotelianism dominated philosophy and science in the late middle ages and the Renaissance, it was vehemently rejected by Descartes and by most of the new philosophers during the rise of early modern philosophy in the sixteenth and seventeenth centuries – a move that culminated with the publication of Newton's Mathematical Principles of Natural Philosophy in 1687 and the general theory of gravitation.

Descartes (section 6) drew a dichotomy between minds (or thinking things) and bodies (extended things), such that bodies are suitable for adequate scientific description but minds are only accessible to those who have them, that is, to human beings. Since Descartes defines minds and bodies as radically different, such that bodies are extended in space and minds are not in space at all, the way they interact becomes a mystery. And this is, briefly, the modern mind–body problem. While we all sense and experience intimate connections between our mental states and physical states, we can give no account of how it comes about. We consider the major responses to this problem in Descartes' time (section 7), and how they lead to the way in which the question is understood today. We briefly consider the response of Malebranche and Leibniz and pay more attention to Spinoza's naturalistic approach, whose spirit – the attempt to capture the mental realm in physical terms – is the most prominent today. We then briefly present Kant's skepticism about the soul and his argument that any attempt to prove its immortality transcends the limits of human knowledge.

In the second section, we fast forward to the twentieth century and present our own approach against the background of the contemporary approaches – both philosophical and scientific – to the study of the mind.

Part I

Psyche–Soma Relations From Socrates to Kant

1. Socrates (469–399 BCE) and Plato (429–347 BCE): The Beginning of Philosophy and the Dualistic Model

1.1 Background

Socrates lived and practiced philosophy in Athens in the fifth century BC. He did not leave anything in writing. But his legacy plays a central role in the history of Western philosophy. Socrates is justly considered as the founding figure of Western philosophy. He has become such a central figure not only because of his philosophy but also due to his character. Since his own time, Socrates has been regarded, with awe and admiration, as a model for practicing philosophy and for living a philosophical life.

While philosophy is often seen as purely theoretical – and often as a mere academic exercise – Socrates shows how one can live a philosophical life. Indeed, Socrates lived such a philosophical life to its bitter end. One of the most significant features of his legacy, as recounted by Plato in some of his most moving dialogues, *The Apology*, *Crito*, and *Phaedo*, concerns Socrates' death. The Athenian authorities accused Socrates of disrupting religion and corrupting the youth through his philosophical activity. In refusing his friends' offer to avoid trial and escape capital punishment, Socrates demonstrates that a true philosopher should live up to, and stand up for, his ideals. Even more relevant to our concerns, he shows that philosophy enables one to face death with equanimity. In the *Phaedo*, Socrates tells his friends that, "the one aim of those who practice philosophy in the proper manner is to practice for dying and death" (64a and 81). For Socrates, the role of philosophy is not merely theoretical but primarily practical and moral: it concerns the proper conduct of life – and a proper conduct of life also means preparing to die properly.

The context of death, in general, and of Socrates' death, in particular, puts questions about the nature of soul and body into sharp focus. In other words, the way we understand death is crucial for our understanding of mind–body relations.[4]

4 The other crucial context concerns questions of health and medicine (of both body and soul).

Indeed, according to Socrates, death is nothing but "the separation of the soul from the body" (*Phaedo* 64c). And the question of the soul's persistence after death is – historically as well as existentially – one of the most pressing motivations for investigating the very nature of soul and body.

The question of death is clearly one the most important sources for the view that soul and body are separable, such that the soul can continue to live without the body – a body that becomes a corpse upon death. Apart from the obvious role this question plays in religious and moral contexts (such as punishment and reward in the afterlife), the question of death is also one that helps us set out the two major positions concerning mind–body relations. Does the soul survive after death? Dualists, such as Plato and Descartes, who hold that a human being consist of two separable entities (body and soul or mind), typically say yes; monists, such as Aristotle and Spinoza, who hold that a human being is a single entity with two inseparable attributes or aspects – mental and physical – typically say no.

The main contrast between body and soul as described by Socrates in the *Phaedo* is this: it is through the soul that we can obtain knowledge and truth, whereas the body is mainly an obstacle to pursuing these goals.[5] Further, whereas the body is ever-changing, the soul is always one and the same. If this is the case, a person who seeks knowledge and wisdom, which is the very definition of a philosopher (for *philo-sophia* in Greek means 'lover of wisdom') should seek to cultivate his soul. As Socrates puts this, "The soul of the philosopher achieves a calm from emotions (such as gluttony, violence, and drunkenness, associated with the body, 81e); it [the soul of the philosopher] follows reason and ever stays with it contemplating the true, divine, which is not the object of opinion. Nurtured by this, it [the soul] believes that one should live in this manner as long as one is alive and, after death, arrives at what is akin and of the same kind, and escapes from human evils" (*Phaedo* 84a).

It is clearly implied here that death can be seen as a flight from the burdens of the body. But, if so, why should a philosopher fear death at all? Indeed, Socrates even seems to rejoice about the prospect of dedicating all his energies and attention in the afterlife for the soul without the obstacles of the body (see *Phaedo* 83, 84e).

5 One of Plato's arguments for the immortality of the soul is that the intellect, the rational aspect of the soul, must be immaterial because what it perceives – truths or ideal forms – are immaterial and the intellect must have an affinity with what it apprehends (*Phaedo* 78b4-84b8).

But what makes him so sure that he, Socrates, will survive his death? Here we come to the most important point in Socrates' view, namely that the soul is that which constitutes our genuine self. And so, if the body ceases to exist, and the soul persists, our true self will persist after death (of the body). Of course, the question how we can know whether the soul remains after death immediately presents itself, as Socrates' interlocutors make clear (*Phaedo*). Later philosophers, notably Emmanuel Kant in the 18th century, will argue that this question goes beyond the limits of possible experience and hence beyond the boundaries of what can be known. We shall return to this point below (section 9). But first let us attend briefly to the historical context in which this discussion takes place.

Since Socrates himself wrote nothing, we only know of his character and extensive discussions of philosophy through the writings of others. Most of his philosophical legacy is passed on to us through the writings of his disciple, Plato. And it is for this reason that Plato, too, plays such a monumental role in the founding of western philosophy.

Plato casts most of his writings as dialogues – extended conversations between Socrates and other intellectuals and friends in the public sphere of Athens. Thanks to Plato's writing style, and his attempts to capture the Socratic debates he attended in the streets of Athens, philosophy has, from its earliest days, taken the particular form of a dialogue; more precisely, it takes the form of a debate or a living discussion based on questions and replies, logic, and arguments, so that the results are shared and agreed upon by the participants. Plato sought to bring out the way in which Socrates did philosophy. In Plato's writings, Socrates serves as the prime model of a philosopher. And his method of probing his interlocutors has come to be known as the Socratic method. As any college student knows, this method still serves as an ideal for class instruction today.

Thus, the figure of Socrates, as presented in Plato's dialogues, exemplifies both a philosophical spirit and a certain philosophical method. This spirit may be described as skeptical attitude towards any authority, on the one hand, and a reliance on human reason alone, on the other. This is remarkable because it is the first moment in history that philosophy assumes this attitude. As John M. Cooper notes, "before Socrates and Plato philosophers usually put themselves forward as possessors of special insight and wisdom: they had the truth, and everyone else should just listen to them and learn".[6] The source of their wisdom and knowledge of truth was usually opaque and mysterious. Pre-Socratic philosophy is characterized by claims to truth that originate from sources such as the Oracle of Delphi. They stand in no need of proof or justification. Knowledge and wisdom are obtained through a special and unnatural relation to an external source, typically a divine source.

Socrates is skeptical of any such authority and pretensions for knowledge. His main effort in the dialogues is to refute those who claim to know the truth and teach others. In particular, Socrates rejected knowledge claims based on authority: those who claim to have truth should be able to provide proper justification, and to demonstrate the source of their knowledge to others, that is, they should be able to provide arguments and stand up to criticism. One crucial feature of Socrates' legacy is his disdain for the convincing power of rhetoric, which was developed and highly praised by those who made rhetoric a profession – the Sophists.[7] By contrast, Socrates sought to base conviction and belief on reason and logic alone. The use of logic, in the sense of providing arguments for one's claims and opinions, has indeed become one of the defining features of philosophy, inherited through Plato's depictions of Socrates' arguments with the sophists.

According to Plato, he was present at some of these conversations in the streets of Athens, and then reconstructed them in writing from his memory. But the extent to which he was describing actual conversations and the extent to which he was composing the dialogues as works of fiction is a matter of speculation. It is, however, reasonable, and standard, to suppose that, at least in some of the middle and late dialogues, Plato uses Socrates to voice his own views. Given this complicated relationship between author, character, and actual historical figure,

6 Introduction to *Plato: Complete Works*, edited by John M. Cooper (Hacket, 1997), p. xix.

7 See, for example, *Gorgias* 452-3, where Gorgias turns out to be a master in rhetoric, seen as the art of convincing and making people believe – but not on the basis of knowledge. As Jeffery Henderson notes, "at first the term *sophistês* was used quite generally and positively, with more less the same meaning as *sophos* ('sage' in the sense of 'learned expert'), [. . .]. But Plato applies it, ironically and with a strongly negative connotation, to a particular group who are linked to one another by a kind of family resemblance. [. . .] They tended to concentrate [. . .] upon rhetorical, ethical, and political issues rather than upon natural phenomena; they wandered throughout the Greek world, including Athens; they demonstrated their knowledge and skills in public lectures and written treaties; they offered instruction and charged fees for it (in some cases apparently becoming quite wealthy); and they provoked strong reactions among the Athenians [. . .]", Jeffery Henderson, *Early Greek Philosophy*, volume VIII, Loeb Classical Library (Harvard University Press, 2016), pp. 3-4.

from a historiographical point of view, the figures of Socrates and Plato are not entirely distinct.

And yet, from a philosophical and interpretive perspective, Socrates and Plato can be distinguished along the following lines. Most of the early Socratic dialogues (in which the historical Socrates is believed to be depicted) end with an *aporia*, that is, a paradox, or a dead-end situation. In these early dialogues, Socrates typically refutes and frustrates his opponent. He demonstrates that the sophists' pretensions to know (and hence to teach) are unjustified since they cannot define the terms they profess to know and teach. Typically, these concern the definition of truth, justice, beauty and other moral virtues. Socrates demands that, if someone claims to teach a certain virtue, they should be able to tell us what they are talking about. For example, if you claim to teach what it is to be a good person, you should be able to tell us what goodness (or virtue) is. However, Socrates casts this demand as a quest for a universal definition, of say goodness or justice, and typically produces counterexamples for any definition proposed by his opponent.[8] At the same time, Socrates himself does not propose any definitions for these terms. For this reason, the result of these dialogues seems to be entirely negative. At the same time, Socrates does not appear to be too troubled by this rather odd outcome. He happily admits his ignorance and claims the virtue of being honest, modest, and, in this respect, wiser. Unlike the sophists, he does not claim to know things he does not.[9] For example, in the context of the *Republic*'s exploration of what justice is, Thrasymachus puts Socrates under pressure to provide some answers of his own, rather than just ask questions. Thrasymachus says: "Socrates can do what he usually does: not give an answer, but, when someone else gives an answer, seize the argument and refute him." Socrates replies: "Yes, dear friend, for how can someone give an answer when one does not know and does not claim to know?" (*Republic* 337 e).

8 One may well question if this demand for a universal definition is fair or even reasonable. While it seems that a definition should cover all cases in all contexts, the Socratic dialogues provide many examples that this is not quite the case. Later philosophers, such as Wittgenstein, argue that our language does not function in this way at all, for our usage of terms may vary according to the context.

9 In the Apology (21d), Socrates says: "So I went away thinking to myself that I am wiser than that man [a public figure reputed wise]. For there is a good chance that neither of us knows what is fine and good, but he thinks he knows something when he does not know it, while I, just as I do not know, so too I do not think that I do" (cited from Henderson, 2016 vol. VIII p. 351). See also Meno 80 c-d; Theaetetus 150 b-e.

This is perhaps the deepest meaning of the Socratic ideal "to know oneself" – maintain your intellectual integrity and do not pretend to know what you don't. This skeptical attitude has certainly been one of the defining features of philosophy in years that followed and, in my own opinion, it constitutes one of the most distinctive features of philosophy at its best – not a particular science, or a discipline that claims to possess a body of positive knowledge, but rather an inquisitive and critical attitude that is not content with facile answers, even if no good alternatives are available. Seen in this way, philosophy is a method for examining theories and concepts for internal consistency and clarity.[10] More than a body of knowledge, philosophy is marked by an inquisitive attitude that seeks to settle conceptual conflicts that arise in our use of concepts. In our own inquiry in this book, we are trying to clarify the tensions that arise in the way we conceptualize the relations between the physical and the mental, the body and the soul.

It is easy to imagine, however, that not everyone would be happy with the negative results of the Socratic dialogues. As it turns out, Plato himself was one of those discontents. The idea that we cannot define virtue is troubling indeed. For how are we going to teach virtue, and how are we to judge those who do not abide by it? And so, while Socrates is seen as establishing this task and setting the standards of definition extremely high, Plato himself comes into the foreground as the philosopher who takes up this formidable challenge and attempts to provide a positive response to Socrates' negative results. In other words, Plato seeks to break from the state of *aporia* or conceptual deadlock produced time and again in the Socratic dialogues.

Plato's response to Socrates' challenge is formulated by means of a theory that was to revolutionize western philosophy, as well as the way western philosophy would conceptualize soul-body relations. This is Plato's most famous invention: his theory of ideal forms and the related distinction between the realm of Being and the realm of becoming. Briefly put, the forms may be seen as pure concepts or essences; they are immaterial, invariable, eternal, and absolute; whereas the things that take part in them or instantiate them in the material world of space and

10 And indeed today there are many branches of philosophy that focus on particular sciences, such as philosophy of physics, or biology, or law, etc.

time are ever changing and relative.[11] For example, the form of goodness (or the definition of the Good) is always one and the same; but events, deeds, or things that are said to be good are only good to a certain extent or in some respect – never absolutely. Any good deed may be contaminated by not-so-good intentions or not-so-good consequences; but the definition of the Good itself remains pure, ideal, and not contaminated by any of the particular circumstances that the deeds or things or events we call good are involved with. Another way to think of the forms is as universal properties. For example, Socrates and Plato are both wise, but wisdom itself is something that they and many others share to a certain extent. Likewise, one can think of many particular red things, such as apples, roses, and watermelons that exemplify or instantiate the pure and universal property of redness.

While Plato's main aim was to capture the definition of moral terms, the theory of forms can be illustrated through geometrical examples (which were probably in the background of Plato's theory). Thus the nature or the definition of a triangle, for example, always remain one and the same; it is a universal and timeless definition that does not tell us anything about the size or color of any particular triangle we may come across or draw. Likewise, any particular example is never pure and ideal. Its lines, for instance, are never true lines because they always admit of some thickness or width (which goes against the very definition of a line as having a single dimension) but they would have some similarity with the definition of a triangle – they are thus said to be instances of triangularity, or to instantiate the form of a triangle in some concrete way. The same goes for beautiful objects, good deeds, and red roses. All particular things exemplify the pure and ideal properties that are seen as universal. For Plato, these universals are true beings; and, as we shall see, for Aristotle, they are not.

1.2 Psyche and Soma, Soul and Body

Socrates is famous for encouraging the Athenians to take good care of their souls as the best way to take care of themselves. This is how he describes his own

11 As already hinted, the soul is not only capable of intellecting (or understanding) the forms; it is also seen as akin to the forms, insofar as it remains one and the same over time and is not material, and thus not subject to the corruption and decay of the body.

agenda: "I go around doing nothing but trying to persuade you, young and old, to care neither for your bodies nor for your possessions before taking care that your soul as good as possible" (*Apology* 30a7-b2). In the *Republic*, we find Socrates stating: "this is what I believe: contrary to the doctrine that soundness of the body produces soundness of the soul, I think that goodness of soul develops excellence in the body's capabilities" (*Republic*, III, 403d).

In these citations, it is clear that Socrates regards the soul as morally superior, and the body as inferior. Furthermore, according to him, effective care of the self is primarily care of the soul. This implies that care of the soul concerns the more important and less superficial aspects of one's person – one's mind and inner life rather than the way one looks or dresses, or one's possessions. It is remarkable how easy it is to understand this phrase today. Socrates says that we should take care of our mind and soul *before* we take care of our looks and possessions (but not instead of doing so).

For Socrates and Plato, this signifies that the true self is identified with the soul rather than with the body. This is all the more important in the context of the significance accorded to the body by the Greeks. It is well known that body was held in high regard in Greek culture and art, as well as taken care of through gymnastics and sport.[12] But, as we shall see in a moment, for Plato, the soul is (or at least should be seen as) our true master. Our conduct should be guided by reason and not by desires and urges associated with bodily needs. This implies that one can take care of one's body in isolation from one's soul, as well as take care of the soul in isolation from the body. Socrates recommends that we take care of the soul first (but not instead of the body). But the idea that care of the body can (and should) be separated from the care of the soul is one that Plato develops in his writings; it is one of the clearest expressions of the split he sees between the soul and the body. The training of the soul has a twofold purpose: (i) so that we can better engage with the world of pure forms and (2) so that we won't succumb to the temptations and inclinations of the body. Socrates holds that,

12 The importance of the Olympic games in Greek culture is a good evidence of this.

> care for the body that goes beyond simple gymnastic is excessive and among the greatest of all such obstacles [. . .]. Above all [care for the body] impedes teaching, learning, or any kind of meditation [. . .]. A man who always supposes that he is being made ill and is constantly anxious about his bodily functions will never find his way to virtue (*Republic* III 407b,c).

For Plato, then, excessive care of the body is harmful because it impedes the more important functions of the soul (teaching, learning, meditating) and, taken together, this prevents us from being virtuous.

The reason for this is that the human soul is seen as embodied; that is, it is captured in a body and constrained by it (*Timaeus* 42b). For Plato, the involvement of soul with matter has morally degrading consequences that define the human predicament. As Brooke Holmes nicely puts this, for Plato (in the *Phaedo*), "embodiment is, in essence, a pathological state".[13] While, for Plato, the soul is often seen as a master using the body as its instrument, "the body being used as an instrument [. . .] is now capable of dragging the soul around, so that it wanders, confused and dizzy, like a drunk man" (*Phaedo* 79c).

For Socrates, the soul is not only superior to the body but constitutes the true self. This is due to the soul's rational ability to rule and guide the self according to reason. Thus, an important part of the use of philosophical practice is to keep the soul free from the concerns and urges of the body. The state of embodiment is likened to the soul being caged in a body, so that it produces an aspiration for disembodiment: "a turning-inward of the soul that minimizes engagement with the world of visible (i.e., material) things and the problems they foster such as gluttony, violence, drunkenness" (Holmes 2016, 46).

This idea of turning our attention (and care) inward to our soul will have an immense impact on western philosophy and culture. The idea will receive a particularly religious twist through its reconciliation with Christianity –

13 Brooke Holmes, "The Body of Western Embodiment: Classical Antiquity and the Early History of a Problem", in *Embodiment*, ed. J. Smith (Oxford University Press, 2016), 17-50, on p. 45.

a reconciliation effected by Augustine in the fourth century.[14] Indeed, the relations between soul and body continue to be the locus of psychological, moral, and religious battlefields.[15]

As we noted, for Plato, the soul is clearly superior to the body. The superiority of the soul is related to its ethical and cognitive virtues. For example, according to Plato, a doctor's mind could cure the body because "it is the mind that cures the body" but not vice versa (*Republic* 408c). At the same time, for Plato, these ethical virtues are also related to an ontological framework; in particular, to the distinction between the realm of Being and that of becoming. The body belongs to the realm of ever-changing material things but the soul is closer to the realm of Being, for the soul is associated with thought (*phronesis*) and judgment, and thus has the ability to rule the body through its higher aspect, viz. reason. The soul also has the ability to contemplate and come to know the eternal forms (which are the true constituents of the realm of Being).[16]

Socrates argues against Alcibiades that, because the body (or soma) can neither use nor rule itself, it must have a user and a ruler. Socrates calls this user and ruler psyche and identifies it with the person (*Alcibiades* 130a-c). Since the soul exercises control over the body, it may be considered as its master and hence as the true self. This relation of soul and body as ruler and being ruled is primarily understood in

14 As we shall see in section 5, according to Augustine, the soul is placed between the material and spiritual realms; it also has the capacity to turn its gaze from the lower realm of material affairs and desires to the realm of eternal truths and laws (seen by Augustine as entailed by the eternal being of a Christian God). The locus of Platonic forms would now become the thoughts of a God. And, unlike the body, the soul can observe and immerse itself with the moral ideals captured by the eternal forms. In this regard, Augustine follows Plato and reconstructs his view in a Christian framework.

15 As we know well, from the medieval period to our own time, this is often cast as a moral battle between flesh and spirit, between the irrational pull of the body and the capacity to elevate ourselves above all of this by virtue of our rational capacity. In this picture, the body is typically associated with vices, and the mind with virtue.

16 "But when the soul investigates by itself [that is, without the body] it passes into the realm of what is pure, ever existing, immortal, and unchanging, and being akin to this, it always stays with it whenever it is by itself and can do so; it ceases to stray and remains in the same state as it is in touch with things of the same kind, and its experience then is what is called wisdom?" (*Phaedo* 79d).

an ethical rather than physiological framework.[17]

In looking at Plato's late dialogue, the *Phaedrus*, Robinson summarizes Plato's view of the relation between psyche and soma, as follows.

> Apart from the remarkable view of the soul as self-moving mover first elaborated in the Phaedros – the picture of the soul is very much (the same as) that found in earlier dialogues: life is a process of purification (from the body) and assimilation to the divine (716e-c); the soul is the true self and enjoys personal immortality (959b3-4); [. . .] a basic substantial distinction of soul and body is taken for granted (Robinson 2000, p.54).[18]

2. Aristotle (384–322 BCE): The Unitary Model of Psychic and Somatic Capacities

We now turn to present the most important alternative to Plato's dualistic model. On this alternative view, developed by Aristotle, the soul is seen as an array of capacities that are intrinsically related to their bodily realizations. Aristotle was born at Stagira in Macedonia. He was the son of Nichomachus, the court physician to the Macedonian king (Amyntas II). It is thus fairly clear that he was acquainted with the medical writings associated with Hippocrates.

17 This is especially evident in Plato's account as found in *Alcibiades* and *Republic*. Brooke Holmes argues that the relation between soul and body is not merely physiological and cannot be understood as a mere description of facts; rather to have a body indicates "a dynamic economy of alien powers" Mind and body are seen as powers whose constant negotiation defines human nature from one of its early and most influential articulations in Plato (Holmes 2016, 49).

18 Robinson summarizes the main points in Plato's account in the *Phaedo* as follows:
Soul is by its nature of greater importance than body in the body-soul nexus; there is an overriding need to care for our genuine self – the soul – over our would-be self – the body; the same soul that is life principle/life carrier is also itself alive – a person constituting the genuine self and endowed with cognitive faculties and moral sensibility; and the happiness of the soul lies not in anything provided by the world of space-time, but in eternal contemplation of the transcendental Forms.
T. M. Robinson, "The Defining Features of Mind–body Dualism in the Writings of Plato", in *Psyche and Soma*, eds. John P. Wright and Paul Potter (Oxford University Press, 2000) [Henceforth: *Psyche and Soma*], 37-56, p. 44.

This background surely played a role in the formation of his views of psyche-soma relations, as well as of his keen interest in the natural sciences. In contrast to Plato, Aristotle paid close attention to the visible world, and his investigations and careful observations of nature – including what we would call today physics, zoology, biology, medicine, and psychology – constitute the very foundation of empirical science in the western world. For Aristotle, an important part of investigating nature was establishing a classification system based on the properties of each particular thing. According to Aristotle, classification proceeds by discerning common and distinct properties of particular things. Thus, for Aristotle, the psyche (the soul) is the common and distinctive feature of all living beings. Hence, Aristotle's main book on the soul – known by its Latin title, *De Anima* – is in fact mainly a book on biology (or living beings) rather than on psychology (even if both terms are used here anachronistically).

At the age of seventeen, Aristotle entered Plato's academy in Athens, and remained there until Plato's death in 347. Between 343 and 340 he served as tutor to the young Alexander the Great, at the invitation of his father, Philip of Macedonia. In 335, he returned to Athens and founded his own school, the Lyceum, on the outskirts of the city. It was at the Lyceum that Aristotle produced the majority of his immense corpus of work. Most of his works are lost, but what survives, which include books on logic, method, physics, metaphysics, biology, zoology, ethics, politics, poetics, and many other topics, dominated science in Europe until the early modern period.

For Aristotle, as for Plato, the soul and the body have different functions. But, according to Aristotle (in contrast to Plato), soul and body are not separate; rather, they are essential features of one and the same individual. While functionally distinct (so that each soul and body performs different functions), for Aristotle, soul and body are inseparable from one another, and from the individual they constitute. In fact, not only is the soul inseparable from its body, but soul and body must co-exist as constitutive elements of a single living being, such that their co-existence is not accidental; rather, their co-existence results from a mutual dependence that defines their very nature, and, together, they define the nature of each living being. Soul and body cannot be separated, because they need one another in order to perform their proper functions. The soul is the source of life and motion through the body, which it uses as its *organon* (instrument).

The soul needs an organic body to operate on, and the (organic) body needs the soul (the psyche) to animate it. "The soul is a first actuality of a natural body which has life in potentiality" (*De Anima* ii 1, 412a27-8). But this is just a general statement about what is common to all living beings, namely their having an animating function, called psyche, for their organic bodies. The intricacy of this dependency becomes clearer when we examine more closely the particular features of living beings, such as self-nutrition, self-motion, reproduction, breathing, sight, etc.

Thus, instead of the 'hostility' and tensions we have observed in Plato, in Aristotle, soul and body not only co-exist with one another but cannot exist separately. As he says, "It's clear that the soul is not separable from the body – or that certain parts of it, if it naturally has parts, are not separable from the body" *(De Anima* ii 1, 413a3-5). Here is an analogy: just as a singer cannot sing without particular features of his vocal organs, the throat and mouth, so do the psychic capacities depend on particular bodily organs to execute their proper functions. Hence, as Philip J. van der Eijk notes, "Not only does the body need the soul in order to exist, but the soul need the body's structures in order to operate: 'psychic' powers such as perception and locomotion need the sense-organs and limbs to become operational, and these sense-organs and limbs must be suitable".[19] In this way, the functional dependence of soul and body is required for all the vital features of living beings, such as motion, nutrition, growth, perception, and generation.

According to Aristotle, the relation between soul and body is but a special case (if a very important one) of a much more general relation that holds for any existing thing whatsoever – a relation between matter and form. The special relation between soul and body (psyche and soma) plays a crucial role in Aristotle's classification scheme, viz., having a soul is the distinctive feature of all animate beings, in contrast to inanimate things. Simply put, while all things consist of matter and form, only living beings are unions of soul (as their form) and a body (as their matter). The soul is seen as the principle or source of life within all livings beings.

Thus, for Aristotle, any true being is a hylomorphic union (*hyle* is matter; *morphes* is form) in which the form and the matter are essential constituents. While this applies to any being whatever, in living beings, the soul is what gives matter some

19 Philip J. van der Eijk, "Aristotle's Psychophysiological Account of the Soul-Body Relationship", in Psyche and Soma, p. 64).

of its features, but the soul can act only through the particular organs of a body. And this is why different kinds of living beings, such as vegetables, animals, and humans have different kinds of soul, vegetative, sensitive, and rational, respectively. The well-known (and historically extremely influential) Latin rendering of the Greek psyche – *anima* – makes this point evident to English readers: at risk of some simplification, we can say that the soul *animates* matter – to animate is to make something live.

For Plato, by contrast, only human beings have a soul. As we shall see, Descartes will resurrect precisely this point. Indeed, Aristotle developed his view in contrast to (and as an explicit alternative for) Plato's view of the nature of being. According to Plato, the only things that truly exist are the unchanging and universal forms, which we can think of as eternal concepts or as essences of things. Any thing that admits of some variation cannot be regarded as a true being because any change necessarily affects the very identity of that thing. Hence, any change would imply that that particular thing no longer exists. This is similar to the reasoning in Heraclitus's famous claim that one cannot enter the same river twice. Any flow of water implies that the river is no longer the same.

Some radical conclusions follow from this observation. It turns out that truly existing things cannot belong to the purely material world, whose very essence is to change, to grow and decay, to generate and degenerate. For this reason, Plato considers the material world to be a realm of mere appearance and phenomena. The truly existing forms, on the other hand, do not belong in the material world of space and time. Because of this, they can only be grasped by reason, and by reason alone. Particular things instantiate the forms in space and time and thus are sensible; these instances, we perceive through our senses. As noted above, for Plato, there is a clear-cut distinction between the intelligible realm, accessible by reason alone, and the sensible material realm, accessible by the senses. What this means is that sensible things, such as chairs, cats, etc., are not true beings (due to their ever-changing nature) but only appearances – things that appear to us but do not truly (or fully) exist.

Aristotle seeks to provide an alternative account, and indeed an entirely different metaphysical picture emerges from his philosophy. For Aristotle, what truly exists are not abstract and universal forms (or properties) but rather individual things that we can perceive with our senses. Aristotle's view gives rise to a metaphysics of individual things, in distinction to Plato's metaphysics of universal forms or properties. *This* man or *this* horse are Aristotle's typical examples – things that are readily familiar to us and thus are easier for our common sense to accept as existing. But how then can Aristotle account for the fact that a particular horse or man are constantly changing – precisely the problem that Plato resolved by abstracting away from material things? It is interesting to observe that Aristotle responds to this problem by means of the (constancy of) the soul. While the material configuration of an individual man or a horse can change, his soul remains one and the same through these changes. In fact, to a large extent, it is the soul that informs these changes; the soul is not only a principle of life but also a principle of change that, nevertheless, itself remains the same.

Aristotle further accounts for the changes that occur in natural things by drawing a distinction between properties that vary and properties that remain the same. While some of the individual's properties may change, their essential properties persist through the individual's life. For example, while the color of a person's hair (or having any, for that matter) typically changes over time, the person's rational capacity, which defines the very nature of the human species, persists through these changes. Thus, the very essence of individual things, informed by their individual forms, remains, according to Aristotle, invariable. In living things, the very dynamical principle, capable of actualizing the thing's nature, and persisting through change, is, as we noted, the soul. In this way, Aristotle places the thing's essence inside it. To be more precise, for Aristotle, the form of an individual is not external to it but rather an intrinsic (and constitutive) part of its nature. One might say that, for Aristotle, the world does not take its shape from ideas (as in Plato) but rather ideas take their shape from the world.

Aristotle often exemplifies the soul-body relation through an analogy (also used by Socrates and Plato) between an art (*techne*) and the instruments it employs. The soul relates to the body as an art relates to its instrument (say, as music relates to a musical instrument), so that, if a musician is to play an instrument, their *techne* and their instrument must be suitable for each another. For example, only an artist who acquired the art of violin playing can play the violin. A drummer, a painter, or a philosopher who lack the proper skills would not be able to play the violin to produce music (let alone good music).

Let us observe, however, that Aristotle's examples of musical instruments and working tools, such as the axe in *De Anima*[20], are artifacts (human-made); and, in the case of artifacts, the fittingness between the art and the instrument is intentionally produced by humans. In organic (living) beings, however, the fundamental fittingness between soul and body is natural and requires no external intervention of an agent (the musician in our example). Rather, the organon of each organic body is the soul's proper instrument (of that individual). In living beings, there is no need for an external agent (say a musician to intervene between the art of music and the actual playing of it) because the soul is seen precisely as the inherent source of life, that is, the source of locomotion, self-nutrition, and generation, which are the distinctive features of living beings. As one might put this, the relationship between soul and body is explained by the fact that the soul is the agent of functions that take place in the organic body.

As Stephen Menn puts this,

> The soul-body relation is like the artisan-instrument relation. Aristotle begins [his *De Anima or Peri psychès*] with this model and refines it into the art-instrument relation. But the soul-body relation is still not like the relation of an ordinary art to its instrument because the soul moves its body from within, as an internal and not merely external entelechy of the organic body, which must therefore be a natural body. Ordinary arts do move their instruments, and use their instruments to perceive individuals, but they do so only from without, by being present in some other body. But the first instrument of any art, or any art-like power, must be some 'marvel' that the power moves from within, [...] And a living body is just such a marvel.[21]

It is worth emphasizing the productive power of the analogy with art; Aristotle is stressing here that the soul has a productive and generative power typical of living things. Aristotle here extends the capacity for self-nutrition (necessary for any living being, on his account) to the capacity to reproduce and multiply, that is, produce offspring, such that "like would beget like." While this observation that, e.g., dogs do not produce cats – may seem trivial, it is not; for its explanation

20 *De Anima* Book 2 chapter 1 412b.

21 Stephen Menn, "Aristotle's Definition of Soul and the Program of *De Anima*" in *Oxford Studies of Ancient Philosophy*, Volume XXII, (2002): 83-139, pp. 138-39.

depends on the individual and unique soul of each animal (or living being), which is naturally suited to a particular organic body. This makes it evident that, for Aristotle, the soul-body relation is not at all accidental but rather necessary for describing and understanding the organic world.

It would be useful to consider a particular case that exemplifies the close and informative relation that Aristotle conceives between the soul and the body as a relation between the capacities of the soul and their manifestation in one's emotional and physiological state. Aristotle goes into a detailed analysis along just these lines, with respect to anger, melancholia, and paranoia. In the first chapter of *De Anima*, Aristotle writes that, "the affections of the soul, insofar at least as they are such things as anger and fear, are in this way inseparable from the natural matter of living things" (403b). Let's look at the telling example of anger (*De Anima* 403a-b). Anger may be given a physical account, in terms of blood boiling around the heart (*De Anima* 403a 31-b1), and it may be accounted for in terms of a desire for revenge; both are legitimate, but the relation with body (i.e., the physical account) is fundamentally constitutive of anger, for there is no psychic process separate from a body – "all the affections of the soul involve the body (*De Anima* 403a 5-15).[22] Health and sanity are likewise associated with balance of cold and hot; and mental trouble, such as melancholia, and paranoia is associated with some physiological imbalances. Thus, we can conclude that, for Aristotle, a full account of the affections must be given in terms of physiological description, such that what we call 'psychology' today is, for Aristotle, psycho-physiology"[23].

While limitations of space, and concern for the reader's patience, dictate that we can only focus here on Aristotle's most influential work on the soul, *De Anima*, it is worth noting that Aristotle implements this approach in investigating the relation between the psychic faculties and their bodily organs in a wide array of contexts, such as the motion of animals, sleep, dreams, memory, breathing, etc. All these topics are the titles of separate treatises that Aristotle dedicates to the investigation of these phenomena. While the medical concepts he employs in his analysis are clearly outdated, the intrinsic connection between psychic capacities and their

22 See Martha Nussbaum, *Aristotle's De Motu Animalium* (Princeton University Press, 1985), pp. 147-48.

23 van der Eijk, 2000, p. 66. See also David Charles "Aristotle on desire and action" in Frede and Reis eds., *Body and Soul in Ancient Philosophy*, 2009 and "Aristotle's Psychological Theory", in *Proceedings of the Boston Area Colloquium of Ancient Philosophy*, 2009.

bodily exercise is not; in fact, we find his approach most useful in order to deal with the problem of mind–body relations at stake here.

To sum up, the soul, for Aristotle, is not a substance separate from the body of a living being; rather, it can be seen as the functional organization of an organic body (*soma organikon*). But, in important respects, talk of the soul is misleading. For while the notion of *the* soul serves as the common feature of all living beings, in reality it breaks down into a variety of capacities and powers that characterize different kinds of living beings, as well as different functions of human beings and other non-rational animals. Thus, for Aristotle, 'soul' is just an umbrella term for a variety of capacities that living beings can exercise. This deflationary account implies that the soul is nothing over and above capacities such as nutrition, growth, sight, perception, imagination, and thought. As we shall see, this position will turn out to play a crucial role in our own approach to the mind–body problem in this book. It is also a view that has been lost on many contemporary philosophers of mind, for they either do not really look back at the history of philosophy beyond Descartes or they fail to see the radical conceptualization of the soul as a name for various capacities, rather than as an entity.

3. Plotinus (205–270 C.E.): Soul and Body, Good and Evil

As we have seen above, for Aristotle, matter involves the potential to receive form and hence has a positive – indeed, an essential – contribution to being. For Plotinus, by contrast, matter is seen as the privation of form and being and, like Plato, he attributes a lower degree of reality to the sensible world.

Plotinus associates matter with evil – for him, evil just is the same as the privation of being.[24] As such, evil stems from a lack of form and/or intelligibility (see

24 In composing this, I was helped by Lloyd Gerson's excellent piece on Plotinus in the Stanford Encyclopedia of Philosophy. Gerson, Lloyd, "Plotinus", *The Stanford Encyclopedia of Philosophy* (Summer 2014 Edition), Edward N. Zalta (ed.), plato.stanford.edu/archives/sum2014/entries/plotinus/.

Ennead II.4[25]). Plotinus holds this in deliberate opposition to Aristotle, who distinguished matter from privation (see *Ennead* II.4.16, 3-8).

In Plotinus, we find a very clear and influential articulation of something that was already present in Plato, namely, a clear affinity between Being and goodness. Indeed, the ultimate source of Being, from which every individual being originates, Plotinus calls the Good or the One. Being and goodness descend down to what he terms the Intellect, and then further down to the Soul. We thus have three degrees of reality: The One or the Good; Intellect; and Soul (see *Ennead* V.1; *Ennead* V.9). At the lowest level, we find matter, which is lack of being or privation; and, as such, matter also constitutes the cause of evil.

The drama of human life is played against the background of this alignment of good and evil. In fact, in the human context, the tension between good and evil is translated into the alignment of soul and matter. In his radicalized version of Plato, Plotinus identifies the soul with goodness and the body with evil. Further, the human person is essentially a soul employing a body as an instrument of its temporary embodied life (see *Ennead* I.1). Plotinus thus draws a line between the person and the composite of soul and body. A person is identical with a cognitive agent or a subject of cognitive states (see *Ennead* I.1.7). An embodied person is, therefore, a conflicted entity, for it is capable both of thought and of being the subject of non-cognitive states, such as appetites and emotions. Needless to say, human beings find themselves torn between and pulled in these opposite directions. Much like in Plato, the body draws us towards evil, and the soul (and intellects) are capable of drawing us towards the Good by contemplating it.

As we have seen, Plato developed Socrates' notion that one should take care of the soul *before* (but not instead) of the body. In Plotinus (as well as other Neoplatonic philosophers), the body is described as the jail of the soul and is vilified completely. Thus, from Socrates' 'take care for the soul before the body', Plotinus moves to a clear 'take care of the Soul *instead* of the body'.

25 The *Enneads* are the complete treatises of Plotinus, edited by his student, Porphyry. The standard citation of the Enneads follows Porphyry's division into book, treatise, and chapter. Hence *Ennead* IV.8.1 refers to book (or *Ennead*) four, treatise eight, chapter one.

The possibility of conducting a good life is premised on a detachment from the objects of embodied desires. For one who is ideally an intellect, longing for the Good can only be satisfied by cognitive identification with all that is intelligible. In this, Plotinus seems very close to Plato. But the ethical dimensions of the opposition between the soul and the body are more clearly marked. If his view is essentially Platonic, one might wonder why, in that case, Plotinus is so important for the history of the mind–body relation. The answer is that Plotinus' writings provide a crucial link between Greek philosophy and its development in the monotheistic western tradition, for the western adoption of Platonism was funneled by Neoplatonic thinkers. This connection was taken up, in an extremely vivid and influential way, through the work of Augustine, to which we now turn.

4. Augustine (354–430): Reconciling the Platonic Soul and Christian Faith

It is hard to exaggerate the impact that Augustine's work exerted on western civilization and philosophy. Appropriating ancient philosophy to the rising Christian religion of his time, his views dominated the west throughout the late Middle Ages, and exerted a strong influence far beyond, right up to the present. His writings, especially his *Confessions*, are still widely read, and there is every reason to think they will continue to be just as widely read in the future. Augustine effects a very powerful reconciliation between Greek philosophy and Christianity, although the impact of Augustine's work has been far wider even than this, since this reconciliation is equally applicable to the Jewish and Islamic traditions as well.

Born in Tagaste in North Africa (currently Algeria) to a pagan father and a Christian mother (St Monica), Augustine studied rhetoric at Carthage, and then taught in Rome and Milan. He was initially drawn to Manichaeism and to skepticism. At the age of 31, through studying Plotinus, he converted to Christianity (386) and later became Bishop of Hippo in North Africa. He produced an immense corpus of written works, among the most well known are his *Confessions*, in which he recounts his spiritual Odyssey, and the *City of God.*

An important aspect of Augustine's influence pertains to the very view of philosophy he articulated – this is the view of philosophy as theology – a view that was to dominate western philosophy until the early modern period (and beyond). According to Augustine, the role of philosophy is to justify by reason the tenets of Christianity accepted on faith.[26] Indeed the major function of philosophy, at least until Descartes, has been theological in character; the aim of theology was not to discover new truths by the light of reason but rather to provide rational explanation for the truths already provided through revealed religion.

Interpretative questions of scripture offered plenty of work for this approach, not to mention the problem of evil, the question of creation, and of the Trinity, all of which receive thorough attention from Augustine. This approach to philosophy was still accepted by some philosophers in the early modern period such as Leibniz, but vehemently rejected by others, such as Spinoza.[27] As we shall see, Augustine's influence on Descartes, both in his style and in the arguments for the existence of God and the soul, is both very subtle and very significant.[28]

Upon his conversion to Christianity, Augustine's main philosophical project became to reconcile Christian faith with Greek philosophy, and especially Plato, as mediated through the works of "some Platonists". As he recounts in his *Confessions*, the effect of his readings of Plotinus was nothing less than an intellectual revelation. Among other things, he sought to reconcile Plato's intellectual elitism with the inclusiveness of Christianity, so that eternal truths – truths that Plato identified with eternal forms – would become accessible to any willing person, and not just to highly educated philosophers. The first step was to reconcile a Christian notion of God, as the Creator and the source of moral law, with the Platonic realm of eternal Forms.

26 See, for example, On the Free Choice of the Will 1.3.6.16 in: Augustine On the Free Choice of the Will, On Grace and Free Choice, and Other Writings, ed. and trans., Peter King (Cambridge, 2010), p. 6

27 In his *Political Theological Treatise* (especially chapter 15), Spinoza draws a sharp distinction between theology and philosophy: philosophy aims to discover truths but religion (and the Bible especially) aims to instill obedience. While philosophy is a theoretical pursuit, religion is a practical one. For Spinoza, they have nothing in common and the major error in theology is to confuse them.

28 On this topic, see Stephen Menn's *Descartes and Augustine* (Cambridge University Press, 1998).

Augustine approached this task by interpreting the Platonic realm of Being – the eternal and invariable Forms – as a realm of divine thought. In this interpretation, the Platonic self-sufficient forms came to be seen as the thoughts in God's understanding. In the Christian Platonic tradition, God was seen as an agent whose intelligible activity – his thinking – consists of the conception of all true Beings, i.e., all Platonic Forms.

Likewise, the Greek distinction between Being and becoming, the intelligible and the sensible, was transposed into a distinction between the objects of God's thought – also seen as the ideal model of creation – and the created world. This transposition introduces both agency (activity) and will into the divine realm as well as into that of creatures.

The next move in Augustine's reconciliation is the following. He integrates the Platonic distinction between degrees of being and Aristotle's hierarchical view of the soul, and thus establishes a hierarchy of being within nature. He distinguishes between three levels: merely existing things or material things, living things, and thinking things. He writes,

> the [kind of] nature that merely exists (and neither lives nor understands) ranks below the [kind of] nature that not only exists but also lives (but does not understand) – the soul of the non-human animals is of this sort. This nature in turn ranks below the nature that at once exists, lives, and understands – for example, the rational mind of a human being. (*On Free Choice of the Will* 2.6.13)

Above the rational soul, there is the realm of being itself, consisting of eternal truths or forms – Augustine identifies this realm with God. Thanks to their having a rational soul, human beings are placed midway below the divine realm and above the realm of other (non-rational) living beings and material things. Further, thanks to the rational soul, human beings are capable of knowledge in general, and knowledge of God in particular. And, as in Plato, knowledge of the realm of Forms can be obtained by means of the rational soul.

Within the hierarchy of nature, the rational soul is above material things, living things, and sensing things; while matter changes in time and place, the soul changes only in time. Still, the soul is below God who is Being itself and does not change at all. At the same time, the soul is created in the image of God[29]: being rational, and being endowed with cognitive capacities, it can access the divine eternal truths. This middle position, between the lowest level of being and the highest, makes human nature susceptible to opposing inclinations: on the one hand, we are drawn downwards through the lower part of our nature – our desires and urges that draw us to the world of sense; but, at the same time, we are capable of turning upwards through reason to the eternal truths entailed in God.

The crucial move for integrating this hierarchy of being with religion and morality is the following: According to Augustine, by an effort of will, a person can turn her gaze inwards to her soul. Looking inwards, however, implies a moral assent by contemplating the good. By looking inwards, Augustine thinks that a person of ordinary intelligence may be drawn to the ideal (Platonic) world – and thus come to know the Truth – rather than to the material world. For Augustine, by turning inside (rather than outside to the world of sense and desires), we can reach God and the moral truths through the mediation of our soul. As he writes,

> I entered into my innermost self [. . .] and with whatever sort of eye it is that my soul possesses, I saw [. . .] an immutable light higher than my mind (*Confessions*, FVP 1-5[30]).

Augustine describes the moment of his conversion as a realization of this highest degree of truth, identified with Being itself (that which is) in distinction from everything that becomes: "So in the flash of a trembling glance [my mind] attained that that which is (*id quod est*)" and "I was certain that you are [i.e., God is or exists]" (*Confessions* 7.17.23).

According to Augustine, when we look inside ourselves, we can all see the very same Truth. Indeed, our mind, our reason, is identified with truth itself (*On Free Choice of the Will* 2.13.35). While the mind exists within the body, for Augustine, the mind is not a prisoner there, but rather this is where its potential for greatest

29 "The human being is made in the image of God in to in the body, but in the mind itself" (Jo. ev.tr 23.10, cited from *The Cambridge Companion to Augustine, 2nd edition* (Cambridge University Press, 2014), p. 139.

30 Cited from David Vincent Meconi, Eleonore Stump, eds., *The Cambridge Companion to Augustine, 2nd edition* (Cambridge University Press, 2014), p. 26.

happiness lies: "By turning down toward the lowest, the soul lives unhappily, but by turning back toward the highest it lives blessedly."[31]

At this juncture the role of the will becomes crucial. Because of the soul's volitional capacity, one can either sin or be virtuous. We can either succumb to lower earthly urges (and thus turn away from God) or, by turning inward and attending to one's rational soul, we can connect with the realm of truth. Both options are open to us. This is the particular situation of human beings that makes us moral creatures. By virtue of the soul, we are capable of either aversion, turning away from God, or conversion, turning back to God.[32]

In line with his emphasis on looking inwards, into our soul, Augustine also produces a new argument for mind–body dualism. This argument, found mainly in his book *On Trinity* (*De Trinitate*) rests on Augustine's assumption that the mind has a unique ability to know itself.[33]

"For what is so intimately known, and what knows itself to be itself, that through which all other things are likewise known, that is, the soul itself?" (*De Trinitate*, 8 6, 9).[34] He goes on to clarify that the soul knows itself best, so that it can attend to its nature or essence, by looking inwards[35]:

> Since our inquiry concerns the nature of the mind [mens], let us remove from consideration all knowledge obtained externally through the senses of the body,

31 Ep. 18.2, cited from Stump, E. and Kretzmann, N., eds., *The Cambridge Companion to Augustine, 1st edition* (Cambridge University Press, 2001), p. 117.

32 This also reveals Augustine's approach to the question of evil, a question that tormented him for many years from his youth to his own conversion. On this point, see *On the Free Choice of the Will* 1.2.4.10. Augustine's solution is that the source of evil lies in our own nature and will, and not in God. But then why did God create us with a will (and a capacity to sin) in the first place? If God were to create us without a will, sin could be avoided. But, in that case, he would also create us without the capacity to become virtuous. And, if so, the whole issue of morality would be meaningless.

33 For this reason, it may be regarded as an internalist argument for mind–body dualism. See Gareth Matthews' "Internalist Reasoning in Augustine for Mind–body Dualism" in *Psyche and Soma*, pp. 133-146.

34 For similar passages, see also *De Trinitate* 9 4.4 and 9 12.8.

35 This is strongly related to what Charles Taylor calls the internalization of the self, that is, the tendency to identify the self through an inward gaze. See Charles Taylor, *Sources of the Self* (Harvard University Press, 1989), chapter 7 and especially pp. 134-35.

> and attend more diligently to that which we have set down: that every mind knows and is certain concerning itself. (*De Trinitate*, 10 10, 14)

By attending to the self-reflective ability of the mind to know itself, Augustine also seeks to remove some troubling doubts. Indeed, he argues that the very awareness of ourselves as doubting can, in fact, serve to remove doubts and arrive at certainty:

> who would doubt that he lives, remembers, understands, wills, thinks, knows, and judges? For even if he doubts, he lives; if he doubts, he remembers why he doubts; if he doubts, he understands that he doubts; if he doubts, he wishes to be certain; if he doubts, he thinks; if he doubts, he knows that he does not know. Whoever then doubts about anything else ought never to be doubt about all of these; for if they were not, he would be unable to doubt about anything at all. (*De Trinitate* 10 10. 14)

Augustine goes further to argue that the mind's self-knowledge and awareness also allow us to know the essence of the mind as something incorporeal. He writes,

> All of these people overlook that fact that the mind knows itself, even when it seeks itself [. . .] But we cannot say that anything is known while its essence is [*substantia*] is unknown. (*De Trinitate* 10 10.16)

Since the mind is certain that it thinks, understands, wills, as we have seen above, it is certain that these are its essential features; but since it is not certain whether it is air or fire or anything bodily, the mind knows that its essence consists in none of these. Augustine concludes that the essence of the mind – thinking, willing, understating – is distinct from any bodily features.

5. Thomas Aquinas (1225–1274): The Aristotelian Soul and Christian Faith

If Augustine is responsible for integrating Plato's philosophy into a Christian (and monotheistic) framework in the early middle ages, Aquinas is responsible for doing the same for Aristotle in the late middle ages, some thousand years later. The rich Aristotelian corpus was unknown in the west for almost a millennium. But once significant parts were rediscovered and translated from the Greek into Arabic and then to Latin, Aristotle's influence became immense. Indeed, the centrality of Aristotle among late medieval thinkers is manifest in the way that he gets referred to simply as "The Philosopher" (whereas Plato and the church fathers are referred to by their names).

Thomas Aquinas thus lived at a critical juncture of western culture, a time in which the west was being exposed to the wide range of texts written by Aristotle. This exposure, among other things, put the *modus vivendi* between reason and faith that had obtained for centuries along the lines articulated by Augustine in question; it questioned the idea that the role of reason and philosophy was to justify faith.

Aquinas also lived during the time of the founding, and subsequent flourishing, of the first universities in Europe. Indeed, Aquinas himself is a product of university education. As a child, he was educated in the abbey of Montecassino and then moved to the University of Naples. He completed his schooling at the University of Paris, where he studied theology. In Naples, he was exposed to the 'new' philosophy of Aristotle. Indeed, one of the most significant attractions of Aristotle, and one of the reasons for his extensive influence throughout the later middle ages, was the product of the new universities' urgent need for textbooks, especially on the secular aspects of education and the sciences. The Aristotelian corpus provided a dream source for this, for it could provide systematic works on any topic one might desire: logic, rhetoric, poetics, physics, ethics, metaphysics, and of course psychology (if we may use this anachronistic term for his book On the Soul (usually referred to, precisely thanks to its popularity in this period, by its Latin title, *de Anima*).

De Anima quickly became *the* medieval textbook of philosophy of mind.[36] The best evidence for this is the sheer number of commentaries on *De Anima* by the central thinkers of the time. Aquinas is among them: he wrote his commentary on *De Anima* late in life, and his most important treatment of the mind appears in questions 75 to 89 in the first part of his *magnum* opus, the *Summa Theologiae*.

36 See Anthony Kenny, *Aquinas on Mind* (Routledge, 1993), p. 19.

Aristotle's view of the soul-body relations poses an obvious difficulty, indeed, a threat for a philosopher of a Christian faith: how can one reconcile Aristotle's view with a belief in the immortality of the soul and its apparent separation from the body upon death. As we shall see, this is precisely the main challenge that informs Aquinas' writing on the relations between body and soul.

Indeed, Aquinas' starting point is clearly Aristotelian: the soul is "the first principle of life" or the distinguishing mark of living or animate things. "In order to inquire into the nature of the [human] soul, we have to presuppose that 'soul' [*anima*] is what we call the first principle of life in things that live among us; for we call living things animate [or ensouled]" (ST I article 75. Ic).[37]

Now, the question that interests Aquinas most concerns the human soul. More specifically, in order to reconcile Aristotle's views with Christian faith, Aquinas needs to account for the soul's subsistence after death, its non-corporeal nature, as well as the unique moral place that human beings occupy in the scheme of nature, now seen as created by a Christian God.

As Norman Kretzmann observes,

> In a theory that recognizes the soul of a plant as a merely nutritive first intrinsic principle of life, and the soul of a nonhuman animal as a nutritive + sensory principle of that sort [i.e., an Aristotelian theory], it comes as no surprise that the soul of a human being is to be analyzed as nutritive + sensory + rational. Aquinas thinks of the human soul not only as three nested, cooperating substantial forms, however, but as a single form that gives a human being its specifically human mode of existence, including potentialities and functions, from its genetic makeup on up to its most creative talents. And so he will often simply identify the human soul as the rational soul, an identification made entirely appropriate by the fact that *rational* is the differentia [the distinctive feature] of the human species in the genus *animal*.[38]

37 See also ST I q.76 art. 1: "It is clear that the first thing with which a body lives is the soul. Life is manifested in different activities at different levels of life, but the soul is that with which first we perform each one of the activities of life" (see Anthony Kenny, *Aquinas on Mind* (Routledge, 1993), p. 147).

38 Norman Kretzmann, "Philosophy of Mind", in *The Cambridge Companion to Aquinas*, eds. Eleonore Stump and Norman Kretzmann (Cambridge University Press, 1993), 128-159, p. 131.

This is clearly consistent with the Aristotelian definition of the human being as a rational animal. Further, Aquinas rejects the Platonic view that the real human being (the "inward man") is the soul which treats the body as a mere instrument. A fully human life and experience are not possible without a body, for even if intellectual activity may not imply a particular organ, having sense experience does. According to Aquinas, a human being is not merely a thinking animal but also a sensing/perceiving animal. If having sense-experience is an essential feature of humans and sense experience implies a body, it follows that the Platonic view is not acceptable.

> Since sense-experience is an activity of a human being, though not restricted to humans, it is clear that a human being is not a soul alone but is a compound of soul and body (ST I 75, 4, cited from Kenny 1993, 137).

At the same time, Aquinas seeks to establish that,

> The principle of the operation of the intellect, which we call the human soul, must be said to be an incorporeal and subsistent principle. For it is plain that by his intellect a human being can know corporeal things (ST 1, 75, cited from Kenny 1993, 132).

This means that "the human soul, which is called the intellect or mind, is something non-bodily and subsistent" (ST 1 75 2c; Kenny 1993, 133). As Anthony Kenny remarks, Aquinas' "argument for immortality stands or falls with the argument for self-subsistence" (Kenny 1993, 143). The argument rests on the Aristotelian view that the soul is the substantial form of the body.

> But the soul is a substantial form, and hence it must be the form and actuality not only of the whole but of every part. That is why when the soul departs, what is left is not a human or an animal anymore, except by a figure of speech, in the same way as a picture or a sculpture may be; and the same holds, as Aristotle says, for hand and eye and for flesh and bone. This is exhibited in the fact that no part of the body continues to function after the soul has departed. (ST I q. 76 art. 8)

Aquinas also relies on Aristotle's remark that the intellectual activity (or thinking), which is the distinctive feature of humans, requires no particular organ and must be seen as "*act per se*", or an act that does not require a bodily organ.[39] Hence, Aquinas maintains that the soul is capable of existing apart from the living body after the death of the body, because the soul is essentially subsistent and thus incorruptible:

> Therefore the nature of the human intellect is not only incorporeal, but it is also a substance, that is, something subsistent (ST 75 art. 2).

In article 6, Aquinas follows up on this point and concludes that "every intellectual substance is incorruptible". And since only the human soul is an intellectual substance, it is the only one that subsists. In this way, Aquinas accomplishes his task of reconciling the immortality of the human soul with Aristotle's doctrine as spelled out in *De Anima*.

6. Descartes (1596–1650): The Rise of Early Modern Philosophy and the Current Mind–Body Problem

René Descartes was born at La Haye, near Tours in 1596. He attended the Jesuit College of La Flèche, took a law degree at the University of Poitiers, and then joined the Dutch army. He traveled widely in Europe and in the winter of 1619 had a vision of composing a new (mathematical) system of the sciences, based on reason alone, thereby ridding himself of the beliefs and prejudices acquired at school. In 1628, he composed his *Rules for the Directions of the Mind* (*ingenii*), which expresses his desire to derive every piece of knowledge from natural reason, as well as a method for doing so. In 1633, upon the condemnation of Galileo by the church, Descartes withdrew the publication of his treatise *The World*. His *Discourse on Method* appeared in 1638, accompanied by essays on optics, meteorology, and geometry. His most influential book, *Meditations on First Philosophy*, was published in 1641, and a second edition with objections from his contemporaries, along with his own replies, was published a year later. In 1649, he went to Sweden on the invitation of Queen Christina and published *The Passions of the Soul*. He died shortly after, in Stockholm, in 1650.

39 "[. . .] the intellectual principle which we call the mind or the intellect has an operation *per se* apart from the body". (ST 75 art. 2)

Descartes' philosophy marks a radical break in western thought. And it is for a good reason that he is regarded as the founding father of modern philosophy (even if this has perhaps been slightly exaggerated). Descartes sought to put an end to the traditional science (*scientia*, understood in the broad sense of knowledge) and to build a new science from scratch. Descartes himself is very explicit about this ambitious agenda. He claims to attempt nothing less than a completely new start and a complete eradication of the scholastic/Aristotelian science and philosophy that had been dominant in the west since the late middle ages.

Indeed, Descartes avows that he will take nothing for granted and will rebuild the whole edifice of knowledge on new, firm grounds. In order to do so, he argues, one must begin by eradicating any belief that may be susceptible to doubt. Only that which cannot be doubted – 'cannot' in the logical, not psychological sense – would be regarded as true and certain. Thus, in the opening paragraph of his *Mediations*, he writes, "I realized that it was necessary, once in the course of my life, to demolish everything completely and start again right from the foundations", in order to establish the sciences on firm and lasting grounds.[40] "Reason now leads me to think," Descartes writes, "that I should hold back my assent from opinions which are not completely certain and indubitable just as carefully as I do from those which are patently false. So, for the purpose of rejecting all my opinions, it will be enough if I find in each of them at least some reason for doubt" (CSM II 12). As he puts it succinctly in his Principles of Philosophy (article 1), "The seeker after truth must [...] doubt everything."[41]

Descartes thus decides to regard any claim to knowledge as false unless it is proven otherwise – that is, unless it proves resilient to doubt.[42] The task Descartes sets himself in his first meditation is to show that what we commonly perceive as true may in fact turn out to be illusory and therefore false. Indeed, he argues that we may not even be able to tell whether we are awake or in a dream,

40 Descartes René, *The Philosophical Writings of Descartes*, ed. John Cottingham, John Cottingham, Robert Stoothoff, Dugald Murdoch (Cambridge University Press, 1985), Vol II, p. 12. [Henceforth: CSM]

41 CSM I 193

42 "Since I now wished to devote myself solely the search of truth, I thought it necessary to do the very opposite and reject as if absolutely false everything in which I could imagine the least doubt, in order to see if I was left believing anything that was entirely indubitable". (*Discourse on Method*, part four, CSM I 126-27)

for dreams often have acute sensations that seem just as real as our perceptions when we are awake. It turns out that even "truths" such as 2 + 2 = 4 may be doubtful, for, as Descartes argues, there may be an evil and powerful demon that twists our perceptions and thoughts, so that we are completely mislead, even in the things that seem most certain. It is possible, Descartes suggests, that "a malicious demon of the utmost power and cunning has employed all his energies in order to deceive me" (CSM II 15). This radical hypothesis renders any presumed knowledge potentially false. Indeed, imagine yourself to be in a *Matrix*-like situation, where all that you take to be reality is in fact an appearance of reality cunningly imposed on you by a sophisticated program that can control your perceptions. Such a scenario, by the way, is directly inspired by the thought experiments in the *Mediations*.

It is worth pausing here to reflect on the boldness of Descartes' call for such radical doubt. Implicit in Descartes' starting point is the rejection of all traditional authority, including the authority of the church, the church fathers, the ancient philosophers, Aristotle, Plato, and Augustine, and indeed a rejection of any previous claim to knowledge or faith. In fact, even the existence and authority of God are put into question. But on top of all this – and this is the most daring point – is the idea that any credible belief must pass the test of *human* reason – what Descartes calls clear and distinct perception by the natural light.

In his earlier works, the *Rules for the Direction of the Mind* and the *Discourse on Method Descartes* makes it clear that his method of doubt is part and parcel of what he takes to be the only valid method of reasoning (and one that he himself never calls into doubt), that is, the method of reason practiced in geometry. What Descartes has in mind is the method of deduction, that is, drawing valid conclusions from true assumptions (or axioms). Descartes calls his method the geometrical method and devotes the two books mentioned above to its exposition.

Descartes' commitment to his geometrical method must, however, make the reader wonder. For, as anyone who has done geometry in school knows, the Euclidean method begins with axioms, that is, propositions assumed to be true. But, as already noted, Descartes will allow for no such thing – any assumption is susceptible to doubt. He wants a completely new start, based on no assumptions at all. And so, in order to apply the geometrical method without any assumptions, as he attempts to do in his *Meditations*, Descartes has to prove, rather than assume, some foundational truths – or at least one such truth. And, indeed, this is the whole point of seeking something that would not be susceptible to doubt. As he notes, "Archimedes used to demand just one firm and immovable point in order to shift the entire earth; so I too can hope for great things if I manage to find just one thing, however slight, that is certain and unshakable".[43] As it turns out, the method of doubt leads precisely to such an indubitable truth.

For suppose "there is a deceiver of supreme power and cunning who is deliberately and constantly deceiving me. In that case, I too undoubtedly exist, if he is deceiving me" (CSM II 17). Even, if there is nothing in the world, no sky, no earth, no minds, no bodies. Does it follow that I too do not exist? No", says Descartes. In this way, the process of casting doubt on everything leads the meditator to see that there is one thing he or she cannot doubt, that is, that I am, or that I exist as long as I doubt or think.[44] Hence, Descartes concludes that "this proposition, I am, I exist is necessarily true whenever it is put forward by me or conceived in my mind" (CSM II 17).

In the *Discourse on Method* (1637), Descartes expresses this point with his famous slogan "I think, therefore I am"[45]. The point is that, if I think, I also know that I think and thus cannot deny that I exist, so long as I think. And so the one thing I cannot doubt (as I attempt to doubt everything) is my own existence. And of this point at least I can be absolutely certain. On the face of it, this

43 Beginning of 2nd meditation, CSM II 16

44 In spite of Descartes' radical stance, the lack of respect he shows towards his predecessors, and the entirely new role he ascribes to human reason, his method closely resembles the way Augustine employed the method of doubt. Recall Augustine's words "if he doubts, he wishes to be certain; if he doubts, he thinks; if he doubts, he knows that he does not know" (*De Trinitate* 10 10. 14). As John Cottingham points out, this similarity cuts deeper. Like Augustine, Descartes has a conception of truth that requires an aversio – a turning of the mind away from the world of the senses – in order to prepare it for glimpsing the reality that lies beyond the phenomenal world. Following Augustine's directive "Go not outside, but return within thyself, in the inward [depth of] man dwelleth the truth", Descartes undertakes an interior journey. Following Augustine's dictum "Go back into yourself", Descartes says: "I turn my mind's eye upon myself" and find the idea of God stamped there (Third Mediation, CSM II 35). Indeed, it is through looking inward into one's soul that one is led to God.

45 CSM I 195

move may not be of great consequence. But, in fact, it allows Descartes to draw important conclusions.

In the *Meditations*, he asks: "what is this 'I' that I know? In the strict sense I am only a thing that thinks [*res cogitans*], that is, I am a mind, or intelligence, or intellect, or reason – words whose meaning I have been ignorant of until now. But for all that I am a thing which is real and which truly exists. But what kind of thing? As I have just said – a thinking thing [*res cogitans*]" (Second Meditation AT III 27; CSM II 18).

In this way, Descartes' method of doubt also turns out to reveal the true nature of the self, that is, that it is a thinking thing. In the *Discourse*, Descartes presents his radical conclusions with even greater clarity. He writes,

> I saw that while I could pretend that I had no body and that there was no world and no place for me to be in, I could not for all that pretend that I did not exist [...] From this I knew that I was a substance whose whole essence or nature is only to think, and which does not require any place, or depend on any material thing, in order to exist. Accordingly, this 'I' – that is, the soul by which I am what I am – is entirely distinct from the body, and indeed is easier to know than the body, and would not fail to be whatever it is even if the body did not exist. (AT VI 32-3; CSM I 127).

One can clearly observe here how Descartes argues for his dualistic position regarding the separation of soul and body. As he also writes in the *Principles*, "this is the best way to discover the nature of the mind and the distinction between the mind and the body".[46] As we can also observe clearly here, Descartes identifies the 'I' with a non-material soul: "a man who doubts everything material cannot for all that doubt his own existence. From this it follows that he, that is his soul, is a being or substance which is not at all corporeal, but whose nature is solely to think (*sa nature n'est pas que de penser*) and that it is the first thing one can know with certainty"[47]. I cannot doubt my existence as a thinking being, but I can doubt the existence of my body. For Descartes, this is a good reason to assign a clear primacy to the soul over the body.

46 *Principles of Philosophy*, I article 8, (CSM I 195).

47 Descartes René, *The Philosophical Writings of Descartes (Vol 3: The Correspondence)*, ed. John Cottingham, John Cottingham, Robert Stoothoff, Dugald Murdoch, Anthony Kenny (Cambridge University Press, 1991), p. 55 [Henceforth CSMK]

Further, the soul for Descartes is distinct from the body and constitutes the true self; it also subsists when the body stops functioning (*Passions of the Soul, 6*). The reason for this is that, by its very definition, the soul does not belong to the material (and thus the destructible) part of nature, since its essence is entirely distinct from that of the body.

In his *Principles of Philosophy* (part I article 53), Descartes spells out explicitly the essential difference between a thinking thing and an extended thing in terms of their respective principle attributes. He writes,

> each substance has a principle property which constitutes its nature and essence, and to which all its other properties are referred. Thus extension in length, breadth and depth constitutes the nature of corporeal substance; and thought constitutes the nature of a thinking substance (CSM I 210).

Furthermore, "Thought and extension can be regarded as constituting the natures of intelligent substance and corporeal substance; they must then be considered as nothing else but thinking substance itself and extended substance itself – that is, as mind and body" (*Principles of Philosophy* I, 63, CSM I 215).

For Descartes, "the nature of body consists not in weight, hardness, colour, or the like, but simply in extension. The nature of matter or body [. . .] consists [. . .] simply in its being something which is extended in length, breadth, and depth" (*Principles of Philosophy*, II 4; CSM I 224).

Now, according to Descartes, the whole of nature, apart from human beings, consists of nothing but extended things. Extended things are made up of bits of matter in motion, so that they can be described in purely mechanistic terms, that is, quantitatively and by using efficient causation alone. The prime example of efficient causation is how bits of matter in motion bring about the motion of other bits of matter, which in turn account for phenomena that we can sense such as heat or cold. It was essential for Descartes' program for a new science to avoid any use of a qualitative language and any reference to final causes – causes that refer to natural ends and purposes. This means that, in the natural, material world, all phenomena, and all explanations thereof, ought to be fully expressed in terms of the size, shape, and motion of the tiny parts that make them up.[48] It is only this kind of explanation that Descartes would regard as scientific. Furthermore, as we shall see, the whole of nature, including, plants, animals, and the human body, should be seen in exactly this way and can thus be regarded as machines. The nature of human beings, however, stands out as an exception, precisely because God endows human beings with a mind (or soul), and thus we are each a union of mind and body.

But, since the mind is non-extended, whatever pertains to the mind cannot be described in along the strictures of the new mechanistic science. Thus, for Descartes, since the mind does not belong to the domain explained by physics, there cannot be natural science of the mind; the mind cannot be explained in terms of its parts since it has none.[49] The soul thus falls out of the domain of natural sciences (and might perhaps require a different kind of science, which is what would eventually happen with the emergence of psychology).

Cartesian metaphysics thus sets out the background for a dichotomy between the study of nature and the study of human thought and consciousness.[50] In fact, it left the field of human thought without a proper method of investigation; it certainly took it out of the domain of a proper scientific method and thereby invoked, probably inadvertently, the need for such a science – which, indeed, would later come to be invented.[51]

* * *

As we have seen above, according to Descartes, the nature and essence of the soul is encapsulated by its principal attribute, viz., thought. In addition to its intellectual functions, the soul according to Descartes includes a variety

48 See Daniel Garber "Descartes on Knowledge and Certainty", in his *Descartes Embodied* (Cambridge: Cambridge University Press, 2001), 111-29, p. 112.

49 For an interesting discussion, see Stephen Voss' article "Descartes: Heart and Soul" in *Psyche and Soma*, 173-196, as well as Gary Hatfield's "Remaking the Science of Mind", IRCS Technical Reports Series (1994). repository.upenn.edu/ircs_reports/159/.

50 See Peter Hacker, *Human Nature: The Categorial Framework* (Blackwell, 2007), p. 23.

51 Psychology has won a scientific recognition but there have been – and indeed there are – many other attempts to form a science of the mind, from Spinoza to Hume, and to much later attempts such as Theosophy, Anthroposophy, and their likes.

of capacities, such as volitions, sensory, imaginative, appetitive, and emotive perceptions (AT VII 28; CSM II 19) – in philosophy, we would call these modes, or modifications, of thought. The soul thus serves Descartes as a broad umbrella term, covering everything mental.[52] The rational aspect of the soul is not a part of the soul; rather, it covers all mental functions. For this reason, the terms 'soul' (*anima*) and 'mind' (*mens*) are, for Descartes, co-referential, that is, they refer to one and the same thing. At the same time, the lower functions of living beings, such as nutrition, breathing, etc. – which were considered by Aristotle to belong to lower kinds of souls – are excluded from the mental realm. For Descartes, only humans are endowed with a soul. Against Aristotle, there is no vegetative or sensitive soul in Descartes (CSM II, 18; CSMK 182); for him these processes are purely material.

The Cartesian soul is both active and passive: in perceiving, it is generally passive; but in willing, it is active (*Principles* I 32; *Passions of the Soul* 17-26). In addition, the soul is one, indivisible, and admits of no parts (*Passions of the Soul*, 30). By contrast, the principal attribute of a body is extension (*Principles* I, 53; II, 4), and the modes of bodies (i.e., of extended things) are particular sizes, shapes, and positions, along with rest and motion, which all admit of parts. Thus, the properties of bodies are quantitative and lend themselves to scientific treatment. Indeed, bodies and their measurable properties are, for Descartes, the objects of science par excellence. As Descartes says, "In my physics I consider nothing apart from the sizes, shapes, positions, and movements of the particles of which bodies are made up" (AT III, 686; CSMK, 224).[53]

Hence, Descartes' definitions of mind and body set them far apart. In fact, mind and body share nothing in common. In particular, while the body is extended in space, the mind is not; while the body (and matter, more generally) is passive, the mind is active; while the body is divisible, the mind is indivisible (Meditation 6, AT 86; CSM II 59). Human beings are the only things that have a mind, whereas the rest of nature consists in extended matter in motion.

52 The realm of thought or the mental incorporates "everything which are aware of as happening within us, insofar as we have awareness of it" (*Principles* part I article 9, CSM I 195). Descartes thus emphasizes the aspect of self-awareness and consciousness of 'inner' experience.

53 In these two paragraphs, I am following Stephen Voss' article, in *Psyche and Soma*, p. 175.

Even if one were to accept Descartes' view according to which plants and animals are entirely reduced to complex mechanisms, his view of human beings would still give rise to a severe problem. As we have seen, human beings are primarily identified with their souls or minds. Indeed, for Descartes, human beings are essentially thinking beings. And yet the human mind is curiously united with, or conjoined to, a body. In his sixth Meditation, Descartes labors to establish a real distinction between body and mind. Such a distinction follows from the distinct natures of the mind and the body. But, when he comes to the description of human beings and the way we experience ourselves, a curious thing occurs: he seems to hold back. It feels as though Descartes is concerned that he might have gone too far in stressing the dichotomy between mind and matter. For, at this point in his argument, when he comes to consider the nature of a human being, he observes that his own sharp dichotomy between mind and body does not fit with his own experience.

If I am essentially a mind, a thinking thing, how is it that I feel a particular attachment to a certain body, rather than to other bodies? Why do I see this body as mine in the first place? And why do I care so much about my body if it is not part of who I truly am? Descartes writes,

> Nature teaches me, by these sensations of pain, hunger, thirst and so on, that I am not merely present in my body as a pilot in his ship,[54] but that I am very closely joined and, as it were, intermingled with it, so that I and the body form a unit. If this were not so, I who am nothing but a thinking thing, would not feel pain when the body was hurt, but would perceive the damage purely by the intellect, just as a sailor perceives by sight if anything in his ship is broken (Meditation 6, AT 81; CSM II 56).

While Descartes is seeking to convey a sense of intimate attachment to his body here, he speaks of it as something rather foreign and strange. For example, he talks of the body being hurt, rather than the person. For Descartes, my feeling of pain serves an indication that something has gone wrong in my body/machine. Descartes' language here conveys that it is not me who is in pain or is hungry; rather, my mind is registering the feelings of hunger and thirst, which in turn

54 I am following the French rather than the Latin version here.

indicates that I need to feed my machine, almost in the same way that the fuel gauge in my car serves to indicate that I need to fill up its tank or the temperature gauge serves to indicate that the car overheats. It looks as though I observe my body as a scientist observes some rather detached phenomena, that is, in an indirect and impartial way, rather than have direct sensation or experience. Thus, my relation to my body is not immediate; rather, it is mediated through the complicated network of nerves that culminate in my brain. Of course, Descartes' point here is that I am not indifferent to my body. But that I feel this way is not at all obvious and requires an explanation; indeed, this intimate relation between mind and body is hardly intelligible in light of the dualist framework that Descartes set up earlier in his *Meditations*.

This conjunction of a mind, seen as a thinking thing, and the body, seen as a machine, gives rise to the mind–body problem as we know it today. For how can such different entities coexist and give rise to a sense of an intimate connection with our body as well as to a sense of two-way interaction between our mind and our body? As anyone knows from his or her experience, at times we feel an influence of our mind on our body, as when I decide to raise my hand, and then, as if by miracle, my hand is rising. And at other times we feel an influence of our body on our mind, as when fatigue and pain might give rise to a sense of despair. Given the definition of the mind as incorporeal and the body as corporeal, such common interactions in our everyday experience seem mysterious, if not utterly incomprehensible. For how can the incorporeal mind interact with the corporeal body, or vice versa? In the poignant words of a later harsh critique, Descartes invokes the mind as "a ghost in a machine".[55]

Even if it does not resolve these obvious difficulties, Descartes' approach to this problem is bold, ingenious, and in many ways remarkably insightful. However, it is worth noting that, as with the Cartesian doubt, many readers were far more impressed with the problem Descartes articulated than by the solution he offered. His solution is roughly following. He argues that the connection between our mind and our body takes place within our nervous system, or more precisely, in its center, that is, in the brain; even more precisely, he terms this locus the "seat of the soul" and argues that it is found in a small gland within the

55 Gilbert Ryle, *The Concept of Mind* (University of Chicago Press, 1949)

brain, viz., in the pineal gland (*Treatise on Man*, article 31; AT X, 130).[56] In The *Passions of the Soul*, he writes:

> Let us therefore take it that the soul has its principal seat in the small gland located in the middle of the brain. From there it radiates through the rest of the body by means of the animal spirits, the nerves, and even the blood, which can take on the impression of the spirits and carry them through the arteries to all limbs. Let us recall what we said previously about the mechanism of our body. The nerve-fibres are so distributed in all the parts of the body, so that when the objects of the senses produce various different movements in these parts, the fibers are occasioned to open the pores of the brain in various different ways. [. . .] To this we may now add that the small gland which is the principal seat of the soul is suspended within the cavities containing these spirits, so that it can be moved by in as many different way as there are perceptible differences in the objects. But it can also be moved in various different ways by the soul, whose nature is such that it receives as many different impressions, [. . .] And conversely, the mechanism of our body is so constructed that simply by this glands' being moved in any way by the soul [. . .], it drives the surrounding spirits towards the pores of the brain, which direct them through the nerves to the muscles; and, in this way, the gland makes the spirits move the limbs. (*Passions of the Soul*, 34; CSM I 341)

The expression 'animal spirits' evokes non-material connotations. But this is not the way Descartes is using it: his 'animal spirits' are very small and agitated particles of blood. As he writes, "For what I am calling 'spirits' here are merely bodies: they have no property other than that of being extremely small bodies which move very quickly, like the jets of flame that come from a torch" (*Passions of the Soul*, 10, CSM I, 331-32).[57]

56 "When a rational soul is present in this machine [a body] it will have its principal seat in the brain, and reside there like the fountain-keeper who must be stationed at the tanks to which the fountain's pipes return if he wants to produce, or prevent, or change their movements in some way" (Treatise on Man, CSM I 141; AT XI 131)

57 As Barnaby Hutchins clarifies, "Cardiac heat rarefies and heats the blood, which pushes it out through the arteries, whereby heat and nutrition are provided throughout the body. Cardiac heat also creates animal spirits, in the form of the smallest, most agitated particles of blood, which are released in the process of heating and rarefaction. The spirits, too, are pushed out of the heart by the rarefaction of the blood, and through the nervous system, whereby they power brain and sensation functions and '[impart] movement to all bodily parts'", Barnaby R. Hutchins, 'Does Descartes Have a Principle of Life? Hierarchy and Interdependence in Descartes's Physiology', in *Perspectives on Science*, vol. 24, no. 6 (2016): 744-769, pp. 758-759.

Descartes' approach is remarkable in at least two significant ways: in his attempt to account for psychophysical relations in physiological terms, and in situating a locus where these connections take place, that is, within the nervous system. In this respect, Descartes's approach points to later developments – in particular, to the direction that cognitive sciences and psychology are taking today, that is, a detailed study of the brain, based on the assumption that understanding the workings of the brain will yield insights into human psychology in general, and psychophysical connections in particular. It goes without saying that while the details of his physiology seem rough today, his approach, which is based on the physiology of the time as well as on his own anatomical investigations, is all the more impressive.

Whether this was for the better or for the worse, there is no doubt that Descartes' attempt to understand psycho-physical relations through the analysis of minute physiological details had an enormous impact on the way that both scientists and laymen have approached this question right up until the present day.

At the same time, we must observe that, from a philosophical and conceptual perspective, Descartes' approach to the mind–body interaction problem is deeply unsatisfying, for it seems to be little more than a restatement of the problem. Even if the transmission of sensation from the extremities of the body to the brain seems very plausible, and indeed verified by later science, if the mind is understood as incorporeal and the body as corporeal, the basic problem remains. For, if this is the case, a physiological description, however precise, cannot reach the mental realm. And the same would hold in the other direction, such that the mental cannot affect the physiological. And the situation looks even worse if we consider the question of free will and the special kind of causality that might be required for it.

While Descartes' approach (in its broad outlines) still exerts a strong appeal today among cognitive scientists, it already encountered strong resistance from his contemporaries.[58] But, more importantly, Descartes' approach has set up a formidable challenge, in the form of the mind–body problem – a challenge that no philosopher since could ignore. Indeed, to a large extent, this challenge set the agenda for philosophy after Descartes, and still does today. In fact, it produced two diametrically opposed approaches: while many believe that the problem will

58 See, for instance, Gassendi's objections in the Objections and Replies to the Meditations.

disappear once our knowledge of the brain is sufficiently advanced, some hold that, given the conceptual difficulty noted above, the problem is in principle insoluble.[59]

Before we can attend to the solutions on offer today, we need to look more closely at Descartes' own agenda and the reactions it evoked in the seventeenth and eighteenth centuries. As we shall see, new notions of causality were discussed, and extremely creative ways of dealing with the metaphysical picture that gave rise to it were invented. Once we have looked more carefully into Descartes' mechanistic agenda, we shall attend to the major reactions to it. Particularly noteworthy will be the following: the approach developed by Malebranche and other Cartesians, occasionalism; Leibniz's notion of pre-established harmony between the mind and the body; and Spinoza's collapse of Descartes' dualistic approach into a monism consisting of a single, unique substance with thought and extension as its two (known) attributes. We will then briefly consider some of the broad reactions in eighteenth-century philosophy, marked by the complete physiologization of human beings (the emblem of which is La Mettrie's *L'Homme Machine* (1748)), on the one hand, and certain anti-mechanistic and anti-scientific reactions, on the other.

On the Aims and Ambition of Cartesian Physiology

As we have seen, Descartes had a very clear and ambitious agenda. In envisaging a new science that would replace Aristotelianism, he sought nothing less than a full mechanization of the natural world. More precisely, he sought a mechanization of our view of the natural world, in which the world is described in quantitative terms alone. In this way, Descartes sought to replace any reference to incorporeal agencies, such as powers, faculties, or forms, as used by the Scholastics, with the quantitative and measurable features of extended matter in motion. The quantification of nature by reducing it to extended matter in motion is at the heart of Descartes' new vision of nature.

Indeed, this vision plays an important role in Descartes' dualism. The world is divided into bodies and minds – extended things and thinking things. But only humans are thinking things and thus have a mind; the rest of nature, including

59 See, for instance, Yeshayahu Leibowitz, *Between Science and Philosophy* (Academon תשמ"ז) [Hebrew], and Hacker 2007. Also see Irving Krakow, ***Why the Mind–Body Problem CANNOT be Solved!*** (University Press of America, 2002).

animals, as well as our own body, must be understood in terms of matter in motion. In short, bodies are likened to mechanisms and the whole world too can be described as a machine.[60] This vision cuts the world in a radically new way. The whole of nature, other than our own minds, is seen as a complicated mechanism. Our own mind is somehow connected (and is united with) such a machine (that is, our own body).

One of the most difficult tasks facing this project was to provide an account of the phenomena of life – especially of some features of living things such as self-nutrition, growth, and generation, which, following Aristotle, were traditionally explained by reference to vegetative and sensitive souls. Descartes maintained that matter is essentially inert, and that nature always follows the laws of mechanics alone. He thus attempted to show that all talk about vital forces in animals is reducible to heat in the heart. Likewise, he argued that any movement in the bodies of animals, as well as in the human body, can be explained by attending to the mere disposition of their organs, so that there is no need to invoke a soul for this purpose.[61]

As Gary Hatfield notes, "Descartes' aim was to mechanize virtually all of the functions that had traditionally been assigned to the vegetative and sensitive souls," and, "[t]o a large extent, Descartes' physiology may be seen as a straightforward translation of selected portions of previous physiology into the mechanistic idiom".[62]

Descartes' aim is very clearly expressed in the conclusion to his *Treatise on Man*:

> these functions follow from the mere arrangement of the machine's organs every bit as naturally as the movements of a clock or other automaton follow

60 *Principles of Philosophy* Part IV, article 188, CSM I 279.

61 In the preface to his *Description* of the Human Body he writes:
It is true that we may find it hard to believe that the mere disposition of the bodily organs is sufficient to produce in us all the movements which are in no way determined by our thought. So I will now try to prove the point, and to give such a full account of the entire bodily machine that we will have no more reason to think that it is our soul which produces in it the movements which we know by experience are not controlled by our will than we have reason to think that there is a soul in a clock which makes it tell the time. (CSM I, 315)

62 Gary Hatfield, "Descartes' Physiology and its Relation to his Psychology", in *The Cambridge Companion to Descartes*, ed. John Cottingham (Cambridge University Press, 1992), 335-370, pp. 341-343.

> from the arrangement of its counter-weights and wheels. In order to explain these functions, then, it is not necessary to conceive of this machine as having any vegetative or sensitive soul or other principle of movement and life, apart from its blood and its spirits, which are agitated by the heat of the fire burning continuously in its heart – a fire which has the same nature as all the fires that occur in inanimate bodies. (CSM I 108)[63]

For Descartes, the autonomous functioning of corporeal substances, in general, and of living and human bodies, in particular, is reduced to the assimilation of the "soul" to the blood.[64] As Descartes says of animals, "the blood is their soul".[65] Following Harvey, Descartes holds that the blood circulates through the body, and that this circulation can be understood mechanically. Descartes disagrees with the details of Harvey's analysis and assigns a crucial role to the heat of the heart as the motor of blood circulation, but the essential point for him remains that blood circulation can be fully explained in mechanistic terms. In this way, all bodies, including living bodies, and the human body in particular, can be regarded as machines.

Further, according to Descartes, the fact all the functions ascribed to animals, including those of memory and corporeal imagination, can be explained mechanically,

> will not seem at all strange to those who know how many kinds of automatons, or moving machines, the skill of man can construct with the use of very few parts, in comparison with the great multitude of bones, muscles, nerves, arteries, veins and all the other parts that are in the body of any animal. For they will regard this body as a machine which, having been made by the hands of God, is incomparably better ordered than any machine that can be devised by man, and contains in itself movements more wonderful than those in any such machine (*Discourse on Method*, part V, CSM I 139).

Descartes' argumentative strategy is rather subtle and sophisticated. His strategy was first to conceive of all living creatures as machines. Once this is established,

63 See also AT XI 202; AT VI, 45-46.

64 See Delphine Antoine-Mahut, «La machine du corps», in *Descartes. Sous la direction*, Frédéric de Buzon et Denis Kambouchner, eds. (Ellipses, 2013).

65 «je ne voudrais pas dire que le mouvement fut l'âme des brutes, mais plutôt, avec la Sainte Ecriture au Deutéronome chap. 12 verset 23, que le sang est leur âme». (1643, AT IV, 65)

Descartes trades on the comparison between a machine manufactured by humans and a machine created by God. Roughly stated, Descartes' strategy is to model natural machines on artificial ones. He argued that the differences between the workings of a complex artificial machine, such as a clock or a fountain, and those of animal bodies are only apparent. He attempted to show that, in essence, animal (and human) bodies are of the same kind as complex machines, and that the differences between them come down to degrees of complexity and the subtlety of the parts involved. Thus, just as we don't need to invoke an occult agency to explain how a clock shows the hour, so there is no need to invoke the agency of the soul in our body: the dispositions of its organs and parts will suffice.

As Descartes states in the *Principles of Philosophy* (part 4, article 203),

> I do not recognize any difference between artefacts and natural bodies, except that the operations of the artefacts are for the most part performed by mechanisms which are large enough to be easily perceivable by the senses – as indeed must be the case if they are to be capable of being manufactured by human beings. The effects produced in nature, by contrast, almost always depend on structures which are so minute that they completely elude our senses. Moreover, mechanics is a division or special case of physics, and all the explanations belonging the former also belong to the latter so it is no less natural for a clock constructed with this or that set of wheels to tell the time than it is for a tree which grew from this or that seed to produce the appropriate fruit. (CSM I, 288)

Aristotle's example of the oak as developing and maturing by realizing the potential (the telos or program) inherent in the acorn, is now, for Descartes, understood in terms of the wheels and springs of a clock. In this way, Descartes can dispense with forms and potentiality, and he certainly no need for a soul as a source of life.

In the *Passions of the Soul* (article 6), Descartes takes the clock analogy a step further. He argues that the difference between a living body and a corpse is akin to the difference between a well-functioning machine and a broken one. He writes, "And let us recognize that the difference between the body of a living man and that of a dead man is just like the difference between, on the one hand, a watch or other automaton (that is, a self-moving machine) when it is wound up and contains in itself the corporeal principle of the movements for which it is designed, [. . .] and on the other hand, the same watch or machine when it is broken and the principle of its movements ceases to be active" (AT 331; CSM I 329-30)

Descartes does not leave any room for doubt that he takes the idea that the human body is a machine very seriously. Similarly, he makes it abundantly clear that he breaks with the traditional picture of the soul as a life-giving principle whose departure from the body is the cause of death. Rather, for Descartes, the soul leaves because the body ceases to function. But this thoroughly mechanistic picture of the body accentuates the gap between body and mind on Descartes' view. Thus, this point serves to highlight the difficulty of accounting for mind–body relations in the Cartesian framework.

7. The Aftermath of Descartes' Dualism: Three Responses

This difficulty was not lost on Descartes' contemporaries. In fact, to a large extent, the mind–body problem has set an important part of the philosophical agenda from Descartes until now. The following three sections present the main responses to this problem, as they were articulated in the seventeenth century: Spinoza's naturalism, Malebranche's occasionalism, and Leibniz's system of pre-established harmony.[66]

7.1. Spinoza (1632–1677): Naturalism

Spinoza's response to Descartes can be summed up in two words: radical naturalism. While Descartes had naturalized the scientific view of nature by excluding vital forces and occult powers, he made a significant exception by placing the human soul or mind outside it. In contrast with the Aristotelian tradition, for Descartes, humans stand out in nature as the only beings endowed

66 For more on this background, see Nadler, Steven, (ed.), 1993, *Causation in Early Modern Philosophy* (University Park: Penn State University Press, 1993).

with a soul. As a union of soul and body, a human being turns out to obey entirely different laws from the rest of nature; and for this reason understanding human beings requires an entirely different analysis- for Descartes, the soul is something that is excluded from the scientific domain and thus from analysis through the scientific method. Spinoza will have none of these exclusions for human beings. According to him, humans and their souls do not occupy any privileged place within nature. In other words, humans do not constitute a peculiar kingdom within the natural world (*Ethics* III, preface). Rather, humans must be seen as an integral part of nature.

This is the heart of Spinoza's critique not only of Descartes but also of all those who had previously written about human beings and the soul. As he writes, "Most of those who have written about the Affects, and men's way of living, seem to treat, not natural things, which follow the common laws of nature, but of things which are outside nature. Indeed they seem to conceive man in nature as a dominion within a dominion. For they believe that man disturbs, rather than follows, the order of nature, that he has absolute power over his actions, and that he is determined only by himself" (*Ethics* III, preface).[67]

For example, human beings perceive themselves as endowed with freedom – that is, the freedom to choose arbitrarily. This self-perception is part of a picture that sets them above (or outside) the regular order of nature. Indeed, for Augustine, Descartes, it is only thanks to the soul that we have free will. The soul is the source of voluntary action, and creatures without a soul have no free will. Without a soul, we would be like the brutes. This picture is deeply ingrained in Descartes' analysis. For, as far as we have a body, we are indeed a part of physical nature; but, in so far as our soul is concerned, we are not. For Spinoza, this is a misconception that philosophical analysis must undermine. According to Spinoza, the only way to achieve some freedom (and ultimately salvation) involves going through a sober realization that we are not above nature; rather, like everything else, we are subject to the necessity of natural laws. For,

> Nature is always the same, and its virtue and power of acting are everywhere one and the same, i.e., the laws and rules of nature, according to which all things

67 *Collected Works* (CW): 491; *A Spinoza Reader*: 152. We refer to the *Spinoza Reader* as well since the *Collected Works* edition might not be available to all readers.

> happen, and change from one form to another, are always and everywhere the same. So the way of understanding the nature of anything, of whatever kind, must also be the same, viz. through the universal laws and rules of nature.
>
> The Affects, therefore, of hate, anger, envy, etc., considered in themselves, follow from the same necessity and force of nature as the other singular things." (*Ethics* III, preface, CW: 492: *Reader*: 153).

In sharp opposition to Descartes, Spinoza holds that the human soul and its affects (that is, our emotions) should be understood in exactly the same way as the rest of nature, for nature is everywhere and always the same. Hence, he writes, "I shall treat the nature and power of human affects, and the power of the mind over them, by the same method by which, in the preceding parts, I treated God and the mind, and I shall consider human actions and appetites just as if it were a question of lines, planes, and bodies" (*Ethics*, end of Preface to Part III[68]). God, our mind and its affects, as well as our body (and any other body), all require the same geometrical treatment through because they are all part of nature and thus must obey its laws.

Spinoza's point in understanding and analyzing the affects of the human mind in a geometrical manner is not only for the sake of disinterested science; rather, the point is also (and most importantly) therapeutic. Spinoza argues that understanding the true causes of our emotions and our mental states as part of a natural network of causal relations will in fact lessen their influence on us and thus increase our self-control. As he writes, "Insofar as the mind understands all things as necessary, it has greater power over the affects, *or* is less acted on by them" (*Ethics* V proposition 6). In understanding the true causes of the affects, we also gain a certain control over them, such that we are not slaves to their power. This, according to Spinoza, is the only sense in which true and meaningful freedom – that is, a partial liberation from the servitude of the affects – can be achieved. The moral point of this analysis is to free ourselves from the illusions and power of the passions and thus gain adequate understanding of nature and of our place within it.

68 *Spinoza Reader*, 153

According to Spinoza, freedom is not (the illusion of) choice among alternatives. A stone falling by the power of gravity might believe that it goes down by its own will – and we are like this stone, says Spinoza (Letter 62). Instead, true freedom, according to Spinoza, is a determination of actions that stems from our own nature.[69] Once we subject ourselves – body and mind – to a rigorous scrutiny of reason, through the geometrical method, we can free ourselves from fears, anxieties, false hopes, and delusions that we are normally subject to. This, in turn, will improve our judgment and conduct. The aim of Spinoza's philosophical analysis is thus ultimately a moral one. For, in the end, understanding our place in nature is a moral project. This is why he calls his major work *Etica ordine geometrico demonstrata* or *Ethics, presented in a geometrical fashion*.

Spinoza's approach to mind–body dualism is also well expressed in his metaphysics. According to Spinoza, thought and extension are not two separate substances, as they are for Descartes; rather, thought and extension are two attributes of one and the same substance.[70] For Spinoza, nature as a whole is seen as a single substance – a unique substance that collapses the traditional distinction between the natural world into and a transcendent God (who creates the natural world) into one entity which is subject to a single set of laws, and in which everything is strictly determined by necessity. If humans are a part of nature, it goes without saying that they too are subject to the same necessity that applies to everything natural, either with respect to their physical nature (body) or with respect to their mental nature (mind).

Recognizing this universal necessity in the human context is a core goal of Spinoza's philosophy. It is also key to the therapy of the passions: such therapy will increase our power of activity (through the employment of our reason) and decrease our passivity (our being subject to passions caused by external things). In other words, being more active will render us less passive and will thus make us act more in line with our own nature rather than being subject to external forces. For this reason, recognizing ourselves – mind and body – as part of the natural causal nexus will make us more spontaneous, in

69 "That thing is called free which exists from the necessity of its nature alone, and is determined to act by itself alone" (*Ethics* I def. 7)

70 The "mind and body are one and the same thing, which is now conceived first under the attribute of thought, now under the attribute of extension" (*Ethics* III proposition 2, scholium). For more detail, see Martin Lin's "Spinoza and the Mark of the Mental" in Y. Melamed (ed.) *Spinoza's Ethics* (Cambridge University Press, 2017), pp. 82-101.

the sense of acting from our own resources. To use a term Spinoza does not, it will make us more autonomous and free in the (Spinozistic) sense of self-determination.

Indeed, a subtle but immensely important message of the *Ethics* is to be active: the more active we are, the less passive we are, and the more freedom and happiness we shall gain. Spinoza argues that an increase in our activity will make us more rational and self-aware, and vice versa. This awareness will enable us to achieve a higher degree of freedom by acting out of our own nature, rather than being affected and constrained by external forces (*Ethics* IV, appendix, iii, v). Thus, maximizing our activity and thus our knowledge of God or nature – the true love of God in Spinoza's sense – is the only path to true salvation, i.e., a kind of knowledge that can liberate us from superstition, delusion, and wishful thinking.

According to Spinoza, such liberation is much needed, for human life is fraught with these kinds of thinking. In particular, we do not usually perceive ourselves as subject to strict necessity; rather, we unreflectively take ourselves to be free. Further, humans tend to think of themselves as the pinnacle of creation, with the whole of nature created in their service. We tend to think, for instance, that animals and plants were created for our nourishment. God himself is seen as a mighty and merciful father who takes care of his children, and whom we can approach and appeal to (through prayer) in order to change the course of nature in our favor (*Ethics* I, appendix). According to Spinoza, nothing could be more absurd than this. This whole personal, anthropomorphic view of God is one of the ways in which we impose our concepts upon nature.[71] As a result of fear, ignorance, and anxiety, human beings have produced a system of beliefs and prejudices that places them so to speak above nature; indeed, they imagine themselves as nature's very end and purpose.

Spinoza's philosophy seeks to undermine the force of such superstitious and wishful thinking, for, in the long run, this kind of thinking can only lead to misery and delusion. For Spinoza, the only source of happiness is a sober realization of the truth: God or nature are different names for one and the same substance, and all particular things, human beings included, are but particular finite modes of this single substance. And, being a particular mode, such as we are, also implies that

71 "Nature does nothing on account of an end. That eternal and infinite being we call God, or Nature, acts from the same necessity from which he exists." (*Ethics* IV preface, CW/*Reader* 197).

our duration is finite.[72] At the same time, Spinoza says, if a bit enigmatically, that there is "something that pertains to the essence of the mind" that will "necessarily be eternal" (E V 23d). Seen under that aspect of eternity, and as part of a system of necessary connection, the essence of the mind has an aspect of eternity too.[73]

Descartes is very explicit that his dualistic view is meant to serve the idea that the soul subsists after death.[74] Spinoza's philosophy seems to convey a completely different message: we have to realize the necessity of our finitude and rescind any false hope for eternal life. The realization of this necessity cannot be a source of sorrow or sadness; rather, the wise cannot hope for something impossible. Instead, it will make us more joyous by increasing our power of activity (which, for Spinoza, is the very definition of joy).

Spinoza's notion of God is very different from the notion held by Descartes and by all monotheistic historical religions. For Spinoza, God is nothing other than nature – and humans (with their minds and bodies) are nothing other than modes of God or Nature. In this way, Spinoza's metaphysics situates human beings as an integral part of nature, just as much as any other individual thing is.

Like anything else in nature, human beings tend to persevere in their existence. This is a natural tendency common to all existing things. But, as all other finite modes, humans are subject to external forces that ultimately cause their destruction and death. If there is something characteristic of human beings, it is their natural rational capacity. Rationality thus is an inherent aspect of human nature. Hence, if we act from our own nature (that is, if we truly act at all), to that extent we are rational; if we are acted upon, such that our behavior is brought about by external forces, we are passive and to that extent irrational. This interplay between reason and passion, action and inaction, in Spinoza is not a binary affair) but rather a matter of degree. Spinoza opposes the traditional picture of a battle between reason and passion in which one wins entirely over

72 For more on this point, see Steven Nadler's *A Book Forged in Hell: Spinoza's Scandalous Treatise and the Birth of the Secular Age* (Princeton University Press, 2013).

73 Interestingly, Spinoza's point here seems to apply as much to the essence of the body as it does to the essence of the mind.

74 Descartes clearly states in his *Meditations* that his philosophy is meant to deliver two main results: to prove that "the soul does not die with the body and that God exists". *Meditations*, Dedicatory letter to the Sorbonne AT VII 2; CSM I 3.

the other. Rather, our self-control and conduct is a matter of increasing our power of action, which is the same is decreasing our susceptibility to the power of the passions. Since the passions – or the passive affects – affect us (as it were from the outside), they also prevent us from being free. As Spinoza makes clear, "Man's lack of power to moderate and restrain the affects I call bondage (or servitude)" (Ethics IV, preface). In Spinoza's picture, we can become free to the extent that we reduce the impact of the passions through understanding their adequate causes.[75] To understand is to exercise reason and thus to act by our proper nature. And this is the true nature of virtue.

> Since virtue (by D8) is nothing but acting from the laws of one's own nature, and no one strives to preserve his being (by IIIP7) except from the laws of his own nature, it follows:
> (i) that the foundation of virtue is this very striving to preserve one's own being, and that happiness consists in man's being able to preserve his being. (Ethics IV 18, scholium)

> Acting absolutely from virtue is nothing else in us but acting, living, and preserving our being (these three signify the same thing) by the guidance of reason, from the foundation of seeking one's own advantage. (Ethics IV, proposition 24).

By grounding virtue in the doctrine of the conatus, Spinoza completes his program of radical naturalization. To be ethical and virtuous is not to act against nature but rather to realize one's true nature. Thus, to act morally is to act naturally. To understand nature and our place in it is the only path to happiness open to humans.

In its historical context, Spinoza's version of naturalism was such a radical break with the tradition that it has been seen as heretical. It is, however, difficult to exaggerate the impact of the naturalistic spirit of Spinoza's philosophy on future generations. While Spinoza's was regarded as a heretic and his writings were banned and derided for centuries, the influence of his work was immense. The fact that the most widely accepted approach to the mind–body problem today is

75 See P. F. Moreau *Spinoza*, Sueil, 1975 p. 98.

a naturalistic one – that is, the idea that both mental and physical aspects must be understood in scientific and physical terms – is clear evidence of the long-ranging impact of Spinoza's naturalistic attitude.[76]

7.2. Malebranche (1638–1715) and Occasionalism

As we have seen above, the most striking problem that Descartes left unresolved for his followers and successors was the causal interaction between the mind and the body. If mind and body are seen as two separate substances, how can we account for the influence (which we feel very clearly) of the mind on the body and of the body on the mind? Since both mind and body are created substances, and since, according to Descartes, a substance is by definition self-sufficient, or more precisely, it depends on God alone, how could we account for the influence of the one over the other? One of the most curious and original solutions to this problem was simply to deny the alleged causal interaction between mind and body altogether. Since God is the only true substance, and the only substance that is indeed entirely self-sufficient, the only true source of causality in the created world has to be God. Whatever happens in the mind or in the body could only be an occasion for God's intervention. In the words of Nicolas Malebranche, the most famous occasionalist of the western philosophical tradition, "there is only one true cause because there is only one true God; [. . .] the nature or power of each thing is nothing but the will of God; [. . .] all natural causes are not *true* causes but only *occasional* causes" (OCM II, 312 / *Search for Truth* 448).

Elsewhere Malebranche writes,

> I agree that God is the sole author of all substances and of all their modes, that He is the author of all beings: not only of all bodies but of all minds. But be careful: I understand by a *mode* of a substance only that which cannot change without there being some real or physical change in the substance of which it is the mode. [. . .] Once again, I agree that God is the sole efficacious cause of all the

76 For the full impact Spinoza had on the development of western culture, see Jonathan Israel's series of books, which make this case very compelling: *Radical Enlightenment* (Oxford University Press, 2001); *Enlightenment Contested* (Oxford University Press, 2006).

> real changes that take place in the world (*Prémotion Physique*, OCM XVI 40).[77]

Thus, at most, "creatures can provide an *occasion* for God's activity, which is direct and immediate in bringing about all effects in nature"[78]. For example, if I wish to raise my hand, this (a mental event) constitutes an occasion for God to intervene and cause my hand to rise (a physical state). What seems like direct influence of the mind over the body turns out to be, in actuality, a divine intervention in all such cases.

If this line of thinking seems like a strange development, note that it is a rather natural consequence of Descartes' position, which is clearly expressed in his *Meditations*, where Descartes holds that "conservation is but continuous creation." As he writes,

> [I]t does not follow from the fact that I existed a little while ago that I must exist now, unless there is some cause which as it were creates me afresh at this moment – that is, which preserves me. For it is quite clear to anyone [...]that the same power and action are needed to preserve anything at each individual moment of its duration as would be required to create that thing anew if it were not yet in existence. Hence the distinction between preservation and creation is only a conceptual one, and this is one of the things that are evident by the natural light. (AT VII 49/CSM II 33)[79]

If the preservation of the world requires continuous intervention of God, as if preservation means a divine re-creation at any moment, this may also be used to settle the question of mind–body interaction. Against this background, the idea of occasional causes, mediation by God seems to be a plausible (or at least less bizarre) development of Descartes' view.

77 Translation is from Elmar J. Kremer, "Malebranche on Human Freedom", in *The Cambridge Companion to Malebranche*, ed. Nadler, S. (Cambridge University Press, 2000), 190-220, on pp. 210-11.

78 Sukjae Lee, "Occasionalism", The Stanford Encyclopedia of Philosophy (Winter 2016 Edition), Edward N. Zalta (ed.), URL = plato.stanford.edu/archives/win2016/entries/occasionalism/

79 See also Principles, Part 1. art. 62. Note that Descartes' physics also requires God's continuous intervention in the world as the source of motion. For if, as he insists, matter is entirely inert, there is nothing to provide power for motion unless God continuously intervenes to provide that power.

7.3 Leibniz (1646–1712): Pre-Established Harmony

Similar considerations motivated Leibniz to develop his system of pre-established harmony. Like the occasionalists, he in effect denies causal influence among created substances. But, according to Leibniz, there is no need for divine intervention in order to account for the relation between body and mind. For Leibniz, each created substance is self-sufficient and inherently active. But, at the same time, God knows its future activities in advance of its creation. Thus, God creates the world, such that the inner activity of all substances result in concurrence and harmony among them. This harmony applies for both inter-substance relations and the relations between body and mind. As he notes,

> From these I constitute a twofold and most perfect parallelism: on the one hand, between the material and formal principles, that is, between body and soul; on the other hand, between the kingdom of efficient causes and the kingdom of final causes.
>
> The parallelism between the body and the soul contains the system of preestablished harmony, of which I am the discoverer.[80]

As he writes elsewhere, "The soul does not act on things, according to my opinion, in any way other than because the body adapts itself to the desires of the soul, by virtue of the harmony which God has pre-established between them".[81] Thus, according to Leibniz, God need not intervene to coordinate between the soul and the body because they are in perfect agreement, due to a pre-established harmony.

Leibniz exemplifies this harmony with an analogy. He writes,

> Consider two clocks or watches in perfect agreement. Now this can happen in three ways: the first is that of natural influence. [. . .] The second way to make two faulty clocks agree would be to have them watched over by a competent workman, who would adjust them and get them to agree at every moment. The third way is to construct these two clocks from the start with so much skill and

80 *The Leibniz Stahl Controversy*, (eds.) F. Duchesneau and J. Smith (Yale University Press, 2016), 21.
81 Roger Ariew (ed.), *Leibniz-Clarke: Correspondence* (Hackett, 2000) Leibniz's fourth letter, remark no. 31.

> accuracy that one can be certain of their subsequent agreement.
> Let us now put the soul and the body in place of these two watches; the agreement will also come about in one of these three ways. The way of influence is that of common philosophy; but since we can conceive neither material particles nor immaterial qualities or species that can pass from one of these substances to the other, we must reject this opinion. The way of assistance is that of the system of occasional causes. But, I hold, that is to appeal to a Deus ex machina in a natural and ordinary matter, where, according to reason, God should intervene only in the sense that he concurs with all natural things. Thus, there remains only my hypothesis, that is, the way pre-established harmony, through prior divine artifice, which has formed each of these substances from the beginning in such a way that by following its own laws, laws which are received with its being, it nevertheless agrees with the other, as if there were a mutual influence.[82]

In his *Monadology*, Leibniz presents the following thought experiment (known today as Leibniz's Mill). He writes,

> [...] *perception*, and what depends on it, is *inexplicable in terms of mechanical reasons*, that is, through shapes and motions. If you imagine that there is a machine whose structure is to think, sense and have perceptions, we could conceive of it enlarged, keeping the same proportions, so that we could enter into it, as one enters into a mill. Assuming that, when inspecting its interior, we will only find parts that push one another, and we will never find anything to explain perception [and thought]. And so, we should seek perception in the simple substance and not in the composite machine or in the machine. Furthermore, this is all one can find in the simple substance – that is, perceptions and their changes. It is also in this alone that all the internal actions of simple substance can consist. (Monadology § 17; in AG 215)

In sharp opposition to Descartes, the foundation of reality for Leibniz is not extended matter but rather animate (active) units consisting of both mind (or an active principle) and matter (seen as a passive principle). In his late writings,

82 Postscript of a Letter to Basnage de Beauval, in AG 147-48. Regarding the pre-established harmony between body and mind see, for instance, *New Essays on Human Understanding* 116; and Leibniz's response to Father Tournemine.

Leibniz calls these units monads. Essentially, these are non-extended units of force; they are akin to atoms in being foundational and indivisible. They do not, however, consist of extended matter; rather, they only consist of force. They have, Leibniz says, a series of perceptions and power (appetite) to move from one perception to another. They constitute the foundation of matter and extension, but each one of them is non-extended.

8. Kant (1724–1804): Skepticism Toward the Soul and the Fallacies of Arguing For Its Immortality[83]

In the preface to his most important and highly influential book, *Critique of Pure Reason*, Emmanuel Kant writes,

> Human reason has this peculiar fate that in one species of its cognitions it is burdened by questions which, as prescribed by the very nature of reason itself, it is not able to ignore, but which, as transcending its powers, it is also unable to answer. (CPR A vii)

As it turns out, the immortality of the soul is precisely such a question. The central aim of Kant's critical philosophy is to criticize and thus to tame this tendency of our reason to go beyond its powers and boundaries. By the nature of our reason, we tend to ask questions that go beyond limits of possible knowledge. For example, we want to know if there is a God; we want to know how things truly are (and not just as they appear to us); we want to know whether we act freely or whether everything is determined; and we want to know if we can hope for life after death. The last question, concerning the existence and the persistence of the soul after death is both most pertinent to our concerns here and also best illustrates Kant's critical attitude. It is also the question about which we care most, since it has crucial moral and existential implications.

83 I would like to thank Noam Hoffer and Reed Winegar for very helpful advice and comments on this section.

For Kant, these three questions exemplify our aspiration to know things in themselves, that is, things as they truly are, independently of our cognitive limitations in general, and of our sensibility in particular. Kant calls these *noumenna* and contrasts them with phenomena, or things as they appear to us. Kant indeed holds that we can think about the *idea* of the way the world is independently of our perception of it; that we can *think* the concept of God and of the soul. Indeed, in the accurate theological sense (the most perfect being, the immaterial immortal soul), we can think of these only as *noumena* rather than as phenomena or appearances. But Kant breaks with the assumption of all previous philosophers that we can come to know whether these things – God, the immaterial immortal soul, or the world in itself – exist, and that we can know things about them. Kant's radical move is to reject the presumption that we can ever come to know anything in particular about these things. The reason is that any knowledge about empirical objects and, more generally, any claim about existing things, requires some input from experience. Such input must come to us through our own sensibility or our own way of receiving sensory material. But, if so, how could we even hope to know what would be the fate of our soul after death, that is, after all our capacities to receive experiential material are no longer in place? In fact, the question holds with the same acuteness for our present situation. For we seek to come to know things that are, by definition, independent of our particular sensibility (i.e., our forms of intuition). But how could we ever know anything otherwise, that is, without our forms of intuition?

According to Kant, this very question and desire for knowledge transcends the boundaries of any experience we could have and thus must be reckoned as lying beyond the limits of possible knowledge. As noted, the question about the immortality of the soul is one that we cannot ignore. But, once we examine it critically, we realize that we cannot answer it either. For it transcends our cognitive powers.[84]

Traditional metaphysics seeks to prove that the soul is a substance, and that it remains the same substance over time. It does so by arguing that the soul is simple

84 Kant's position should be also contrasted with the radical empiricist position that the self is just an illusion, a contingent bundle of perceptions, as David Hume famously argued in his *Treatise on Human Nature*. According to Kant, our awareness of the unity of consciousness cannot be detached from experience. This feature may have also inspired the phenomenological approaches that flourished after Kant.

rather than complex. If a substance is simple, then it cannot naturally be destroyed; for only complex things can naturally decompose (i.e., they come apart into simpler components). The rational doctrine of the soul seeks to establish that the soul is a component of the created world – but an immortal one, as it cannot be destroyed with the natural destruction of the body (CPR B410-411).

According to Kant, however, we can think of the soul as an idea but not as a reality or as a substance. For the sense in which the soul is considered a substance does not involve any intuition (or experiential material) and thus does not belong to the realm of experience at all. The soul, just like God and the more general category of things in themselves, is something that we can think of but cannot know (CPR preface to the second edition).[85]

Allen Wood summarizes Kant's position on the soul as follows:

> Kant is far more skeptical than any view that has a widespread following today. He is neither a materialist nor a dualist. He does not think we can ever know whether the soul is material (whether thought or consciousness are bodily functions)... If the soul is an immaterial thing, Kant finds that there are three theories of the relation between it and the body: (i) "physical influence" (a mutual natural causal relationship, as maintained by Crusius and Knutzen) [this is in effect Descartes' view]; (ii) "pre-established harmony" (as held by Leibniz); and "supernatural assistance" (the occasionalism of Malebranche and others). Kant roundly rejects all three, claiming that they are all equally unprovable and even of doubtful intelligibility. In sum, Kant holds that the nature of the soul and its relation to the body are matters of transcendent metaphysics that lie entirely beyond the bounds of what we can ever know. (Allen Wood, *Kant*, Blackwell, Great Minds series, p. 89)

While this renders the soul, as a thing in itself, to be entirely unknowable, Kant's view also gives rise to a new direction for investigating the soul and its relation to the body. This stems from thinking of the self not as *noumenon* but as a phenomenon instead – that is, as it appears to us. This field has later come to be called phenomenology. On the one hand, Kant's critique relegates the

85 It is worth adding why Kant thinks that that reason (and rationalist philosophy) is tempted to think of the soul as a substance: we mistake the functional features of consciousness (unity, simplicity, etc..) for a substance which has these attributes.

investigation of the soul to the non-scientific domain. And indeed Kant himself thinks that, in spite of his critique, there is a *moral* reason for believing in the immortality of the soul (see the Canon of Pure Reason in the *Critique of Pure Reason*, and the postulates of practical reason in the *Critique of Practical Reason*). But, on the other hand, Kant's distinction between the self as a noumenon and the self as phenomenon – the self as it appears to us – seems to suggest that a phenomenological (rather than a metaphysical) approach to the study of soul-body relations remains possible. And, indeed, the phenomenological school has flourished in post-Kantian philosophy and has many adherents today.

Part II

Contemporary Approaches to Mind–Body Relations

Introduction

In this section, we turn to presenting our own view. We present our view against the contemporary scene of the main disciplines and methods – both philosophical and scientific – that are currently used to investigate mind–body relations. We begin by quickly reviewing the thread that led from the seventeenth century to the twentieth, and then present the main approaches in the study of the mind over the twentieth century in more detail. This will set the stage for our own approach. We use Wittgenstein in order to break from the grip of the Cartesian picture that splits human nature into body and mind, and this will allow us to recover the Aristotelian picture of human nature in which human beings are seen as a single entity – a psychophysical unity – endowed with a variety of capacities. The classification of these capacities into mental and physical can be useful as well as confusing, since the distinction between them may not be so clear.

We present our approach against the background of contemporary debates, so that the reader will gain a better understanding of the current trends and positions and in order to better demarcate our own approach. It goes without saying that our approach has some affinity as well as diversity from current approaches. Our general strategy – using Wittgenstein to break away from the Cartesian picture in order to go back to Aristotle – draws on the historical survey presented in the first part. We primarily seek here to present a clear exposition of this approach rather than engage in arguments and debates with other positions and thinkers. We also don't make any claim for originality here. We rather aim at a clear and (as much as possible) accurate presentation.

Our approach does diverge from the mainstream of contemporary approaches. It is not a scientific approach and does not pretend to be a scientific-like approach. In its broad outlines, the approach we are presenting is similar to the approach presented in recent years by (the philosopher) Peter Hacker and (the neuroscientist) Maxwell Bennett in a series of books that both criticize the current tendency in cognitive neuroscience and lays out the more positive approach.[86] The reader is strongly encouraged to consult these books. At the end of this section, we indicate some of our (rather minor) differences from Hacker and Bennett.

9. A Quick Tour From Descartes to the Twentieth Century

During the seventeenth century – the early days of modern science – Descartes drew a sharp dichotomy between two kinds of things: thinking things and extended things. According to him, these are two distinct and entirely separate substances that share nothing in common. For Descartes, the physical aspect of nature consists of bits of matter in motion – and nothing else. The principle attribute of matter is extension. This implies that matter is passive, inert, and divisible, and that it lacks any internal powers or built-in properties beyond extension itself. It also lacks any ability to enact motion or activity. A mind or a thinking thing, on the other hand, is active and is capable of initiating thoughts and actions. A mind is one and indivisible; but it is *not* extended or situated in space. According to Descartes, human beings are the only creatures that possess a mind or mental capacities, and all other living beings are seen as intricate machines of various degrees of complexity. Even the human body, considered in isolation from the mind, is taken to be nothing but a mechanism. Given this disparity between mind and body, the question of how the human mind and body interact becomes rather enigmatic. However, as Descartes himself was the first to note, we feel and experience ourselves as one being – a union of mind and body in constant interaction. The discrepancy between the way we experience ourselves and the distinct nature of body and mind gives rise to the mind–body problem.

The Cartesian framework not only had an immense influence on the development of western science, philosophy, academic and medical institutions; it also constitutes

86 In *Philosophical Foundations of Neuroscience* (Wiley-Blackwell, 2003) and *History of Cognitive Neuroscience* M. R. Bennett and P.M.S. Hacker critically explore the history and the philosophical presuppositions of cognitive neuroscience. In three successive volumes, Hacker lays out his positive view of human nature: *Human Nature: The Categorial Framework* (Blackwell, Oxford, 2007); *The Intellectual Powers: A Study of Human Nature* (Wiley-Blackwell, 2013); *The Passions: A Study of Human Nature* (Wiley-Blackwell, 2018). Here we mainly draw on Hacker (2007).

the conceptual framework in which we still think about the body and the mind. In response to the schism advanced by Descartes, some tended to stress the body/ the material side, and others tended to stress the mind/the mental side. This is expressed in an opposition that developed between materialist and idealist outlooks. Already in the seventeenth century, Thomas Hobbes was arguing for a strict version of materialism.[87] In the eighteenth century, taking the bodily side (so to speak) led to a strict physiologist agenda that saw the mind (and everything mental) as an entirely redundant category, or as something that could be understood in bodily and physical terms alone. This natural extension of Descartes' approach resulted in a view that takes not only the human body (as well as all other animals) as machines but also in taking the whole human being as a machine. This tendency was evident among the French *lumières* (enlightenment thinkers) in the eighteenth century, and one can see the emblematic manifestation of this trend in La Mettrie's *L'Homme-machine*. For La Mettrie (as well as for other French physiologists), 'soul' was a "merely a vain term".[88] Thinking as well as all other mental attributes could be fully understood within the framework of extended things, so that thinking things as a separate category could drop out of the picture.[89] Indeed, the idea of thinking matter had already appeared in

87 In the very first lines of his *Leviathan*, Hobbes writes: "For seeing life is but a motion of limbs, the beginning whereof is in some principal part within, why may we not say that all *automata* (engines that move themselves by springs and wheels as doth a watch) have an artificial life? For what is the heart, but a *spring*; and the nerves but so many *strings*; and the joints, but so many *wheels*, giving motion to the whole body, such as was intended by the artificer?" (Hackett edition, edited by Edwin Curley, 1994, p. 3)

88 'Soul', in itself, "is merely a vain term of which we have no idea and which a good mind should use only to refer to that part of us which thinks" (de La Mettrie JO. *Machine Man*. In: Thomson A, editor. *Machine man and other writings*. Cambridge: Cambridge UP, 1996; 1-39.) See also, de La Mettrie JO. *Histoire naturelle de l'âme*. The Hague: Jean Neaulme, 1745.

89 It should be observed that the physiologist trend encountered some strong resistance, especially within medicine, in the second half of the 18th century. The vitalist movement in France, mainly associated with the Montpellier school of medicine, rejected the consequences of Cartesian dualism. As Roselyne Rye points out "The vitalists' primary thesis was an affirmation of the unity of man, a being which must always be studied as a whole, and whose *physical* and *moral* aspects are closely conjoined". [. . .] In their rejection of the two main contemporary medical currents [mechanism and animism], the vitalists took up a positions whose central feature was the requirement that account be taken of the 'sense of the vector' which moves 'from the moral to the physical'." "Psyche, Soma, and the Vitalist Philosophy of Medicine" in *Psyche and Soma* pp. 256-57. For a clear example of this attitude, see the article on Melancholy in the *Encyclopédie*.

John Locke's influential book *Essays on Human Understanding*.[90] Locke's suggestion that God could have superadded thinking to matter in a similar manner as motion is added to bodies in Newtonian physics is certainly ingenious. But more influential was the reform of medicine and physiology in ways that made no reference to the mind. Through this route, the Cartesian framework became extremely influential not only in philosophy but also in medicine.[91] This tendency, to view the human being through the physical (bodily) category of the Cartesian divide, is certainly the most influential trend in cognitive sciences and philosophy to this very day.

At the same time, it is important to recall that, in Descartes' framework, the mind is in effect excluded from the domain of science.[92] While the body is in principle fully describable by the new mechanical science, the mind cannot be so described. It can only be sensed from within: only *I* have direct access to my mind. According to Descartes, natural science is to be carried out in rigorous quantitative terms (because the natural world is ultimately nothing but extension, and extension is geometrical). It follows that talk about the mind necessarily becomes either subjective or a topic for a religious and moral discourse. This consequence of the dualistic Cartesian framework, in turn, created a need for a special science (and a scientific language) suitable for investigating the mental domain. And indeed, the nineteenth century saw the rise of theosophy, anthroposophy, and ultimately psychology (which, until the latter part of the century, was largely concerned purely with introspection) as precisely such (more or less successful) attempts.

90 "We have the Ideas of Matter and of Thinking, but possibly shall never be able to know, whether any material being thinks, or no; it being impossible for us, by the contemplation of our own Ideas, without revelation, whether Omnipotency has not given to some System of Matter fitly disposed, a power to perceive and think, or else joined to matter so disposed, a thinking immaterial substance [. . .] For I see no contradiction in it, that the first Eternal Thinking Being, should, if he pleased, give to certain systems of created, senseless matter, put together as he thinks fit, some degree of sense, perception and thought" (Book IV chapter 3, article 6).

91 For a clear and influential expression of this view see the article *Mécanicien* in the Encyclopedia of Diderot and d'Alembert – a text that can be considered as expressing the main agenda of the French Enlightenment. "The term *Mécanicien* – a mechanic – is the name by which one calls those modern physicians who, after the discovery of the blood's circulation (by Harvey) and the establishment of Descartes' philosophy shaken the yoke of authority, have adopted the method of the geometers [. . .] according to which all the operations of bodies in nature obey mechanical laws" (our translation).

92 Or, to be precise, of what we today would call science.

The details of this historical development are rather complicated and go far beyond the scope of this section. Regardless of how exactly this took place, the emergence of psychology and its recognition as a science and a dignified therapeutic method resulted in a sharp schism within the medical institutions, such that we got one branch of medicine for treating the body and a wholly separate branch for treating the psyche. An immensely important part of this division of labor is that physicians are trained (and are thus competent) to take care of what's defined in anatomical and physiological terms alone (or one might say of the physical aspects of health and disease alone). Likewise, the medical system distinguishes between mental, bodily, and psychosomatic illnesses, the latter which being those illnesses that somehow cannot be classified into one of the standard (mental or physiological) categories.[93]

Despite severe criticism, by and large, medical institutions still operate along these fault lines – that is, they are still professionally split between treating the body and treating the mind. With the rise of specialization within medicine, the division of labor has only increased: it is rare to find a physician whose concern is the health of the whole person rather than this or that specific aspect or body part.

Indeed, we are all too familiar with the situation today. If one suffers from severe headaches, or stress, or is unable to sleep at night, or has a persistent lower back pain, the question of whom should one consult, a physician or a psychologist, or a psychiatrist, or a chiropractor, or a naturopath, or some other sort of healer, typically presents itself.

The point we are trying to make is, quite simply, that the current division of labor in the medical institutions between physical and mental health still strongly corresponds to (and to a certain extent stems from) the Cartesian division between two kinds of entities, body and mind. The ontological division that was drawn in the seventeenth century played an important role in the branching of the medical institutions and medical schools that we are familiar with today. This philosophical and historical point has clear practical implications. For, as noted, in choosing whom to consult, one necessarily makes a decision as to whether one assumes the condition one is suffering from to be, so to speak, physical, in which case one goes

93 It is worth noting that other medical traditions, such as Chinese and Ayurvedic medicine, do not employ such a sharp division.

to see a medical doctor/physician, or mental, in which case one would consult a psychologist or a psychiatrist.[94] Other implications pertain to issues such as whether one's health insurance covers (or does not cover) mental health treatment, psychological counseling, and so on.

It is partly for these reasons that our conception of human beings as psychophysical creatures – creatures endowed with both mental and physical capacities (and limitations) – matters. For, as we can see, the way we conceptualize mind–body relations has many practical implications as well.

In order to present our own view of the issue, we still need a few pieces of background. We shall now pick up the thread of our very cursory historical story and turn to mapping the main contemporary conceptions of mind–body relations as they were shaped in the twentieth century. The immediate context is the rise of psychology and the attempt to make it a true and legitimate *science* of the mind.

10. Behaviorism and Its Shortcomings

Behaviorism in psychology was mainly born from the concern to make psychology an adequate, objective, and respectable science. On the traditional view of the mind, a view accepted without question by psychologists in the nineteenth century, states of mind were taken to be private conscious states that are not amenable to public scrutiny. While 'access' to my own states of mind is direct, others can only observe their effects. The pioneering behaviorists J. B. Watson (1878-1958) and B. F. Skinner (1904-90) argued that only what is publicly observable is an appropriate subject for science. And they sought to turn psychology into such a science. Watson, for example, wrote that, "psychology as a behaviorist views it is a purely objective experimental branch of natural science. Its theoretical goal is [...] prediction and control" (1913, p. 158).

In order to meet this objective, they sought to exclude (the private and obscure) states of mind from psychology. The main idea was that a description of human

94 In this connection, see this interesting article: nytimes.com/2017/09/11/well/alternatives-to-drugs-for-treating-pain.html

psychology can be given as a description of human behavior. More specifically, human behavior was to be described in terms of a stimulus-response mechanism. The paradigmatic example here was that of a reflex, such as when the doctor taps on your knee (stimulus) and then the knee jerks up (response). In order to describe what's going on here, no reference to a mind or a mental realm is required. Thus it was argued that the mental realm should be left out of psychology.

As John Heil explains,

> On the behaviorist conception, talk of minds, conscious experiences, and the like is pointless. Appeals of such things in explanations of behavior reflect only a superstitious past in which observable characteristics of objects were explained by reference to ghosts and spirits taken to animate them. To deny ghosts and spirits – and mental states – is not to deny that objects and intelligent creatures have complex observable traits, nor is it to deny that these are susceptible to rigorous scientific explanation. Just as we have put behind us explanations of pathological behavior that appeal to possession by evil spirits, so we must put behind us explanations that appeal to private inner occurrences. This is what behaviorists set out to do (Heil 2013, p. 63)[95].

One phenomenon that seemed particularly important and apt for an explanation in terms of a stimulus-response mechanism is that of learning, in general, and language acquisition, in particular. Since language has always been seen as one of the defining features of human nature, and as a particular mark of the mental, explaining language acquisition in behavioristic terms would be extremely important. Skinner's efforts to provide such an account were summarized in his book *Verbal Behavior*, which was published in 1957. In 1959, Noam Chomsky published a review of Skinner's book. In a later edition of his review, Chomsky made it utterly clear that his intention was not to attack Skinner but to "discuss his proposals as a paradigm example of a futile tendency in modern speculation about language and mind and to propose an alternative to this behaviorist tendency."[96]

What Chomsky refers to as the futile tendency of behaviorism, I take it, is the attempt to describe (and explain) human learning (and language acquisition

95 Heil, J., Philosophy of Mind: A Contemporary Introduction (Routledge, 2013).
96 An online version of this review can be found here: chomsky.info/1967____/

in particular) without taking into account the set of capacities that must be presupposed, even if they are invisible, in order to explain the way children master a language at such a young age (between two and three years old). Behaviorists explicitly focus on linguistic *performance* and ignore the *competence* aspect because it seems to invoke a mental realm that appears to transcend the scope of observable science. But for the explanation of childhood language acquisition, the behavioristic approach fails quite miserably. In Chomsky's words, "a refusal to study the contribution of the child to language learning permits only a superficial account of language acquisition" (Review of Skinner's *Verbal Behavior*, section XI).

Chomsky observed that, by the age of four, the average child has an almost limitless capacity to produce sentences they have never heard before. Chomsky argued that it seems plainly untrue that language learning depends on the application of reinforcement, as the behaviorists maintained. Most children learn a language without explicit teaching and instruction from adults; rather, they are introduced to a language by growing up in a language-speaking environment.

As it turns out, our behavior and behavioral capacities often surpass the limitations of individual reinforcement histories. Our history of reinforcement is often too impoverished to determine uniquely what we do or how we do it. This is clear in the case of language acquisition, but the point extends to other capacities. Historically, Chomsky's attack on these central behaviorist themes had a devastating effect on the behaviorist program.[97]

11. Chomsky's Critique of Behaviorism and Methodological Naturalism

Chomsky's critique of behaviorism leads to the recognition that it is not so easy to eliminate the mental realm by focusing on behavior alone. One cannot fully

97 "Then Chomsky pulled the rug out from under us . . . [We] were very busy trying to provide the apparatus for a theory of linguistics that at that moment was being discredited. It's a very disappointing position to be in . . . [By] the time we could supply the right kind of theory, the nature of what language was believed to be had changed. The whole theory was no longer appropriate. Very grim, very grim" (Jenkins 1986: 243; cited in Boden 2006: 297)

express human capacities in terms of behavior – behavior that can presumably be described in scientific terms – and by ignoring mental capabilities that cannot be so described. In other words, a psychology that ignores the content of the mind (seen as a black box whose content can be ignored) but focuses instead on stimulus and response alone does not work very well for explaining complex learning processes, in general, and language acquisition, in particular. The stimulus-response mechanism does not do well in accounting for language acquisition because the linguistic response of children who are learning a language is much richer than the stimulus they are exposed to. Since children produce sentences they have never heard, the response is going to be richer than the stimulus. According to Chomsky, in order to account for this creative aspect, we must assume a built-in linguistic (or mental) capacity. Chomsky relates this capacity to an innate grammatical capability that enables the producing of new sentences from a finite set of words – what he calls innate universal grammar.

However, how exactly to understand and conceptualize this linguistic capacity, even within Chomsky's research program, has been a matter of controversy. Some argue that it is merely syntactic, and others (e.g., Fodor) that it includes semantics. The program itself has been developed and modified and very seriously contested.[98] But this controversy is behind our concerns here. The important take-home point for us is that some linguistic – or more generally mental – capacities cannot be explained away by the behaviorist method. In general, some apparently mental capacities must be presupposed in order to account for our language use and acquisition.

For his part, Chomsky does not think that such mental competence should be identified with a mysterious entity or some substance called mind.[99] In other words, according to Chomsky, while we must assume some linguistic competence innate in human beings – a competence that he does sometimes identify with the mind – the necessity of such competence for explaining linguistic creativity and behavior need not invoke anything that is not physical or that cannot in principle

98 See, for example: scientificamerican.com/article/evidence-rebuts-chomsky-s-theory-of-language-learning/
99 Rules and Representation 1980: p. 227.

be described by natural science.[100] To paraphrase Chomsky, we might think about the investigation of mental capabilities as an investigation of the body – especially of the brain – which takes place at a certain level of abstraction.[101]

12. Methodological Naturalism (and Some Current Instances)

Chomsky thus clearly articulates an extremely important approach – and one that constitutes the most widely shared methodology among scientists, psychologists and philosophers alike. It can be called *methodological naturalism*. And this is a second take-home point from this discussion. According to methodological naturalism, we should proceed with a research program that seeks to explain everything in a scientific (and physicalist) manner, even if the present state of science does not allow us to provide such an explanation.[102] In fact, Chomsky himself holds that current science does not even have a clear notion of what a body is, let alone of the mind. It goes without saying that articulating mind–body relations in scientific terms poses huge difficulties. But, according to Chomsky, we should not give up on the scientific course. We should not accept ghosts in the machine or occult properties because present science does not yet know how to explain competences that, for lack of a better word, we call mental; rather, we should be patient and let science develop more adequate tools and concepts to explain these away or to describe our innate capacities in physical and biological terms. For the most part, this lack of knowledge is now associated with the huge task of understanding the structure and functioning of the human brain.

The prominent biologist, Francis Crick, has nicely articulated this approach. In 1953, Crick and Watson (along with Rosalind Franklin) discovered the structure of DNA. Crick later turned his attention to exploring the "mystery of consciousness." In his book, *The Astonishing Hypothesis, The Scientific Search for the Soul* (1994), he writes:

100 For instance, see his discussion in *On Nature and Language* (edited by Belletti and Rizzi) (CUP 2002) pp. 55-60.

101 Rules and Representation 1980: p. 31.

102 See Boden *Mind as Machine*, Oxford University Press, 2006: p. 12.

> This book is about the mystery of consciousness – how to explain it in scientific terms. I do not suggest a crisp solution to the problem. I wish I could, but at the present time this seems far too difficult. Of course some philosophers are under the delusion they have already solved the mystery, but to me their explanations do not have the ring of scientific truth. What I have tried to do here is to sketch the general nature of consciousness and to make some tentative suggestions about how to study it experimentally. I am proposing a particular research strategy, not a fully developed theory. What I want to know is exactly what is going on in my brain when I see something (Crick 1994, p. xi).

Indeed, the methodology Crick recommends here, to discover what is going on in the brain when a certain mental state takes place, is one that dominates much of current research programs in brain sciences and one that exerts immense influence in other disciplines.[103] The idea that research into the structure and functioning of the brain will yield insight into human psychology and improve our understanding of both pathological and normal human functioning informs current research in medicine, psychology, economics, philosophy, computer science and, of course, the brain sciences. These are sometimes grouped together under the title of cognitive sciences.[104] In any event, there is a huge growth in the efforts and in the resources currently allocated to brain research. This can be gauged by the (number and amount of) funds allocated to this growing field of research[105], the number of research positions in universities, new research centers, etc.[106] In Israel alone, a new brain science center has been built in all major universities; and millions of dollars have been allocated by the European Union to the new brain research center in Jerusalem alone.[107] Huge sums are invested in ambitious projects such as

103 See the Forward to *Philosophical Foundations of Neuroscience*, by Bennett and Hacker (Blackwell, 2003).

104 As Boden notes "the main disciplines involved in cognitive sciences are psychology, linguistics, AI, A-Life, neuroscience, and philosophy" (Boden 2006, 12).

105 In 2013, the European Union allocated around a billion Euros to brain research. They write, "The brain is much more than an organ. It is a system whose secrets can help us not only cure diseases, but also build better computing systems, able to do things that today we may not even imagine". See: ec.europa.eu/digital-single-market/en/programme-and-projects/brain-research.

106 It is reported, for example, that, in October 2016, the American National Institute of Health (NIH) nearly doubled investment in its BRAIN Initiative research.
For some details, see: nih.gov/news-events/news-releases/nih-nearly-doubles-investment-brain-initiative-research

107 See: elsc.huji.ac.il

reconstructing biological and electronic models of the brain.[108]

We can see evidence for the impact of brain studies in psychology in the curricula of undergraduate courses in psychology, in which it is currently standard to include many courses on empirical studies of the brain and neurology, at the expense of more theoretical approaches and previously dominant traditions and schools (e.g., Freud, Jung, etc.).

Also indicative is a significant trend toward unifying strands from psychology and economics with neuroscience in what has come to be called neuroeconomics. For example, a course titled 'Introduction to Neuroeconomics: How the Brain Makes Decisions' describes itself as follows: "Economics, psychology, and neuroscience are converging today into a unified discipline of Neuroeconomics with the ultimate aim of creating a single, general theory of *human* decision-making."[109] Note how quickly the course description moves from describing human decision-making to supposing that it is the *brain* that makes these decisions. Much of this research is conducted under the assumption that we can gain insight into decision making if we observe what is going on in the brain when humans make decisions (by using fMRI, eye response, and other empirical methods). In paraphrasing Crick's point above, we can say that what neuroeconomists want to know is exactly what is going on in the brain when a person makes a decision. Just how this would help understand the logic of decision-making or whether or not a certain decision is good is, however, very far from clear. But we will come to this point in due time. It suffices to observe here that much the present scientific research is predicated on the assumption that looking into the brain is the best way to understand human mind and psychology.

108 See for instance, bluebrain.epfl.ch/page-56882-en.html
and also: scientificamerican.com/article/why-the-human-brain-project-went-wrong-and-how-to-fix-it/

109 coursera.org/learn/neuroeconomics

13. The Contemporary Philosophical (and Scientific) Scene

The attitude we see in psychology, neuroeconomics, and so on is very evident in philosophy as well. With some few exceptions, all contemporary positions in the philosophy of mind (which studies mind–body relations, among other things) are versions of 'physicalism'. Physicalism is the thesis that everything is physical or, in other words, that the real world is nothing more than the physical world. In particular, physicalism implies that what we call 'mental' is in fact physical. Physicalism is a later version and a direct consequence of the materialistic view that was prominent in eighteenth-century France.[110] Originally, physicalism was considered to be mainly a linguistic thesis according to which every mental state has the same meaning as some physical state. As the term suggests, it also conveys the idea, popular among philosophers, that what truly exists corresponds to what can be described by science, in general, and by physics, in particular. Indeed, most current positions in the philosophy of mind take their cues from developments in the sciences – currently most prominent are neuroscience and computer science – and hold that any approach should be scientific or science-like (e.g., Dennett, Searle, Fodor).

Thus today 'physicalism' designates mainly the metaphysical thesis that mental phenomena supervene on physical-biological nature. This means that mental phenomena strongly depend on physical phenomena, so that, if the physical realm is eliminated, the mental realm will be eliminated as well. But this does not hold in the inverse direction, such that if the mental realm is eliminated, the physical will stand fast.

Versions of physicalism differ in the form they assign to the dependency of the mental on physical nature. In other words, all versions of physicalism assume that the physical is fundamental, and they differ in how they account for the mental.

110 Otto Neurath (1931) and Rudolf Carnap (1932/1959), both of whom were key members of the Vienna Circle, a group of philosophers, scientists and mathematicians active in Vienna prior to World War II introduced the word 'physicalism' into philosophy. See the item Physicalism in the Stanford Encyclopedia of Philosophy. See: plato.stanford.edu/entries/physicalism/

Indeed, some versions regard mental phenomena as a mere illusion.[111]

13.1 Searle's 'Biological Naturalism'

John Searle suggests replacing physicalism with 'biological naturalism'. His agenda is to make neurobiological processes in the brain central for the account of consciousness. For Searle, "Consciousness [. . .] is caused by neurobiological processes and is as much a part of the natural biological order as any other biological features such as photosynthesis, digestion, or mitosis" (Searle, 1992: 90). He writes:

> There is exactly one overriding question in contemporary philosophy – the question is, How can we square this self-conception of ourselves as mindful, meaning-creating, free, rational, etc., agents with a universe that consists entirely of mindless, meaningless, unfree, nonrational, brute physical particles? The short answer to the question of how consciousness fits in with the basic facts is that conscious states are entirely caused by neuronal processes in the brain and are realized in the brain.[112]

How does Searle's reference to the brain's activity – activity that causes consciousness – addresses the gap between our self-conception and the scientific outlook is not so clear. What is clear is that Searle argues that consciousness is "entirely caused by lower level neurobiological processes in the brain," even though it exists only "at a level higher than that of neurons and synapses," which are not conscious themselves (Searle J. R., *Mind: A brief introduction*. Oxford: Oxford UP, 2004). For Searle, "consciousness stands to the brain as digestion stands to the

111 Type physicalism, also called 'psycho-physical reductionism', is the strongest form of physicalism, and was defended as late as the 1970s (D. Armstrong, *A Materialist Theory of the Mind*). Type physicalism is the position that a given type of mental state reduces to, or is identical to, a determinate type of brain state. One issue with type physicalism is that mental states appear to be multiply realizable – it is at least conceivable that different physical systems other than brains, such as computers or the physiology of aliens, can realize identical mental states. In addition, it seems that identical mental states should be realizable by different physical states of a single brain (or other physical system). This is called 'token physicalism' (N. Block, "Antireductionism Slaps Back").

112 Searle, J. R., *Freedom and Neurobiology* (Columbia University Press, 2004), pp. 4-5.

movements of the stomach". Incidentally, it is very interesting to note how similar this formulation is to Aristotle's analogy between sight and the eye. But it is also worth remarking that the distinction between a "lower level of neurobiological processes" in the brain and a higher level of consciousness is at best metaphorical and risks begging the question. Searle further writes,

> The brain is a biological machine, and we might build an artificial machine that was conscious; just as the heart is a machine, and we have built artificial hearts. Because we do not know exactly how the brain does it we are not yet in a position to know how to do it artificially. ("Biological Naturalism", 2004)

Thus, for Searle, as to many others, the deep question will be resolved once we understand the complex mechanisms of the brain. Indeed, huge funds are currently invested in seeking to construct an artificial brain. In 2013, the European Commission awarded neuroscientist Henry Markram and his team $1.3 billion to pursue the audacious goal of building a simulation of the human brain.[113] It is also worth remarking that the Cartesian question of understanding the relations between the body and the mind is currently transformed into a question about the relations between the brain and the mind. The prevalent attitude among neuroscientist is nicely expressed in the following passage from an interview with leading neuroscientist:

> It is not pleasant to think of ourselves as machines, but in all my studies of the brain I have not seen a soul running in the brain. All I have seen are physical materials, electrical signals and chemistry. Yes, we – you, and I and everyone – are machines, machines that can generate all the beauty, the sense of 'self,' of feelings and creativity.[114]

The next section illustrates some of the ways in which philosophers sought to deal with this unpleasant thought, viz., that our mental life is best described in terms of the neural processes in our brain.

113 For a report on this project see: scientificamerican.com/article/why-the-human-brain-project-went-wrong-and-how-to-fix-it/

114 Idan Segev in an interview with Ziv Hellman in the Jerusalem Post, August 14, 2010.

13.2 Functionalism

In the late 1960s, the strong version of the identity thesis between the mind and the brain evolved into a more nuanced version of physicalism called functionalism. Functionalism drew its main inspiration from the distinction between software and hardware in the development of electronic computers. Functionalists were impressed by the fact that different hardware can run the same software.[115] Think of an application that the can run on a PC and on a Mac, for example. If the mind can be likened to the software and the brain to the hardware, this does seem to imply that mental states can be realized in many ways and in different physical states.

As John Heil explains,

> If something like this were right, then there would seem to be no deep mystery as to how minds and bodies are related. Minds are not identifiable with brains, as an identity theorist would have it; but neither are minds distinct immaterial substances mysteriously linked to bodies. Talk of minds is at bottom talk of material systems at a 'higher level', a level that abstracts from the 'hardware'. Feeling a pain or thinking of Vienna are not brain processes, any more than a computational operation, summing two integers, for instance, is a vacuum tube process or a transistor process. Brains and brain processes are analogous to the hardware and electrical processes that, in a particular kind of computing machine, realize computations. Thoughts and feelings are, as computations are, multiply realizable. They are capable of being embodied in a potentially endless array of organisms or devices. Your mind is a program running in your brain (Heil 2013, p. 90).

Minds then can be related to brains in something like the way that computational processes are related to computing machines. Minds are not brains for just the reasons that programs or computational operations are not identical with components of the hardware on which they run. Just as in describing the operation of a computing machine at the 'program or algorithm level', you would be describing the machine's causal structure without regard to its hardware, so in

115 See Hilary Putnam's 'Minds and Machines' (1960) and Jerry Fodor's 'The Mind–Body Problem' (1981). Putnam later changed his mind. In the late 1980s, he abandoned functionalism and any other computational model of the mind.

describing mental operations, psychologists are describing the causal structure of intelligent agents without regard to their biological hardware (Heil 2013, p. 121).

13.3 Mind as Machine, Cognitive Science, and the Project of Artificial Intelligence

In fact, the analogy between mind and body, software and hardware, cuts much deeper: the digital computer now serves as the most prominent model of the mind and for understanding human intelligence. Roughly stated, the idea is that thinking is similar to (or even identical with) computing. Or at least, computation is regarded as the best model we have for understanding thinking.[116] Since we can build machines that provide a very clear example of computation, we can also embark on the project of understanding and modeling human intelligence by means of artificial intelligence, i.e., through machines and the algorithms that run them. Specifically, we are trying to build artificial networks that would model neural networks in the brain. This is precisely the business of cognitive science, a science largely inspired by the conception (and invention) of computing machines.

As Margaret Boden puts this, "Broadly speaking, cognitive science is the study of mind as machine. [. . .] More precisely, cognitive science is the interdisciplinary study of mind, informed by theoretical concepts drawn from computer science and control theory" (Boden 2006, pp. 9-12); and she points out that "the huge attraction of the field [cognitive science] lies largely in its promise to help solve one of the greatest philosophical puzzles of all: the mind–body problem" (Boden 2006, 1337).

If we follow the computer analogy, then what cognitive science is concerned with is the software, while the hardware is the preserve of neuroscience.[117] These two sources, the informational and the biological, are the main ways in which science

116 For a rare divergence from this view, see *In Our Own Image* (2015) George Zarkadakis. A shorter presentation of this view can be seen at: aeon.co/essays/your-brain-does-not-process-information-and-it-is-not-a-computer

117 Although this is something of an oversimplification: cognitive science often integrates plenty of neuroscience. As we might expect, studying software will sometimes have to involve looking at the hardware as well. After all, hardware limitations, for instance, restrict what the software can do.

now goes about investigating the mind. No wonder that they now often come together in what's come to be called 'brain science'.

Some of the interesting questions these sciences study concern what we can learn about the human mind by constructing machines, or devices, or algorithms, that seek to imitate certain human capacities. In short, we study the human mind by making machines that resemble it in certain respects. This enterprise rests on the assumption that the best way to understand something is to make it. This has been a fruitful approach since at least Descartes' time: in his terms, we can study God's creation through human production.[118] It is important to emphasize that the main presupposition here is to investigate the human mind in a *scientific* way – that is, to create a *science* of the mind. But one must wonder if this is not altogether misguided. For does it even makes sense to say that 'machines think'?

13.4 Can Machines Think?

The question of whether machines can think was explicitly in the mind of one of the most important figures in the theory of computing, and in the invention of the universal machines we now call computers, Alan Turing. In his article 'Computing Machinery and Intelligence', published in 1950, Turing proposes to examine the question 'can machines think'?[119] He begins by noting that both concepts, 'machine' and 'thinking', are poorly defined. He proposes to bypass this difficulty by suggesting a game, the 'Imitation Game'. The game is played among three participants, a man, a woman, and an interrogator. The interrogator stays in a room apart from the other two. The object of the game is for the interrogator to determine through written questions, mediated via a teleprint (something like a modern texting device), which of the two is the man and which is the woman. Turing also stipulates that the man is trying to mislead the interrogator. The game can be played a number of times and the interrogator's success is recorded.

118 One leading proponent of this *verum factum* (truth is made – roughly, to know something is to be able to make it) tradition was Giambattista Vico (1668-1744). Vico argued that the humanities can provide us with genuine knowledge, because they study the creations (not of God but) of human beings

119 Turing's article was published in *Mind*, Vol. LIX no. 236, October 1950, pp. 433-460.

Turing then turns to putting a machine into the game, taking the role of the man. He writes:

> We now ask the following question: What will happen when a machine takes the part of A [the man] in this game? Will the interrogator decide wrongly as often when the game is played like this as he does when the game is played between a man and a woman?

Turing proposes that these questions replace the original question whether machines can think (p. 434). In other words, this test would stand in for the question of machine intelligence.

Some versions of this game have come to be known as the Turing Test for whether machines can think. It is often presented in the following, much-simplified form: if you exchange text messages with either a person or a computer, would you be able to tell the difference? If you cannot, there does not seem to be a substantial difference between them. As it happens, in real life, we now often play this sort of game whether we like it or not. Often, you call your bank or write an email or text message and you really don't know if there is a person replying, or whether the reply is generated by an algorithm. But, of course, the algorithms that run these machines are specifically designed to imitate the way humans would respond. And there are now very good technologies to create such convincing imitations.

Thus, the project of artificial intelligence (AI) is not only alive but can probably be said to be a great success in superseding human intelligence in many respects.[120] A computer won the world champion in chess long ago (IBM's Deep Blue beat the world chess champion Gary Kasparov in New York on May 11, 1997); and no one even mentions anymore the facility of machines in calculation, as we now simply take this for granted. With the development of deep learning methods, and big data science, there have been many more advances. In 2015, Google's AlphaGo beat one of the world's best players at Go (a game whose complexity makes it far harder to address computationally than chess). And while it previously seemed impossible to program computers to recognize faces, they now seem better –

120 As Boden puts this, "Artificial Intelligence tries to make computers do the sorts of things that minds can do. These things range from interpreting language or camera input, through making medical diagnoses and constructing imaginary (virtual) worlds" (Boden p. 4).

certainly faster – than humans at this task; and AIs are already driving automated cars. Even language translation, though still far from being fully accurate and reliable, has advanced to the point of being quite useful (as every user of Google Translate knows).

Observe that all these achievements are in some respect due to Turing's initial insight of defining a particular task rather than asking a general (and, as Turing suggested, meaningless) question about thinking or intelligence – what's come to be called 'strong AI'.[121] Nor has it become clearer what intelligence (in a general sense) means. It is also noteworthy that none of these amazing feats says anything about the more basic question of whether it makes sense to say that a computer (or a machine) thinks, or calculates, or *plays* a game, or drives a car. It is not at all clear that imitating a human being or even doing better than humans at certain tasks implies that the machine plays the game in the sense we use the word for humans. It is not even clear that saying that a machine plays chess makes sense: it is questionable whether it makes sense to say that the machine wants to win, for instance. As Chomsky put it, Deep Blue beating Kasparov was no more interesting than a bulldozer winning a weight-lifting contest. Likewise, we are not very excited by the fact that a motorbike, or a cheetah for that matter, runs faster than Usain Bolt. As a matter of curiosity, it is worth pointing out that in spite of all the marvelous feats of AI, no computer program has passed something much narrower than Turing's original imitation game.[122] As Boden notes, among AI researchers, the question is no longer, 'What should we do to pass the test?' but, 'Why can't we pass it?' (Boden 2006: 1355).[123]

121 As Turing writes, "The question 'Can machine think?' is too meaningless to deserve discussion" (1950, p. 442).

122 See Boden, 2006, 1353-54 and en.wikipedia.org/wiki/Loebner_Prize.

123 But see: en.wikipedia.org/wiki/Eugene_Goostman for some later claims to have passed the Turing test as well as skepticism about it. Also, as a matter of curiosity, here is an amusing point made by the computer scientist, Avi Wigderson in 2017 at the Institute of Advanced Study in Princeton. In a short talk entitled "Why AI will Succeed this Time", Wigderson suggested that, since smartphones now navigate for us, complete sentences for us, provide information for us, etc., AI will reach the level of the human intelligence by debilitating humans (rather than reaching up to it) and thus win the intelligence contest. In my view, this can be seen as a *reductio ad absurdum* of the whole project of machines 'beating' humans. Not because we are smarter but because, as Turing already observed, the project is not very well defined.

13.5 An Evolutionary Approach to the Emergence of the Mind

Another important way in which science investigates the nature of human beings as psychophysical creatures is to take an evolutionary approach. Such an approach asks the following question: how did our psychic and linguistic capacities, or the mind, or consciousness, develop, and how were they shaped through the long and complicated course of evolution?

This approach is similar in spirit to the one evolutionary biologists take in investigating the origin and development of life, in which they try to track the process through which complex organisms developed from simple ones. How, in this long and complex process, did sensitive and linguistic capacities arise? Some philosophers (e.g., Dennett) argue that this is in principle the research program that will resolve the (apparent) mind–body problem. But some evolutionary biologists take up the challenge by delving into the details; and some have come up with rich and interesting accounts.

A recent example of this approach is summarized in a new book, *The Evolution of the Sensitive Soul*, co-authored by Simona Ginsburg and Eva Jablonka.[124] Ginsburg and Jablonka write,

> The nature of consciousness is one of the greatest enigmas scientists face. We approach this problem from an evolutionary perspective, which focuses on the origin of consciousness during the history of life. We argue that consciousness is a facet of the capacity for open learning and that it was the evolution of learning that led to the emergence of consciousness in the Cambrian era. 542 million years ago.[125]

Ginsburg and Jablonka argue that, "just as scientists have found markers indicating the existence of life, so can one find markers of consciousness." And they suggest

124 The book is forthcoming with MIT Press in 2019.
125 Source: a booklet published in advance of *The Evolution of the Sensitive Soul*, by the Van Leer Institute in Jerusalem, p. 2.

open-ended learning as an evolutionary marker of consciousness (booklet p. 15).[126]

They are also fully committed to the naturalistic approach, according to which, "mental states and processes are complex states of a sophisticated physical system that is part of an embodied, world situated animal. This complex system is the central nervous system (which includes the brain), in which representations and representations of representations – a recursive mapping of the world, the body, and their relation – are formed."[127] Thus, this evolutionary approach is very much within the framework of methodological naturalism; it focuses on the origin of the nervous system and its functions, assuming that we can better understand the psychic capacities by investigating their origin and development.

13.6 Daniel Dennett (1942–)

Daniel Dennett is one of the most influential living philosophers in contemporary philosophy of mind. His work integrates (and thus illustrates) the main strands of methodological naturalism presented above: taking the hard sciences as the prime model for explaining all phenomena; and building on the advances in computer science and neurophysiology. Dennett is an anti-Cartesian and strives to get rid of Descartes' split metaphysics. He clearly prefers one of the Cartesian substances, namely, extended substance – or bodies. And he rejects entirely the alleged authority of the first-person stance over experience. His program is the explanation of all phenomena in naturalistic terms alone, and he seeks to approach the question in a purely scientific (rather than common-sense or phenomenological) manner. Building

126 For some caution and skepticism about the general project of providing an evolutionary account of cognition, see Richard Lewontin's "The Evolution of Cognition: Questions We Will Never Answer" in *Methods, Models and Conceptual Issues*, (eds., Scarborough and Sternberg) Vol. 4 MIT Press, 1998 pp. 107-131. Lewontin's main line of caution derives from the simple fact that is very hard to come by hard evidence for the phenomena of language and cognition. His critique is aimed at the early work of Lumsden and Wilson (1981), and even more so of Pinker and Bloom (1990). He writes, for instance, "Lumsden and Wilson can martial no evidence at all, for none exists" and, for lack of evidence, Pinker and Bloom fall back on the old argument from design (p. 112). I think that Ginsburg and Jablonka are mindful of these dangers, but it is worth bearing in mind Lewontin's words of caution in light of the popularity of Pinker's work. See for example his How the Mind Works (Norton, 1997). For a critical review of Pinker see: bostonreview.net/archives/BR23.2/berwick.html.

127 Booklet published in advance of *The Evolution of the Sensitive Soul*, pp. 6-7.

on Wilfrid Sellars' distinction between the manifest image and the scientific image, Dennett holds that the things we see and hear and interact with (the manifest image) are "not *mere* fictions but different versions of what actually exists: real patterns." But the underlying reality, what exists in itself and not just for us or for other creatures, is accurately represented only by the scientific image – ultimately in the language of physics, chemistry, molecular biology, and neurophysiology.[128] The details of Dennett's approach and the controversy between him and his main opponent, David Chalmers, merit a longer discussion. But in order to avoid digression from our main line of argument, we present this controversy to an appendix.

14. Is the Mind–Body Problem Soluble?

Against the dominant strand of methodological naturalism, however, there is a small counter-current that holds that the mind–body problem can never be solved, no matter what progress science makes. Even if, at some point, we fully understand how the brain works, the argument goes, we'll remain in the dark about its relation to the mind. Some, like Chalmers, argue that this problem is really hard because we don't have a clue as for how to go about solving it. But, some hold a stronger position. According to this position, the problem is in principle insoluble. Arguments to this effect were articulated by Hilary Putnam later in his career, Collin McGinn, John McDowell, Thomas Nagel, and the whole tradition that emphasize the irreducible character of qualia. A very crisp (if much less known) version of this position was held and tenaciously argued for by Yeshayahu Leibowitz. Leibowitz gave many lectures on this topic but most of his publications remain in Hebrew.[129] Even if his position didn't have a significant impact outside Israel[130], his crisp formulation of the problem serves our purpose

128 See Thomas Nagel's review of Dennett's recent book *From Bacteria to Bach and Back: The Evolution of Minds*, Norton, 2017 in the New York Review of Books, March 9, 2017 Issue.

129 Here, we translate from his most influential lecture series at the Broadcast University and published under the title *Body and Mind: The Psycho-Physical Problem* (in Hebrew) Ministry of Defense Publication, 1989.

130 It curious to mention the Nobel prize winner, Daniel Kahneman's hypothesis that, as a result of Leibowitz's teaching in Jerusalem, it is the city with the highest percentage of people preoccupied with the mind–body problem. For Kahneman's response to Leibowitz's views, see *Mind and Brain*, Van-Leer Publications, 2005, pp. 59-73).

well here, namely to highlight the point that the mind–body problem may not be a scientific problem at all.[131]

Leibowitz argues that the gap between a scientific description of the body (and specifically of the brain) and the non-scientific immediate way in which our psyche is given to us is unbridgeable. The acute problem for him is thus epistemic. By definition, science must be objective and deal with what is public and accessible to anyone. But the mind is a subjective/private domain accessible only to its holder. As he notes: "In spite of himself, human beings recognize and discern two worlds – an external world and an inner world [. . .] but these are distinct worlds from the perspective of immediate human perception and recognition" (Leibowitz, 1989, p. 14).[132] Science cannot investigate the human psyche or the domain of human experience with its quantitative methods and instruments of measurement and observation; it can only investigate the intricate mechanisms and workings of the brain. But no matter how far our scientific understanding of the brain advances, it must remain in the descriptive mode of chemical interactions, degrees of energy, and electronic measurements. And, for this reason, it will never tell us anything about how a person feels, or what he or she experiences simply because such a description will not be expressed in the quantitative language of science.

As he writes,

> We tend to fuse psychic reality with nervous processes in the brain: how is the world of these quantities transformed into a world of qualities? We confront here a question that not only can we not answer, but we also have trouble understating what we mean by this question. We realize that we presuppose something impossible. We presuppose that brain processes are transformed in psychic processes, and on the basis of this supposition we are forced to ask the absurd question – how do quantities become qualities? [. . .] These two questions, how processes in the public domain become facts in the private domain and how quantitative categories are turned into qualitative ones, still await a rational response.[133]

131 For a more nuanced position, distinguishing clearly between the empirical business of the sciences and the conceptual business of philosophy, see Bennett and Hacker, *Philosophical Foundation of Neuroscience*, 2003.

132 For the sake of the argument, Leibowitz disregards the metaphysical and ontological question whether these two worlds truly exist.

133 *Body and Mind: The Psycho-Physical Problem* (Hebrew) Ministry of Defense Publication, 1989, p. 55.

The problem, Leibowitz stresses, is not "**how the brain works**. This is a problem of physiology; and physiology indeed advances towards its solution. The problem is **how the person (who has a brain) works**, that is, how does a psychic process take place in her as a result of (or in relation to) what is going on in her brain? How does a physical event that takes place in the public domain of space and time turn into a psychic event in the private domain of a certain living creature's mind?"[134]

For Leibowitz, whatever science reveals, it is not about our psyche; and, on the other hand, our psychic world of experience can never be expressed in the mode and methods of science. This point can be rephrased as follows: the mind–body problem is not a scientific problem and cannot even be articulated in scientific terms. This is partly because Leibowitz (as well as Chalmers) accepts the Cartesian framework according to which the realm of the mental is purely subjective and accessible only through introspection. The realm of the mind, therefore, must remain outside the domain of science.

But even thinkers who are much more optimistic about the scientific approach to the investigation of the psyche, agree that the mind–body problem cannot be resolved by science alone. Margaret Boden, for example, puts this as follows:

> In sum, the existence of qualia – and therefore of mind–body correlations, as normally understood – isn't as "obvious" as it's typically assumed to be. And if their existence is in doubt, their explanation is necessarily problematic. The jury's still out. The discussion is often bedeviled by disagreements rooted in a clash of intuitions wholly impervious to argument. [. . .] But one thing's sure: *mind-brain correlations aren't a purely scientific problem*. The philosophy has to be sorted out too. (Boden 2006, 1246)

For our part, we shall reject the assumption about an unbridgeable gap between the internal/private and external/public realms. But we think that emphasizing (as Leibowitz does) the distinction between the methods and objectives of science and the realm of human experience and meaning is on the right track. And, indeed, it is arguable that even if we have a very good understanding of what's going on

134 *Body and Mind: The Psycho-Physical Problem* (Hebrew) Ministry of Defense Publication, 1989 p. 67.

in the brain, it will not solve or even get us closer to clarifying the logic and the meaning of a certain decision, let alone to solving the mind–body problem. This is because, after all, the brain is a physical organ and its scientific description seems radically different from the ways we express ourselves, both logically and emotionally. An accurate description of my nervous system when I reminisce about my past, for instance, will not tell me anything I'm interested in when I reflect on my past, or about its bearing on my present situation. Even if cognitive science could tell me what exactly is going on in my brain when I make a certain decision, and even if this phrase had a clear meaning, it is hard to see how this information would tell me anything about its significance.

There is, indeed, we believe, a certain gap between the objectives of the natural sciences and the meaningfulness of the conversations we carry out with others and with ourselves about many things that concern us. This point was argued forcefully in the late works of Hillary Putnam and John McDowell. In the philosophical jargon, the issue of meaning is called intentionality. For Putnam (both middle and late) and McDowell, intentionality is regarded as pre-scientific and hence not something that can be explained by science. If so, neuroscience has nothing to say about meaning. At best, neuroscience can only describe what goes on in our brains when we have meaningful thoughts (see Boden 2006, 1245).

In his early work, the *Tractatus Logico-Philosophicus*, Wittgenstein argued (rather dramatically) that "even if all scientific problems be solved, the problems of life would not even be touched" (TLP 6.52). In the context of Wittgenstein's early work, the scope of science is limited to the realm of facts, that is, descriptions or propositions that can turn out to be either true or false. Anything else falls out the domain of science. Wittgenstein's point can be paraphrased thus: precisely in order to be able to describe the natural world clearly, science must stay away from human questions about the meaning of life, and the meanings of events, phrases, etc. And the radical conclusion that Wittgenstein himself draws in his *Tractatus* was accordingly "of what one cannot speak clearly, one should remain silent" (TLP proposition 7) – and for 'clearly' here, we might read 'scientifically'. After this, Wittgenstein himself left philosophy. But he picked it up again (about a decade later) once he realized that philosophical problems cannot be solved once and for all through a logical/metaphysical analysis of the relations between language and reality, so that a clear line would be drawn between what can be said clearly (the realm of facts) and what cannot be said at all. According to his later view, philosophy is an on-going activity that seeks to clarify conceptual confusions by observing the way words and concepts function in the normal use of language.

15. Our Approach

This brings us to our approach, which is inspired by Wittgenstein in being explicitly non-scientific. Nor is it scientific-like. Unlike most current philosophical positions, it does not seek to resemble the scientific approach in its methods and aims. But, lest there be any mistake, it is not *anti*-scientific. Rather, we find current brain research as well as attempts to understand human intelligence through analogies with artificial intelligence extremely interesting and promising in many respects. But we don't think that they even begin to address many of the questions that concern humans with respect to mind–body relations. We do not think that the mind–body problem is a scientific or a scientific-like problem; it is rather a philosophical question that rests on some misleading (but deeply entrenched) suppositions. The philosophical task is to clear up the confusion. Another way to put this is that our approach is *orthogonal* to the various scientific investigations noted above – it is entirely independent of them.[135] The scientific (and most philosophical) approaches noted above seek to provide *causal* explanations: they seek to explain the causes of certain mental states and, in the case of medicine, to find out how a pathological state can be cured or relieved. To be sure, this research has very important implications for both practical and conceptual levels. For instance, understanding the chemistry related to states of depression or pain can obviously be very useful, so that certain drugs (such as SSRIs or NSAIDs) may be used. The growing use of antidepressants to treat many kinds of depression (and their frequent use by many who are not diagnosed with clinical depression) is surely a very significant development on both individual and sociological levels.[136]

135 Denis Noble nicely put this thus: "philosophy and science are not in opposition. Rather they deal with different kinds of questions" (in *Philosophical Foundation of Neuroscience*, xiii).

136 Incidentally, it might also have an impact on the fact that so many people are currently diagnosed as suffering from depression. It only makes sense that physicians will prescribe and use the tools they have; especially if they see those as effective and non-harmful drugs.

But our approach here does not concern itself with whatever it is that is going on in the brain, and certainly not with some opaque descriptions (favored by many philosophers) of brain states, or C-fibers firing, etc. The point we seek to highlight is quite an obvious one, namely that the relations between physical and mental states can be observed directly; and that such observations can be usefully employed in contexts such as attentive yoga practice. When I straightened my back and roll my shoulders back, I can observe the impact. It would certainly be interesting to know what is going on in my nervous system and the role it plays; but this would involve a scientific approach that is not a component of the direct observation and the sensations we have.

Indeed, in our philosophical approach, we do not seek to provide causal explanations; rather, we seek to provide a conceptual and historical clarification that aims at dissolving the problem. In other words, we aim at providing a framework in which such direct observations make sense. The scientific search for causes and accurate descriptions of our neuronal states and more broadly chemical and biological states seems to be after something quite different from expressing feelings and sentiments such as the sensations we have of our own body; or longing for someone; or responding to scenes we read in books or see on the screen. If I would describe my neuronal state and the complicated chemistry involved to the person I am missing and longing to be with, our relations would probably not last very long; for the scientific quest for an explanation is quite different from that of the general human quest for expression. As Wittgenstein noted, "The existence of the experimental method (in psychology) makes us think that we have the means of solving the problems that trouble us; though problem and method pass one another by" (PI II xiv, p. 232 in Blackwell edition).

As noted, we seek to clarify how the mind–body problem has arisen and how we can get rid of the assumptions that give rise to this seemingly insoluble problem. While the approach we present here is inspired by Wittgenstein's work, Wittgenstein never expressed it in this explicit way. Peter Hacker, a Wittgenstein scholar and a philosopher who researched the foundations of neuroscience deeply and widely, presents a similar approach.[137] Hacker writes,

137 See, for example, *Philosophical Foundations of Neuroscience* by M.R. Bennett and P.M.S. Hacker, (Blackwell, 2003).

> The mind/body problem is insoluble. For it is a hopelessly confused residue of the Platonic/Augustinian/Cartesian tradition. It cannot be solved; but it can be dissolved. The mind is not an entity that could stand in a relationship to anything. All talk of the mind that a human being has and of its characteristics is a talk of the intellectual and volitional powers that he has, and of their exercise.[138]

Our task thus involves two steps: first, undoing the major premises of the Cartesian picture that gives rise to the current mind–body problem, and, second, articulating an alternative approach in which the problem does not even arise. Both moves require reference to the history of how these concepts were shaped. Given our extended survey (at the first part of this chapter), we can now do this with relative ease. The first move seeks to undercut the grip of the Cartesian picture, and the second seeks to promote an Aristotelian model, according to which the mind is not an entity, a substance, and mental events are not shadowy entities in the mind; rather, the mind is a name for an array of capacities that are functionally dependent on physiological capacities and organs for their realization.

15.1 Wittgenstein's Attack on the Cartesian Picture

Wittgenstein's attack on the Cartesian picture – a picture that splits human beings into two kinds of substances, a thinking thing or mind and an extended thing or body – does not operate by providing specific counter-arguments; rather, it operates by attempting to dismantle the whole picture. Wittgenstein does so by attacking the main presuppositions that *give rise* to the mind–body problem. If one can show that these presuppositions are without basis, the whole picture will collapse. The main presuppositions of the Cartesian picture are the following. First, it rests on the distinction between two realms: an inner realm of mental and psychological states that are accessible only to the subject of experience, and an external physical world, observable and accessible to all. While the inner world is subjective and private, the external world is objective and public; while the first ream is expressed in the first person, the second is expressed in the third person; while the second realm can be investigated by

138 *Human Nature: The Categorial Framework*, Blackwell, 2007, p. 283

science, the first realm cannot. The mind–body problem rests on the supposition that the gap between these realms is unbridgeable. The second presupposition is that the word 'mind' refers to an entity; and likewise, that mental predicates and utterances (such as 'I am in pain', 'I am upset', 'I feel anxiety building in me') refer to inner and private entities, or events, called sensations, emotions, or intentions, or some other kind of inner-like objects. We proceed by arguing against the first presupposition and then turn to the second.

15.2 Can There Be a Private Language?

Wittgenstein's attack on the first presupposition can be presented through the following thought experiment. If the Cartesian picture is an adequate picture, then in talking and thinking about my inner experiences – experiences that are presumably private – I could, and normally would, use a language that is essentially private, that is, a language no one other than myself could understand; for what it is about, what it refers to, is essentially inner entities in my own private domain.

But, asks Wittgenstein, is such a language possible? Does the idea of a private language even make sense? Could there be a language that only I can understand? If only I can understand the meaning of words in this language, it goes without saying that I will not be able to share it with anyone else and express my inner experiences in a way that others could understand.

But how would I come to know the meaning of the words in my own private language? How do I learn to use words such as 'I am in pain'? Well, presumably, I just decide the meaning of the words for myself. But how do I decide this and on what basis? And if I myself know the answer to these questions, why can't I explain them to others (in which case it would not be a private language)? Wittgenstein illustrates this question by drawing an analog with money:

> Why can't my right hand give my left hand money? – My right hand can put it into my left hand. My right hand can write a deed of gift and my left hand a receipt. – But the further consequences would not be those of a gift. When the left hand has taken the money from the right hand, etc., we shall ask: "Well,

> and what of it?" And the same could be asked if a person had given himself a private definition of a word; I mean, if he has said the word to himself and at the same time has directed his attention to a sensation. (PI 268)

As the exchange of money requires that a note or coin would have some value, a linguistic exchange requires that the words would have some meaning. But how does it come about that pieces of paper acquire value? And how does it come about that words have meaning? The exchange of words, as well as the exchange of money, presupposes some human institutions and practices that give words meaning and money value. Such institutions and practices, however, are clearly public, not private. Thus, defining the meaning of a word privately makes as much (or as little) sense as for my right hand to give money to my left hand. Wittgenstein suggests that the idea of a private language is analogous to the idea of a private monetary system. And why can't I institute my own private currency, as a government does, print a lot of it, and become rich? The question is what use could such a currency serve, and what value would it have? We know of various non-standard monetary systems, such as money in a monopoly game, prison money, cryptocurrency, etc.[139] But all these are systems that presuppose some institutions and agreed upon conventions – the exact opposite of the idea of a private language.

The conclusion Wittgenstein draws from this thought experiment is radical. Our talk about presumably inner and private sensations is no less public than our talk about external behavior. For my talk about my inner sensation – say, 'I am in pain', 'I am anxious', 'I am excited' – requires some relation to human behavior and external context in order for these expressions to have sense. If someone told us, 'I am terribly distressed' while looking entirely cheerful, what could we make of it? We might think that such a person does not know English very well.

Consider another argument against the idea of a private language. Assuming that a language rests on rules, such that learning a language requires learning its rules, and using the language requires following its rules, what could it mean to say that I follow the rules of my own private language? Obviously, only I can decide if I follow the rules or not, based on my inner private feelings. But, if so, it looks like

139 In some prisons in the US where cash is not allowed, the prisoners establish other currencies for exchanging goods between them. I myself heard of a prison where cans of tuna provide the equivalent of a monetary unit.

I could never go against the rule. And if I could never go against the rule, does it make any sense to say that I follow a rule correctly or that I follow a rule at all? In *Philosophical Investigations*, (remark 202), Wittgenstein writes, "'obeying a rule' is a practice. And to *think* one is obeying a rule is not to obey a rule. Hence it is not possible to obey a rule 'privately'; otherwise thinking one was obeying a rule would be the same as obeying it."

Inventing a private language would make as much (or as little) sense as inventing a private game. Of course, I can invent a game and play it alone. But if I can play the game with myself, why can't I play it with someone else? Or, more precisely why can't I teach its rules to someone else? Wittgenstein reply is very clear and simple: if I can set out rules for a game and play it with myself, I can surely teach these rules to others. Thus, if we have a language through which we express our inner sensations, it cannot be any more private than my pointing to colors or describing buildings.

Thus, it seems that to the extent that we are expressing our inner world by linguistic means, to the extent that we discuss our experiences, with ourselves or with others, this 'inner' mental realm is no more private than our external physical realm. Of course, it is patently true that only I *have* my pain, but it is also true that only I have my money. And it is far from obvious that the cases are so different as they initially appear to be. Certainly, in most cases, other people can see that I suffer. That I am in pain has fairly obvious behavioral manifestations. The fact that I can express and discuss my pain, with myself or with my doctor or a friend, shows that it is not hidden in the inner and mysterious depths of my soul. In other words, to the extent that I know how to express my sensations, I can express and convey them to other people.

15.3 How Do We Use the Word 'Mind'?

Let us now turn to examining the second presupposition, namely that the mind is seen as an entity, a substance. According to Wittgenstein, the meaning of words can only be understood through the way they are used. We have to observe how words function in a particular context or, to put it differently, how words function and what work they do in a particular language game. In our context, the right method would be not to ask what the mind is but rather how the word 'mind' is used in particular contexts. This will help us in clearing up confusions about the adequate use of the word 'mind', and in seeing what kind of thing it is, and, more importantly, what kind of thing it is *not*.

Wittgenstein's method is encapsulated in the following remark: "Grammar tells us what kind of object anything is" (PI 373).[140] According to Wittgenstein, rather than engaging in metaphysical speculation, we should try to clarify philosophical puzzles by attending to the way in which we employ concepts in our daily use of language. This, however, is tricky. For often it is the very use of language that gives rise to philosophical puzzles. Consider, for example, expressions such as 'I have a mind' or 'I have a body'. Do I have a mind in the same sense that I have a house, or money, or a friend? We do often say that someone 'lost his mind'. But what does that mean? Do we mean that he is searching for his mind as one searches for a lost key or a hat? Or rather that he is behaving abnormally, or is just very seriously confused? Similarly, when we say that someone is mindful, we certainly do not mean that he is full of mind but rather that he is an attentive, caring person. Thus, our language gives rise to certain puzzles. In particular, it leads us, perhaps unconsciously, to suppose that a mind is something that we can possess. And, on a deeper level, that it is some*thing*, an entity, in the first place.

But then we should examine closely the context in which such expressions make sense. In which context (if at all) do we say things like 'I have a mind' or 'I have a body'? Is there a non-philosophical context in which someone would say such phrases? And does the negation of such a phrase make any sense? What could it mean to say, 'I don't have a mind' or 'I don't have a body'? Do such expressions make any sense?

Gilbert Ryle (1900-76) makes this point more explicit. According to Ryle, the supposition that minds are kinds of entity is a 'category mistake': 'it represents the facts of mental life as if they belonged to one logical type or category [. . .] when actually they belong to another' (1949, 16). Ryle illustrates this with the following example. Suppose you take a visitor on a tour of your university. You stroll through the grounds; you take him to the library; you show him

140 See also "Essence is expressed in grammar" (PI 371).

the classrooms; the cafeteria; you introduce him to students and to members of the faculty. When you are done, you ask whether there is anything else he would like to see. The visitor replies: 'you've shown me the grounds, academic and administrative buildings, the library, students, and faculty; but where is the *university*?' The visitor's confusion reflects a category mistake. He has taken the term 'university' to designate something similar to, but distinct from, those things he has seen already.

If such a visitor persisted in the belief that 'university' designates such an entity despite failing ever to encounter it, he might come to imagine that the entity in question is a spectral, immaterial edifice. An analogous mistake, says Ryle, encourages a spectral notion of the mind. You begin with the idea that minds are entities. But when you examine all the candidate entities – bodies and brains, for instance – you fail to find mentality. If minds are entities, then, they must be entities of a special sort, *nonmaterial* entities. You come to see the mind, in Ryle's colorful phrase, as a *ghost in the machine*. But, Ryle holds, the mistake was made at the outset. Minds are not entities at all, ghostly or otherwise, a fact we should appreciate if only we kept firmly before us the way 'mind' functions in ordinary English.[141]

Wittgenstein's view is nicely expressed in his saying that "The human body is the best picture of the human soul" (PI p. 178). But this is not because the soul is something bodily (MS. 124. 7); rather, the human body is the best picture of the human soul because the best manifestation of the human soul is human behavior.[142]

Our view is that it would be better to say that human behavior is not the best manifestation of the human *soul* but rather of the whole person. We prefer the medieval adage, 'the body is the paintbrush of the soul'. But even this can be slightly misleading. And it would be better to say that the most fitting way of describing a *person's* state – both physical and mental – is his or her behavior. You can probably imagine some of the implications this has for yoga practice.

But then one must wonder whether human mental life ultimately comes down to nothing more than behavior, or is fully expressed by one's behavior. Is there nothing beyond behavior? Or, to put it differently, aren't there many things that

141 This bit on Ryle is a paraphrase of Heil 2013, pp. 54-55.
142 This is a paraphrase of Hacker 1990 p. 253.

somehow remain hidden and are not expressed in our behavior? Wittgenstein addresses this question by considering the case of pain. He writes,

> 'But you will surely admit that there is a difference between pain-behaviour accompanied by pain and pain-behaviour without any pain?' -Admit? What greater difference could there be? -'And yet you again and again reach the conclusion that the sensation itself is *nothing*.' --Not at all. It is not *something*, but not a *nothing* either. The conclusion was only that a nothing would serve just as well as a something about which nothing could be said. We have only rejected the grammar which tries to force itself upon us here.

The paradox disappears only if we make a radical break with the idea that language always functions in one way, and serves the same purpose: to convey thoughts – which may be about houses, pains, good and evil, or anything you please. (PI 304)

The key word here is 'about'. We tend to take the sole function of language to be the expression of thoughts that are *about* something, that refer to certain entities. In our case, thoughts that are supposed to be *about* some inner experiences, such as pain. But, for Wittgenstein, expressions such as 'I am in pain' or 'I have a headache' are not *about* anything; rather, they serve to *express* the way we feel. They do not refer to some mysterious inner entities; they are part of a behavior that typically manifests pain.

As Ray Monk comments, Wittgenstein's entire later philosophy begins and ends with an attack on this misunderstanding, namely, that we tend to think of the function of words as referring to objects, or to something on the model of an object, an entity, a thing like a chair or an apple. This view of language is very clearly presented through the Augustinian picture at the very first remark of *Philosophical Investigations*.[143] In this first remark, Wittgenstein cites a the following passage from Augustine's *Confessions*: "when my elders named some object, and accordingly moved towards something, I saw this and I grasped that the thing was called by the sound they uttered when they meant to point it out." Wittgenstein comments that Augustine's words "give us a particular picture of the essence of human language. It is this: individual words in language name objects –

143 Monk R. *How to Read Wittgenstein*, p. 93.

sentences are combinations of such names." In this picture, the meaning of a word "is the object for which it stands" (PI 1). Wittgenstein does not regard this picture as false. The problem is that it is true of a very small part of our language, and the variety of ways in which it functions, namely the part that concerns names and nouns. The main cause of error is that we take this idea and apply it to all kinds of words and to all variety of uses. Thus, we create a prejudice of thinking that every word must correlate with or refer to a certain object.

In the case of sensation, this prejudice turns out to invoke a rather strange inner object, to which the word 'pain' presumably refers. But rather than thinking that my words "I am in pain" refer to some mysterious object (pain) hiding in me, we could think of the words as part of the behavior through which we express pain.[144] Thus, pain need not be seen as something internal seeking external expression; rather, pain is simply expressed by our typical pain behavior. Linguistic behavior – what we say and how we say it – is part of our behavior: "'So you are saying that the word 'pain' really means crying?' – On the contrary: the verbal expression of pain replaces crying and does not describe it" (PI 244).

In this context, it is important to ask how one learns to use expressions such as 'I am in pain'. When a child falls down and cries, his parents ask him: "are you in pain"? "Where does it hurt"? etc. Wittgenstein's general response is this: "The concept of 'pain' is acquired with learning a language" (PI 384). Learning to use expressions such as 'I am in pain' is something that comes with typical behavior in particular circumstances, and is no different from learning to use other words or phrases.

Similar considerations hold for our learning to use other mental predicates (I intend, I think, I imagine, I recall, etc.). Indeed, the mind–body problem itself rests on the

144 PI 293. "If I say of myself that it is only from my own case that I know what the word 'pain' means – must I not say that the same of other people too?
Now someone tells me that *he* knows what pain is only his own case!----Suppose everyone had a box with something in it: we call it a 'beetle'. No one can look into anyone else's box, and everyone says he knows what a beetle is only by looking at *his* beetle. – Here it would be quite possible for everyone to have something different in his box. One might even imagine such a thing constantly changing. – But suppose the word 'beetle' had a use in these people's language? If so it would not be used as a name of a thing. The thing in the box has no place in the language game at all; not even as a ***something***: for the box might be empty. [. . .]
That is to say: if we construe the grammar of the expression of sensation on the model of 'object of designation' the object drops out of consideration as irrelevant." (PI 293)

(false) picture that the words 'mind' and 'body' refer to entities in their own right. A person, a human being, is an entity, a psychophysical unity. Of course, for various purposes, it is convenient to think of our body as a thing, so that we can talk about its weight, shape, etc., but when we talk about ourselves, the kind of creatures we are, we don't have to think of our body and of our mind as entities that are independent of one another. The deep assumption in this picture is not so much that mind and body are *separate* entities but that we tend to treat them as entities (as things or as substances) in the first place. When we say that the mind and body are separate, we already operate within the misleading picture that presents them as substance-like things.

Instead, we can think of a human being in an Aristotelian fashion, such that, just like any other living being, it is endowed with various powers and capacities. Some of these capacities, like the linguistic/rational capacity, seem to be distinctive of human beings; but it does not follow that human beings have an extra thing like a soul or a mind hidden in them that is responsible for these capacities.[145] To talk and think are behaviors that form part of our nature, just as being able to navigate across continents is an ability of migrating birds.

Sometimes, it is convenient and useful to distinguish mental capacities from physical ones. But in many cases, our various capacities are not so clearly distinguished, and the boundaries between them may be quite fuzzy. Walking gracefully, playing a piece of music well, pretending, mimicking, pointing at a certain target, or being irritated by someone's voice all clearly involve both our physical and mental capacities and limitations. Along these lines, we can think of what is often called 'the mental' as an array of capacities whose exercise often involve not just mental faculties but requires physical ones as well. Perception, for example, involves many of our physiological systems. Even the ability to concentrate involves ignoring all sorts of physical and mental distractions. Capacities such as recollection, imagination, intention, and reflection are naturally

145 It might be objected that on the model we're proposing here, talking of capacities would invoke exactly the same kind of error as talking of minds. When I say 'I recall', it's a part of recalling-behavior – to infer from that that there's some recalling-capacity behind the behavior is either a further, metaphysical step or a just convenient way of speaking about different kinds of behavior. The point is that there is no need to invoke some entity (other than our whole selves) standing behind the behavior. We would like to thank Barnaby Hutchins for this clarification.

classified as mental. And there is no harm in this. But let us note that the exercise of such capacities is normally related to many other features (rather than just our so-called mental features). Further, we usually exercise these capacities (as when we say 'I recall', 'I think', 'I wish', 'it makes no sense to me', etc.) while making no explicit mention of something called the mind. And, as Peter Hacker points out, talk of the mind is often "a convenient *façon de parler*, an oblique way of speaking about human faculties and their exercise" (2007, p. 250).

16. Some Consequences and Brief Discussion[146]

Wittgenstein writes,

> 'But doesn't what you say come to this: that there is no pain without *pain behavior*'? – It comes down to this: only of a living human being and what resembles (behaves like) a living *human* being can one say: it has sensations; it sees; is blind; hears; is deaf; is conscious or unconscious. (PI 281)

This seemingly trivial point has important ramifications. Let us note here the most central ones. First of all, the subject of mental (and other) capacities is not the mind, or the brain, or the body, or some other body part; rather, it is the whole person, the human being.

> But isn't it absurd to say of a body that it has pain?----And why does one feel an absurdity in that? In what sense is it true that my hand does not feel pain, but I in my hand?
> What sort of issue is: Is it the body that feels pain?---How is it to be decided? What makes it plausible to say that it is not the body?----Well, something like this: if someone has a pain in his hand, then the hand does not say so and one does not comfort the hand, but the sufferer. (PI 286)

It is not, then, my mind or my brain or my body that suffers pain or has a good time; it is me, a person, a human being. Likewise, it is not the stomach that suffers

146 In this section, I draw on Hacker 2007, pp. 252-55.

from stomachache or the head that has a headache; it is the person who suffers and experiences pain or pleasure, and not the brain or one of my body parts. This point cuts across much of contemporary philosophy of mind, debates about artificial intelligence, and especially the very common view that the mind is identical with the brain and that the brain and some of its components may be regarded as agents.[147]

Thus, it is also useful to remind ourselves that neural, cortical states are features of the brain or the nervous system,[148] but mental states, such as perceptions, intentions, concerns, and desires, are features and states of human beings; that is, they may be ascribed to persons rather than to their brains. A human being can be in a cheerful or miserable mood, but what would does it mean to say of the brain that it is cheerful, or in a cheerful state?[149] It might be a challenging scientific project to describe what is going on in ones' brain (or nervous system) when one experiences such states or feelings. But it is important to keep in mind that this is would be a different kind of enterprise. It is also worth mentioning that the common reference among philosophers to 'brain states' is extremely vague. The human brain consists of billions of neurons, each of which has thousands of synapses. These neurons form a network of immense complexity – a network that is also in constant change and interaction (both internal and with the environment). We don't have a clear idea of what it means to describe a brain state, let alone correlate such a state with a certain mental state that supposedly takes place at the same time.[150] This is not to deny that many things can be observed about the brain and that this is a scientific project worth pursuing. But the goals and possible achievements of this project must be critically examined. A description of my 'brain state', whatever this may turn out to be, would not express my mental or emotional state and the meaning it has (or does not have) in my life. This is not something that a description of the brain, however accurate, is about. It might instruct us about the *causes* of my state but not what it means.

147 As in the example noted above, some neuroeconomists talk of the brain as making decisions. For much elaboration and substantiation of this point, see *Philosophical Foundations of Neuroscience*, chapter 3.

148 The notion of a brain state as often used by philosophers is entirely opaque; it lacks any clear description of the immensely complex neural system and is no more than a fiction of something that sounds empirically clear but is not. It is basically vacant as currently used.

149 For instance, in a televised conference, Professor Idan Segev of the Hebrew University of Jerusalem describes the present state of the art by saying that "the brain now investigates the brain and can even cure the brain". This can only mean, I take it, that he Prof. Segev, or we as human beings, investigate our brain. See: youtube.com/watch?v=AG6nKwTALWo.

150 See Hacker 2007, p. 252.

We do say that someone has a creative or a narrow mind; but we do not normally speak of the mind as if it were an agent in its own right (Hacker 2007, 253). A man who has a sharp mind is a man with intelligence – but this is not a statement about the person's mind, seen as something independent of the person. Someone who has a curious mind is a curious person; it is not that his mind can be abstracted from him and discovered to be curious. All these examples reiterate the point that the use of physical and mental capacities, while very common and useful, need not be seen as conflating the human person with his or her mind or her body or her brain. This is not a new point. In fact, Aristotle noted this long ago: "to say that the *psyche* is angry is as if one would say that the *psyche* weaves and builds. For it is surely better not to say that the *psyche* pities, learns, or thinks, but that the man does these things with his *psyche* (*De Anima* 408; cited from Hacker, 255).

We can, and normally do, see human persons as having intrinsically related mental and physical capacities, which also imply mental and physical limitations. But it often happens that the scientific explanation of the causal story in the background gets confused with the way we express ourselves. It is therefore worth reminding ourselves that it is not the eyes that see or the legs that walk; rather it is the person who walks and sees; though without the functioning of the eyes and legs, no seeing or walking would be possible. In principle, activities such as imagining and recalling should not be understood all that differently. None of them would be possible without the functioning of the nervous system; but this does mean that what we see or recall or imagine can be described by describing our nervous system.

Before concluding let us address three questions and objections.

1. One might wonder how our view differs from functionalism. Functionalists also argue that the mind is not a thing and that it can be likened to something like a computer program. While functionalists are certainly not dualists, it seems to us that they, like all contemporary philosophical positions, are deeply entrenched in the Cartesian picture in the sense that they feel obliged to give an account of the mental in terms of the physical. This means that their deep concern is to account for the alleged mystery of the mental in terms of the (scientifically described) physical nature of extended matter.

We, on the other hand, don't accept this challenge. We don't think that the mental is a mystery that needs to be accounted for, let alone in physical terms. We think that the mental looks mysterious *within the Cartesian framework*. But more broadly, we don't seek to provide a scientific account of the mental at all. That project seems misguided to us. We think that mental and physical capacities evoke no particular mysteries within an Aristotelian framework that sees human living beings as psychophysical unities with various capacities that stem from their nature.

2. But one might wonder whether capacities are not things as well, such that the whole problem just comes up at another level. On our view, capacities are not names for things hidden in the background. They merely indicate the functions a certain system can perform. The capacity of sight requires nothing over and above the eye and the entire complicated system that enables it; just as the capacity for walking and standing is related to our having two legs, as well as to many other enabling mechanisms; but these are not entities that stand, as it were, behind the walking behavior – they are not anything that exists in its own right.

3. One might also wonder how our view differs from Hacker's. We see not only the mind as a set of capacities; we also think that this is the best way to think about the body. Indeed, our conviction is that the mind–body dichotomy is one in which the two concepts are mutually constitutive – that is, our concept of the body serves to define what the mind is, and our concept of the mind serves to define what a body is. But again, mind and body are not entities; they are just names for different features of a single entity. This is more clearly the case in living beings, but it is also arguable that other things also don't have a body in this sense. Thus, observe that we don't normally talk about the body of a chair or a stone or a river, though there is a tradition of talking about bodies in the history of science. We also don't think that the distinction between mental and physical capacities and limitations is sharp and clear; rather, we think that the lines between them are often not clearly delineated. As we discuss in chapter 2, some qualities and capacities have different senses – stability of the body is the not the same as stability of the mind (though they may be related). Much would depend on the particular context we are considering.

In addition, we also don't feel that the boundaries between the empirical domain of science and the conceptual domain of philosophy are as sharply delineated as Hacker makes them out to be. Relatedly, we also feel that advances in science and technology can (and do) change our language as well as our concepts. So, we are a little reticent about drawing too easy a distinction between science and philosophy. Here, too, the lines are not so easily drawn, and clarification is always needed in each particular context.

17. Conclusion

In our approach, we have sought to dissolve the post-Cartesian mind–body problem by rejecting the picture in which it arises. Dissolving the problem means dismantling the assumptions of the conceptual framework within which it arises – that is, dismantling the whole picture in which the problem as we know it today arises. This may not be an easy thing to do, for both conceptual and psychological reasons. The main idea is to get rid of a very powerful presupposition underlying this debate – and the difficulty of getting rid of it may be as difficult as getting rid of a deeply ingrained habit, because it is embedded into the way we are habituated to talk and think about mind and body. The presupposition we are referring to is a basic one, namely, that mind and body are *things* of some sort – that they are entities, or substances, in the philosophical jargon. If we are able to free ourselves from the picture in which mind and body are seen as things, and hold instead that only the human being *as a whole* may be seen as a thing, then we might be ready to replace the problematic presupposition with the Aristotelian insight that we are beings with mental and physical capacities that are intimately and inseparably related – both conceptually and empirically. Aristotle's insight is that soul and body are related as the capacity of sight is related to the organ of sight (i.e., the eye). The eye enables us to see, and its particular structure and mechanism allow us to see in certain ways and not in others. It thus both constitutes the ability to see and imposes certain limitations on what and how we see. Instead of thinking of ourselves as creatures with minds that are *things*[151], we can think of ourselves

151 On this point, see also Lowe *Introduction to the Philosophy of Mind*, p. 1. Lowe notes that much of the usual way of doing the philosophy of mind presupposes minds to be things. The main reason for this is that "Indo-European languages such as English are overburdened with nouns and those whose native tongues they are have an unwarranted tendency to suppose that nouns name things" (p. 1). Lowe suggests referring to minded things as "subjects of experience" (Lowe 2004, p. 8). This seems rather technical and we prefer using the more natural 'persons' instead.

as creatures endowed with mental capacities or powers – such as sensibility, imagination, memory, thought, calculation – that are bound up with physical features (and capacities) that are necessary for their realization, and are manifest in our normal activities.

In this picture, there is no mystery in a bodily position – such as a *yogasana* – expressing a person's mood; nor is there any serious problem, as far as we can see, in our ability to improve our well-being by working on our physical posture along the lines we describe in chapter 2. Rather, studying and investigating our physical and mental capacities and limitations in their curious and complex interactions seem to be a reasonable method that can, in our own experience at least, improve our well-being and extend our horizons in various ways. The conclusion here is not meant as a once-and-for-all resolution that would put an end to all questions about mind–body relations; rather, it is meant as an invitation to experience, explore, and use the subtle and complicated relations among our mental and physical capacities. The point of the philosophical exercise taken up here – apart from its inherent interest – is to carve out a conceptual space for such an exploration (which we designate as a 'psychophysical lab'), without invoking the paradoxes that come up within the Cartesian framework. We hope to have articulated a framework in which exploring ourselves as psychophysical creatures (or our psychophysical nature) makes some sense.

Appendix: The Debate Between Daniel Dennett and David Chalmers[152]

In this appendix we present the views of Dennett and Chalmers, whose views are probably most influential in contemporary philosophy of mind. There is an ongoing debate (both direct and indirect) between these philosophers, and it is worthwhile to become familiar with their influential positions.

1. Daniel Dennett

Daniel Dennett (born 1942) is one of the most influential living philosophers in contemporary philosophy of mind. Dennett is an anti-Cartesian and strives to get rid of Descartes' split metaphysics. He clearly prefers one of the Cartesian substances, namely, extended substance – or bodies. His ultimate goal is explaining all phenomena in naturalistic terms alone and he seeks to approach the question in a scientific (rather than common sense or phenomenological) manner.

Building on Wilfrid Sellars' distinction between the manifest image and the scientific image, Dennett holds that the things we see and hear and interact with (the manifest image) are "not *mere* fictions but different versions of what actually exists: real patterns." But the underlying reality, what exists in itself and not just for us or for other creatures, is accurately represented only by the scientific image – ultimately in the language of physics, chemistry, molecular biology, and neurophysiology.[153]

One of the challenges that are laid out before anyone who rejects the dichotomous split between body and mind is to explain how such a peculiar (and wonderful) thing as the capacity to experience the world from a first-person point of view could arise out of supposedly nothing but a lump of cells. In other words, what makes consciousness possible? Dennett believes that, due to progress in science

152 This section was composed by Benyamin Eisner (and then revised and edited by Ohad Nachtomy)

153 See Thomas Nagel's review of Dennett's recent book *From Bacteria to Bach and Back: The Evolution of Minds*, Norton, 2017 in the New York Review of Books, March 9, 2017 Issue.

– especially in biology and neuroscience – since the late twentieth century, the investigation of consciousness is in a much better starting point than ever before.

The solution he proposes (and the reason he considers our generation to be in a better position to develop such a solution) can be presented through the analogy he draws between the problem of consciousness and the problem of life. For many years, the phenomena of life posed a hard challenge for science. The challenge was to explain the possibility of the unique features of life such as metabolism, growth, self-repair, self-defense, and reproduction. Since mechanistic-naturalistic explanations, which we are familiar with today, were not available back then, Dennett claims, it was very common, even among scientists, to assume a mysterious ingredient – *a life force* or *élan vital* – which was supposed to be responsible in some way for the miracles of life. There are almost no proponents of this idea (which is called *vitalism*) remaining nowadays, because the motivation behind it weakened dramatically due to successful naturalistic explanations that the scientific progress provides us with.[154] Dennett expects that something similar will happen with the problem of consciousness. Although we do not yet have an explanation of that phenomenon, once a good naturalistic explanation is offered, the need to posit the existence of some mysterious substances like mind or soul in order to explain what makes consciousness possible will disappear.

Not all contemporary philosophers share Dennett's view. They claim that the nature of this particular problem is different, and that it couldn't, in principle, be solved by any mechanistic account whatsoever.[155] Consciousness – which is taken to be mainly the ability to experience reality from a first-person perspective – seems to be something non-physical in its very nature. We know that the processes of perception and sensation are accompanied by first-person perspective experience, but, supposedly at least, they could also happen 'in the dark', that is, without the experience, without the awareness; it is difficult even to imagine what a naturalistic explanation that can show why and how a first-person experience is derived from physical states would be. According to Dennett's dualist opponent's view, we must look somewhere else, or just accept that we will never solve that mystery. The proponents of this position, whom Dennett calls *mysterians*, often use

154 This is in fact not entirely historically accurate, for many versions of vitalism were raised as a *response to* a mechanistic explanation (and not because it was not available).
155 See for example, Chomsky 1994; Nagel 1998; McGinn 1999.

thought experiments to show the alleged impossibility of a physicalist explanation of consciousness. One of those experiments is a few hundred years old and named after its creator: 'Leibniz's mill'. In his *Monadology*, Leibniz constructs the following thought experiment:

> If you imagine that there is a machine whose structure is to think, sense and have perceptions, we could conceive of it enlarged, keeping the same proportions, so that we could enter into it, as one enters into a mill. Assuming that, when inspecting its interior, we will only find parts that push one another, and we will never find anything to explain perception [and thought]. And so, we should seek perception in the simple substance and not in the composite machine or in the machine. Furthermore, this is all one can find in the simple substance – that is, perceptions and their changes. It is also in this alone that all the *internal actions* of simple substance can consist. (*Monadology* § 17; in AG 215)

Dennett is not moved by Leibniz's thought experiment. Such experiments, he argues, are nothing but 'intuition pumps': they are designed to stimulate a certain intuition but contain no rational arguments to support those intuitions. Leibniz insists on looking for the source of a specific point of view – a first-person perspective. Admittedly, he could not find anything, but can it be the case, Dennett wonders, that there is actually nothing to find? In Dennett's words:

> Might it be, however, that Leibniz, lost in his giant mill, just couldn't see the woods for the trees? Might there not be a bird's eye view – not the first-person perspective of the subject in question, but a higher-level third-person perspective – from which, if one squinted just right, one could bring into focus the recognizable patterns of consciousness in action? Might it be that somehow the organization of all the parts which work one upon another yields consciousness as an emergent product? And if so, why couldn't we hope to understand it, once we had developed the right concepts? (2005, p. 5)

Dennett believes that what finally broke "the spell of Leibniz's intuition pump" was the appearance of computers. Computers are 'mind-like' in many ways, at least from a third-person point of view. They can perform tasks that call for inference, memory, judgment, anticipation; they can gain new knowledge, find new patterns, and do many things that heretofore only minded human beings (or, perhaps in some cases, animals) could do. According to Dennett, the lesson we ought to learn from computers is that "what is well-nigh invisible at the level of the meshing of billions of gears may nevertheless be readily comprehensible at higher levels of analysis" (2005, p. 6).

The idea that the mind can be explained by computational models of the kind naturalists recruit may still seem counterintuitive, at least at first glance. It appears that such explanations would always leave out something important. Modern versions of Leibniz's mill thought-experiment try to capture this intuition. One version, which has been the focus of many contemporary debates, asks us to consider the possibility of a philosophical zombie. A philosophical zombie is a creature that, by definition, behaves indistinguishably from a conscious being. In any possible test, the zombie will perform exactly as if he is conscious. Nevertheless, by definition, it has no consciousness at all, so that it does not experience the world from a first-person point of view – so, just as Leibniz's mill suggest that all the mechanisms of the brain are not sufficient to explain consciousness, so the philosophical zombie suggests that all the behavior of humans is similarly insufficient.

The question is whether there is any real difference between a conscious person and a perfect philosophical zombie. Intuitively, the answer to this question seems to be positive. Apparently, we understand what a philosophical zombie is and are able to determine that it is different from a conscious person. This answer gives rise to a position, according to which "The fundamental flaw in any mechanistic theory of consciousness is that it cannot account for this important difference" (2005, p.14). Dennett holds that those philosophers who claim they can *conceive* of a philosophical zombie are mistaken. He claims that the idea of an unconscious zombie of the kind proposed is incoherent, and therefore there is nothing to learn from it (Dennett 1991, esp. chapters 10-12). One widely-accepted contemporary view that strongly supports this line of reasoning is the view according to which the mental supervenes upon the physical. In a nutshell, according to this view, a physical duplicate is a complete duplicate, and specifically, it is a mental duplicate (because the mental supervenes entirely on the physical: it is not something that can be separated from it). Hence, if a zombie is a physical duplicate of a conscious person, then it just is a mental duplicate of that person, i.e., it is not a zombie at all.

The alternative that Dennett offers is an optimistic one: "Consciousness, on this optimistic view, is indeed a wonderful thing, but not that wonderful – not too wonderful to be explained by using the same concepts and perspectives that have worked elsewhere in biology" (2005, p.6).

By "the same concepts", Dennett means specifically the method of third-person investigation. There is a tradition of regarding consciousness as something accessible only "from the inside", i.e. only from the first-person point of view. From a third-person point of view, according to that tradition, we can only infer indirectly, or speculate, about the existence or characteristics of consciousness, but we can never be sure about it. This tradition, Dennett declares, "is not just a mistake, but a serious obstacle to ongoing scientific research that can explain consciousness" (2005, p. 25).

As we can clearly see here, Dennett seeks a *scientific* account of consciousness. And he relegates the common sense and subjective experience we have of ourselves as conscious agents to the manifest image. Rejecting the first-person point of view tradition, Dennett embraces a different approach to the investigation of consciousness. He calls his approach *Heterophenomenology*. For the heterophenomenologist, the ultimate data is the data available to everyone, i.e. the third-person accessible data. What about the first-person point-of-view data? Should we just ignore that? Of course not. After all, we come to learn about others' first-person point-of-view through their speech and other acts, which he counts as third-person point-of-view data. We should account for that sort of data, but we need to treat it with caution and bear in mind that, contrary to the common belief, one can be wrong even about his own so-called 'first-person point-of-view' experiences.

Here is how Dennett describes his method in his book *Consciousness Explained*:

> You are not authoritative about what is happening in you, but only about what seems to be happening in you, and we are giving you total, dictatorial authority over the account of how it seems to you, about what it is like to be you. And if you complain that some parts of how it seems to you are ineffable, we heterophenomenologists will grant that too. What better grounds could we have for believing that you are unable to describe something than that (1)

> you don't describe it, and (2) confess that you cannot? Of course you might be lying, but we'll give you the benefit of the doubt. (1991, pp. 96-97)

Heterophenomenology, according to Dennett, is just a natural extension of the regular method that rules over the objective physical sciences. It is "the *neutral* path leading from objective physical science and its insistence on the third-person point of view, to a method of phenomenological description that can (in principle) do justice to the most private and ineffable subjective experiences, while never abandoning the methodological principles of science" (1991, p. 72). Heterophenomenology requires us to take nothing for granted – even a person's claims about their own experience from their own point of view – unless we can confirm that data from a third-person point of view (2005, pp. 47-49). Using Heterophenomenology, Dennett hopes to achieve his primary goal of eliminating the mystery around the phenomenon of consciousness by means of scientific explanation that does not leave unexplained gaps.[156]

2. David Chalmers

Born and raised in Sydney, Australia and presently a philosopher at New York University, Chalmers is a prominent figure in the field of philosophy of mind and especially in the problem of consciousness.

Chalmers (1995) distinguish between 'the easy problems of consciousness' and 'the hard problem of consciousness'. The easy problems include those of explaining phenomena like the ability to react to environmental stimuli, the ability of a system to access and report its own internal condition, the difference between wakefulness and sleep, and other phenomena related to the term 'consciousness'. The hard problem is the problem of *experience*. Chalmers takes it for granted that when we think and perceive, there is a subjective

156 For lack of space, we only mention Dennett's Intentional Stance Theory here, which culminates in his (1996) *Kinds of Minds: Toward an Understanding of Consciousness* (1996). The Intentional Stance Theory provides an interesting development, namely, the mental as the product of us interpreting other people (and likewise other systems, e.g., thermostats), i.e., taking an 'intentional stance' towards them.

aspect – in Nagel's famous phrase, "There is *something it is like to* be conscious" – and this subjective aspect is what Chalmers calls *experience*. Experience goes along with perception in different modes. When we see, for example, we experience the felt quality of color (redness, darkness, and so on). Experience also takes place when we hear, smell, or touch. We experience emotions and thoughts too. There is definitely something that it is like to be in those states; hence, those are also states of experience.

It is important to note that 'experience' for Chalmers means something slightly different from 'experience' for Dennett. For Chalmers, an experience is essentially subjective. Unlike Dennett, who strives to describe an experience in objective terms, Chalmers holds that such an objective description, by definition, will never be a complete description of an experience as long as it leaves out the subjective aspect.

Chalmers assumes that at least some organisms are subjects of experience. The hard problem is explaining why:

Why is it that when our cognitive systems engage in visual and auditory information-processing, we have visual or auditory experience: the quality of deep blue, the sensation of middle C? How can we explain why there is something it is like to entertain a mental image, or to experience an emotion? (1995, p. 201)

The 'easy problems' are easy because they concern the explanations of abilities and functions. It may still be difficult to actually explain them, but at least the existing methods of cognitive science are well-suited for producing this kind of explanation. Explaining a function involves specifying a mechanism that can perform that function. For example, to explain the ability to react to environmental stimuli, we need to explain how a system could be affected by environmental stimuli and react in a specific manner. Chalmers holds that 'It is a *conceptual* fact about these phenomena that their explanation only involves the explanation of various functions, as the phenomena are *functionally definable*' (1995, p. 202). All we mean by 'to be awake' is to be receptive to information from the environment. Therefore, all it could possibly take to explain such phenomena is an explanation of how the relevant functions are performed.

By contrast, the 'hard problem' is hard precisely because it is not a problem about functions and abilities. Even when all the relevant functions and abilities concerning consciousness are perfectly explained, the hard problem will remain untouched (just like in Leibniz's mill).

Even when we have explained the performance of all the cognitive and behavioral functions in the vicinity of experience - perceptual discrimination, categorization, internal access, verbal report - there may still remain a further unanswered question: *Why is the performance of these functions accompanied by experience?* A simple explanation of the functions leaves this question open (1995, p.203). According to Chalmers, this further question is the key question in the problem of consciousness. It is also a unique question, because it goes beyond problems about functions, and for that reason solving it requires a new approach.

As we have seen above, Dennett thinks that consciousness should be addressed by using the same methods scientists used in order to solve the problem of life. Chalmers, however, believes that the analogy between the problem of consciousness and the problem of life is wrong and misleading. Unlike consciousness, Chalmers considers life as a phenomenon that is functionally definable: "To explain life, we ultimately need to explain how a system can reproduce, adapt to its environment, metabolize, and so on" (1995, p.203). Lacking detailed knowledge of biological and chemical mechanisms, the vitalists doubted whether any physical mechanism can perform the remarkable functions of life and put forward the hypothesis of 'vital spirit' as an alternative. But overall, they do accept the conceptual claim that what is needed here is explanations of functions. In the case of consciousness, on the other hand, explanations of functions will never suffice because the problem is not about functions but about the subjective experience that accompanies them. It is also important to note that there is a significant difference between *experience* and *vital* spirit. The vital spirit, Chalmers suggests, was posited in order to explain the functions of life, so it can be discarded once those functions are explained by other means. Experience, by contrast, is an *explanandum* (it is the very thing we wish to explain); hence, denying it will be avoiding the problem rather than facing it.

Apparently, there are many ways of denying experience. We can equate 'experience' with particular functions and abilities such as the capacity to discriminate and report. If we identify consciousness with a certain function, once we explain that function, our job is done, and there is nothing left to explain. Alternatively, we can insist with Dennett that what we cannot verify and describe from a third-person point of view is not real. Indeed, choosing one of those ways will lead to a simpler theory of the mind. But, for Chalmers, denying experience is not an option.

> Experience is the most central and manifest aspect of our mental lives, and indeed is perhaps the key explanandum in the science of the mind. Because of this status as an explanandum, experience cannot be discarded like the vital spirit when a new theory comes along. Rather, it is the central fact that any theory of consciousness must explain. A theory that denies the phenomenon "solves" the problem by ducking the question. (1995, p.206)

Chalmers concludes that the 'hard problem' cannot be solved using the usual methods of cognitive science and neuroscience. Nevertheless, he does not turn into what Dennett calls a 'mysterian' and does not give up trying to explain consciousness. Rather, he considers a few alternative explanations.

In his early work (1995), he suggests that we take experience as fundamental. Taking experience as fundamental means adding it to our ontology as a non-physical component which stands on the same level with the basic physical components of the world such as mass and space. This position, Chalmers says, "qualifies as a variety of dualism, as it postulates basic properties over and above the properties invoked by physics" (1995, p.210).[157] Recently, Chalmers has considered panpsychism - the hypothesis according to which consciousness is not only fundamental but ubiquitous in the natural world (2013) - as well as idealism, which holds that consciousness is the ultimate foundation of all reality (2018). What unifies all these positions is that all of them take conscious experience for granted rather than seeking to eliminate it. Dennett would probably see this as a rather mysterian approach. Thus, it is hard to see a common ground for the debate between them.

157 Note that Chalmers would need to address the problem of *the closure of the physical realm*, which every dualist position faces.

CHAPTER FOUR

Practice Sequences

Introduction

The effects of yoga practice are highly sensitive to the order in which the *asanas* are performed in a particular session. This is called *Vinyasa* or *Vinyasakrama*. The sequence of *asanas* is to be selected according to the purpose and intention of the session. In selecting a sequence, one ought to take into consideration one's practice experience and maturity; one's current physical and mental condition; the purpose of performing the sequence, as well as the characteristics of the environment in which the practice takes place. This may include your age, your physical and mental condition, your occupation, the time of the day, the season, and much more.

This section presents five sequences designed for enhancing the following mental states and qualities:

1. For confidence building (reducing anxiety)
2. For emotional balance (enhancing *sattva*)
3. For optimism and joy (countering *tamasic* mood)
4. For calming and pacifying (countering *rajasic* mood)
5. For restoration (recovering from fatigue)

In these sequences we make extensive use of props, so that one has to be well acquainted with the use of props. In composing these sequences, I draw on my own experience and practice as well as on my teaching experience. I have tried them on my own and with my students and find them very useful and very effective in transforming our mental state.

However, note that such sequences can't be standardized, since they must be adapted to the constitution, age, physical and mental state, and so on, of the practitioner. Use these sequences as general guidelines. If you suffer from mental problem you must seek an advice of a knowledgeable yoga teacher, which should guide you and tailor the sequence to your special condition and needs.

How to Use the Sequences

Once you have selected a sequence you wish to practice, you can use it in several ways:

- Follow the sequence every day, for a period of a few weeks or months.
- Follow the sequence often (2-3 times a week), and at other days practice other *asanas*.
- Incorporate the selected sequence in your practice routine and use it whenever you feel the need.
- It is recommended to repeat the key poses in the sequence (indicated by an asterisk (*)) more often.

The sequences presented vary in their length; some require 30 min. to complete, while the longer ones will take 90 minutes. It is recommended to follow the entire selected sequence; however, if your time is limited, you may skip the *asanas* that are not marked with an asterisk.

Since the practice should suit the special needs and conditions of each individual practitioner, it is hard to give general advice about the application of these sequences. A good sequencing requires intimate knowledge of the energetic properties of each *asana* and its anatomical, physiological, neurological, sensory and mental repercussions.

The journey for mastering any subject can be described by four stages: ignorance, information, intelligence, and integration. When you are ignorant about a subject you have to learn it in order to acquire the necessary information and rules. After some learning you can use the information and rules more intelligently and apply them a more sophisticated manner. Finally, when you have internalized the rules and master the subject, you can forget the rules and improvise. This is the integration stage in which you have integrated the knowledge, so you don't need to remember the rules anymore. But it may take several decades of practice and study to reach this level!

If you are a beginner, try, as much as possible, to follow sequences given by experienced teachers. Of course, you should always be prudent and use discrimination, and if necessary, adapt your practice according to your health condition and any limitations you may have. Consult an experienced teacher in any case of doubt. If the sequence includes a pose you are not familiar with, avoid it or seek guidance.

More experienced practitioners may use these sequences as guidelines and add or skip *asanas* according to the day to day conditions and circumstances.

CAUTION

- In Chapter 1, the Explorations, I have included cautions and contra-indications for some of the *asanas*, as well as guideline for practicing during menses. Before practicing an *asana*, make sure you are not suffering from any of the symptoms which are contra-indicated for that pose. If you are menstruating, avoid the poses that are contra-indicated for these days (see the Introduction to chapter 1, on page 16).

Generally, I assume you know the *asanas* in the sequence you select. However, for some *asanas*, I added special instructions, that are numbered and referred to in the sequence, next to the name of the *asana*. These instructions are meant to guide you to do the *asana* in a way that will contribute to creating the desired effects of the sequence (see pages 349 to 352). For more information about the use of props, see Eyal's books: *A Chair for Yoga* and *Props for Yoga Vol. I, II & III.*

• We use the abbreviations: ACFY and PFY •

4.1 *For Confidence Building (Reducing Anxiety)*

Standing poses strengthen the Earth Element (which symbolizes solidity, stability, heaviness and steadiness), hence they constitute the foundation of building confidence. The Hero Poses (*Virabhadrasana I, II* & *III*) in particular strengthen the body, open the chest and induce power and courage. It is said that *Shiva* – the Lord of yoga – gave these poses in order to help us face fear.

To improve stability and to increase the opening of the chest, the standing poses are done with a chair support (However, if a suitable chair is unavailable, you can do these poses without a chair).

Balance poses, inversions and backbends present challenges; mastering these poses strengthen physical and mental confidence (see the section about 'Confidence and Courage' in Chapter 2, for a discussion of this topic).

Here are two sequences for building self-confidence and overcoming low self-image. The first is intended for all levels, and the second is for practitioners with at least 2-3 years of practice.

4.1.1 Building Confidence For All Levels

Level: all levels
Time: 30 min.
Props needed: 2 blocks, belt, blanket, bolster (or other support)
Optional props: chair

1. *Tadasana* with belt on elbows. See PFY Vol. I, p. 14

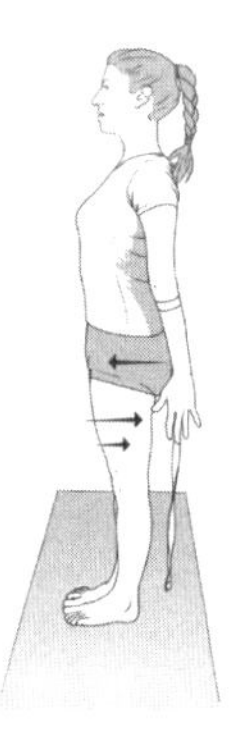

1 m.

2. ** Urdhva Hastasana* belt on arms, block between hands. See PFY Vol. I, p. 21

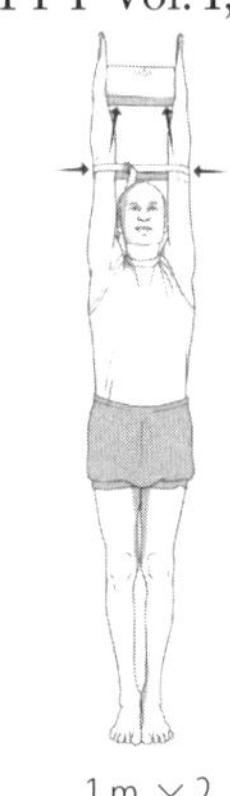

1 m. × 2

3. *Vrksasana* See PFY Vol. I, p. 25

45 sec. on each leg

4. ** Utthita Trikonasana* back against a chair. See ACFY p. 13

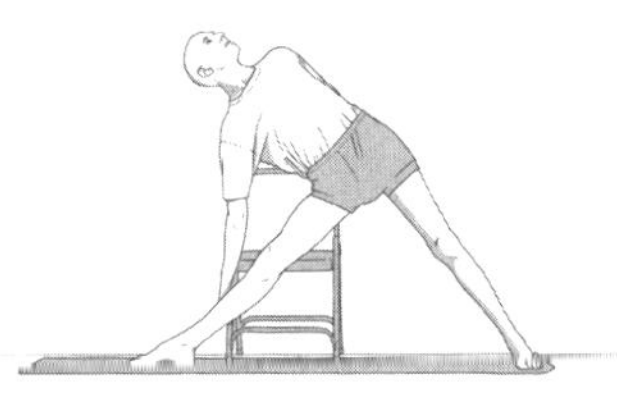

45 sec. each side × 2

5. ** Virabhadrasana II* with a chair in front. See ACFY p. 17

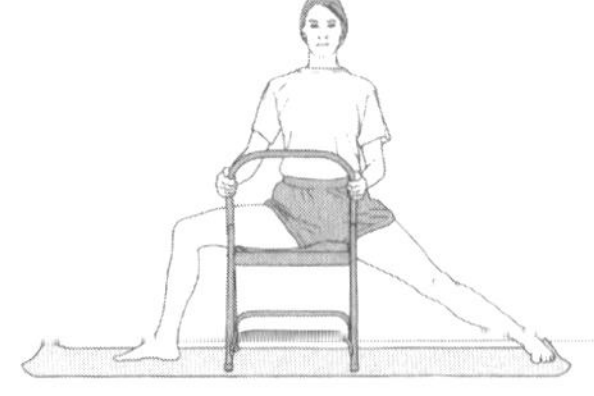

45 sec. each side

6. ** Paryankasana* blocks support. See 8 on p. 351

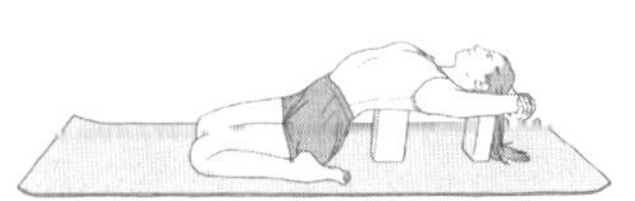

3-4 m.

7. *Shavasana*
block support.
See p. 65

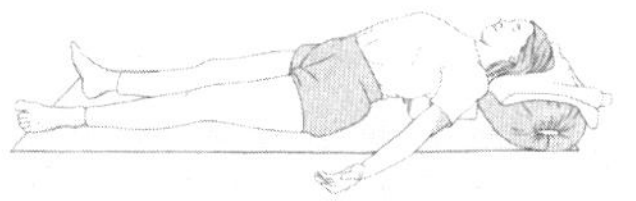

3-4 m.

8. ** Supta Baddha Konasana*
on lengthwise (spine-wise)
block. See p. 131

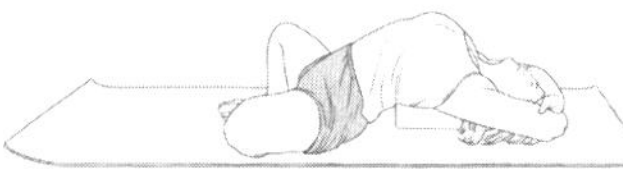

3-4 m.

9. *Shavasana*
on a bolster.
See 6 on p. 351

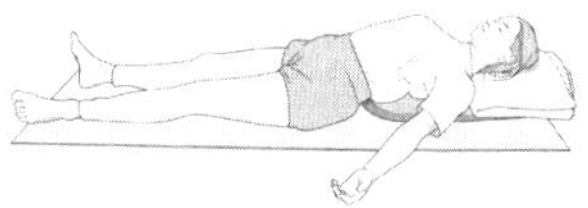

5 m.

4.1.2 Building Confidence For Intermediate and Advanced Levels

Level: Intermediate and advanced
Time: 90 min.
Props needed: chair, bolster, block
Optional props: blanket

1. *Tadasana*
See p. 21

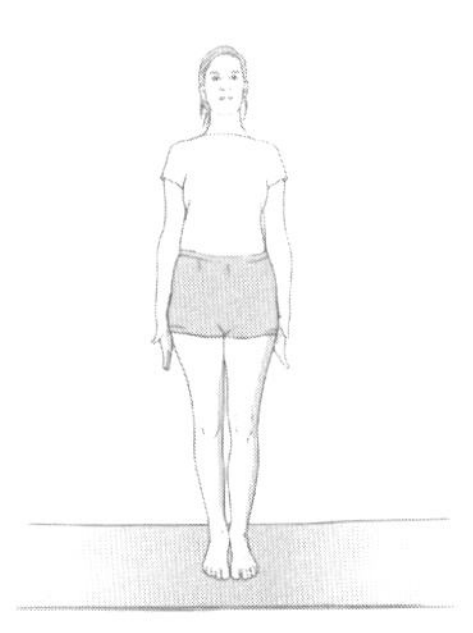

1 m.

2. *Vrksasana*
See PFY Vol. I p. 25

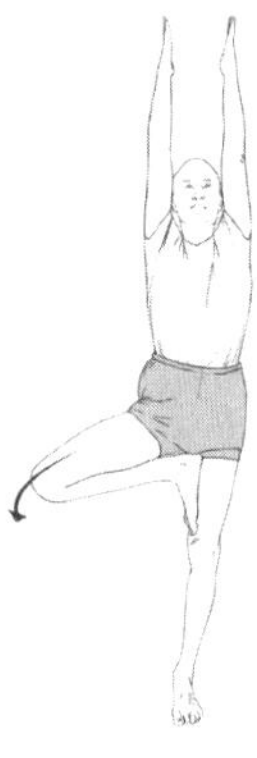

1 m.

3. * *Utthita Trikonasana*
back against a chair.
See ACFY p. 13

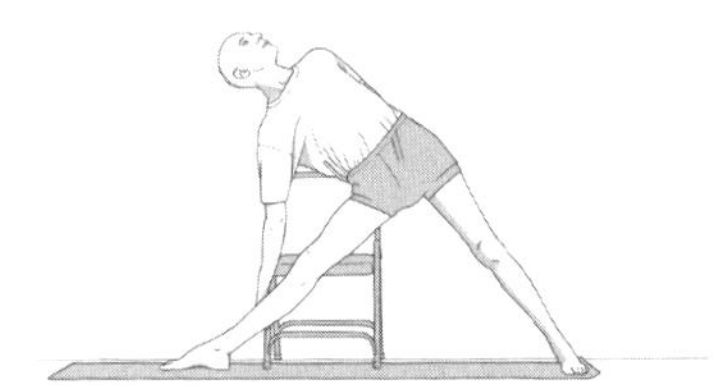

45 sec. each side × 2

4. * *Virabhadrasana II*
with a chair in front.
See ACFY p. 17

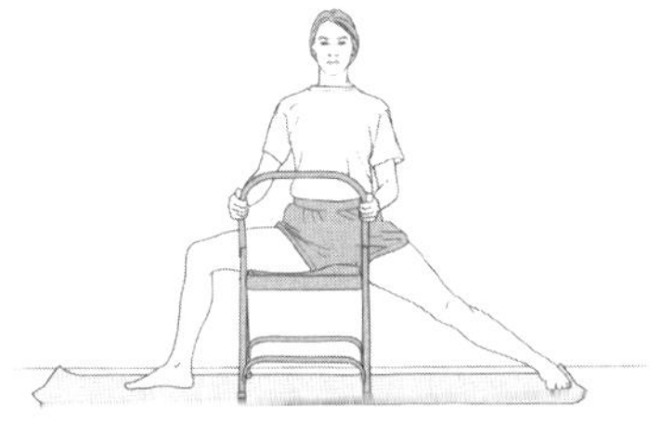

45 sec. each side

5. * *Virabhadrasana I*
front leg under the backrest. See ACFY p. 21

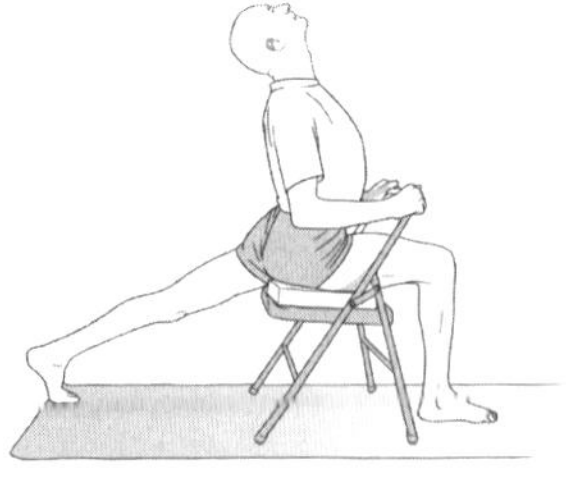

45 sec. each side

6. *Uttanasana*
leaning on a folded chair.
See ACFY p. 11

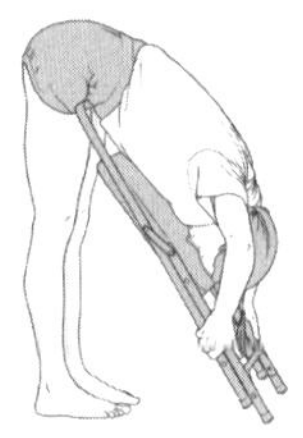

40 sec.

7. *Ardha Chandrasana*
back against a chair.
See ACFY p. 23

45 sec. each side

8. **Virabhadrasana III*
hands on the backrest.
See ACFY p. 30

45 sec. each side

9. *Uttanasana*
leaning on a folded chair.
See ACFY p. 11

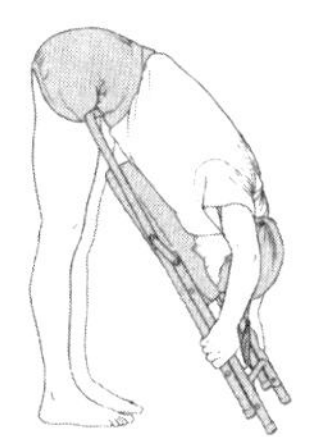

40 sec.

10. *Parsvottanasana*
leaning on a folded chair.
See ACFY p. 33

45 sec. each side

11. *Supta Virasana*
on a chair support
See ACFY p. 155

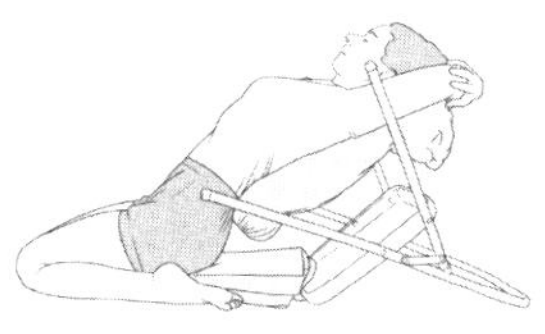

3-5 m.

12. **Shirsasana*
shoulder blades
supported by chair.
See PFY Vol. III, p. 28

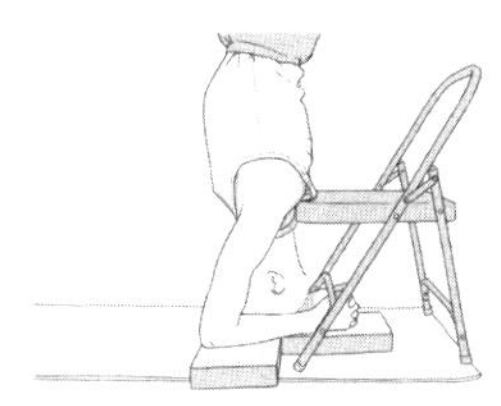

5-8 m.

13. *Adho Mukha Shvanasana* hands on inverted chair. See ACFY p.4

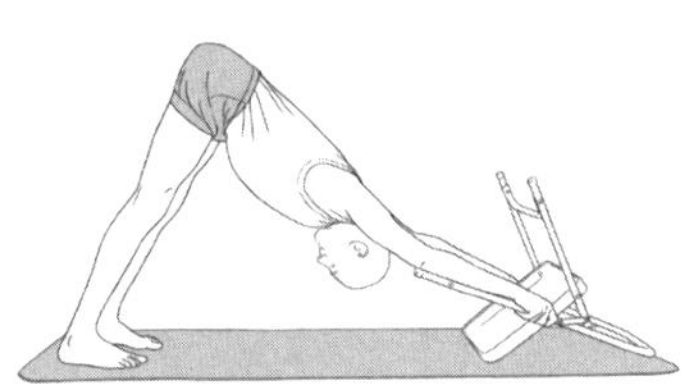

1 m.

14. *Urdhva Mukha Shvanasana* hands on chair. See ACFY p. 110

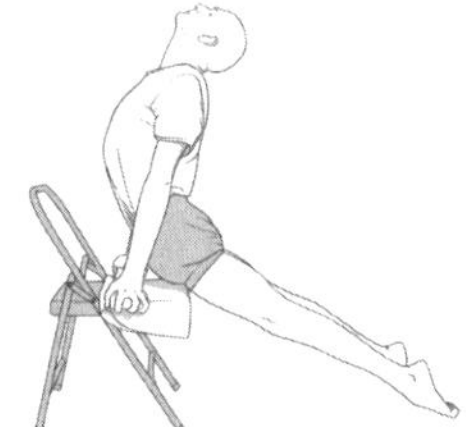

1 m.

15. * *Viparita Dandasana* on a chair. See p. 139

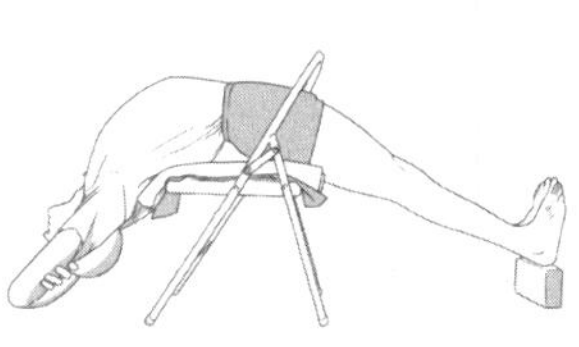

3-5 m.

16. *Setu Bandha Sarvangasana* a bolster supporting the back. See PFY Vol. III p. 106

3-5 m.

17. *Shavasana* on a bolster. See 6 on p. 351

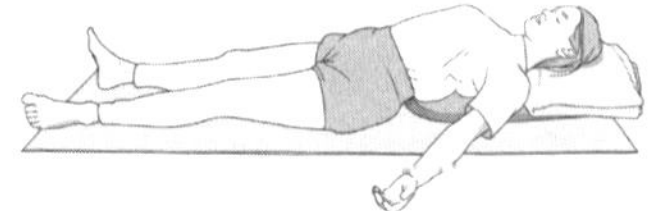

45 sec. each side

4.2. For Emotional Balance (Enhancing Sattva)

Level: Intermediate and advanced

Time: 60-90 min.

Props needed: 2 blocks, chair, belt, bolster

1. **Adho Mukha Shvanasana* head support. See 4 on p. 350 and PFY Vol. I p. 52

2-3 m.

2. *Uttanasana* head support. See 2 on p. 349

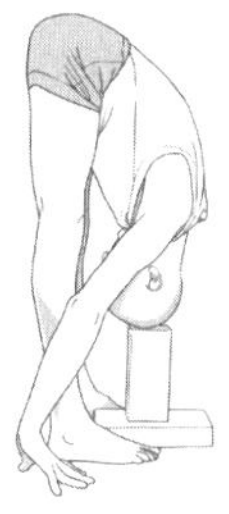

3-4 m.

3. *Supta Virasana* bolster support. See 3 on p. 349

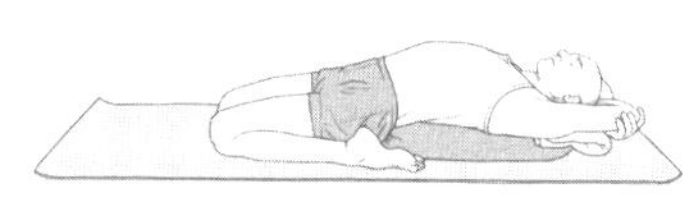

4-5 m.

4. **Viparita Dandasana* on chair with head support. See p. 139

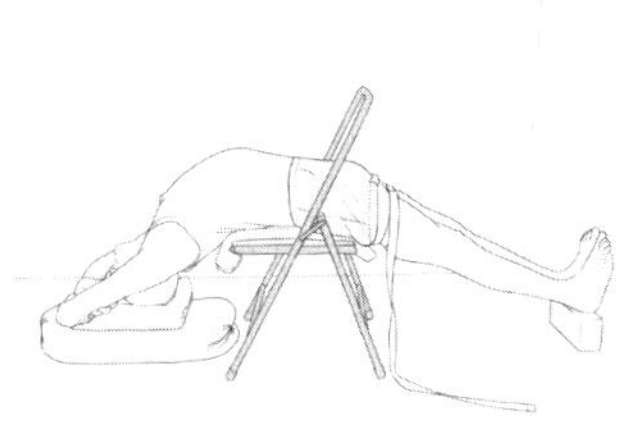

3-5 m.

5. **Shirsasana* upper back support. See p. 113

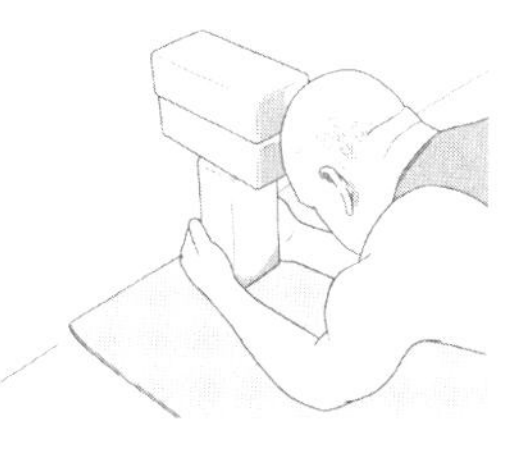

5-8 m.

6. **Sarvangasana* from a chair. See PFY Vol. III p. 85

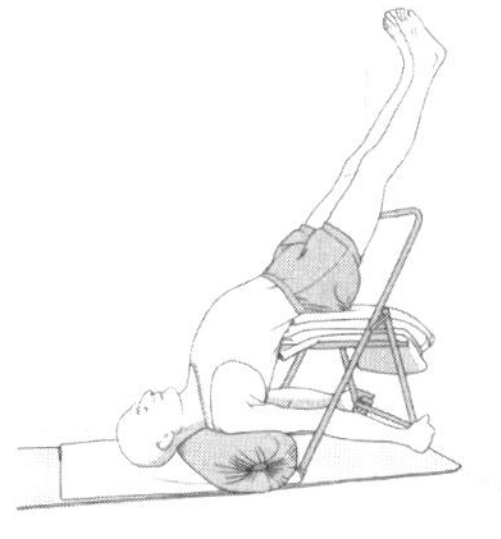

5-10 m.

7. *Ardha Halasana* supporting the legs on chair (or bench). See PFY Vol. III p. 92

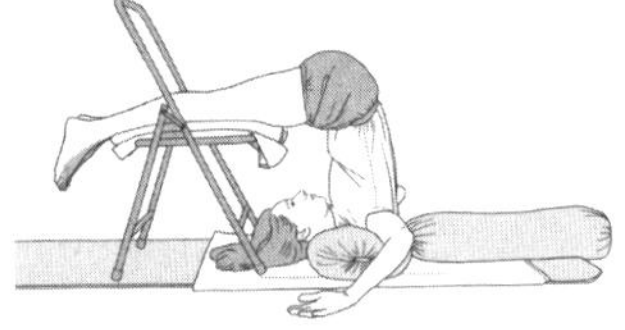

5-10 m.

8. *Setu Bandha Sarvangasana* on bolster. See PFY Vol. III p. 106

5 m.

9. **Paschimottanasana* head support. See p. 127

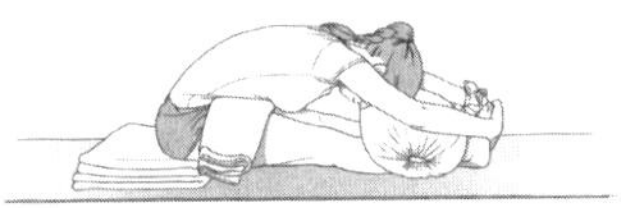

3-5 m.

10. *Upavishta Konasana* **bolster support** See PFY Vol. II p. 131

2-4 m.

11. *Baddha Konasana* chair **support** See ACFY p. 41

2-4 m.

12. **Ujjayi Pranayama* sitting on chair. See ACFY p. 48

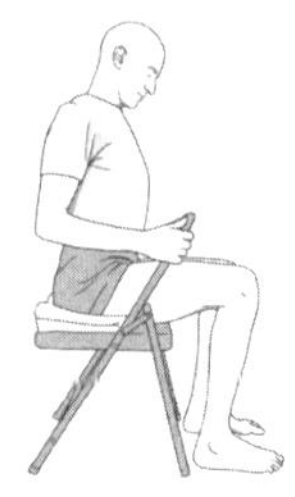

5-10 m.

13. *Shavasana*
on a bolster.
See 6 on p. 351

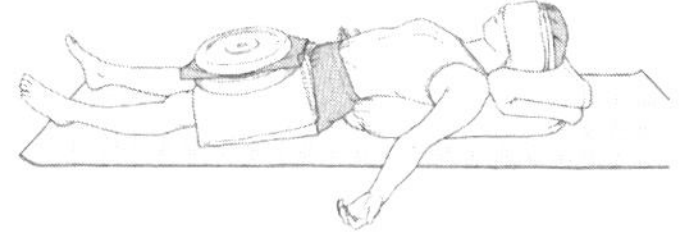

5-10 m.

4.3. *For Optimism and Joy (Countering Tamasic Mood)*

Level: Intermediate and advanced

Time: 90 min.

Props needed: 2 blocks, chair, bolster or a few blankets

General guidelines

This sequence is intended to help you overcome a *tamasic* mode. *Tamas* is a state were one lacks energy, and there is lethargy and laziness. Mentally this state is characterized by inertia, or resistance to change. One may feel down and even depressed. The sequence is energetic, opens the chest and encourages deep inhalations to clear up the clouds of despair.

Specific guidelines:

- We can think of inhalation as the positive side of the breath; as it helps spreading awareness to the extremities of the body. Use inhalations to pump energy and optimism and exhalations to expel negative feelings and thoughts.
- Practice backbends to open the chest and uplift the spirit.
- Use props to keep the chest open also when resting in supported *asanas*. Make sure to spread well your arms to open the 'windows' of the armpits.
- In restorative *asanas* and *Shavasana* don't force yourself to close your eyes; it is better to keep the eyes open and soft.
- Make your practice dynamic and light. Use movements, but don't over-work; don't exhaust yourself.
- In the standing *asanas* avoid looking down; raise your chin up and look slightly above eye-level.
- After each pose, stand in *Tadasana* for 30 seconds; lift your head, look slightly up and breathe deeply.
- Practice *Adho Mukha Vrksasana* (Full Arm Balance); it is an energizing and joyful pose.
- Practice *Sarvangasana* from a chair in order to open your chest and deepen your breath. Avoid *Halasana*.

1. *Tadasana*
See 1 on p. 349

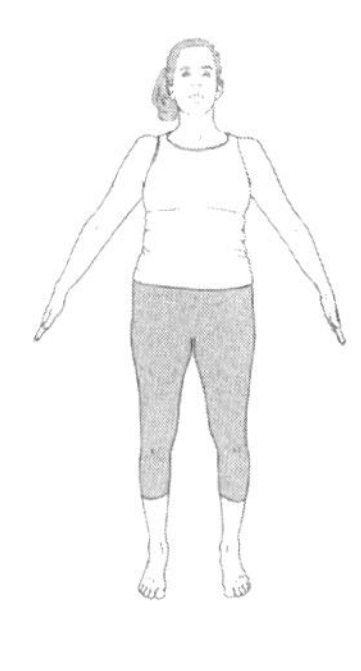

1 min.

2. ** Urdhva Hastasana*
dynamic. see 7 on p. 351

6-8 times

3. *Vrksasana*
see p. 33

45 sec. on each leg

4. ***Urdhva Hastasana***
Uttanasana
dynamic

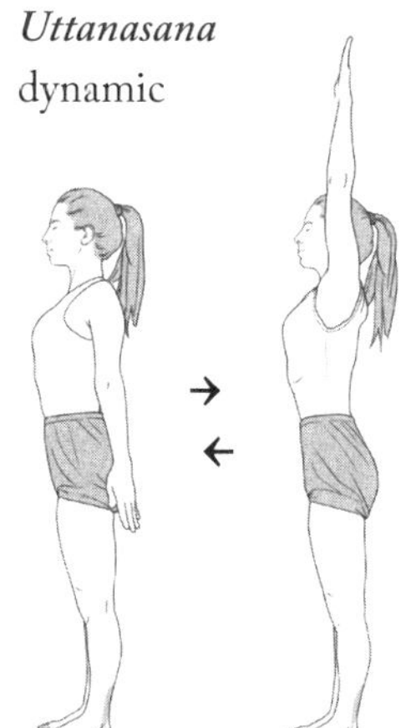

10-12 times

› Inhale and stretch up, exhale and bend to *Uttanasana*.

› Repeat following the rhythm of your breath

5.1 *Tadasana*
Exhale

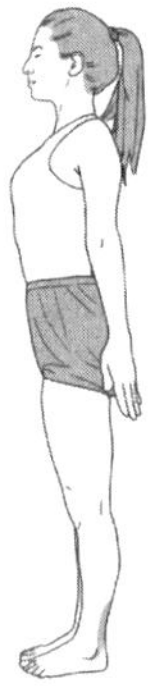

→

5.2 *Urdhva Hastasana*
Inhale

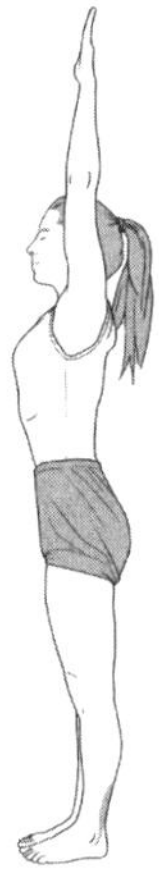

→

5.3 *Uttanasana*
Exhale

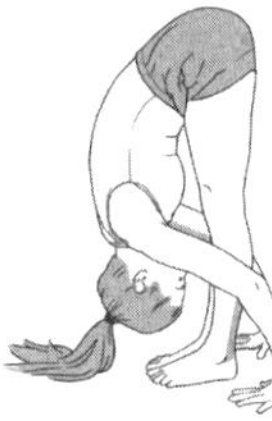

↓

5.4 *Uttanasana* back concave
Inhale

Jump
←

5.5 *Adho Mukha Shvanasana*
Exhale

Jump
←

5.6 *Uttanasana*
Inhale

↑

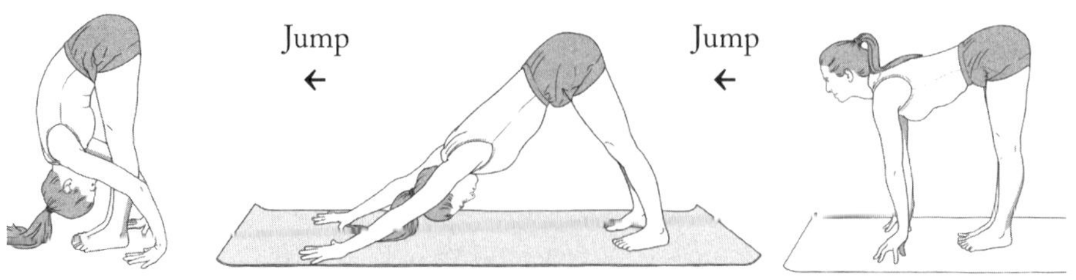

6-8 times

6. Half *Uttanasana*
hands on wall. Support your hands on the wall, keep your back concav.

30 sec

7. **Virabhadrasana II*
See p. 99

40 sec each side

8. **Utthita Trikonasana*
holding a block (or any object weighing 1-2 kgs or 4-5 lbs).
See PFY Vol. I p. 90

40 sec each side

9. **Virabhadrasana I*
catching a belt.
See PFY Vol. I p. 106

40 sec each side

10. *Adho Mukha Shvanasana*
hands on blocks. See p. 82

45 sec

11. **Adho Mukha Vrksasana*
wall support. See p. 123

30 sec × 4

12. *Supta Baddha Konasana*
lengthwise block support.
See p. 131

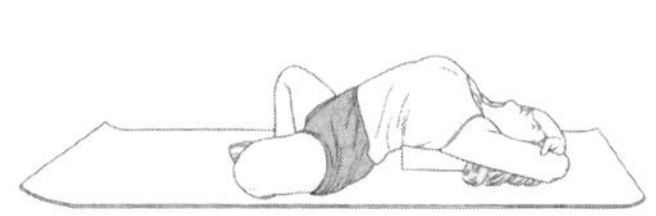

3-5 min

13. *Paryankasana*
block support.
See 8 on p. 351

3-5 min

14. * *Viparita Dandasana*
on a chair.
See p. 139

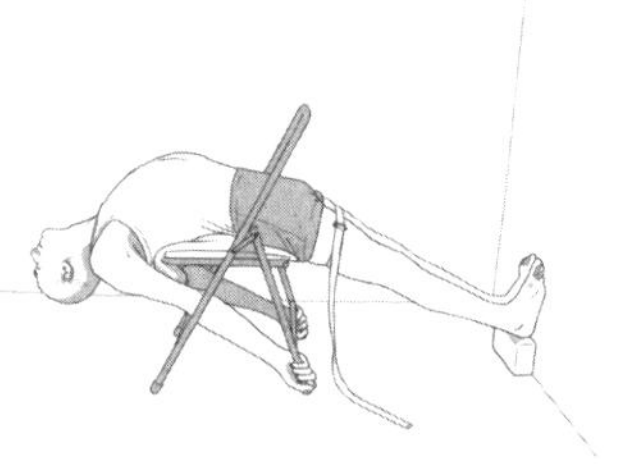

3-5 min

15. * *Urdhva Dhanurasana*
on the backrest.
See 9 on p. 352

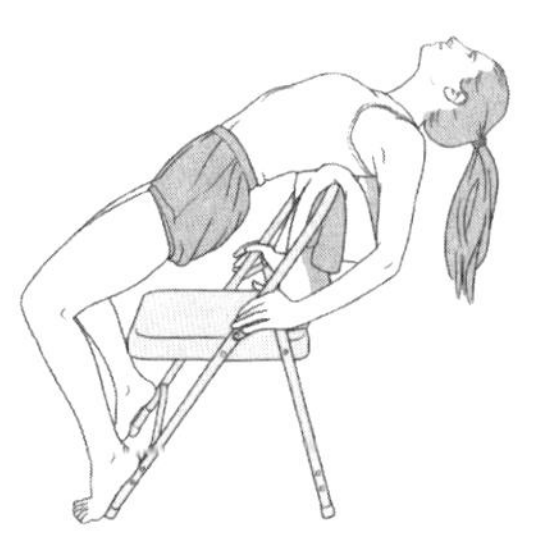

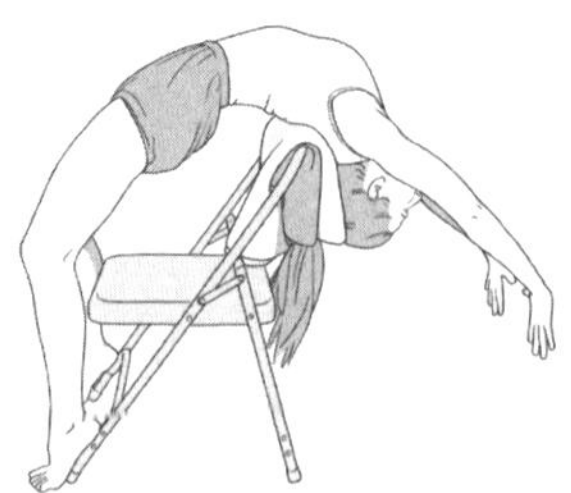

2 min × 2

16. *Bhardvajasana*
sitting on chair.
See p. 143

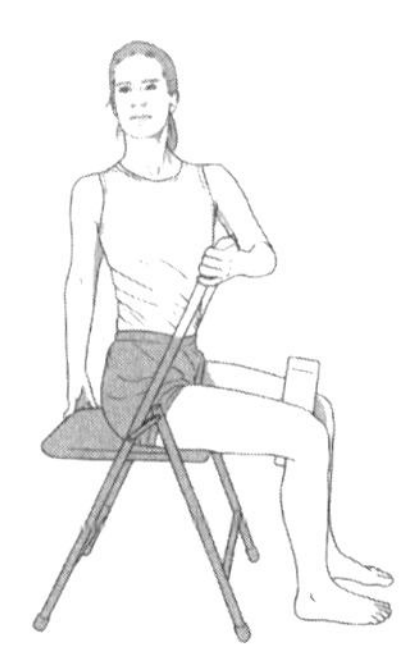

40 sec × 2 on each side

17. *Adho Mukha Shvanasana*
hands on blocks.
See p. 82

1 min

18. * *Sarvangasana*
from a chair, shoulders on bolster.
See PFY Vol. III p. 85

5-8 min

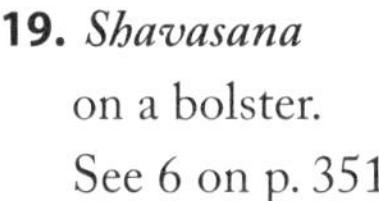

19. *Shavasana*
on a bolster.
See 6 on p. 351

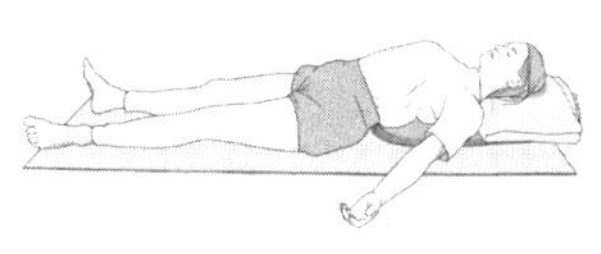

5-8 min

4.4. For Calming and Pacifying (Countering Rajasic Mood)

Level: Intermediate and advanced
Time: 90 min.
Props needed: 2 blocks, 2-3 blankets, bolster, long belt
Props needed: chair, bolsters

Note: It is recommended to do this sequence without breaks, moving from one *asana* to the following with minimal disturbance. For this reason, it is recommended to prepare all the props needed beforehand (including the platform for *Sarvangasana*).
Time: 60–80 min.

1. ** Uttanasana*
head support.
See 2 on p. 349

2. **Adho Mukha Shvanasana*
head support.
See 4 on p. 350 and PFY Vol. I p. 52

3. *Prasarita Padottanasana*
see 5 on p. 351

4 min

4 m.

4 m.

4. **Paschimottanasana*
support for head, back of the knees and lower abdomen. See p. 127

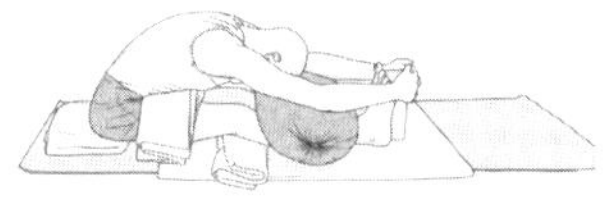

4-5 min

5. *Janu Shirsasana*
head support. Use the same supports you used for *Paschimottanasana*.

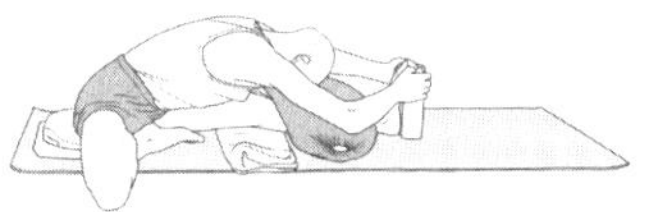

2-3 min on each side

6. **Shirsasana*
with belt hanging from the big toes. See p. 110

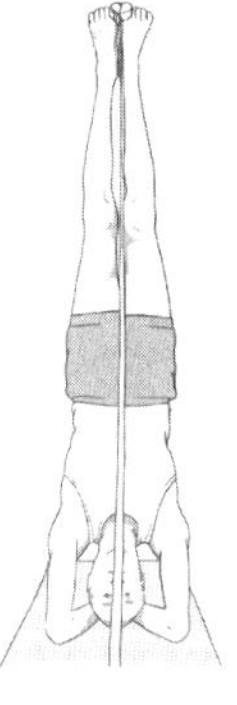

6-10 min

7. **Niralamba Sarvangasana*
wall support.
See PFY Vol. III p. 74

6-8 min.

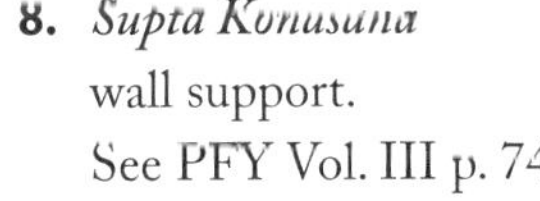

8. *Supta Konasana*
wall support.
See PFY Vol. III p. 74

3-4 min.

9. *Karnapidasana*
wall support.
See PFY Vol. III p. 75

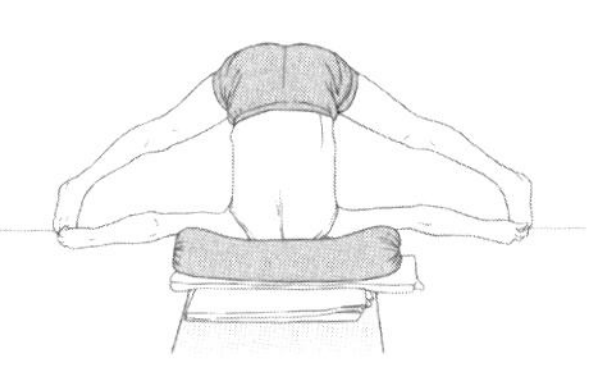

1-2 min.

10-14. **Repeat steps 1- 5 in the reverse order (start from *Janu Shirsasana*, and continue up to *Uttanasana*)**

Use the same timing as before

15. * *Tadasana*
facing a wall.
See 10 on p. 352

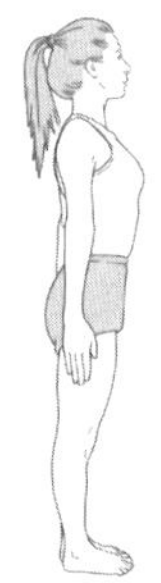

5 min

16. *Shavasana*
shins on chair; block on top of an eye cover and block on abdomen

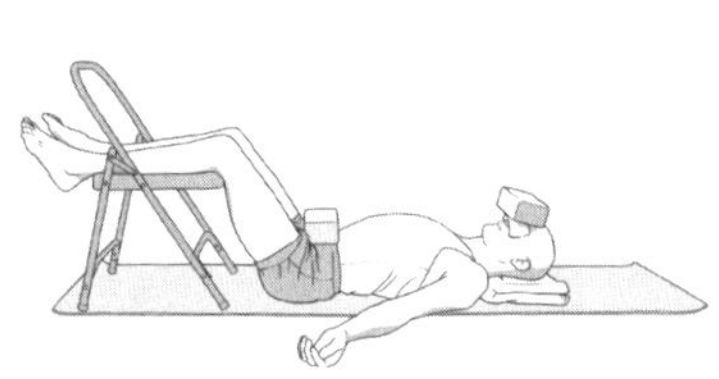

5-10 m.

4.5. Restoration (Recovering From Fatigue)

Level: All levels
Time: 30 min.
Props needed: belt, chair, bolsters, 2-3 blankets
Optional Props: *Viparita Dandasana* bench, *Setu Banda Sarvangasana* bench

1. ** Supta Baddha Konasana*

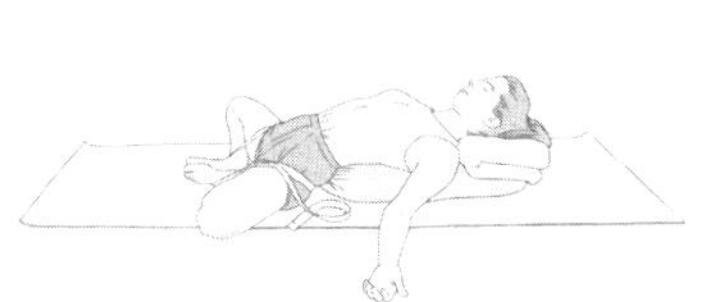

3-5 m.

2. ** Supta Virasana*
See 3 on p. 349

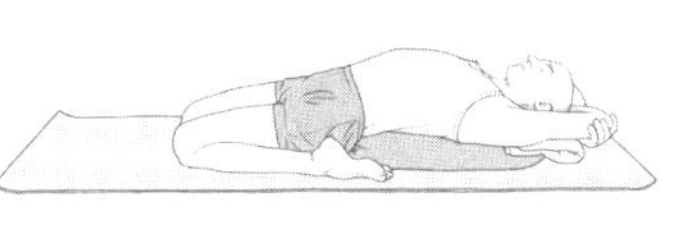

3-5 m.

3. *Viparita Dandasana* on a support.
See p. 139

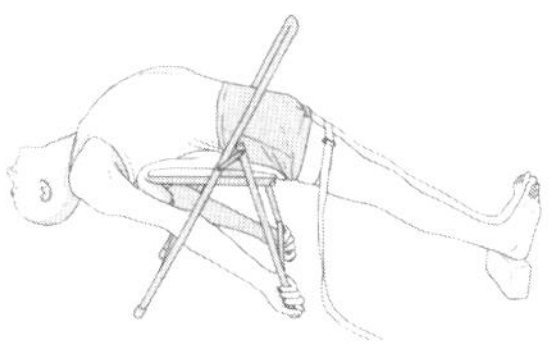

3-5 m.

4. ** Shirsasana*
hanging from rope

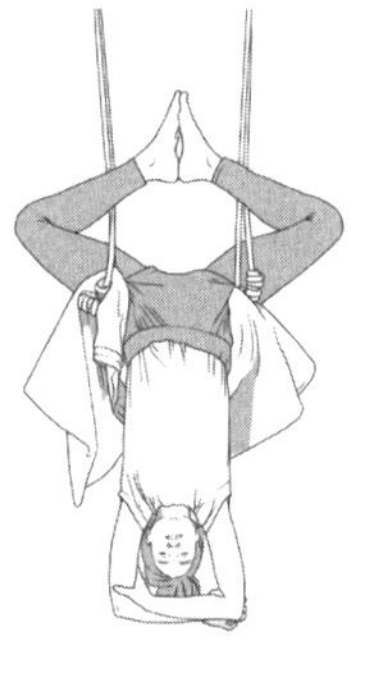

3-5 m.

If you know how to use a rope to hang in 'Rope-*Shirsasana*', then it's a great restorative pose. Otherwise, skip this step (or if you can, do independent *Shirsasana*)

5. *Setu Banda Sarvangasana*
on a bolster or a bench.
See PFY Vol. III p. 106

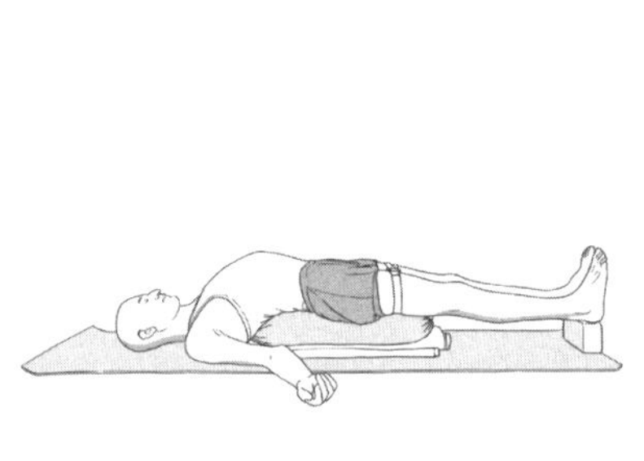

5 m.

6. ** Viparita Karani*
on a bolster.
See PFY Vol. III p. 140

5-7 m.

7. ** Shavasana*
with head hanging under a chair. See ACFY p. 160

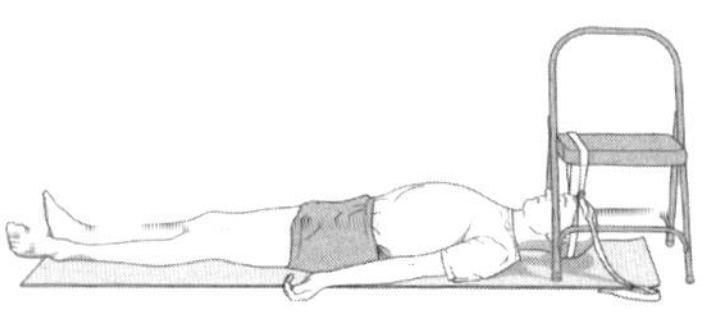

5-7 m.

Instructions

1. Instructions for *Tadasana*

- Move your arms sideway such that your upper arms are slightly away from your armpits. Roll your biceps out and turn your palms to face outward.
- Widen your collar bones and open your chest.
- Lift your chin and look slightly above eye level. ∫

2. Instructions for *Uttanasana* With Head Support

- Depending on the length of your legs and your flexibility, adjust the blocks such that you can rest the top of your head on them.
- If the two blocks are not enough, use a chair and support your head on the seat.
- Stand in front of the block or blocks.
- Spread your legs slightly and bend forward.
- Use your hands to align the head: place the tips of your thumbs in the opening of the ear and the fingers on the back of your skull. Roll your head forward until it is vertical.
- Place the top of your head on the support and place your finger tips on the floor on the sides of your feet. You may use two additional blocks to support your hands.
- Widen and lift your shoulders away from your neck.
- To fine-tune the height of your head, slightly increase or decrease the spread of your legs, until your head is supported, but your neck is long and not compressed. ∫

3. Instructions for *Supta Virasana* With Bolster Support

- Place a lengthwise bolster along the center of the mat and place a folded blanket on it (for head support).
- Sit in *Virasana* in front of the bolster. Loop a belt around your legs to keep your knee joined, or at pelvis width (but not wider).

Note: If sitting in *Virasana* on the floor is difficult, use support for our buttocks and lift the bolster at the same amount (for example, you can use a 3-folded blanket under the buttocks and the bolster).

› Recline back, place your elbows on the floor and lift your chest. Extend your buttocks away from the bolster and your back to the head side.
› Place your back on the bolster, spine on the center.
› Move your shoulders one-by-one away from your neck (toward your elbows). Adjust the blanket to support the back of your neck and head. ʃ

4. Instructions for *Adho Mukha Shvanasana* With Head Support

If you don't know how much support is needed to support your head, do the pose first to estimate the distance between your head and the floor. You can use a bolster, folded blankets, block or any combination of these.

› Place the support 50 to 70 cm (2 feet) away from the front edge of your mat, at the center of the mat.
› Place your hands on the mat aligning your finger tips with the front edge of the mat.
› Go to *Adho Mukha Shvanasana* and place the top of your forehead (hairline) on the support.
› Rest only the weight of your head on the support, and keep moving your front thighs back and up. ʃ

Notes:

- Keep moving your trunk back and up. Avoid collapsing your entire weight on the support. Support only the weight of your head.
- If keeping your elbows straight is too challenging, loop a belt around them, or hold the edges of your mat.

If you have wall hook, you can use them (see instructions in: *Props for Yoga*, Vol. I, p. 53-54).

5. Instructions for *Prasarita Padottanasana*

- Spread your legs wide and bend forward to *Prasarita Padottanasana.*
- Rest the top of your head on the floor, or on a support (block, folded blanket or similar support)
- You can hold your outer ankles or place your hands on the floor.
- Widen and lift your shoulders away from your neck. ʃ

Optionally you can use the wall and a block to support your outer feet as explained in *Props for Yoga* Vol. I, p. 139

6. Instructions for *Shavasana* on a Bolster

- Use a lengthwise bolster to support your back.
- Sit on the mat in front of the support and lie with your spine in the center of the bolster.
- Use a folded blanket to support the back of your head and neck.
- Optionally you can use an eye wrap or an eye pillow. ʃ

You can also place weights on your thighs (up to 50 Kgs. or 100 lbs.).

7. Instructions for *Urdhva Hastasana*

- Inhale and lift your arms and join your hands to clap above your head, then exhale and lower your arms.
- Move your arms while they are well extended. ʃ

8. Instructions for *Paryankasana* with block support

- Place a Highest-height block on the center of the mat.
- Sit in *Virasana,* lift and arch your upper back, to place it on the block.

› The block should be under the center of your chest (to support the heart center).
› Arch back your neck and head. ʃ
• You can use another block to support the top of your head.
• If *Virasana* is difficult, do the pose with straight legs (as in *Supta Tadasana).*

9. Instructions for *Urdhva Dhanurasana* supporting on the back of a chair

› Place a chair with its back at about a meter (3 feet) away from the wall.
› Sit on the chair. Place your heels on the front legs of the chair (to prevent the chair from rolling).
› Lift slightly your pelvis and place your mid-back on the backrest.
› Extend your arms to place the palms on the wall. Straighten your elbows and push against the wall.
› In the 2nd attempt you can move the chair slightly closer to the wall and once in the pose, walk your hands down to increase the back arch. ʃ

10. Instructions for *Tadasana* Facing the Wall

› Stand in *Tadasana* facing the wall, at a distance of about 20 cm (5 inches) away from it.
› Join your big toes and heels.
› Keep your eyes open but not focused.
› As you stay observe if you swing from one foot to the other. As much as possible, attempt to center yourself and keep your weight distributed evenly on both feet. ʃ

APPENDIX A.

My Path to Peace: A Yogic Journey Through Dystonia

In this Appendix we bring a real-life story of a young woman, Atar Rabina[1], who suffers from a congenital neurological disease that affects her both physically and mentally. Her story demonstrates how yoga has helped her to deal with this psychophysical disease.

I started studying yoga with Eyal 7 years ago at the age of 23. Since that time, I never stopped studying and practicing yoga. In 2017 I was certified as an *Iyengar Yoga* teacher, and I am currently teach yoga on a small scale. I am also an artist and taught art in high-school in Tel-Aviv. Since the age of 12, I have suffered from dystonia, a congenital disease[2] that causes uncontrolled movements in my left hand, lack of control of my left shoulder and right foot, as well as general laxity in other regions of my body. When standing or walking, I am unable to ground my right leg properly, and this affects the entire right side of my body, often causing pain in my lower back.

This disease has marked mental correlations; for example, when I am stressed or exposed to external noise, the tremor in my left hand increases and I experience more internal 'noise'. This catalyzes a 'snowball effect', whereby the stress increases the tremor, which in turn generates more stress, which further increases the tremor, and so on. Before I started practicing yoga I didn't know how to get out of this snowball effect and retain my serenity.

The disease also affects my yoga practice, my breath and my ability to relax in a pose. When I started studying yoga, I found it hard to sit quietly or to relax in *Shavasana* (Relaxation Pose). The mere expectation (mine and presumably that of the teacher) to be quiet and to be able to relax my hand, created more stress, which again increased the tremor. The more I tried to stop the uncontrolled movement or to place a weight on my hand in order to subdue it, the more my hand shook.

In my practice, I observe my mental state and its connection with my nervous system. My biggest challenge is to find quietude and relaxation in every pose. For example, forward bends are typically naturally pacifying and relaxing. When practicing forward bends, like *Paschimottanasana* (Seated Forward Bend Pose), my nervous system often becomes more irritated. I need to adapt the pose in

1. Atar also demonstrated for some of the figures in this book.
2. Wikipedia definition: Dystonia is a neurological movement disorder syndrome in which sustained or repetitive muscle contractions result in twisting and repetitive movements or abnormal fixed postures. The movements may resemble a tremor. Dystonia is often intensified or exacerbated by physical activity, and symptoms may progress into adjacent muscles.

various ways (like keeping the legs slightly spread, placing my feet against a wall, supporting my forehead on a bolster, and so on) in order to find peace and poise. Often it happened however, that the attempt to relax, and the struggle to bring quietness, increase the tremor and the disturbance.

This disease forces me to find ways to work with the instability, and the more intimate knowledge of my body and my nervous system I get, the more my understanding develops. I have learnt to adapt many *asanas*, often by using props to create a closed circuit and to center my nervous system down. For example, in *Shirsasana* (Headstand) I hold a block in order to maintain the stability of my hands. In *Virabhadrasana II* (Warrior Pose II), I hold a belt stretched between my two hands to avoid my left hand from shaking. In restorative *asanas* I often use weight on my forehead.

My disturbance is not clearly visible from the outside; in a classroom situation I often relinquished practicing the necessary adaptations, in order to avoid drawing too much attention to myself from the teacher and the other students. I used to sacrifice the quality of my practice to avoid designating myself as a 'special case'. I was not confident enough to share my condition with everybody.

Additionally, in teaching, the issue of demonstration naturally arises. When demonstrating, I am continually faced with questions like: Can the students see the tremor? Should I tell them about my condition, or just demonstrate the pose to my best ability? The answers vary from pose to pose, as in some poses the problem is almost invisible, while in others it is very noticeable. These dilemmas were obstacles that accompanied me while teaching.

I sense that the tremor and the shakiness travel through my entire nervous system, affecting my entire body, my mental and emotional state, my behavior and my inner experience. I often felt moody and emotionally imbalanced. During the first years of yoga practice, and through my teacher training, I tried to ignore this limitation and struggled to do the poses like the rest of the class. When I did adapt some *asanas*, I felt miserable and inferior.

However, persisting in my yoga practice has helped and continues to help me across several dimensions. Physically, I sense better awareness in my posture and better connections between my body parts. My body has become stronger, more flexible and I have better mobility and coordination. I learned to align my body and to use *asanas* to reduce my shakiness and my lower back pain. The improved stability of my body supports me mentally and emotionally.

Additionally, and significantly, I am better connected with my breath; in fact, whenever I am fully attentive to it, the tremor immediately decreases. This is available to me not only during my practice, but throughout my day.

Many *asanas* create a feeling of openness and space; this seems to break inner barriers within my nervous system, and brings about emotional stability and balance. Today I can better handle negative emotions and emotional upheavals, and can find stable ground and serenity.

Maturity in yoga practice has helped me to accept my condition, without ignoring or concealing it- this in itself quiets my nervous system and reduces the tremor. I am more confident and able to share my condition. It's ok that there is this perpetual movement; I can live with it and be happy. I don't need to prove anything to anybody, nor to try and make the impression that my *asanas* are perfect. It's ok to adapt my poses and to use props, and I don't need to struggle so much. I have learnt to observe the fluctuations of my nerves, like one may observe movements of clouds in the sky, and to allow the changes to take place, without trying to cling to an ideal, non-realistic notion of how my practice should be. I can see the impermanence (*anitya*) of life, and be more open to accept my condition (and my practice) every day as it comes. Sometimes my *Paschimottanasana* comes easily and I can stay calmly, without adaptations, but on other days, I need to use support.

Learning to cope with my laxity and instability has made me a better teacher. I can more easily identify when students are struggling and exerting themselves and offer them the tools that I have developed in my own practice. Often I instruct them to listen to their body attentively and sincerely and to be more compassionate toward their bodies, to release tension and undue effort and to be more receptive. The lessons that I have learned as a result of this specific disease are in fact universal in nature, and subsequently, I can share them as a teacher in a more general way, as we all can benefit from accepting both the changing nature of our bodies and our practice.

Yoga has taught me *viaragya* – acceptance, surrender and dispassion. Instead of trying to prove to myself and to others that I can perform perfect *asanas*, I work more towards finding softness, flow and smoothness. Though I am still at the beginning of what I hope to be a lifelong journey, with many more lessons to learn, I am confident that yoga is the correct path for me. Yoga has educated me to accept whatever my nervous system allows for in each day and in each moment! I am so grateful for this life-changing lesson!

APPENDIX B.

Glossary of Sanskrit Words

words in bold and initial capitals are explained in the glossary. The numbers are page numbers.

Ahimsa (190) – non-violence, non-injury. It is the first ***Yama***.

Aparigraha (167, 192)– non-possessiveness, non-greed and non-attachment. Living a simple life without unnecessary possessions and consumption. It is the fifth ***Yama***.

Asana – a posture done with attention and reflection. The third component of the ***Ashtanga Yoga***, where Patanjali defines *asana* as 'to be seated in a position that is firm, but relaxed'.

Ashtanga yoga (190) -the eight component (literally eight-limbs) yoga included in Patanjali's *Yoga Sutras*. These are: ***Yama***, ***Niyama***, ***Asana***, ***Pranayama***, ***Pratyahara***, ***Dharana***, ***Dhyana*** and ***Samadhi***.

Chitta (7) – consciousness, psyche, mind stuff, or 'the lower mind'. *Chitta* allows for subjectivity and has the functions of thinking and feeling. However, according to yoga, *chitta* is part of *prakriti* and borrows it's conscious from *Purusha*, while in itself, it is unanimated.

Dharana (95, 186) – concentration, focused attention. The sixth limb of the *ashtanga yoga*; the first of the three internal limbs which together constitute ***Samyama***.

Dharmendriya – the organ of righteousness; conscience.

Dhyana (95, 188) – meditation, contemplation. The seventh limb of the *ashtanga yoga*; the second of the three internal limbs which together constitute ***Samyama***.

Dvesha (178) – aversion. One of the five ***Kleshas***.

Guna (195) – A quality of nature. Everything in mature (*prakriti*) is made of a combination of three qualities. These three *gunas* are: *tamas* – inertia, dullness; *rajas* – dynamism, energy; *sattva* – luminosity, purity, clarity. These qualities apply equally to the material as well as to the mental domains

Ishvara Pranidhana (201) – Surrender to *Ishvara*, the impersonal God; devotion.

Klesha – affliction. A deep tendency in our consciousness that causes us unhappiness and suffering. A term from Indian philosophy and yoga, meaning a 'poison'. The *Yoga Sutras* identify five *kleshas* (YS, II.3):

1. ignorance (in the form of a misapprehension about reality) – *avidya*,
2. egoism (in the form of an erroneous identification of the Self with the intellect) – *asmita*,
3. attachment – *raga*,
4. aversion (*dvesha*), and
5. fear of death (which is derived from clinging ignorantly to life) – *abhinivesha*.

Kosha (7) – usually rendered "sheath", is a covering of the *Atman*, or Self according to yoga philosophy. There are five *koshas*, and they are often visualized as the layers of an onion.

Niyama (167, 201) – literally means positive duties or observances. The *niyamas* and its complement, ***yamas***, are recommended for healthy living, spiritual enlightenment and liberated state of existence.

The *niyamas* are the second limb of the eight limbs of yoga, the five *niyamas* given by *Patanjali* are:

1. ***Shaucha:*** purity, clearness of mind, speech and body
2. ***Santosha:*** contentment, acceptance of others and of one's circumstances as they are, optimism for self
3. ***Tapas:*** austerity, self-discipline, persistent and zeal in practice, perseverance
4. ***Svadhyaya:*** study of self, self-reflection, introspection of self's thoughts, speeches and actions
5. ***Ishvarapranidhana:*** contemplation of the *Ishvara* (God/Supreme Being, True Self, Unchanging Reality), attunement to the supreme consciousness

Pranayama (19, 44, 68, 146) – literally means extension, prolongation and expansion of the *Prana* (the cosmic vital energy), breath control. The fourth limb of *Ashtanga Yoga*, as set out by Patanjali in the *Yoga Sutra*.

Pratyahara (75) – sense withdrawal or non-attachment. The fifth limb of *Ashtanga Yoga*, as set out by Patanjali in the *Yoga Sutra*.

Purusha (7) – cosmic man or Self, spirit, pure consciousness, and Universal principle. *Purusha* is eternal, indestructible, without form and is all evasive. *The Purusha* concept is explained with the concept of ***Prakriti***. According to this, the universe is envisioned as a combination of the perceivable material reality and non-perceivable, non-material laws and principles of nature. Material reality (or *Prakriti*) is everything that has changed, can change and is subject to cause and effect. *Purusha* is the Universal principle that is unchanging, uncaused but is present everywhcre and the reason why *Prakriti* changes, transforms and transcends all the time and which is why there is cause and effect. *Purusha* is what connects everything and everyone according to the various schools of Hinduism.

Prakriti (7) – material reality or the entire nature. see ***Purusha***.

Rajas (195, 343) – dynamism, energy. see ***Gunas***.

Raga (178) – attachment; one of the five ***Kleshas***.

Sadhana (180) – literally 'a means of accomplishing something'; a spiritual path and discipline aimed at achieving ultimate realization.

Santosha (167) – the second ***Niyama***; contentment; being satisfied with what one has, acceptance of others and of one's circumstances as they are, optimism for self.

Samadhi (76, 99) – meditative absorption or trance, attained by the practice of ***Dhyana***.

Samyama – literally, *sam-yama* means holding together, tying up, binding, integration. Combined simultaneous practice of ***Dharana*** (concentration), ***Dhyana*** (meditation) and ***Samadhi*** (union). A tool to receive deeper knowledge of qualities of the object. Complete absorption in the object of meditation.

Sattva (195, 334) – luminosity, purity, clarity. See ***Gunas***.

Satya (193) – the second ***Yama*** – means truth, truthfulness, honesty, sincerity, and authenticity. It means living honestly, being sincere to yourself, not deceiving others, being truthful in thought, speech, and deed.

Siddhis (184) – spiritual, paranormal, supernatural, or otherwise magical powers, abilities, and attainments that are the products of spiritual advancement through yoga practice.

Svadhyaya (126, 188, 193) – literally means "one's own reading" and "self-study"; it is the second component of the *kriya yoga* (YS, II.1).

Tamas (195, 337) – inertia, dullness. see ***Gunas***.

Tapas (182) – derived from the Sanskrit root *Tap* which means 'to heat'. Spiritual practices that often involve a high degree of self-discipline; burning zeal in practice. Sometimes translated as austerity.

Yama (167, 190) – The first component (or *anga* – limb) of the *ashtanga yoga*. Patanjali mentions five *yamas*, specifying ethical-social rules of conduct. Patanjali designate them as eternal and universal ethical vows. These five are:

1. ***Ahimsa*** (or non-*himsa*) – the practice of non-violence, or more generally of non-injury.
2. ***Satya*** (or non-*Satya*) – the practice of truthfulness, sincerity and authenticity in action, speech and thoughts.
3. *Asteya* (or non-*steya*) – the practice of not stealing, nor having the intent to steal another's property through action, speech and thoughts.
4. *Brahmacharya* – literally means 'going after *Brahman*'. It is the practice of chastity, marital fidelity or sexual restraint.
5. ***Aparigraha*** (or non-*parigraha*) – the practice of non-avarice, non-possessiveness, non-grasping and non-greediness.

BIBLIOGRAPHY

Chapters 1 & 2

Clennell B., *Yoga for Breast Care* (Rodmell Press, 2014).

Clennell B., *The Woman's Yoga Book* (Rodmell Press, 2007).

C., Pisano., *The Hero's Contemplation* (the English language edition published by Yoga Words Ltd 2011).

Iyengar, B.K.S., *Light on Life* (Rodale, 2005).

Iyengar, B.K.S., *Light on Pranayama* (Harper Collins, 1981).

Iyengar, B.K.S., *Light on Yoga* (George Allen & Unwin, 1966).

Iyengar, B.K.S., *Light on the Yoga* Sutras of Patanjali (Harper Collins, 1993).

Iyengar, B.K.S., *The Tree of Yoga* (Shambhala, 2002).

Iyengar, B.K.S., *Yoga – the Path to Holistic Health* (Dorling Kindersley 2008)

Iyengar, B.K.S., *Astadala Yoga Mala Vol. I-VIII* (Allied Publishers 2008).

Iyengar, P., *Alpha & Omega of Trikonasana*, (YOG, Mumbai, 2004).

Kofi, B. (ed.), *Iyengar the Yoga Master* (Shambhala, 2007).

Nivedita J., *Guruji Uwach* (2004).

Radhakrishnan, S., *The Bhagavad-Gita* (Harper Collins, 1948/2010).

Ravindra, R., *The Wisdom of Patanjali's Yoga Sutras* (Shaila Press, 2015).

Shapiro, D., Cook, A. I., Davydov, M. D., Ottaviani, C., Leuchter F. A., Abrams, M., "Yoga as a Complementary Treatment of Depression: Effects of Traits and Moods on Treatment Outcome", eCAM, 2007. See: yoganga.com/iyengar-yoga/yoga-as-a-complementary-treatment-of-depression/

Shifroni, E., "Establishing and Structuring Self-Practice,"*Iyengar Yoga News*, no. 26 (Spring 2015) and no. 27 (Autumn 2015). iyengaryoga.org.uk/resources/articles/

Shifroni E, *A Chair for Yoga – A complete Guide to Iyengar Yoga Practice with a Chair*, 2nd ed. (2013).

Shifroni E, *Props for Yoga – A Guide to Iyengar Yoga Practice with Props – Volume I: Standing Asanas* (2014).

Shifroni E, *Props for Yoga – A Guide to Iyengar Yoga Practice with Props – Volume II: Sitting Asanas and Forward Extensions* (2015).

Shifroni E, *Props for Yoga – A Guide to Iyengar Yoga Practice with Props – Volume III: Inverted Asanas* (2017).

Steinberg, L., *Geeta S. Iyengar's guide to a Woman's Yoga Practice*, Volume I (2006).

Woolery, A., Myers, H., Sternlieb, B. and Zeltzer, L., "A yoga intervention for young adults with elevated symptoms of depression", *Alternative Therapies in Health and Medicine*, Vol. 10 no. 2 (2004): 60-63.

Chapter 3

Introduction

Snell, B., *The Discovery of the Mind*, translated by T. G. Rosenmeyer (Harvard University Press, 1953).

Spencer, H., *Principles of Psychology*, 3rd Edition (William and Norgate, 1890).

Williams, B., *Shame and Necessity*, Sather Classical Lectures, Volume 57 (University of California Press, 1993).

Wright, J. P. and Potter, P. (eds.), *Psyche and Soma* (Oxford University Press, 2000).

Section I

1. Socrates and Plato

Cooper, J. M. (ed.), Introduction to *Plato: Complete Works* (Hacket 1997).

Henderson, J., *Early Greek Philosophy*, volume VIII, Loeb Classical Library (Harvard University Press, 2016).

Holmes, B., "The Body of Western Embodiment: Classical Antiquity and the Early History of a Problem", in *Embodiment,* edited by Smith, J. (Oxford University Press, 2016), 17-50.

Robinson, T. M., "The Defining Features of Mind–Body Dualism in the Writings of Plato", in *Psyche and Soma*, edited by Wright, J. P. and Potter, P. (Oxford University Press, 2000), 37-56.

2. Aristotle

Charles, D., "Aristotle on Desire and Action", in *Body and Soul in Ancient Philosophy*, edited by Frede, D. and Reis, B. (de Gruyter, 2009), 291-309.

Charles, D., "Aristotle's Psychological Theory", in *Proceedings of the Boston Area Colloquium of Ancient Philosophy* 24, issue 1 (2009): 1-49.

van der Eijk, P. J., "Aristotle's Psychophysiological Account of the SoulBody", in *Psyche and Soma*, edited by Wright, J. P. and Potter, P. (Oxford University Press, 2000), 57-78.

Menn, S., "Aristotle's Definition of Soul and the Program of De Anima" in *Oxford Studies of Ancient Philosophy*, Volume XXII (2002):83-139.

Nussbaum, M., *Aristotle's De Motu Animalium* (Princeton University Press, 1985).

Nussbaum, M. and Rorty, E. O. (eds.), *Essays on Aristotle's De Anima* (Oxford University Press, 1992).

3. Plotinus

Ennead	The Enneads are the complete treatises of Plotinus, edited by his student, Porphyry. The standard citation of the Enneads follows Porphyry's division into book, treatise, and chapter. Hence E IV.8.1 refers to book (or Ennead) four, treatise eight, chapter one.

Lloyd, G., "Plotinus", *The Stanford Encyclopedia of Philosophy* (Summer 2014 Edition), edited by Zalta, E. N., plato.stanford.edu/archives/sum2014/entries/plotinus/.

4. Augustine

Augustine, On the Free Choice of the Will, On Grace and Free Choice, and Other Writings, edited and translated by King, P. (Cambridge University Press, 2010).

Matthews, G., "Internalist Reasoning in Augustine" in *Psyche and Soma*, edited by Wright, J. P. and Potter, P. (Oxford University Press, 2000), 133-146.

Meconi, D. V. and Stump, E. (eds.), *The Cambridge Companion to Augustine, 2nd edition* (Cambridge University Press, 2014).

Menn, S., *Descartes and Augustine* (Cambridge University Press, 1998).

Stump, E. and Kretzmann, N. (eds.), *The Cambridge Companion to Augustine* (Cambridge University Press, 2001).

Taylor, C., *Sources of the Self* (Harvard University Press, 1989).

5. Aquinas

ST *Summa Theologiae*

Kenny, A., *Aquinas on Mind* (Routledge, 1993).

Kretzmann, N., "Philosophy of Mind", in *The Cambridge Companion to Aquinas*, edited by Stump, E. and Kretzmann, E. (Cambridge University Press, 1993), 128-159.

6. Descartes

AT Descartes, R., *Œuvres de Descartes*, 11 vols., eds. Adam, C. and Tannery, P. (Paris: J. Vrin, 1996).

CSM	Descartes, R., *The Philosophical Writings of Descartes*, vols. 1, 2, edited and translated by Cottingham, J., Stoothoff, R. and Murdoch., D. (Cambridge University Press, 1984-5).
CSMK	Descartes, René, *The Philosophical Writings of Descartes*, vol. 3, edited and translated by Cottingham, J., Stoothoff, R., Murdoch., D. and Kenny, A. (Cambridge University Press, 1991).

Antoine-Mahut, D., «La machine du corps», in *Descartes. Sous la direction*, edited by Buzon, F. et Kambouchner, D. (Ellipses, 2013).

Garber, D., "Descartes on Knowledge and Certainty", in his *Descartes Embodied* (Cambridge University Press, 2001), 111-129.

Hacker, P., *Human Nature: The Categorial Framework* (Blackwell, 2007).

Hatfield, G., "Descartes' Physiology and its Relation to his Psychology", in *The Cambridge Companion to Descartes*, edited by Cottingham, J. (Cambridge University Press, 1992), 335-370.

Hartfield, G. "Remaking the Science of Mind", IRCS Technical Reports Series (1994). repository.upenn.edu/cgi/viewcontent.cgi?referer=https://www.google.com /&httpsredir=1&article=1159&context=ircs_reports .

Hutchins, B. R., *Obscurity and Confusion: Nonreductionism in Descartes's Biology and Philosophy*, PhD dissertation, Department of Philosophy and Moral Sciences, Ghent University, 2016.

Krakow, I., *Why the Mind–Body Problem CANNOT be Solved!* (University Press of America, 2002).

Leibowitz, Y., *Between Science and Philosophy* (Academon). [Hebrew]

Ryle, G., *The Concept of Mind* (University of Chicago Press, 1949).

Voss, S., "Descartes: Heart and Soul" in *Psyche and Soma*, edited by Wright, J. P. and Potter, P. (Oxford University Press, 2000), 173-196.

7. The Aftermath of Descartes' Dualism

Nadler, Steven, (ed.), 1993, Causation in Early Modern Philosophy (University Park: Penn State University Press, 1993).

7.1 Spinoza

Ethics	Benedictus de Spinoza, The Collected Works of Spinoza, in (CW). I notes the part of Ethics followed by A= axiom, cor.= corollary, dem.= demonstration, P= proposition, or Schol.= scholium, with their respective numeration, e.g. "2P47" refers to Part Two of the Ethics, Proposition 47.
CW	Spinoza, B. de: *Collected* Works, vol. 1, edited and translated by Curley, E. (Princeton University Press, 1988)

Israel, J., *Radical Enlightenment* (Oxford University Press, 2001).
- *Enlightenment Contested* (Oxford University Press, 2006).

Lin, M., "Spinoza and the Mark of the Mental", edited by Y. Melamed *Spinoza's Ethics* (Cambridge University Press, 2017), 82-101.

Moreau, P. F., *Spinoza* (Sueil, 1975).

Nadler, S., *A Book Forged in Hell: Spinoza's Scandalous Treatise and the Birth of the Secular Age* (Princeton University Press, 2013).

Spinoza, B. de: A *Spinoza Reader: The Ethics and Other Works*, edited and translated by E. Curley. (Princeton University Press ,1994).

7.2 Occasionalism

Search for Truth	Malebranche, N., *The Search for Truth and Elucidations of the Search for Truth*, translated by Lennon and Olscamp (Cambridge University Press, 1997).
OCM	Malebranche, N., *Oeuvres compl.tes de Malebranche*, edited by André Robinet (Vrin, 1958-84), cited by volume and page number.

Kremer, E. J., "Malebranche on Human Freedom", in *The Cambridge Companion to Malebranche*, edited by Nadler, S. (Cambridge University Press, 2000), 190-220.

Lee, S., "Occasionalism", *The Stanford Encyclopedia of Philosophy* (Winter 2016 Edition), edited by Zalta, E. N., URL = plato.stanford.edu/archives/win2016/entries/occasionalism/

7.3 Leibniz

NE	Leibniz, G. W., *Nouveaux essais sur l'entendement humain*, translated and edited by Remnant, P. and Bennett, J.(Cambridge University Press, 1981, 2d ed. 1996), cited by book, chapter and section.
AG	Leibniz, G. W., *Philosophical Essays*, edited and translated by Garber, D., and Ariew, R. (Indianapolis: Hackett, 1989).

Ariew, R. (ed.), *Leibniz-Clarke: Correspondence* (Hackett, 2000).

Duchesneau, F. and Smith, J. (eds.), *The Leibniz Stahl Controversy* (Yale University Press, 2016).

8. Kant

CPR Kant, I., *Critique of Pure Reason*, edited and translated by Guyer, P. and Wood, A. W. (Cambridge: Cambridge University Press, 1998).

Kant, I., "Critique of Practical Reason", in *Practical Philosophy*, edited and translated by Gregor, M. J., introduction by Wood, A. W. (Cambridge: Cambridge University Press, 1999).

Karl Ameriks, *Kant's Theory of Mind*, Cambridge University Press.
Allen Wood, *Kant* (Blackwell, Great Minds Series: 2005).

Section II

Armstrong, D. M., *A Materialist Theory of the Mind* (Routledge, 1968).

Bennett, M. R. and Hacker, P.M.S., *Philosophical Foundations of Neuroscience* (Wiley-Blackwell, 2003).

Bennett, M. R. and Hacker, P.M.S., *History of Cognitive Neuroscience* (Blackwell, 2013).

Block, N. "Antireductionism Slaps Back", *Philosophical Perspectives 11: Mind, Causation, and World*, edited by Tomberlin, J. (1997). Reprinted in *Nous* 31, issue 11 (1997): 107-132.

Boden, M., *Mind as Machine* (Oxford University Press, 2006).

Carnap, R., "Psychology in Physical Language" [1932/33], in *Logical Positivism*, edited by Ayer, A. J. (The Free Press, 1959), 165-198.

Chalmers, D. J., "Facing Up to the Problem of Consciousness", *Journal of Consciousness Studies* 2, issue 3 (1995): 200-19.

Chalmers, D. J., "Panpsychism and Panprotopsychism", *The Amherst Lecture in Philosophy* 8 (2013): 1-35.

Chalmers, D. J., "Idealism and the Mind–Body Problem", in *The Routledge Companion to Panpsychism*, edited by Seager, W. (Oxford University Press, 2018).

Chomsky, N., "Review of B. F. Skinner's *Verbal Behavior*", in *Readings in the Psychology of Language*, edited by Jakobovits L. A. and Miron, M. S. (Prentice-Hall, 1967), 142-143. marxists.org/reference/subject/philosophy/works/us/chomsky-skinner.htm

Chomsky, N., *Rules and Representation* (Columbia University Press, 1980).

Chomsky, N., "Naturalism and Dualism in the Study of Mind and Language", *International Journal of Philosophical Studies* 2, Issue 2 (1994): 181-209.

Chomsky, N., (1994). "Naturalism and Dualism in the Study of Mind and Language", *International Journal of Philosophical Studies* 2: 181-209.

Chomsky, N., *On Nature and Language*, edited by Belletti, A. and Rizzi, L. (Columbia University Press, 2002).

Crick, F., *The Astonishing Hypothesis: The Scientific Search for the Soul* (Simon and Schuster, 1994).

Davidson, D., *Essays on Actions and Events* (Clarendon Press, 1980).

Dennett, D., *Consciousness Explained* (Little, Brown and Company, 1991).

Dennett, D., *Kinds of Minds: Toward an Understanding of Consciousness* (Weidenfeld & Nicolson, 1996).

Dennett, D., *Sweet Dreams: Philosophical Obstacles to a Science of Consciousness* (MIT Press, 2005).

Dennett, D., *From Bacteria to Bach and Back: The Evolution of Minds* (Norton, 2017).

Fodor, F. A., "The Mind–Body Problem", *Scientific American* 244 (1981): 114-25.

Ginsburg, S. and Jablonka, E., *The Evolution of the Sensitive Soul*, (MIT Press, forthcoming in 2019).

Hacker, P.M .S ., *Wittgenstein, Meaning and Mind* (Blackwell, 1990).

Hacker, P.M .S ., *Human Nature: The Categorial Framework* (Blackwell, 2007).

Hacker, P.M .S ., *The Intellectual Powers: A Study of Human Nature* (Wiley-Blackwell, 2013).

Hacker P.M .S ., *The Passions: A Study of Human Nature* (Wiley-Blackwell, 2018).

Heil, J., *Philosophy of Mind: A Contemporary Introduction* (Routledge, 2013).

Hobbes, T., *Leviathan*, edited by Curley, E. (Hackett, 1994).

Jenkins, J. J., "Interview with James J. Jenkins", *Baars* (1986): 239-52.

Kahneman D., "The Psychology of the Mind–Body Problem", in *Mind and Brain: Fundamentals of The Psycho-Physical Problem*, (Van Leer Jerusalem Institute Hakibbutz Hameuchad Publishing House, 2005), 59-73.

Leibowitz, Y., *Body and Mind: The Psycho-Physical Problem* (Israeli Ministry of Defense Publication, 1989). [Hebrew]

Leibowitz, Y., *Mind and Brain: Fundamentals of The Psycho-Physical Problem*, Van Leer Jerusalem Institute Hakibbutz Hameuchad Publishing House, 2005. [Hebrew]

Lewontin, R. C., "The Evolution of Cognition: Questions We Will Never Answer", in *An Invitation to Cognitive Science: Methods, Models and Conceptual Issues*, Vol. 4, edited by Scarborough, D. and Sternberg. S. (MIT Press, 1998), 107-131.

Locke, J., *Essays on Human Understanding*, edited by Woolhouse R. (Penguin, 1997).

Lowe, E. J., *Introduction to the Philosophy of Mind* (Cambridge University Press, 2004).

Lumsden, C. J. and Wilson, E. O., "Genes, Mind, and Ideology", *The Sciences*, 21, Issue 9 (1981): 6-8.

McDowell, J,. *Mind and World* (Harvard University Press, 1994).

McGinn, C., *The Mysterious Flame: Conscious Minds in a Material World* (Basic Books, 1999).

de La Mettrie, J.O ., "Machine Man", in *Machine Man and Other Writings*, edited by Thomson, A. (Cambridge University Press, 1996).

Monk, R., *How to Read Wittgenstein* (Norton, 2005).

Nagel, T., "Conceiving the Impossible and the Mind–Body Problem", *Philosophy* 73, Issue 3 (1998): 337-352.

Nagel, T., "A Review of Dennett's From Bacteria to Bach and Back: The Evolution of Minds", *The New York Review of Books*, March 9, 2017.

Neurath, O, "Physicalism: The Philosophy of the Vienna Circle" [1931], in *Philosophical Papers 1913-1946*, edited by Cohen, R.S . and Neurath, M. (D. Reidel Publishing Company, 1983), 48-51.

Pinker, S. and Bloom, P., "Natural language and natural selection", *Behavioral and Brain Sciences* 13, Issue 4 (1990): 707-27.

Pinker, S., *How the Mind Works* (Norton, 1997).

Putnam, H., "Minds and Machines", *Journal of Symbolic Logic* (1960): 57-80.

Rye, R. "Psyche, Soma, and the Vitalist Philosophy of Medicine", in *Psyche and Soma*, pp. 254-65.

Searle, J. R., *The Rediscovery of the Mind* (MIT Press, 1992).

Searle, J. R., *Mind: A Brief Introduction* (Oxford University Press, 2004).

Searle, J. R., "Biological Naturalism", in *The Blackwell Companion to Consciousness*, edited by Velmans, M. and Schneider, S. (Blackwell, 2007).

Searle, J. R., *Freedom and Neurobiology* (Columbia University Press, 2004), pp. 4-5.

Skinner, B. F., *Verbal Behavior* (Appleton-Century-Crofts, 1957).

Stoljar, D., "Physicalism", *The Stanford Encyclopedia of Philosophy* (Winter 2017 Edition), edited by Zalta, E. N., URL = plato.stanford.edu/archives/win2017/entries/physicalism/.

Turing, A., "Computing Machinery and Intelligence", *Mind*, Vol. LIX no. 236 (1950): 433-460.

Watson, J. B., "Psychology as the Behaviorist Views it", *Psychological Review*, 20 (1913): 158-177.

Wittgenstein, L., *Tractatus Logico-Philosophicus*, translated by Ramsey, F. P. and Ogden, C. K. (Routledge & Kegan Paul Ltd, 1922).

Wittgenstein, L., *Philosophical Investigations*, translated by Anscombe, G. E. M. (Basil Blackwell, 1953).

Wittgenstein, L., *Remarks on the Philosophy of Psychology*, Vol. I (Blackwell 1980).

Zarkadakis, G., *In Our Own Image: Savior or Destroyer? The History and Future of Artificial Intelligence* (Pegasus, 2016).

ASANAS INDEX

NOTES

NOTES